FURIOUS MINDS

Furious Minds

THE MAKING
OF THE MAGA NEW RIGHT

LAURA K. FIELD

PRINCETON UNIVERSITY PRESS
PRINCETON & OXFORD

Published by Princeton University Press
41 William Street, Princeton, New Jersey 08540
99 Banbury Road, Oxford OX2 6JX

press.princeton.edu

GPSR Authorized Representative: Easy Access System Europe - Mustamäe tee 50, 10621 Tallinn, Estonia, gpsr.requests@easproject.com

ISBN 978-0-691-25526-2
ISBN (e-book) 978-0-691-25530-9

British Library Cataloging-in-Publication Data is available

Editorial: David McBride, Bridget Flannery-McCoy, and Alena Chekanov
Jacket design: Karl Spurzem
Production: Erin Suydam
Publicity: James Schneider
Copyeditor: Anita O'Brien

This book has been composed in Arno

Printed in the United States of America

10 9 8 7 6 5 4 3 2

MIX
Paper | Supporting
responsible forestry
FSC
www.fsc.org   FSC® C008955

In memory of Ruth Florence Field (1922–2003)

The idea that it takes extreme experience to produce great literature should never be left unexamined. The great literature that arises from extreme experience covers a very narrow band, and does so at the cost of bleaching out almost the whole of life—the everyday world that enjoys, in Nadezhda Mandelstam's great phrase, "the privilege of ordinary heartbreaks." Catastrophes like the Holocaust—and if it is argued that there have been no catastrophes quite like the Holocaust it can't usefully be argued that there won't be—have no redeeming features. Any good that comes out of them belongs not to them but to the world they try to wreck. Our only legitimate consolation is that, although they loom large in the long perspectives of history, history would have no long perspectives if human beings were not, in the aggregate, more creative than destructive. But the mass slaughter of the innocent is not a civics lesson. It involves us all, except that some of us were lucky enough not to be there. The best reason for trying to lead a fruitful life is that we are living on borrowed time.

—CLIVE JAMES

CONTENTS

ACKNOWLEDGMENTS

I LEFT MY faculty position at American University in 2018. That choice eventually gave me time to write this book, but it was a stressful decision that led to some big moves and upheavals, first to Wichita, KS, then Frederick, MD, and back to DC again. The pandemic hit while we were in Frederick; our kids were very small. All in all, it was a time in life when I needed the support of friends and family. And I had it. To my astonishment and delight, there have also been, as they say, new friends made along the way.

But first: Thank you to Leon Craig and Heidi Studer for being wonderful teachers and a gateway to something like the life of the mind, as well as to friendships with so many others numbered on these pages. The same goes for Tom Pangle, Lorraine Pangle, Devin Stauffer, and Dana Stauffer. Gary Jacobsohn is also a great teacher to whom I owe sincere thanks.

Mark Verbitsky and Mijke Rhemtulla have been in my corner for as long as I have known them, as have Andi Kowalchuk and Laura Rabinowitz. Thank you for believing in me, and for all of the wonderful talks over the years.

Thanks to Shannon Bazil of Wichita for a burst of friendship at just the right time.

Thank you to Damon Linker for help and advice when I first tried writing for a nonacademic audience, and to Bill Kristol and Jonathan V. Last for publishing my first articles in *The Bulwark*. Bill Kristol has been a kind and trusted friend since that time. So has Jeff Tulis, who I knew first as an inspired and generous teacher at UT Austin. Thanks to you both for your support and insight over the years. And thank you to *The Bulwark* for allowing me to reproduce selections from my articles in this book.

I owe special thanks to Adam Keiper and Tom Merrill for being terrific friends and constant interlocutors as I wandered deeper into the world of American politics than anyone ever could have imagined. Adam: You are a joy to work with and so thoughtful and kind, and you give the very best pep talks. Tom: You are a model of intellectual integrity, decency, and intelligence in a world that could use a lot more. Thanks to you both.

Thank you to many friends and colleagues who are (or were at one point) connected with the Niskanen Center and who have been so supportive: David Dagan, Soren Dayton, Geoffrey Kabaservice, Jacob Levy, Brink Lindsey, Gabriel Schoenfeld, Louisa Tavlas, Jerry Taylor, Steve Teles, Kevin Vallier, and Will Wilkinson. Thanks to Jacob for being an exemplary political thinker and public scholar. Thank you to Gabe for feedback on this project early on, and to Soren for helpful insights closer to the end. Thank you to David for being such a great collaborator over the years and for commenting on parts of the book. Geoff: Your feedback on the whole manuscript was truly invaluable. Thank you so much. Same goes for you, Kevin. A major upside of working on the New Right has been getting to know you and your work. I am also so glad to know you, Steve. A big thanks to Niskanen, also, for permission to reprint passages here that first appeared as publications with them.

Thank you to Emily Chamlee-Wright, Mike Tolhurst, Matthew Kuchem, and others at the Institute for Humane Studies for supporting my work, for good conversations, and for all the good work that you are doing. Thanks also to the IHS for a grant that helped with the early stages of this project.

Thank you to Paige Harden for help with navigating the early professional stages of book writing, as well as for her insights at key moments along the way. Thank you also to Heather Cox Richardson for great advice early on. Thank you to Liz Anderson, Aurelian Craiutu, and Russ Muirhead for their early support for this book. And a big thank you to Niki Hemmer for being such a wonderful scholar herself and for supporting me as I got this project off the ground.

I pinched myself when I landed Lisa Adams of The Garamond Agency as a literary agent and have been so lucky to have her by my side throughout this process. Thank you, Lisa. Thank you to Bill Frucht for helpful early advice on this kind of work. To Bridget Flannery-McCoy: I owe tremendous thanks to you for acquiring this book and for understanding what I was doing; I thank you for your thoroughness, your casual excellence, and all of the thought and care you put into what you do. Thank you to my three anonymous reviewers who were all so thorough and insightful. And thank you to the whole terrific team at PUP: Alena Chekanov, Eric Crahan, Rob Tempio, Jenny Wolkowicki, and James Schneider. Thank you in addition to Anita O'Brien, Virginia Ling, and Lachlan Brooks. I am especially thankful to David McBride who joined the press as my book entered its final stages and has been so wonderful to work with.

I want to thank Jim McAdams for inviting me to the University of Notre Dame in 2022 to create an edited volume alongside some wonderful scholars, too many to list here, all of whom helped me think about the global right more clearly. Jim: You are a generous spirit and it has been a pleasure to get to know you. Thank you for your sharp and thoughtful comments on the manuscript. Thanks also to Agnieszka Bień-Kacała, Tímea Drinóczi, Samuel Piccolo, Steven Pittz, Sarah Shurts, and José Pedro Zúquete, for their conversation and feedback at various stages. Particular thanks to George Hawley and Josh Vandiver for reading chapters and offering feedback as this book progressed. And thank you to Routledge Press for permission to reproduce passages from my essay, "Forced to Be Free? America's 'Postliberals' on Freedom and Liberty," from our collection, published as *Far-Right Newspeak and the Future of Liberal Democracy* (2024).

A big thank you to George Thomas for hosting a workshop for this book through The Salvatori Center for the Study of Individual Freedom at Claremont McKenna College in Fall 2023. Thank you, George, for providing insightful comments and suggestions at various stages, and for your own good work in public law. Thank you to all the Salvatori workshop participants—among them Zachary Courser, Ioannis Evrigenis, Lily Geismer, Stephanie Muravchik, Seth Lobis, Jack Pitner, and Jon Shields—for such helpful feedback on early chapter drafts. Massive thanks to Nicholas Buccola, whose own books are such an inspiration, for great feedback and advice as I worked on this manuscript.

Ronnie Biener read and commented on drafts of every chapter: Thank you Ronnie, both for your help and for all the good work that you do.

Jerome Copulsky invited me to join a panel on populism and religion with the Berkley Center for Religion, Peace, and World Affairs at Georgetown University and the Pulitzer Center in 2023 and soon became a generous friend and comrade-in-writing. Thank you, Jerome, for reading and commenting on the whole book, for being such a tremendous sounding-board, such a generous champion of this book, and such a terrific local social convener!

Thank you to new friends Libby Anker, Sidney Blumenthal, Matt Dinkel, Ger FitzGerald, Sam Goldman, Benjamin Leff, Peter Montgomery, Martyn Oliver, Brad Onishi, Sarah Posner, Adele Stan, Katherine Stewart, Matthew Taylor, Julian Waller, and Doug Wolfe. All of you have read some portion of the book at some stage, or answered questions as they arose, and I am grateful for your input, conversation, and friendship. Sarah and Ger went above and beyond with their comments on the manuscript: Thank you.

Patrick Thaddeus Jackson has been a terrific conversation partner and friend for over a decade now. I am grateful for your support, Patrick, and thank you for your excellent and thorough feedback on the manuscript. Thank you as well to Jonathan Marks for providing characteristically astute comments on the book, and for being so evenhanded and good-humored always.

Others who have read and commented on chapters, or the whole book, or otherwise answered questions or shared insights as I was writing, include: Marco Bherer, Corey Brettschneider, Holly Brewer, Max Bodach, Sarah Burns, Shikha Dalmia, Borden Flanagan, Bill Galston, Bryan Garsten, Jim Goldgeier, Gareth Gore, Tim Haglund, Lena Hunsicker, Will Inboden, Jeff Isaac, Brad Jackson, Andy Koppelman, Julius Krein, Michael Luchese, Peter Minowitz, James Patterson, Jacqueline Pfeffer Merrill, Greg Sargent, Logan Sawyer, Suzanne Schneider, Anne-Marie Schultz, Tim Shenk, Stephanie Slade, Constanze Stelzenmüller, Liz Suhay, Joshua Tait, Nicholas Tampio, Brandon Turner, Emily Wilson, Ben Wittes, Richard Wolin, Mark Yellin, Elisabeth Zerofsky, and

Michael Zuckert. My sincere thanks to each of you for your help and support.

Thomas Zimmer has become a great friend and collaborator over the years, and his sharp insight is a benefit to us all. Thank you for your work and friendship, Thomas.

Thank you to *The New Republic* and *Politico* for allowing me to reproduce passages from articles here ("Ivory Power," *The New Republic,* October 26, 2021 and "JD Vance Has a Bunch of Weird Views on Gender," *Politico,* July 23, 2024). Thank you to Patrick Caldwell for great editing in both cases.

As work on this book was wrapping up, I started working with the Illiberalism Studies Program at George Washington University, which is under the direction of Marlene Laruelle. Thank you, Marlene, for the wonderful work you are doing, and to John Chrobak and Aaron Irion for being great collaborators.

Nacona Nix: It is hard to find people who are hyper-literate, funny, have encyclopedic brains, and with whom one almost always agrees. You're it! A perfect friend. Thank you for all the texts and conversations. Your ideas are everywhere in this book. All remaining errors are Nacona's.

Sarah Snyder is a most gracious friend who introduced me to the fine world of living historians, and whose generosity and good will have impacted this book in more ways that I can count. I am so thankful to you, Sarah. Thanks as well to Claire Brunei, Danny Fine, Mike Schroeder, and Molly Smith. You are all so brilliant. Thank you to Annie Claus for being simply the best through all of these years of young kids and tumult: A top-shelf friend whom I adore. Thank you to Jen Gauck—so smart and big-hearted—for being our family through the pandemic and beyond. And to Tom Zlamal and the kids, too. And to Martine Tcheuga. You all are the people who make DC (and Frederick) home.

Thank you to my old friend Tracy Wadlington, and to new ones Brenna and Daniel Van Stone.

Thank you to Trish Gerald, Midori Hyndman, and Christie Nichols for a lifetime of friendship. And to Erin Collins, Ben Hass, and their kids for summertime friendships.

Rubina Hussein, thank you always for your boundless good humor, for the spiritual sustenance you give, for the example you set, and for your uncanny ability to be there right when people need you. Erin Dolgoy, thank you for your overall excellence, and for your steady goodness and integrity all these years. To Lori Ritland: you are such an important presence in my life and I am so grateful for the community that flourishes around you. Thank you to the kind and talented Shilpa Saroop.

Natalie Elliot is a friend whom I'm not sure I could live without, who has shaped the course of my life, and whose courage, honesty, and creative verve make the world so much more interesting and alive. Thank you for sharing this wild ride, dear Natalia.

George Jamieson, an old friend of my dad's, provided feedback on this book during what turned out to be his last year with us—a gift for which I will always be grateful. Rest in peace, George.

I dedicated this book to my grandmother Ruth Florence Field because she never went to university but made it possible for me to go. She was so good to me. She was also a great reader with a warm, cackling spirit and would have loved more formal education. There are many such cases.

To my many wonderful aunts and uncles and cousins in Edmonton and beyond: Thank you for the love, kindness, and fun you have given me my whole life. I can't list you all. But Margy: No one else understands me quite like you do, and boy do I love you for it. And Jeanie: your goodness has been a steadfast presence in all our lives for as long as I can remember. Thank you. Everyone should be so lucky as to have family like this.

Robert, Norah, William, and Martin: It would make us all uncomfortable if I said all that much about how much you mean to me and my little family. Thank you for everything. I love you.

My mother, Lois Donna Field, is one of the smartest people I know: so curious and sharp, so funny, and also so endlessly generous with her kids and grandkids. My mom didn't just tolerate my intensity as a young person: she listened and asked questions and argued and even seemed mostly entertained. She read this whole manuscript before almost anyone else, and then read the proofs, again, with apparent enthusiasm.

Thank you for pouring your love into us always, mom; we are so lucky to have you.

My in-laws are too good to be true, in every way. Joyce and Darrel: Your constant kindness shapes our spirits and our lives every day and means more than I can express in words. Thank you.

Finally, thank you to my Austin, and our two sons. To our boys: You two are the big stars in the constellation of my happiness. You brighten every day with your sweetness, hilarity, and popping energy, and I'm so lucky to be your mom. Austin: I never really thought I'd settle down until you came along and, in your quiet Kansan way, swept me off my feet. I got the best one out there and am still flying high. Thank you for all of it.

Dramatis Personae

SOHRAB AHMARI	Postliberal. Journalist and founder of *Compact* magazine.
COSTIN ALAMARIU ("Bronze Age Pervert")	Hard Right. Yale PhD in political philosophy. Influencer.
MICHAEL ANTON ("Publius Decius Mus")	Claremonter and "Paleo-Straussian." Wrote for *The Journal of American Greatness* and author of "The Flight 93 Election."
LARRY P. ARNN	Claremonter. Claremont Graduate University PhD. President of Hillsdale College.
STEVE BANNON	Hard Right. Former executive chairman at *Breitbart News* and chief strategist for President Trump.
DARREN BEATTIE	Hard Right. Duke PhD in political philosophy. Founder of *Revolver News*.
ALLAN BLOOM (1930 – 1992)	Straussian. Professor and Writer. Author of *The Closing of the American Mind* (1987).
TUCKER CARLSON	Hard Right. Journalist and media personality, formerly of Fox News.

CHARLES CORNISH-DALE ("Raw Egg Nationalist") — Hard Right. Oxford and Cambridge graduate. Anon body-builder and health guru.

CHRIS DEMUTH — National Conservative. Former president of the American Enterprise Institute.

PATRICK DENEEN — Postliberal. Professor at the University of Notre Dame. Author of *Why Liberalism Failed* (2018) and *Regime Change* (2023).

RON DESANTIS — Governor of Florida. Candidate in the 2024 GOP presidential primary.

JOHN C. EASTMAN — Claremonter. Director of the Claremont Institute's Center for Constitutional Jurisprudence. Author of the "Coup Memos."

SAMUEL T. FRANCIS (1947 – 2005) — Paleoconservative. Writer and intellectual. White supremacist.

ROBERT P. GEORGE — Leading Catholic conservative intellectual. Professor at Princeton University and director of the James Madison Program in American Ideals and Institutions.

PAUL GOTTFRIED — Paleoconservative. Writer, intellectual, and far-right organizer.

JOSH HAMMER — National Conservative. University of Chicago Law School JD. Media personality and proponent of "Common Good Originalism."

YORAM HAZONY — National Conservative. Israeli-American political organizer and author of *The Virtue of Nationalism* (2018).

HARRY V. JAFFA (1918 – 2015) — West Coast Straussian. Intellectual forebear of the Claremonters. Scholar of Lincoln and author of *Crisis of the House Divided* (1959).

CHARLES R. KESLER	Claremonter. Professor at Claremont McKenna College and editor of *The Claremont Review of Books*. Author of *Crisis of the Two Constitutions* (2021).
THOMAS KLINGENSTEIN	Claremonter and National Conservative. Chairman of the board at the Claremont Institute and major donor to the institute and to National Conservatism.
JULIUS KREIN ("Plautus")	Harvard BA. Wrote for the *Journal of American Greatness*. Cofounder of *American Affairs*.
HARVEY C. MANSFIELD	Straussian. Professor at Harvard University. Machiavelli and Tocqueville scholar and author of *Manliness* (2006).
STEPHEN MILLER	Right-winger. Duke BA. Worked as a speechwriter and policy advisor in the first Trump White House and as deputy chief of staff for policy in the second.
GLADDEN PAPPIN ("Marcus Manlius Capitolinus")	Postliberal and Catholic integralist. Harvard PhD. Wrote for the *Journal of American Greatness*. Cofounder of *American Affairs*. President of the Hungarian Institute of International Affairs.
R. R. RENO	National Conservative. Yale PhD in religious studies. Editor of *First Things* magazine and author of *The Return of the Strong Gods* (2019).
KEVIN D. ROBERTS	National Conservative. University of Texas at Austin PhD in history. President of the Heritage Foundation.

CHRISTOPHER RUFO	National Conservative. Activist and employee of the Manhattan Institute.
CARL SCHMITT (1888 – 1985)	German legal scholar and Nazi jurist.
LEO STRAUSS (1899 – 1973)	German scholar and émigré to America. Known for the rediscovery of the "esoteric" tradition in political philosophy.
PETER THIEL	New Right billionaire influencer. PayPal cofounder, investor, Strauss aficionado, and donor to Trump, National Conservatism, and JD Vance.
JD VANCE	Postliberal. Senator and vice president. Author of *Hillbilly Elegy* (2016).
ADRIAN VERMEULE	Postliberal and Catholic integralist. Harvard Law professor and author of *Common Good Constitutionalism* (2022).
STEPHEN WOLFE	Hard Right. Louisiana State University PhD. Author of *The Case for Christian Nationalism* (2022).
CURTIS YARVIN ("Mencius Moldbug")	Hard Right. "Techno-monarchist" Silicon Valley influencer and founder of the "neoreactionary" movement. Friend of Peter Thiel.

WE WERE SEATED at a round table in a banquet hall in Charlottesville, at the University of Virginia's Colonnade Club. It was a beautiful room—high arched windows, buttercream walls, crisp white linens—and a lovely evening, sometime in summer 2010. Fireflies flickered in the warm air outside.

The dinner that night was hosted by a conservative educational organization devoted to American history and the founding. It was the opening soirée for a summer program in which a couple dozen young scholars would hear lectures from prominent intellectuals, meet with book editors, and otherwise schmooze. These events are lavish. They offer a level of luxury that many graduate students have never experienced in their young lives: open bars, nice wines, beautiful grounds and rooms.

At the time, I was in my fifth year of graduate school in political theory and public law at the University of Texas at Austin and about to enter a cutthroat academic job market. I was excited and nervous. My doctoral supervisor was one of the guest speakers that year, and the banquet room was full of others who might have a hand in shaping my career.

At dinner, I was seated to the right of one of the high-level staff members of the organization running the program. Let's call him Todd. I had heard about Todd from friends who had attended the program in the past and imagined him to be an engaging and friendly sort of person. To my left was an old friend of mine, someone who had also gone to graduate school in political theory. I'll call him Ronnie.

We were barely into the first course, during the first event of that first day, when Todd mentioned that he had recently been at an event with

First Lady Michelle Obama. He described his impressions succinctly: "She was truly statuesque. Very tall, very impressive. I'd really like to fuck her."

An awkward grimace and head shake from Ronnie. I didn't know what to say, so I set down my napkin and excused myself to the restroom.

I'm not an especially buttoned-up person. At the time I was writing a dissertation about Rousseau and Nietzsche. Rousseau abandoned all his (four or five) newborn children to an orphanage in Paris, and Nietzsche has often been called the intellectual godfather of fascism. I am pretty inured to offensive behavior and ideas, and I try to carry this into everyday life. And that summer wasn't my first time at the conservative rodeo—I had been in these circles for nearly a decade. But Todd's remark got under my skin. Maybe he was showing off for Ronnie, but it felt like a provocation aimed my way—a little jab meant to test my prudishness, or inversely my philosophic coolness. It was also clear that it had to do with more than sex, and with more than me. It had to do with women, and it had to do with Michelle Obama, a Black woman, and the first Black president's wife.

In the ladies' room at the Colonnade Club, I remember looking in the mirror—the moment felt surreal and cinematic even at the time—and shaking my head and thinking: "What a total asshole." And then I asked myself: "What on earth am I doing here?" It was the beginning of the long, slow process of extricating myself from the world of conservative intellectualism.

My timing was good.

1

Introducing the MAGA New Right

BETWEEN 2016 AND 2024, over the course of less than a decade, American conservatism capitulated to—and took a part in fomenting—a far-right populist movement that led to the nomination of Donald J. Trump as the Republican Party's candidate for the US presidency, and then catapulted him into power, twice. This new movement was inspired by Trump, but the seeds were there long before him, and the movement reached well beyond. It transformed US conservatism, including its dominant intellectual wing. Over the course of the first Trump administration, various groups of conservative thinkers coalesced, at different times and for different reasons, and more or less enthusiastically, behind Trumpism.

In short order, the conservative intellectualism I thought I knew had all but vanished from the discourse that dominated the Republican Party. Champions of the US Constitution, and of originalism, were now sympathetic to a man who obviously cared very little for constitutional niceties and was eventually willing to throw the entire electoral system—the foundation of American government—into chaos for his own power. People who excelled at the identification of demagogues and would-be tyrants—who had railed against Barack Obama for his rhetorical excesses and overweening message of "hope and change"— were denying that Trump's enthusiastic deployment of hate, resentment, and fear was a matter of concern. Former defenders of "family values," high culture, and Christianity were suddenly lining up behind an adulterer, purported rapist, and obvious misogynist who was also an anti-intellectual and failed capitalist with a record of six bankrupted businesses. In a separate twist, Trump and the GOP now supposedly stood for a protectionist style of economics—the opposite of the laissez-faire approach that had long been the mainstay of the American right.

By 2024, matters had become much worse. In addition to ongoing right-wing indulgence of President Trump's "Big Lie" about the 2020 election, and their refusal to contend honestly with the implications of January 6, 2021, right-wing thought leaders were talking about ending liberal democracy and installing a "Red Caesar."[1] They were calling themselves Postliberals and publishing books with titles like *Regime Change*.[2] Establishment groups like the Heritage Foundation and Intercollegiate Studies Institute joined arms with Trump-supporting groups like National Conservatism and the Claremont Institute. Together they began to work on "Project 2025"—a plan for action should Trump retake the White House, which involved firing thousands of public servants and replacing them with far-right stalwarts. A doctrine of "No Enemies to the Right," or NETTR, started to take hold in some of these right-wing circles. Trump, for his part, shamelessly praised foreign dictators, admitting at one point that he *would* like to be a dictator if reelected, but only for one day.[3] He then chose Senator JD Vance—a true darling of the new movement—as his running mate.

By then, "New Right" had become the catch-all term for the energetic group of intellectuals and political activists who together formed the brain trust and influencer arm of the new populist Republican politics. This book documents the emergence and coalescence of this movement between 2016 and 2024. It is a book about PhDs and intellectuals who, almost by definition, exist outside of the political mainstream. They are up in the ivory tower, writing articles and books, perhaps an occasional op-ed in *The Wall Street Journal* or *The New York Times*. These are men (yes, they are almost all men) who most people, including many conservatives, have never heard of, but who matter greatly because they articulated the ideas that have shaped a movement.

I had heard of them and had met a few. And I watched closely—and with genuine surprise—as their authority within the Trumpist GOP grew. This book chronicles how it happened—the writings, conferences, groupings, and schisms. The intellectuals of the New Right did us the favor of articulating their visions for the future, leaving behind a lengthy public record of their project. Over the course of this book, you will meet the men who first endorsed Trump, see their talks, learn about the books they wrote, and read the tweets they tweeted.

The story is one of ideological radicalization—the mutually reinforcing radicalization of intellectuals, politicians, and the movement they led. The men of the New Right saw Trump as a major opportunity; they egged him and his supporters on, and they brought others into the fold. They saw that he shared some of their extremist, old-school conservative views, and they appreciated that he would use whatever means necessary—including unconstitutional means—to gain and exert power. They are people who sought to leverage real problems, as well as known vulnerabilities of liberalism, to impose their own homogenizing moral and political vision on the rest of the country. They wanted to turn back the clock on pluralistic liberal democracy, and even on modernity itself. Many were also articulating new visions for the future: new laws, schemas for education, modes of constitutionalism, traditionalist communities, and technological utopias.

The New Right as a whole consists of many extremely smart people who occupy positions of power and prestige in American institutions. They are professors at Harvard and Notre Dame and have graduate degrees from Duke and Yale; they are concentrated in places like the Claremont Institute in Southern California and Hillsdale College in Michigan, but also have a footing in Silicon Valley, Viktor Orbán's Hungary, edgy New York neighborhoods, and the think tanks of Washington, DC. The Republican staffers on Capitol Hill know all about the New Right. And more than a couple prominent American politicians—like Senators Josh Hawley, Tom Cotton, and Marco Rubio, as well as Vice President JD Vance—have embraced the movement. Ron DeSantis, Florida's governor and one-time presidential hopeful, was first to enact a full-fledged New Right policy suite at the state level.

Michael Anton, who was one of the first to defend Trumpism in intellectual terms, defined it in September 2016 as "secure borders, economic nationalism, and America-first foreign policy."[4] This is a useful shorthand that captures some of the fundamentals. The New Right is indeed, with very few exceptions, anti-immigration. It stands against free trade and globalism. And it represents a turn against the neoconservative interventionism in foreign affairs that characterized the first part of the twenty-first century. But if those are the ribs of the New Right's politics, Anton's formulation hides the spine, which is a staunch social traditionalism and rejection of liberal pluralism and egalitarianism; in other words, the various New Right policy prongs are organized around a traditionalist (usually white, Christian, and patriarchal) social vision and homogenizing nationalism meant to counter and replace pluralistic liberalism. The New Right views mainstream liberal America—the "woke" America that embraces plurality and equality, including across various formerly marginalized identities—as an all-encompassing, monolithic "regime" of elite oppression (which they often also refer to as the "enemy"). Culture warriorism—which we might define as an excessive emphasis on rhetoric and media performance over policy formulation and real-world political negotiation—plays a major role on the New Right because at bottom this is a movement driven by reactionary social values and principles, not specific policy concerns.

R. R. Reno, the editor of an important conservative Christian journal *First Things*, has framed the right's turn toward nationalism and populism in terms of a "return of the strong gods." In a book by that title published in 2019, he celebrated this return, which he identified with strong, solidaristic forms of love and juxtaposed with liberalism. "Liberalism," wrote Reno, "hearkens to the gods of weakening . . . when liberalism becomes dominant, as it has done in the postwar consensus, civil life withers, for liberalism offers no vigorous language of love." He claimed that the liberalism of the last half-decade or so "trains us to be loveless and therefore to be something less than human." It is a refrain that you will hear across the New Right. It is based on misunderstandings both of human nature and of liberalism, but Reno is confident: Whatever comes next, he says, "will require a restoration of love.

And love is roused by the strong gods, which is why they are return-ing."[5] However much it rejects liberalism, the New Right does not un-derstand itself in strictly negative terms. It thinks it has a monopoly on things like "the good, the true, and the beautiful." In other words, it does not really care about (or for) Donald Trump. The New Right has bigger plans—cultural, political, economic, local, and international visions for a new old-fashioned world.

Who's Who

The New Right does have a defining core—Reno's reactionary "strong god" spine, supported by Anton's ribs of "secure borders, economic na-tionalism, and America-first foreign policy." But it is not a monolith. I divide the New Right into three groups: the Claremonters, the Postlib-erals, and the National Conservatives. In brief, the Claremonters idolize the American founding, the Postliberals a particular (religiously in-spired) conception of the "Common Good," and the National Conser-vatives the myth of a traditional American nation. These camps are not mutually exclusive; it is best to think of the New Right as a highly net-worked movement with distinct clusters and modes of thinking, that is home not only to intellectuals, but also to activists, influencers, staffers, and politicians.

The Claremonters are closely networked with the Claremont Insti-tute, a think tank in California, and the political science faculty and administrators at Hillsdale College in Michigan. Many of the scholars in this cluster identify as West Coast Straussians—a school of thought inspired by the twentieth-century political philosopher Leo Strauss and his student Harry V. Jaffa. They rally around a particular vision of the American founders—a vision that they are desperate to recover but that they believe can only happen through radical change. Its ideology is in some respects spiritually adjacent to originalism, except that rather than appeal to the text of the Constitution, the Claremonters appeal to the first principles of the founding (an approach that some scholars have called "Declarationism").[6] Between 2016 and 2024 it became attached to a radical form of counterrevolutionary activism, inspired by Anton's famous essay "The Flight 93 Election," from September 2016, in which he had defined Trumpism. This younger generation of Claremonters even took inspiration from an older group of conservatives called the Paleoconservatives or Paleos, opponents of Jaffa's who disliked his emphasis on equality (and whom one historian described as "the embittered heirs of failed traditionalism, many with longings for the antebellum South.")[7] Some Claremonters have also embraced an emergent Christian nationalism.

JD Vance has spoken at Claremonter events, and the Claremonters were jubilant when he was chosen as Trump's running mate. The aesthetic here is youthful, bitter, masculinist, and counterrevolutionary. The Claremonter crowd signals their toughness with the phrase "knowing what time it is." If you know what time it is, you know that the hour is late, and it is time for radical action in America.

Compared to the Claremonters, the Postliberal camp is less enamored of the American founders and instead embraces many elements of communitarianism and traditional Catholic social teaching, including a greater role for the state in shaping public life and morality. Some American Postliberals are also part of the Catholic integralist movement, which promotes a radical effort to end the separation of church and state, thus making political life subordinate to spiritual aims. It includes thinkers like Patrick Deneen, a professor at the University of Notre Dame whose book *Why Liberalism Failed* (2018) helped to launch the New Right, and Adrian Vermeule, a legal scholar at Harvard University and Catholic integralist who has gifted the New Right a constitutional defense of far-right conservative authoritarianism. These are the most sophisticated thinkers of the New Right, and the ones who appear the sincerest in their critique of capitalism and commitment to the populist economic reforms that Trump and the New Right have sometimes promised. The Postliberals sometimes lean on mainstream Catholic thought to sustain their views; at other times they deploy ideas from much more controversial figures, like the German jurist (and Nazi) Carl Schmitt. The Postliberal aesthetic is sober, traditionalist, and highbrow. Vance has identified closely with the "postliberal right" and is an admirer of Patrick Deneen.[8]

National Conservatives

Chris DeMuth
Yoram Hazony
Josh Hammer
Josh Hawley
Christopher Rufo
Viktor Orbán
R.R. Reno
Kevin Roberts

The Edmund Burke Foundation
First Things
The Heritage Foundation

Postliberals

Sohrab Ahmari
Patrick Deneen
Gladden Pappin
JD Vance
Adrian Vermeule

Claremonters

Michael Anton
Larry Arnn
John Eastman
Charles Kesler
Thomas Klingenstein

Claremont Institute
Hillsdale College

Darren Beattie
Nathan Pinkoski
Stephen Wolfe
Curtis Yarvin ("Mencius Moldbug")
Costin Alamariu ("Bronze Age Pervert")
Charles Cornish-Dale ("Raw Egg Nationalist")

Hard Right Underbelly

FIGURE 1: Key people and institutions of the MAGA New Right

"National Conservatism" serves as a big tent and umbrella for the movement. It is organized and formal in a way that the rest of the New Right is not, with regular conferences in the United States and abroad. Ideologically, National Conservatism promotes the notion of a single, relatively homogenous nation-state that is under threat from within and without and needs to be protected. This embrace of nationalism— at times the open endorsement of Christian nationalism—is highly exclusive. It cuts against America's tradition of religious pluralism, as well as against the Declarationist creedal elements of America's traditional self-understanding and civil religion.[9] Vance was a speaker at three of the four NatCon conferences that took place in the United States between 2019 and 2024. The mood of National Conservatism is fervent and unyielding.

Finally, there is a rather capacious underbelly to the New Right movement, which I generally call the Hard Right. I do not consider them their own camp because ideologically they span the other three. They are distinct insofar as they are more hard-line, racist, misogynistic, and violent in their rhetoric. The aesthetic here is hypermasculinist, desperate, and ruthless; several figures from the Hard Right are open racists and fascists.[10] They push the movement ever further to the extremes.

―――――

Furious Minds tells the story of ideals and grievances, aspirations and self-delusions. It is about what the New Right was trying to achieve, how it succeeded, and how it has at times flailed. The New Right gained outsized influence within a Trump-led Republican Party and succeeded in transforming the party. In other respects, it faltered. But the New Right is dynamic and sees itself as youthful, fresh, and hardcore. Carl Schmitt has more purchase in some quarters of the New Right than Abraham Lincoln, and a writer named Bronze Age Pervert is a favorite for GOP staffers on Capitol Hill.[11] In many instances, these conservatives have more in common with European defenders of monarchy and reactionary antimodernists than with anything that has been mainstream in the United States for the past hundred or more years. The movement is, in many respects, untethered from the ordinary decency and common sense that characterize America at its idealistic best—and from the pluralistic reality of the country as it exists today.

The New Right is also bigger than it seems. It extends beyond Washington, DC, into movement conservatism—the still broader webs of pundits, funding organizations, media operators, and churches that also give shape to American conservatism. When I look back at the people from that summer program in Charlottesville, I was meeting a cut of professors from the conservative mainstream, and I never would have expected them to turn toward Trump. But some became Trump's defenders or collaborators, and very few repudiated him in public, even after January 6. Most have gritted their teeth and watched the show unfold. They are patient enough—and, justifiably or not, trusting enough in America's capacity to resist Trumpism's excesses—to wait it out and see what comes next. This book is about them, too: about all the people on the elite right whose silence, acquiescence, and bad judgment allowed Trumpism to grow, who could have spoken up and helped things go a different way but didn't.

That said, the contours of contemporary American conservatism—and the American right—are broader than the currents I investigate here. There are still many conservative intellectuals who oppose Trump and Trumpism; they just have less power than they did before. And this book does not fully address Trumpism as a popular phenomenon. While the New Right has reshaped the Republican Party, the extent to which men like Steve Bannon, Elon Musk, and other New Right figures represent or influence the views of ordinary voters remains unclear.[12] Furthermore, I do not investigate the rise of the QAnon conspiracy, or the ongoing impact of the Prosperity Gospel, or the many ways in which Trump has become a cultlike strongman figure on the American right. The rise of Trump has meant—or coincided with—the rise and spread of apocalyptic, Manichean, and conspiratorial thinking across the country reminiscent of earlier phenomena like the Birchers and the Birthers. Some of the thinkers I discuss in this book suffer from versions of these same pathologies, at times acutely. But I leave the connections for others to untangle.

Historical and Global Context

The New Right movement of the early twenty-first century represents the most radical and successful iteration of a pattern on the American right that goes back at least to the start of the twentieth century. And while this is not a book about the history of American conservatism, it is worth saying more about this dynamic to clarify what is and isn't "new" about the MAGA New Right. It is also useful to put the American case in global perspective. So reader be warned: For a few pages now I will take a more historical and academic turn, to set the stage for everything to come.

As a descriptor, "New Right" is somewhat confounding since it has been used many times by many groups to describe other waves of incipient change spanning the 1950s through the 1990s. Overall, such terms—and others, like "paleoconservatism" and "neoconservatism"—reflect the push and pull of ideological influence, which tends to oscillate between an isolationist, socially conservative style and one that is more internationally minded (or interventionist/imperialist) and socially moderate. As these waves come, the moniker "New Right" has been used repeatedly, the result being that it can refer to various strands of conservatism, including ones that are in some mutual tension. The matter is complicated still more by the fact of partisan realignment. For much of the twentieth century, the Republican and Democratic Parties did not represent the conservative and liberal sides of the political spectrum. The second half of the century saw progressives, moderates, and Black voters leave the GOP in waves and white Southerners migrate into it, as the GOP pursued its infamous "Southern Strategy."[13] The overall story of the twentieth century is one of a gradual, conservative, populist takeover and consolidation of the GOP—away from the progressivism championed by President Theodore Roosevelt or the progressive moderation of President Eisenhower and toward something more ideologically homogenous.

The MAGA New Right is the most successful and forward-looking expression of far-right politics in recent memory, but there have been several cycles or turnings of the push-pull within American conservatism—each with their own permutations and particularities. On an abstract level the dynamic goes something like this: American conservatism, at its ideological core, tends to be isolationist, socially traditionalist, and devoted to small government. This was the basic character of what was called the "Old Right"—which describes the conservatism of the first half of the twentieth century.[14] (The libertarian thinker Murray Rothbard called the Old Right "a coalition of fury and despair against the enormous acceleration of Big Government brought about by the New Deal.")[15] When conservatives win elections and have to govern, however, this ideological core has to soften: They make compromises and tend to moderate, gradually calcifying into a more centrist, power-wielding "establishment." We might here think of Eisenhower, who was elected as a conservative but did not turn against the New Deal, or of Reagan's eventual acceptance of the Civil Rights Act, or of George H. W. Bush's tax increase. Such compromises are part of holding power in a large democracy, where realities are complicated, and constituencies diverse.

But it also means that governing coalitions are vulnerable to challenges from the extremes—and especially to the charge of having sold out on conservative principles. This too is part of the cycle and has happened repeatedly over the past century. Barry Goldwater's movement in the late 1950s and early 1960s took this shape—i.e., of an extremist flank accusing older conservatism of weakness and betrayal, and claiming that they, the true believers, could do a better job. Something similar happened with Pat Buchanan and the Paleoconservatives in the 1990s, and then with Newt Gingrich and with the Tea Party, too. To the extent that such efforts succeed, the party shifts rightward. And often the rhetoric ratchets up: To maintain the affections of the movement, the true believers become more hardened and uncompromising, their rhetoric more militant and violent.

Such a dynamic has played a major part in the story of Donald Trump and the New Right intellectuals, who have been involved in a mutually reinforcing radicalization process that operated mainly against the former GOP establishment (though they were certainly egged on at times by the left and understood themselves to be reacting to a left-wing, "woke Marxist" takeover of the country). Over the course of eight years, they cycled further into extremism of various types—from Red Caesarism and "regime change" to Catholic integralism and Christian nationalism. And as went the New Right intellectuals, so too did many prominent public figures and politicians. JD Vance's political rise was in nearly perfect—and radicalizing—lockstep with the growth of the New Right movement. So was Elon Musk's.

So what exactly did the New Right oppose? In brief, they turned against the Reagan/Buckley establishment that had dominated the Republican Party since the 1980s, moving farther right on social issues and foreign policy and left on economics (in the sense of questioning the tenets of neoliberalism and being open to greater state involvement in the economy). William F. Buckley (1925–2008) was one of the most important conservative voices of the twentieth century. In 1955 he founded *National Review*, which served as the intellectual anchor of the American right for many decades. Buckley and the people he gathered near the magazine sought to raise the tenor of conservatism in America—or, as he put it, to "articulate a position on world affairs which a conservative candidate can adhere to without fear of intellectual embarrassment or political surrealism."[16] This endeavor was, for a time, successful.

President Reagan famously and succinctly defined his conservative movement as a three-legged stool ("the Gipper's Stool"), and very much along the ideological lines forged by *National Review*. The three legs that sustained his movement were (1) social conservatism; (2) free-market economics (i.e., fiscal conservatism); and (3) anticommunism (along with foreign interventionism). The first two legs had been part of the Old Right, but the third was distinctive and new. The Soviet Union was now the sole other great power, and it needed countering, even if that meant compromising, for a time, with big government on the domestic front.[17]

The Reagan/Buckley movement of the 1970s was sometimes labeled the "New Right"; for the sake of clarity, in this book I use Reagan/Buckley conservatism, "fusionism," and "establishment conservatism" synonymously to describe the dominant ideological umbrella of the conservatism of the last half-century. ("Movement conservatism" is another relevant term, and encompasses the broader coalition of activists and organizers who worked to shape the GOP in the same period.)[18] Reaganism began as a reprise of Goldwaterism and, as with Goldwaterism, was championed by the minds at *National Review*—intellectuals like Frank Meyer, James Burnham, Paul Weyrich, and Buckley—as well as by institutions like the American Enterprise Institute and the Heritage Foundation.[19]

As the theorist of so-called fusionism, Frank Meyer argued that traditional conservative values, liberal economics, and opposition to communism were all essential to freedom (and that interference by the state meant interference with freedom).[20] James Burnham was an editor at *National Review*, where he wrote a regular column in which, according to one scholar, he "excoriated every president from Truman to Carter for appeasing the Soviets."[21] The social conservative leg of the Gipper's Stool was galvanized by the growing Christian Right movement, and by populist figures like Buchanan, Rush Limbaugh, Jerry Falwell, Phyllis Schlafly, and Richard Viguerie (Falwell founded Moral Majority in 1979).[22]

The Reagan/Buckley style of conservatism won elections and dominated the Republican Party for many years. Trumpism demonstrates the extent to which Reagan/Buckley fusionist conservatism was a temporary and fragile settlement that masked the enduring id of old-fashioned American conservatism, including the Hard Right fringe, and today's New Right ascension represents the latest push-pull in America's cycle of conservative extremism.

The flipside of right flank attacks on conservative "sell-outs" is gatekeeping from the center, and among America's conservative elites, concerns about the extremist fringe have waxed and waned. As early as 1960, Republican leaders and intellectuals like Russell Kirk and Buckley worried about the extent to which the GOP tolerated (or encouraged) extremists like the John Birchers in their midst. (The Birchers were anticommunist activists distinguished for their paranoia, conspiracism, and antisemitism.)[23] In 1964 the Goldwater Republicans refused to admonish extremists like the Birchers and the Ku Klux Klan in the party, and Goldwater won the primary—an obvious victory for the Birchers and Klansmen. But he lost the election, badly. And when Reagan ran for governor of California in 1965, he began openly denouncing the Birchers. Buckley did too, issuing a special report in the October 1965 issue of the *National Review* that was critical of them. Over the course of the coming decades, Buckley would keep Birchers from having bylines at the *National Review*.[24]

Conservatives will sometimes speak as though these actions succeeded in establishing a cordon sanitaire around the conservative establishment. As today's New Right plainly demonstrates, that was always something of a myth.[25] Behind the burnished images of the establishment players, the rest of the party was not so punctilious, and boundaries proved porous. The forces that sustained the Birchers never went away; they went underground and festered. "Paleoconservatism"—an intellectual counter to neoconservatism rooted in the Old Right—was a persistent thorn in the side of the fusionist establishment through the 1990s and early 2000s. As the establishment faltered at the end of the last century and liberal social victories continued to accrue at the beginning of this one, these older forces raged forth like the chthonic Furies of the ancient world.

The nomination of Donald Trump as the GOP candidate for president in 2016 was a reactionary eruption of buried conservative ideas and sentiment against a compromised and stagnating conservative mainstream and their liberal friends. If the old establishment stood on the three pillars of social conservatism, fiscal conservatism, and foreign interventionism, the New Right stands on four: social conservativism (Reno's strong gods), economic nationalism, isolationist foreign policy, and anti-immigration (Anton's trifecta). Between 2016 and 2024, the New Right was most consistent in its commitment to old-fashioned traditionalist values and opposition to immigration; the legs of economic nationalism and isolationism were wobblier. In these years, the MAGA New Right excelled at culture warriorism but was less effective at escaping the Republican Party's prior commitments to big tax breaks and the American establishment's interventionism in foreign affairs. The early days of 2025 revealed a second administration much less cowed and confused than the first.

———

The reconfiguration we have seen within the conservative intellectual universe has been dramatic. At the end of the Cold War, the fusionist coalition faltered, and then there were new crises, like 9/11, the (second) Iraq War, and the economic crisis of 2008. The American right also saw both the election of Barack Obama in 2008 and the 2015 Supreme Court decision in defense of marriage equality as major national crises. With Trump, a new opportunity emerged, and the New Right seized the day, breaking hard with the recent past. Whereas conservative intellectuals, with some important caveats, have often served as a brake and restraint on the right's worst impulses, the MAGA New Right fast became an engine and accelerant for extremism. The old cordons were soon *épuisés*; the guardrails all but vanished. And though the various New Right camps may disagree about what an ideal future looks like, in each instance they are backward-looking socially and antiliberal politically. They want, in the words of the libertarian thinker Murray Rothbard (as newly recollected by John Ganz), to "break the clock" and "repeal the twentieth century," or perhaps to take us back to before the Civil Rights Act, or to the founding era, or even the Middle Ages.[26] And unlike Rothbard and his friends in the 1990s, or Goldwater in the 1960s, the New Right, thanks to Trump, has had extraordinary success in gaining proximity to power and fueling change. They are finding enormous audiences and achieving an illiberal renaissance.

As these conservatives broke with the fusionist establishment, they also came into their own. I count three main differences between today's New Right and its precursors like the Goldwater movement, paleoconservatism, and the Tea Party.

First, it is populated by savvy and sophisticated young people who understand populism as well as the transformed landscape of modern media.

Second, it is misogynist and obsessed with masculinity in a way that the older iterations were not (they were often antifeminist and masculinist, but not so openly misogynist as the New Right is today). Kristin Kobes Du Mez, in her book *Jesus and John Wayne* (2020), describes how evangelical support for Trump was not an aberration or a merely pragmatic compromise but rather "the culmination of evangelicals' embrace of militant masculinity, an ideology that enshrines patriarchal authority and condones the callous display of power, at home and abroad." The MAGA New Right is playing catch-up with the world that Du Mez describes.[27]

The final and most obvious difference between the far-right conservatisms of the past and today's movement is that, under Trump, the far right ascended unambiguously to the center of power in the Republican Party. For some on the far right—as we will see in this book—even Reagan seemed like a great capitulator: someone who had betrayed their cause by ceding ground to the center and the left. That is not how they talk about Trump.

———

The New Right also qualifies straightforwardly as a right-wing populist movement. The Dutch political theorist Cas Mudde defines populism as an ideology "that considers society to be ultimately separated into two homogeneous and antagonistic groups, 'the pure people' and 'the corrupt elite,' and which argues that politics should be an expression of *volonté générale* (general will) of the people."[28] For Mudde and others, the twin pillars of populism are anti-elitism and antipluralism, and populists will claim an exclusive right to govern on behalf of "the real people" and in opposition to elites.[29] (In the American context, there are stark differences between right-wing populism and left-wing populism, in that, for example, Bernie Sanders and his supporters tend to reject nativism.)[30] The New Right takes aim against elites of all stripes, despite being powerful elites themselves, and against pluralism, despite the disagreements within their movement. They argue that the system is failing because elites have not protected the true (and always singular) American way of life. These discussions often echo older forms of racism and antisemitism. The New Right doesn't care. Its adherents are opposed to pluralism in principle and do not believe in the egalitarian, multiracial, pluralistic democracy that has gained real traction in the United States in recent decades—what Frederick Douglass called "the composite nation."[31] Increasingly, and as part of its radicalization, the New Right is openly minoritarian and antidemocratic in its theoretical principles.[32]

If some of what I have described of the New Right vision sounds contradictory, that is largely because it is. It is not clear, however, how much the incoherence of the New Right movement matters in the rough and tumble of real politics. As the political theorist Matthew McManus—who has also written extensively about the New Right—explains, "Being unable to live with ideological contradictions has never been a major weakness of the hard right." He continues: "Indeed a willingness to sublimate and affirm contradiction as expressing some allegedly deep truth, such that subordination to a revanchist aristocracy is really a populist rejection of liberal elitism, is almost a requirement to play the part."[33] Most camps of the New Right are not bothered by the inconsistencies and hypocrisies of their movement. But there have been some schisms in the movement since it started to take shape in 2016, which I address in this book.

The New Right movement in the United States is also part of a trend toward right-wing extremism and populism in democracies around the world. The shift began with the newly unsettled Great Power landscape that came with the end of the Cold War, the austere economic programs of the late twentieth century, the failures of American foreign policy in the Middle East after 9/11, the decline of American manufacturing, and rolling economic, refugee, and emigration crises of the twenty-first century. By the time Brexit happened and Donald Trump was elected in 2016, right-wing populist movements opposing free trade and foreign interventionism were gaining ground all over. Many of these movements were also nationalist and xenophobic, favoring one national cultural identity over all others, and usually lining up behind a strongman—or strongwoman—who promised to restore the dominance of that supposedly more authentic group. The list of such figures is long: Jair Bolsonaro in Brazil, Marine Le Pen in France, Viktor Orbán in Hungary, Narendra Modi in India, Benjamin Netanyahu in Israel, Giorgia Meloni in Italy, and, of course, Vladimir Putin in Russia have all fueled the international turn to chauvinistic nationalism. It is a response to a sense of growing international instability and insecurity that is not unique to any one place, and, increasingly, these groups learn from one another and collaborate. The MAGA New Right often imitates Orbán, who has called his approach "illiberal democracy" or "Christian liberty," and which involves using majority democratic support to install an authoritarian regime.[34]

Paradoxically, the New Right fully cohered only after January 6, 2021. The attack on the US Capitol was a major point of consolidation and loyalty testing—the moment Republican leaders briefly questioned the New Right dispensation, only to see it more and more openly affirmed. Eventually, Trump and the New Right's lie about a stolen election became orthodoxy on the right and, as David A. Graham observed, took the shape of a "New Lost Cause" myth, the recitation of which became a (bizarre) symbol of patriotism.[35] This subversion was a clear sign of the power of the New Right, and of its autocratic nature. The writer and Russian expatriate Masha Gessen has written that, "unmoored from lived reality, the autocrat has no need to be consistent. In fact, the ability to change his story at will is a demonstration of power."[36] Gessen named this phenomenon "The Power Lie." The phrase nicely describes how Trump and the New Right have approached January 6, 2021. This is a destabilizing approach to truth and reality that puts them firmly in the authoritarian camp.

My Background and Approach

My perspective on American politics is shaped, for better and worse, by my education in political philosophy. I was born in Edmonton, Alberta, Canada, to bourgeois, hippie parents and had ambitious plans to be a doctor in the developing world until a required university course in political theory with a conservative professor—Leon Craig—changed the course of my life.

A former US marine, Craig had a knack for drawing out the seriousness of old books, and the one he taught best was Plato's *Republic*. I happened into a small Plato study group while I took Craig's course; we met every week—often gathering at a restaurant called Plato's Pizza (really)—and went through the Allan Bloom translation of Plato's great dialogue on justice line by line.[37]

Reading through the *Republic* slowly like that was exhilarating; it allowed us to experience the subtlety of the dialogue, to puzzle at the details together, and to wonder at how much of it resonated in our lives. Plato came to feel like my own personal soul whisperer and diviner. I remember reading Emerson's rapturous essay "Plato, or The Philosopher" at around that time. Emerson declares that "Plato is philosophy and philosophy, Plato" and concludes with the beautiful line, "The great-eyed Plato proportioned the lights and shades after the genius of our life."[38] At the time, I read that and thought: "Yes, that's exactly right." I was totally hooked—and so were my friends. Many of us stayed on and did MA degrees with Dr. Craig and Dr. Heidi Studer, who was also a wonderful teacher. Many went on to do PhDs in Straussian political philosophy. Jump ahead some twenty years, to January 2025, and one of us, Jonathan Pidluzny, was appointed deputy chief of staff for policy and programs in the US Department of Education under Trump and Vance. Another, Murray Bessette, was hired as a senior advisor in the Office of Postsecondary Education the following month.

The sort of encounter I had with Plato at the University of Alberta is hardly reserved for Straussians, but that was my entry point to the world of political philosophy.[39] The "Straussian" moniker describes a dispersed group of intellectuals and academics (many of whom we will meet in the pages to come), typically conservative in their politics, who work in the style of the political philosopher Leo Strauss (1899–1973). Strauss was an émigré who left fascist Germany in the early 1930s and eventually came to the United States, where he devoted himself to the careful reading and exegesis of diverse works of political philosophy, mainly from what we call the Western canon—Plato, Aristotle, al-Farabi, Maimonides, Aquinas, Machiavelli, Hobbes, Spinoza, Rousseau, and so on through the messy centuries.

When I say "careful" I mean more than just attentive: Strauss believed (and made a good case) that many of the most significant texts in the history of political thought were multilayered and highly stylized works of tremendous literary and political sophistication. He held that such masterpieces were intentionally crafted to speak to different readers in different ways, and even, in some instances, secretly to shape or influence historical events. He called this the tradition of "esotericism."[40] A big part of my education involved reading and decoding political texts in accordance with this Straussian approach—an approach that many on the New Right share. Indeed, many of my teachers' teachers were also their teachers' teachers.

Strauss's legacy as a scholar and teacher is mixed and highly controversial. This reflects the complexity and pluralism of the vast tradition he inhabited, as well as his distinctive approach to that tradition (esotericism—like many other modes of thought—bears some similarities to conspiracy thinking; it's also just a very standard artistic device—think of fans decoding secret messages in Taylor Swift's lyrics). Another factor in this legacy is the number of Strauss's students, or students of students, who have been engaged in American politics and culture at the highest levels for decades—to the extent that there was speculation in the early 2000s about a Straussian neoconservative cabal controlling Washington. At times the speculation was fanciful and overheated, but the influence of Strauss on a certain strata of Washington insiders was undeniable, and West Coast Straussians certainly figure prominently in the growth of the New Right (they form, as we will see, the core of the Claremonter camp).

This book bears the marks of my Straussian education. Not only do several chapters—especially the early ones—concentrate on the influence that Straussian thought has had on the conservative movement, but in some ways my approach itself is Straussian. I focus squarely on the intellectuals and ideas behind right-wing populism, so I pay less attention than others, for example, to contemporary media dynamics, QAnon, "following the money," technology, race, gender, and economics. This is not to say these other factors matter less. Rather, I focus on what I know. My hope is to shine light on the political scene in the United States as it unfolded between 2016 and 2024, in order to contribute to a better and truer collective sense of the whole.

In practice, I have concentrated on each actor's speeches and writings and arguments, trying my best to give their ideas a fair shake, and assuming a degree of good faith. I take for granted the notion that ideas—and not just or even primarily material conditions—have power in shaping our world. Words and ideas obviously do not fully constitute human life, but they play an important role. The ideas of the New Right have been powerful, despite being in many ways untethered from empirical reality. The New Right thinkers are immensely successful propagandists and culture warriors who can show us the power of cultural politics.

They can also reveal the hard limits of such an approach, and indeed the limits of what I, throughout this book, call "Ideas First" political philosophy. The Ideas First approach is typical of the conservative intellectual world and is captured by popular right-wing catchphrases like "politics is downstream from culture" and "ideas have consequences," as well as by the proliferation of ideological institutions (like the one I attended in Charlottesville) that educate young conservatives and initiate them into right-wing discourses and traditions.

Ideas Have Consequences was the title of a book by Richard Weaver in 1948 that could be considered the urtext of Ideas First thinking. Weaver traced modernity's ills to the abandonment of transcendentals (or to "nominalism"—the belief that universals exist only as categories of the human mind, and not "out there" as permanent things). "Like Macbeth," he wrote, "Western man made an evil decision, which has become the efficient and final cause of other evil decisions." Weaver's Western man had fallen for the seductions of "the witches on the heath" and "the powers of darkness," of all those who denied objective moral truth and embraced "man is the measure" relativism. This was an intellectual move that invited a bundle of problems that have since become trigger words for conservatives: not only relativism, but also materialism, historicism, and politics as will to power. Without a transcendental metaphysics, in their view, there is nothing to limit political turpitude, and no reason for people to be good and true. Only philosophical traditionalism can ground and limit politics.[41]

The New Right generally agrees with Weaver (whereas I want to hear out those witches), but they also show why the Ideas First approach is confused. Too often, New Right thinkers find themselves in the awkward position of using intellectual abstractions to defend nativism, rooted-ness, and love of one's own. Too often, the recitation of moral ideology is privileged over the practice of good and virtuous deeds. And too often, highbrow abstractions smother straightforward real-world truths— about, say, who won which election, who invaded which country and when, or which demographic is being abused and oppressed. And in many instances, "intellectual abstractions" and Ideas First are too gener-ous as phrases, for we are in fact talking about myths, ideology, and lies. As someone who tends to gravitate toward an Ideas First approach my-self, I hope to be your guide to this particular New Right pathology— and a few others besides, like monomania (the idea that there is only one legitimate perspective on anything) and catastrophism.

If my focus on ideas is typical of Straussians, in other ways the book is very un-Straussian. For one thing, I am focused on very recent history, whereas most academic Straussians home in on figures from the canonical past. I also take it for granted that historical context matters a great deal, both for interpreting texts and ideas and for understanding—and evaluating—the relationship between theory and action. Many Straussians show a limited interest in the empirical details of history (I would not say quite the same thing of Strauss, who emphasized the importance of context for rhetoric—something that distinguishes the Straussian tradition from analytic philosophy). I also care what others, including non-Straussian conservatives, have to say about politics, and big parts of this book are about them. The intellectual movement in support of Trumpism began with a group of Straussians, and Straussians constitute important parts of the movement but the New Right is something quite distinct, and certainly not all Straussians are part of it. Many prominent "Never Trump" conservatives and anti-Trump liberals have Straussian backgrounds.[42]

Perhaps the most important difference between me and the Straussian world in general is that I am not a conservative and never have been, while many Straussians are and always were. Strauss himself declined to identify as a conservative, as did Allan Bloom (who was perhaps his most influential student). But Strauss's legacy in the academy and beyond is conservative. And I am more liberal in my politics than either of them.

I came to my belief in multiracial, pluralistic, liberal democracy slowly, and partly through a decades-long intellectual sojourn through the history of political thought. That academic work informs this book in obvious ways. But I also want to be clear that my own belief in liberal democracy does not come primarily from my study of political philosophy (especially in the Straussian context, which tends to be oblivious both to public policy and to post-Rawlsian liberal thought). It comes from my study of constitutional law and of history (especially the atrocities of the twentieth century and the wave of liberal constitutionalism that emerged in the aftermath), and from my own experiences in the world—including the experience of becoming a parent.

I want to be direct about this because it bears on material in the book, especially when it comes to the Hard Right's contempt for women and nontraditional families (and, indirectly, their contempt for children, too). Becoming a mother has made me ferociously attached to liberalism—to its hospitals, doulas, and midwives; to its everyday domestic comforts; to the time it affords me (because I'm lucky) with my children, husband, friends, and family; to the hope that I can live a long and rich life in community with them while also freely pursuing some of my own interests and loves; and to the hope that my kids will grow up and live good, free lives, too. A person would have to be an ingrate and a fool not to feel immense gratitude for a life like mine—full of what the Russian Jewish writer Nadezhda Mandelstam called the "privilege of ordinary heartbreaks"—and for the political system that makes it possible.[43]

Having my own kids has also made me see the glaring injustices and stupidities of contemporary American life more clearly. You know the list. It includes grotesque and rising economic inequality and the absurd consolidation of economic and political power in the hands of the few (and ever fewer!), manic careerism, persistent and degrading racial inequities, dystopian gun violence, drugs and deaths of despair, the brutalities and accountability failures of American policing, cruel attacks on LGBTQ communities, consumption and materialism, relentless environmental destruction, and the new barrage of AI. To this long list I'd add the contemporary degradation of public common goods and public education (in the trades as well as the liberal arts and humanities), and the evergreen democratic dangers of groupthink and intellectual monomania that make honest discussion of these matters so hard.

I want these things to change. One of the most frustrating things about politics today—and here I am thinking about the New Right mainly, but certainly not exclusively—is the amount of money, energy, and talent that it churns through, wasted, when there is always so much to be done.

————

Many others have done excellent work on the past and present of American conservatism, in articles, Substacks, podcasts, and books. I am constantly learning from others' insights and excavations and have tried my best to give credit where it is due. My core purpose is not to examine historical precursors to the New Right; I focus on the intellectual world that has grown up under the cover of Trumpism more than on the intellectual roots of these changes. This approach shines a light on an area of critical discontinuity with what came before. Understanding the deep continuities between today's political realities and those of the past can help us all to grasp the depth and scope of today's political problems; understanding the shift among conservative intellectuals can enable us to see the acuity of the challenges that the liberal world faces today. Ultimately, it's best to have a clear sense of both.

I have been writing about New Right intellectuals since 2019. The most common response I get when I mention this to liberals is something along the lines of "Trumpy intellectuals? Now that's an oxymoron!" or "Hahaha, I think you mean dumb fascists!" While the impulse is understandable, it's also mistaken and counterproductive.

Many on the left assume that the only serious reason to support the GOP has to do with finance and tax returns, and that right-wing voters are racists. But people's motives are mixed, and America's reactionary intellectuals are armed with more than greed and prejudice. They also have reasons and arguments that they appear to care about, whole epochs and libraries full, ready-to-hand. What the writer Matthew Rose says about the radical right is true of the New Right, too:

> Almost everything written about the "alternative right" has been wrong in one respect. The alt-right is not stupid; it is deep. Its ideas are not ridiculous; they are serious. To appreciate this fact, one needs to inquire beyond its presence on social media, where its obnoxious use of insult, obscenity, and racism has earned it a reputation for moral idiocy. The reputation is deserved, but do not be deceived. Behind its online tantrums and personal attacks are arguments of seductive power.[44]

The New Right's questions, ideas, and arguments may not be of the sort to convince the average *New York Times* subscriber, but they are effective in their contexts, and it's not like they are easy to refute. Education and specialization being what they are today, the people I focus on in this book know more than your average JD or political science PhD about early American political history and about the history of the so-called West, and of course many of them have other specialties and areas of expertise besides. I am generally not an admirer of the people I write about here, but it would be foolish to deny that they are smart and well-informed in their own way. It's obviously possible to be highly knowledgeable and to have terrible judgment or dangerous politics.

To presume otherwise—to believe that there is nothing to learn from these thinkers and no compelling noneconomic reasons to support something like Trumpism—is naive and dangerous. It misunderstands and fetishizes intelligence, by presuming that real brains never chase after raw power. It fails to see the possibility and power of genuine intellectual fanaticism—and the allure of people who have strong convictions backed by strong arguments. And it assumes a deep sameness about one's fellow citizens and so refuses to contend with real, protracted ideological disagreement and conflict. In other words, it refuses to reckon with what might be the greatest challenge posed by political life: the fact that people really do think differently and disagree, about just about everything, and especially about the most important things, like the meaning of life, God, and the soul, and what is good.

Above all else, the naive view overestimates liberalism's immediate appeal and underestimates liberalism's fragility. Growing right-wing extremism has not emerged in a vacuum but in many instances is a response, however misguided, to real problems, and to the real vulnerabilities of liberal democracy. It reflects some of the actual failures of modern liberal politics and economics, of modern liberal culture, and of the corporate neoliberal academy. One of the major advantages of spending time with the New Right is that it allows us to see these challenges more clearly, and to think through future possibilities for a pluralistic liberal order more deeply. And with some urgency.

2

The Claremonters

ON JULY 16, 1964, Senator Barry Goldwater of Arizona accepted the Republican nomination for the presidential race. He did so at the Cow Palace in Daly City, on the outskirts of San Francisco. Goldwater's nomination was a major event in the history of American conservatism, and even in the history of American politics. It was a galvanizing, transformative moment, one that perhaps more than any other signified the departure of moderates and liberals from the GOP and its realignment into a fully conservative party. It also signaled the rise of westerners over East Coasters in the upper echelons of the GOP.[1]

The principal contest that year was between Goldwater, on the one side, and moderates like New York governor Nelson Rockefeller, Michigan governor George Romney, and Pennsylvania governor William Scranton, on the other. A poll just prior to the convention showed Scranton with a major advantage, but Goldwater ended up winning handily.

Goldwater was a staunch conservative with a reputation as a principled renegade, and was often styled a "cowboy conservative." He stridently opposed communism and centralized government, including the New Deal, and he was a libertarian who could make a strong moral and spiritual case for free markets; Goldwater subscribed to the idea that bigger government was coeval with an emasculated citizenry, and as a Senator had argued that left-wing philosophy had weakened the American people by serving up "a dole of inflated greenbacks as a pacifier for lost manhood."[2]

He was also perceived as a loose cannon—and presented as such by his opponent, President Lyndon B. Johnson. In his smash-hit book from 1960, *The Conscience of a Conservative*, Goldwater was hawkish on nuclear weapons, arguing against disarmament and for the development of nuclear capacities.[3] During the campaign, he made several remarks about his willingness to use atomic and nuclear devices in Vietnam.[4] Johnson turned that against him, as Rockefeller had done before. When Goldwater chose "In your heart, you know he's right" as his campaign slogan—often interpreted as a nod to white southerners and extremists—the Johnson campaign responded with "In your guts, you know he's nuts."[5]

The strongest opposition to Goldwater concerned his position on civil rights. His relationship with the movement was complicated. He had been a lifelong member of the NAACP in Arizona and was an early advocate of desegregation in his state. But he voted against the 1964 Civil Rights Act due to concerns about constitutional overreach in several of its clauses—a choice that likely cost him many votes in the general election. The progressive left was extremely critical of Goldwater and blamed him not only for the 1964 vote, but for what they saw as the dangerous, and racist, implications of his "states' rights" political ideology.

Dubbed the "Woodstock of the Right" by Goldwater biographer Rick Perlstein, the Cow Palace convention was a tension-filled, raucous spectacle that would also become something of a referendum on civil rights.[6] The new national law had been passed in June 1964, and Goldwater was one of only six GOP senators to vote against it. It was signed into law by President Johnson on July 2, 1964. Martin Luther King Jr. had spoken at the Cow Palace in May 1964 at an interfaith Human Dignity rally, and he returned to the Bay Area in July to testify at the GOP Platform Committee, hoping to persuade the party to acknowledge the full constitutionality of the new national civil rights law.[7] The initiative was voted down, 68–31.

Governor Rockefeller subsequently addressed the full convention to defend a minority resolution meant to denounce extremism in the party. "It is essential," he said, "that this convention repudiate here and now any doctrinaire, militant minority whether Communist, Ku Klux Klan or Birchers." And he warned that the Republican Party was in danger of subversion by a radical and well-financed attack that was "wholly alien" to the "sound and honest Republican liberalism that has kept this party abreast of human need in a changing world."[8] Though there were some boisterous Rockefeller supporters in the audience, it was, in the words of the journalist Theodore White, as if he "were poking with a long lance and prodding a den of hungry lions—they roared back at him." Early in the speech, the Goldwater crowd erupted against Rockefeller, "hating and screaming and reveling in their own frenzy."[9] The motion was defeated "by an overwhelming standing vote."[10] Jackie Robinson, another outspoken critic of Goldwater who was present at the Cow Palace, described it as a waking nightmare.[11]

The culminating event of the convention was when Goldwater, "Mr. Conservative" himself, took to the stage. The reception could not have been warmer. He gave a rousing speech that culminated with some famous lines: "I would remind you," Goldwater intoned, "that extremism in defense of liberty is no vice. And let me remind you also that moderation in the pursuit of justice is no virtue." When Goldwater got to these lines, which had been composed by a political theorist named Harry V. Jaffa, he had to pause twice for extended applause.

The message did not play so well on the national stage, where Goldwater was broadly viewed as an extremist, and where his movement was sometimes viewed as fascistic.[12] King, who had formerly followed a policy of not endorsing political candidates, compromised that principle to denounce Goldwater.[13] And months later, Goldwater would lose the election in a landslide to Lyndon B. Johnson. As the historian Rick Perlstein writes, "The political world's near unanimous judgment was that Goldwater's landslide loss to LBJ that November was a disaster for all Republicans, not just conservative Republicans." Perlstein also notes, however, that 1964 catalyzed fervent grassroots organizing and inaugurated a Republican Party that was "surer of its identity and better positioned to harvest the bounty—particularly in the South."[14]

For the next half century, the forces that had lined up behind Goldwater moved in and out of national psyche. But they did not go away—thanks in part to the intellectual fire kept burning by Harry Jaffa, the author of Goldwater's famous lines, and his students.

————

On September 7, 2016, Rush Limbaugh—the right-wing radio personality who, prior to his death in 2021, averaged fifteen million listeners a week—spent most of his show reading from the pages of the *Claremont Review of Books*, the flagship journal of the Claremont Institute, a conservative think tank some four hundred miles south of the Cow Palace. The institute was founded by students of Harry Jaffa in 1979. "2016 is the Flight 93 election," Limbaugh announced, "Charge the cockpit or you die. You may die anyway. You—or the leader of your party—may make it into the cockpit and not know how to fly or land the plane. There are no guarantees. Except one: if you don't try, death is certain."[15]

Rush was exuberant: "The piece is so good. It is just a home run, every paragraph." He explained that the best thing about it was how, unlike the Never Trumpers, the author conveys a sense of urgency and outrage about the state of the country. Here is how Limbaugh summed it up: "The point of this whole piece is that Donald Trump's the only hope, that conservatism no longer applies. We're way past that. Conservatism, as has been applied the last ten years, what do we have to show for it? We have a bunch of midterm election victories, but nothing done with them." He titled his show that day "The Shaming of the Never Trumpers."

Much ink was spilled over "The Flight 93 Election" essay, which was published in September 2016 under the pseudonym Publius Decius Mus, and which Limbaugh helped turn viral. Publius's essay made such a big splash in part because of its sensational rhetoric. The imagery deployed referred to United Airlines Flight 93, which on September 11, 2001, was hijacked by terrorists who intended to crash the plane at the US Capitol or the White House. The essay's author was comparing a potential Hillary Clinton presidency to the worst-ever terrorist attack on American soil, and Trump supporters to would-be heroes of the republic. "If you don't try, death is certain," Decius wrote. "To compound the metaphor: a Hillary Clinton presidency is Russian Roulette with a semi-auto. With Trump, at least you can spin the cylinder and take your chances."[16]

The essay was riddled with this kind of apocalypticism and conspiracism. The last big section was about how everything was stacked against genuine conservatism and Trumpism. The media and universities who control the culture were against them; conservative leaders were in the habit of playing way too nice and so were in effect acting against themselves; and the electoral system was on the brink of being overrun through the "ceaseless importation of Third World foreigners" who were not "traditionally American" and so voted against Republicans. (This mode of thinking has since come to be known as the Great Replacement conspiracy.)

But the essay was also distinctive because it made a positive analytical case for Trump. "The truth is," Decius wrote, "that Trump articulated, if incompletely and inconsistently, the right stances on the right issues—immigration, trade, and war—right from the beginning." Trump was a "worse than imperfect candidate," but America was in dire straits, and it would probably take a "loudmouth" like Trump to do something about it—to stop immigration, put an end to the endless wars, and create a more equitable economy.

The most interesting thing about the essay was how it grappled with the limits of conservatism. The core argument was that anyone who called themselves conservative should be willing to vote for Trump, and that anyone who went along with the status quo by voting for Hillary Clinton was in fact not a real conservative. That strikes me as true in a sense, and the Trump years continued to reveal how hard-line and uncompromising conservatism like this is incapable of contending with historical change. That is one of its major liabilities.

Weeks later, Limbaugh was elated at the election outcome. "There are so many vibrantly great feelings to share. We have not lost our country," he said.[17] In the tumultuous months after Trump's victory, Decius's identity was disclosed in the pages of the soon-to-be-defunct neoconservative magazine *The Weekly Standard*. It was Michael Anton, who had recently been hired by the Trump administration as part of the National Security Council (Anton was given the equivalent of Ben Rhodes's job in the Obama White House). He was also a thinker of the West Coast Straussian school and an admirer of Harry V. Jaffa.

Jaffa and Anton are not the only Straussians who have caused upset on America's national stage. And though the extent to which their lives and work have been true to Strauss's thought is questionable, Strauss has had an indelible impact on conservative intellectual discourse for decades, and his legacy—as interpreted by his students on the West Coast—is palpable in the New Right movement, especially with its emphasis on the American founding, culture, and higher education. Several of the main characters in this book have a Straussian intellectual lineage, including, most worryingly, some of the most influential thinkers of the Hard Right, whom we will meet in chapter 6.

In this chapter we move through Strauss's influence in American political thought, tracing the lines from Strauss to Jaffa to Anton and Limbaugh, as a way of seeing the early seeds of New Right conservatism and New Right extremism. Our main purpose here is to understand West Coast Straussianism, which is the political philosophy of the Claremonters, our first of three intellectual factions of the New Right.

The two most important thinkers in this Straussian trajectory are Harry Jaffa and Allan Bloom. Jaffa was one of Strauss's most political students and the founder of West Coast Straussianism as a school of thought. Bloom was Strauss's most successful culture warrior, with his 1987 hit *The Closing of the American Mind*. Jaffa and Bloom were very different people and thinkers, but they were both devoted to an Ideas First style of engagement. Jaffa also indulged in his fair share of monomania and catastrophism. Michael Anton speaks glowingly of both men.

Leo Strauss and Harry Jaffa

Here is how Harry Jaffa described his encounter with Leo Strauss:

Nothing had prepared me for Leo Strauss. Unlike his students at Chicago, I encountered him unadorned by any distinction of position or place. [He] was a physically insignificant little man with a weak voice.

His presence was as unimpressive as the dilapidated classrooms provided by the New School. But he was pure overwhelming intellectual force. After a few minutes into one of his seminars, the little man became a giant. Every great book was a kind of Treasure Island, or more particularly a map of an island holding a treasure.

But you had to decipher the map, and do the work of discovery, overcoming the obstacles by which great art, imitating nature, trains the mind to be worthy of its gifts. One of Strauss's secrets was that he made you feel not a passive receptacle of his insights, but as his partner in a voyage of discovery. He was the captain of the ship. But you were part of the crew. And you sailed together.[18]

Strauss was born in 1899 and grew up in a Jewish household in Prussia. He served with the German army in World War I, after which he enrolled at the University of Hamburg, where he earned his doctoral degree. He studied under Ernst Cassirer and sat in on classes with some of the most renowned philosophers of the era, including Edmund Husserl and Martin Heidegger. When the Nazis gained power in Europe, Strauss sought opportunities elsewhere and spent a period in England before landing with his family in the United States in 1937. He taught at the New School in New York for ten years, where he had Jaffa as a student, and then for twenty years at the University of Chicago. Before his death in 1973, Strauss spent time at Claremont Men's College (now Claremont Mckenna) in California, and at St. John's College in Annapolis, Maryland.

Leo Strauss spent the second half of his life in the United States, but his mind was firmly anchored in Europe. Though much of his early work focused on Maimonides and al-Farabi, his fifteen-plus books focused exclusively on European thinkers, as did his teaching schedule, with pride of place given to the ancient Greeks.[19] Generally speaking, he left the subject of America to students like Jaffa.

As we will see, there have always been major feuds among Strauss's students, which hinge on their different ways of reading Strauss, and different interpretations of old canonical books.[20] Harry Jaffa came to represent West Coast Straussianism, which sees the American experiment as resting largely on premodern foundations. The various kinds of regimes and foundings are core themes throughout Straussian thought, and most Straussians—though not all—betray a preference for ancient political thought. (Strauss himself spoke in terms of sweeping, world-historical dichotomies and antagonisms: "Athens v. Jerusalem," the "Ancients v. the Moderns," and "Reason v. Revelation.") But for orthodox West Coast Straussians, or Claremonters, the American founding stood apart. Whereas other Straussians would speak, echoing Strauss himself, of how modernity was built on "low but solid ground," the Claremonters believed that the American founding was based largely on premodern ideas, which saved it from being quite so low. For them, America's founding-era thought was the result of a grand synthesis of biblical political thought, ancient Greek philosophy, and modern political thought—or, as one commentator memorably put it, referring to the thought of Harry Jaffa, "of Athens, Jerusalem, and Peoria."[21]

Jaffa was originally from New York. He earned his doctorate from the New School of Social Research in 1951, where he was one of Strauss's first graduate students. (He had also studied with Harvey Mansfield Sr., a government professor, as an undergraduate at Columbia University. Mansfield Sr. was father to Harvey Mansfield Jr., one of the country's other famous Straussians and conservatives, who would land at Harvard.) Upon graduation, and reportedly thanks to the help of Mansfield Sr., Jaffa gained a professorship at Ohio State University, where he remained for over a decade.[22] In 1964 he moved to California, where he joined the faculty at Claremont Men's College. He remained there for twenty-five years, until his retirement in 1989, at which point he joined the Claremont Institute as a senior fellow.[23]

The Claremont Institute was founded in 1979 by some of Jaffa's students; it had no formal connection to the Claremont group of colleges, but, as with other conservative institutions that run adjacent to America's colleges and universities, there is overlap among the faculty and scholars, and the ideological influence often goes both ways.

The institute has not always been in the political spotlight, but since its founding in 1979 it has always represented the more politically engaged part of the Straussian landscape. While it has been far less policy-oriented and wonkish than most American think tanks, it has also been more overtly political than other conservative groups in higher education.

The Claremont Institute's political bent has everything to do with Harry Jaffa. Jaffa's students founded the institute, and it was Jaffa's thinking that inspired them. He had politicized Leo Strauss's thought in two significant respects: First, he was among the first to apply Strauss's interpretive methods to the study of American political thought, in what would become his best-known work, *The Crisis of the House Divided*, published in 1959.[24] Second, he became involved in American politics. In 1963 he joined a grassroots group of Goldwater devotees in Ohio, which is how he ended up writing parts of Goldwater's historic acceptance speech at the Cow Palace.

The Crisis of the House Divided was a close study of the Lincoln-Douglas debates. It was not Jaffa's first book, but it was by far his most influential, and widely regarded as a classic by historians. When Jaffa approached the Lincoln-Douglas debates in the 1950s, he did so as someone deeply ensconced in the Straussian outlook and interpretive method, which involves very close reading, including for esoteric teachings and nuances. There was some novelty in his choice of subject—Abraham Lincoln was more statesman than philosopher, and so not the standard choice for Straussian inquiry—but the encounter paid high dividends. In *Crisis*, Jaffa argued that the Lincoln-Douglas debates did not merely represent a series of important moments in the historic 1858 campaign but brought to life an essential political question. Against Douglas's majoritarian claims about popular sovereignty and the rights of states to decide their own fates with regards to slavery, Jaffa argued, Lincoln mounted a much weightier moral argument about the meaning of freedom and equality, as defended in the Declaration of Independence, and their radical incompatibility with the practice of slavery.

As a Straussian book, *Crisis* stands apart for its thick engagement with the historical record. The book is long, and the first third of it consists of an extended, deep, charitable read of Douglas's side of the debate. At the core of Douglas's "popular sovereignty" argument was the principle of democratic self-government: A given population (meaning its white, male portion—a point that Jaffa does not emphasize) should able to decide their own fate, including the fate of slavery in their state or territory. Jaffa's reading presents Douglas as committed to finding a moderate path through the explosive political thickets of the time, and it credits Douglas with the presumption that westward expansion (or "manifest destiny") would lead to the eventual collapse of the slave system. Lincoln, in contrast, argued not only that slavery was unlikely to die out on its own but also that the Dred Scott decision and other midcentury developments were set to transform slavery into a national phenomenon.

Jaffa's approach was novel at the time. Against contemporary historians who downplayed the threat of slavery's expansion or attributed to Lincoln a reckless opportunism in speaking so stridently against such expansion, and then in waging war, Jaffa suggested that Lincoln was a clear-sighted statesman endowed with a deep understanding of the moral logic of freedom and of the Declaration of Independence. Slavery was such a grave injustice and violation that it put America in contradiction with itself—especially with its core principle that "all men are created equal"—and undermined the republican character of the country. Unlike other conservatives of his day, Jaffa did not minimize the evil of slavery.

For Jaffa, it was something of a historical miracle that Lincoln was able to act out that understanding on the stage of American history. He saw a universal philosopher in Lincoln, in one place likening him to the philosopher Socrates in the contest against the sophist Thrasymachus from Plato's *Republic*, engaged in one of the quintessential political debates of the ages. Jaffa's book is strange to read today, partly because it is just so darn Straussian—he turns Lincoln's story into something of a theoretical contrivance; we are witness here to obvious Ideas First philosophizing, even if Jaffa was better on this point than many others—but also because today we take Lincoln's moral seriousness for granted, thanks in part to Jaffa's ideas, and are more familiar with arguments about the deep hypocrisy and contradictions of the founding era.[25]

———

In his second book on Lincoln, *A New Birth of Freedom*, published forty years after the first, Jaffa famously changed his mind about Lincoln's relationship to the framers and the founding.[26] Whereas in *Crisis* he had presented Lincoln as deepening and even transcending the original meaning of the Declaration, through a type of second founding, in *New Birth* he argues that the depth of meaning was there from the start—i.e., Lincoln's actions were a fulfillment of, rather than an improvement on, the founders' ideals. (As Thomas Merrill put it, "By the time of *A New Birth of Freedom*, Jaffa had concluded that the Founding needed no correction.")[27] In this book, not for the last time, Jaffa argued that the American system amounts to the best possible political regime.[28] The main reason for this was that the framers were able to resolve, in practice, the eternal tension between politics and religion (or Athens/Jerusalem, reason/revelation).

These were bold claims that rested on a series of arguments that Jaffa made throughout the last few decades of his life. The core claim was that the American founders had forged a limited constitutional order that made space not only for civic freedom, but also for true moral and religious liberty, and so for something like the true, positive exercise of the human moral faculties. Crucially, Jaffa argued that the Establishment Clause of the US Constitution—which disallows the establishment of a national religion and is understood by many as something that facilitates sectarian disagreement and moral pluralism—had strengthened civic, moral, and religious bonds and agreement.

Writing in 2007 for the *Claremont Review of Books* in an essay entitled "The American Founding as the Best Regime," Jaffa argued that "by strengthening this moral consensus, disestablishment promoted confidence and even friendship among the citizens." He went on to refine the point: "The virtue of the American Founding rests not only upon its defusing of the tension between reason and revelation, but upon their fundamental agreement on a moral code which can guide human life both privately and publicly."[29] For the later Jaffa, the American regime rested as much on a strong moral consensus as it did on religious freedom, for there was a near-perfect harmony, a "fundamental agreement," between the two. By Jaffa's lights, the separation of church and state simply made space for people to act within the shared, highly homogenous, moral universe that he calls "our inheritance from the ancient cities of Athens and Jerusalem." At one point in the essay he writes, "As the Virginia Bill of Rights shows, the Framers never conceived the blessings of liberty in nonmoral terms. They never imagined it to encompass the exhibitionism of lesbians, sodomites, abortionists, drug addicts, and pornographers."

That last sentence is typical of Jaffa's later writings. Indeed, Jaffa's understanding of the Establishment Clause sounds nice enough, until you realize that the moral universe he subscribed to excludes huge swaths of modern philosophy and political thought (and perhaps much of ancient thought, too), as well as much of modern liberalism. "Radical modernity," Jaffa wrote, "is the enemy equally of autonomous human reason and of biblical revelation." He continued: "The core of radical modernity is radical skepticism, a dogmatic skepticism that denies that we do have, or can have, any genuine knowledge of the external world." There are clear echoes here of Richard Weaver's attacks on nominalism. But what Jaffa called "dogmatic skepticism" is hard to distinguish from ordinary philosophical questioning, which need not tailspin into relativism, nihilism, amorality, scientism, Nazism, or Stalinism (which is the declinist narrative that Jaffa presents in his essay and a common refrain on the right). In other words, it is quite possible—perhaps even quite common!—to be a hard skeptic about the possibility of having "genuine knowledge of the external world" in the sense that Jaffa and Weaver meant while also holding on to the possibility of knowledge. Many liberals and pragmatists operate according to such assumptions every day, living good and wholesome lives governed by strong convictions. And of course, most people's worldviews are not entirely consistent, and ideas don't always come first.

Here's another way of putting it: The implication of Jaffa's statement is that, to count as morally viable, we must positively assert that we do have, or can have, "genuine knowledge of the external world." Modern philosophy retorts: "How can we ever really know?," and Jaffa balks. Modern philosophy says, "It's ok: we can still know things, just in a different way," and Jaffa takes it as an attack on everything he's ever held true and good. For him, "The triumph of Western civilization is to be found in the evidence, supplied by both philosophy and revelation, that the human soul, no less by the questions it asks than by the answers it believes it has discovered, participates in a reality that transcends all time and change." Modern philosophy responds with questions like: "OK, but what if we disagree?," or "What if nature is more changeable than you think?," and it makes Jaffa angry. In the essay, he eventually trains his attention on the universities: "It is the outright denial—within the very citadels of learning, the universities—of the dignity of reason and of revelation that threatens the eclipse of the American Founding, and therewith of Western civilization itself."

The final paragraph of the essay is an exhortation to action in the face of the supposed decline of the West, which Jaffa says includes "unprecedented" threats to biblical religion, human reason, and political freedom. "The threat is, above all, an internal one, mining and sapping our ancient faith, both in God and in ourselves." Historically, despairing narratives like this one have done plenty to threaten healthy civic life, but Jaffa seems not to have considered that dimension of the problem.

I am sympathetic to the idea that there is an excess of skepticism and criticism in many contemporary universities, and not enough space in which to take the possibility of genuine knowledge—especially moral knowledge—seriously. We will return to that problem again throughout this book. But ultimately what we get with Jaffa by the end of his career is a political thinker who went very far—much farther than his teacher Strauss—in asserting and defending what can only be called a dogma. For Jaffa, there was a singular moral core to the American regime, and this core was so thick and substantive (and intolerant) that it put a hard cap on actual religious pluralism, political liberty and contestation, and philosophical freedom. This is a way of thinking that lends itself in obvious ways to political extremism. There is a desperation to the late Jaffa's writing—an early glimpse of the kind of grasping monomania and insistence on political simplicity that we will see throughout this book—that has no analogue in Strauss's thought.[30]

I find Jaffa's later writings unreadable. I am sure there is much to learn here—he was clearly an erudite person full of knowledge and insight. But what, for instance, could anyone mean by "ancient Greek morality"? Does this refer to Spartan morality or to Athenian? To

Homer's tragic pessimism, to Aristotelian virtue ethics, or perhaps to Epicureanism? Doesn't it matter that these were each dramatically different orientations toward the world? Doesn't it matter that Greek metaphysics and morality bear little resemblance to the biblical outlook (to the extent that we can speak of a single biblical outlook)? Some of the late Jaffa's claims about America seem fundamentally silly to me: soaked in hubris, anathema to a genuinely philosophic orientation, and inconsistent with the humility demanded by the biblical traditions as I understand them.

Harry Jaffa at the Cow Palace

Grasping moral zeal was, in a way, Harry Jaffa's signature move, and his impact on American politics—like that of many on the New Right— arguably stems from his willingness to disregard the orthodoxies of modern liberal pluralism and argue instead from moral conviction. That willingness was memorialized in those famous words from Barry Goldwater's nomination acceptance speech. Jaffa's lines, wittingly or not, played a part in the demise of the moderate liberal wing of the GOP.

As Jaffa later told the story in interviews, he had joined the Goldwater campaign while he was still teaching in Ohio and was invited to the nominating convention in his role as a scholar. He was sitting at a hearing for the platform committee when he became frustrated by the constant talk of "extremism this, extremism that." This led to his drafting a paragraph on the subject, which made its way to Senator Goldwater, who then asked him to draft the entire acceptance speech for the convention. (Jaffa's story is disputed by Goldwater's regular speechwriter at the time, Karl Hess.)[31]

Later in life, Jaffa would credit Martin Luther King Jr.'s *Letter from a Birmingham Jail*, which was written the year prior, as his main inspiration for the Goldwater speech. This revelation suggests a strange disregard for King's opposition to Goldwater as a candidate.[32] King was among Goldwater's most determined critics, and for him the stakes of the campaign were not merely intellectual. Goldwater's speech took place on the same day as the killing of James Powell, a fifteen-year-old Black boy, by an off-duty New York City policeman—an event that led to the Harlem uprisings and riots of 1964. This was also the year of Freedom Summer, which saw a massive campaign on the part of civil rights activists to register voters in Mississippi against a background of anti-Black lynching and violence. In June 1964, three civil rights workers went missing after being arrested in Mississippi. Their bodies were discovered on August 4.

Dr. King wrote about these events in chapter 23 of his autobiography, which began with a discussion of his unprecedented opposition to Barry Goldwater. In Goldwater, King saw a major threat to the "health, morality, and survival" of the nation. He explained: "All people of goodwill viewed with alarm and concern the frenzied wedding at the Cow Palace of the KKK with the radical right. The 'best man' at this ceremony was a senator whose voting record, philosophy, and program were anathema to all the hard-won achievements of the past decade."

King went on to discuss his concerns with Goldwater's foreign policy ("a narrow nationalism, a crippling isolationism, and a trigger-happy attitude that could plunge the whole world into the dark abyss of annihilation"), before turning to domestic policy. "On social and economic issues," King wrote, "Mr. Goldwater represented an unrealistic conservatism that was totally out of touch with the realities of the twentieth century." He had no understanding of the issue of poverty, and on civil rights "Senator Goldwater represented a philosophy that was morally indefensible and socially suicidal." King then tackled the question of Goldwater's racism head-on:

> While not himself a racist, Mr. Goldwater articulated a philosophy which gave aid and comfort to the racist. His candidacy and philosophy would serve as an umbrella under which extremists of all stripes would stand. In the light of these facts and because of my love for America, I had no alternative but to urge every Negro and white person of goodwill to vote against Mr. Goldwater and to withdraw support from any Republican candidate that did not publicly disassociate himself from Senator Goldwater and his philosophy.[33]

King understood what Harry Jaffa and Goldwater appear to have missed—that, in the churn of politics, shining abstract principles could be untethered from reality on the ground and so serve extreme injustice. Goldwater's commitment to individual freedom and local independence also meant turning his back on the Black freedom movement and winking at violent racists.[34]

———

The fact that Jaffa could blithely claim King as his inspiration for the Goldwater speech nicely encapsulates his grandiose, Ideas First approach to politics. What mattered to Jaffa was that an idea made sense in the abstract; how it played out in real life was less concerning. There is a lurking ruthlessness here.[35]

Besides Arizona, the only states that Goldwater won were in the Deep South. As Louis Menand put it in a perceptive profile of Goldwater in 2001, "His campaign realigned the South . . . [his] longest-lasting political legacy was to drive African-Americans out of the party of Lincoln."[36]

This is not how conservatives tend to articulate this history. For a long time, the basic consensus among mainstream conservatives was that although Goldwater had failed in his bid for the presidency, and badly, he was vindicated insofar as he had realigned the party behind his brand of conservatism and paved the way for Ronald Reagan. The conservative commentator George Will observed in *The Washington Post* in 1994 that "Goldwater lost 44 states but won the future. . . . He catalyzed conservatism's breakthrough."[37]

Others on the right disagreed with the new fusionist conservatism championed by Reagan, and with the growing consensus around Goldwater's legacy. The far-right scholar Paul Gottfried argued in 2008 that Reaganism was in truth a betrayal of Goldwater's truer style of conservatism: "After Goldwater, the conservative movement made its peace with the New Deal and the leftward drift of the country." For Gottfried, the new movement had abandoned what made Goldwater unique: his radicalism and willingness to court controversy, including those things that alienated King. Gottfried's subsequent writings and collaboration with far-right white supremacists suggest that he considered efforts to police the boundaries of respectability in the conservative mainstream to be a major error. They had had the right idea back at the Cow Palace in 1964.[38]

Gottfried further argued, presciently and deftly anticipating the arguments of Michael Anton and others on the New Right, that "the catalyst for changing course will not come from the compromised conservative movement. Getting rid of what now passes for movement conservatism, with its establishment journalists and D.C. bureaucrats and insiders, and replacing it with a genuine oppositional force would be necessary to reform the Right."[39]

Gottfried was an early and prominent "paleoconservative"—a scion of the Old Right, and someone who opposed the old fusion of social conservatism with economic liberalism. He was also one of the first "alt-right" thinkers (who was at one point closely allied with Richard Spencer). He became a prominent presence within the Hard Right, and we will meet him again in chapter 6.

For his part, Harry Jaffa was unfazed by the Goldwater loss and held tight to the consensus view that Goldwater was the obvious and triumphant intellectual precursor to Ronald Reagan.[40] Jaffa seldom engaged in electoral politics directly again but would have a voice in conservative politics for the rest of his long life, and the men who founded the Claremont Institute were clearly inspired by his activism.

Claremont, Harry Jaffa, and Allan Bloom

The Claremont Institute was founded in 1979 by four of Harry Jaffa's graduate students: Peter W. Schramm, Thomas B. Silver, Christopher Flannery, and Larry P. Arnn. Schramm and Silver were both professors (since deceased); Flannery is a senior fellow at the institute; and Arnn was president there through 2000, at which point he left to run the increasingly influential Hillsdale College (Arnn and Hillsdale are major subjects in chapter 8).

The mission of the Claremont Institute—"to restore the principles of the American Founding to their rightful, preeminent authority in our national life"—is clearly inspired by Jaffa's life work. For decades, the institute has shaped American public discourse indirectly through the summer fellowships it offers to ambitious young conservatives. A quick glance at the alumni lists of these programs reveals a who's-who of contemporary right-wing media personalities, from Ross Douthat to Mollie Hemmingway to Ben Shapiro.

There has often been tension between the Claremont group and other Straussians—a tension captured by the so-called West Coast and East Coast divide. The West Coast Straussians tend to be more politically engaged than the East Coast group and more wedded to the American founding as the peak of political achievements.

Harry Jaffa was by all accounts the sort of person who took his famous line about extremism to heart, and he was widely known as a seriously cantankerous individual. He had major public quarrels not only with East Coast Straussians like Harvey Mansfield, Thomas Pangle, and Walter Berns, but also with other political actors on the right, such as Judge Robert Bork and Justices William Rehnquist and Antonin Scalia.[41]

William F. Buckley, who was friends with Jaffa, had a famous line that went, "If you think Harry Jaffa is hard to argue with, try agreeing with him. It is nearly impossible." Buckley went on to provide at least a partial explanation for why Jaffa could be so disagreeable: "The relentless Jaffa logic pries at apparently trifling differences until they open like chasms. What is more, he is able to convey the full gravity of these differences." Many of Jaffa's insights were like this: simple but also weighty, and so worth a good fight. He always sided with Lincoln and Declarationism against those who sought to minimize the importance of the principle of equality. "The genius of Abraham Lincoln," he once wrote in response to Frank Meyer in the pages of the *National Review*, "consisted above all in the clarity with which he perceived and demonstrated the inner connection between free, popular, constitutional government, and the mighty proposition, 'that all men are created equal.'"[42]

One of Jaffa's most substantive exchanges involved the conservative thinkers George Carey and Wilmoore Kendall. In their book *The Basic Symbols of the American Political Tradition* (1970), Carey and Kendall argued that the most important symbol of American politics was a "virtuous people deliberating under God," an argument that leaned more in the majoritarian direction of Douglas. It was also an argument for localism and particularity against abstract principle, and it meant the displacement of the Declaration of Independence in the tradition, as well as a demotion of Lincoln and the principle of equality. Carey and Kendall argued that Lincoln's emphasis on equality had "derailed" the American tradition and implied that he had teed things up for the rights revolution of the 1960s—and possibly for even worse forms of "Caesarism" and tyranny in the future. (Jaffa's heirs at the Claremont Institute would later draw similar links between liberalism, progressivism, and twentieth-century forms of tyranny.) Jaffa wrote a withering review of the book, taking Carey and Kendall to task for, among other things, writing a work targeting Lincoln and equality without so much as mentioning slavery.[43]

The public record is also full of unsavory exchanges between Jaffa and his fellow Straussians, and often Jaffa does not come off well.[44] The messiest dispute concerned his old friend Allan Bloom (1930–1992), the quintessential East Coast Straussian, and, in the end, the most famous. Bloom was a student of Strauss who earned his PhD at the prestigious Committee on Social Thought at the University of Chicago in 1955. He had a long career as a professor of political philosophy, teaching at Yale, Cornell, and the University of Toronto, returning to the University of Chicago in 1979. Bloom's first book was a collection of essays on Shakespeare's politics, which he coauthored with Jaffa in 1964 (the year of Freedom Summer and Goldwater's campaign). He subsequently published important translations of Plato's *Republic* and Rousseau's *Emile*— both major texts on philosophy and education—and wrote extensively about other literature.

Then, in 1987, Bloom took the conservative academic world by storm with his wildly popular commentary on the state of higher education in America. That book, titled *The Closing of the American Mind: How Higher Education Has Failed Democracy and Impoverished the Souls of Today's Students*, was, in its way, a late follow-up to Buckley's breakthrough book, *God and Man at Yale* (1951).[45] Taking aim primarily at the social transformations of the 1960s, Bloom argued that young people in America had become soulless relativists, devoid of any serious passion or interest in the questions that matter for life (with a heavy emphasis on failures in the humanities and philosophy). The book's reigning thematics—cultural relativism, nihilism, the perils of feminism and rock-and-roll, and the supposedly crazed incoherence of social justice activism—would preoccupy a generation.[46]

Everyone had something to say about the book in the 1990s, and it seeded a small cottage industry of follow-up books on higher education, from authors across the political spectrum, which lasted for decades.[47] Bloom gained a small fortune from the book sales, which allowed him to spend time in Paris during his final years. The writer Saul Bellow memorialized his friend Bloom's life in the novel *Ravelstein* (2000).

But things turned ugly between Jaffa and Bloom, because Jaffa was homophobic and Bloom was gay. The public record is full of Jaffa's extreme antigay bigotry, which he himself tied neatly to his own hard-line moralism.[48] There is no sugar-coating Jaffa's homophobia, which is well-documented, and there is no denying that it derived from his rigid teleological views about nature, morality, and "right." (Claremont Institute senior fellow Ken Masugi defended Jaffa's views on homosexuality in *First Things* as recently as 2015 with an extensive explanation of how they derive from his principled philosophical orientation.)[49]

In his review of *Closing of the American Mind* in 1988, Jaffa blamed Bloom for failing to discuss the gay rights movement, which he claimed had far surpassed feminism as "the most radical and sinister challenge, not merely to sexual morality, but to all morality."[50] For Jaffa, it was all-or-nothing: "The demand for the recognition of sodomy as a moral and political right represents the most complete repudiation—theoretical as well as practical—of all objective standards of human conduct . . . The so-called 'gay rights' movement is then the ultimate repudiation of nature," he wrote. He went on to thank the AIDS pandemic for providing clarity about the moral evils of homosexuality: "Thanks to AIDS then, we have a little breathing time to reassert the true arguments—the 'enriching certitudes' (as in the *Nicomachean Ethics*), not merely Bloom's 'humanizing doubts.'" I have no idea where Jaffa found "certitudes" in Aristotle, and it is worth noting that in general the ancient Greeks were not homophobes.

Allan Bloom died in October 1992. The cause is widely thought to have been AIDS (thanks in part to an insinuation in Bellow's *Ravelstein*).[51]

Harry Jaffa's line about extremism in the service of liberty and justice is intuitively appealing, since most everyone loves liberty and justice. But it also conceals a zealous and unforgiving certainty about the full scope and meaning of those virtues, and that hubris and dogged self-certainty is part of Jaffa's legacy at the Claremont Institute.

————

From this and similar presumptions about monopolized moral and political knowledge, many Claremonters made a jump to a crude, absolutist politics that serves as a pattern for similar moves across the New Right. The substance of the moralism shifts around, but the monomania stays the same. And it signifies a failure to contend with the hard realities of moral and political difference—and so also a failure to grapple with the origins and foundations of liberal democracy. Stated simply, liberal democracy has emerged over the course of the last few centuries, often against the background of violent religious strife, to allow people with very different values and belief systems to live together in relative peace. The New Right rejects the possibility of deep pluralism at a national level and seeks to impose homogeneity instead.

A related problem—and one that also plagues factions across the New Right movement—is that of intellectual abstraction, and what I have called Ideas First politics (which is also connected to culture-warriorism). Here, the Claremonters, in their philosophical mode as Straussians, provide a useful paradigm.

At their best, Straussians are very good at reading and interpreting texts and at understanding the broad strokes of political history. They are charitable toward authors, and this helps them attend to nuance, rhetoric, and layers of meaning. Jaffa's *Crisis of the House Divided* was like this in some respects. But in its worst iterations, the Straussian love of abstraction liberates them from any due diligence about on-the-ground facts, and the preference for the world of ideas and big thinking releases them from normal intellectual constraints of empiricism and historical accuracy. By some Straussian thinking, Lincoln's speeches alone settled the question of American racism. In *Closing of the American Mind*, for example, while trying to explain an already abstract proposition of Tocqueville's (about the paucity of genuine disagreement in democratic societies), Bloom argued that "the only quarrel in our history that really involved fundamental differences about fundamental principles was over slavery." He then claimed that this question "was really already settled with the Declaration of Independence." He goes on: "Black slavery was an aberration that had to be extinguished, not a permanent feature of our national life. Not only slavery, but aristocracy, monarchy, and theocracy were laid to rest by the Declaration and the Constitution."[52]

This is a good example of putting Ideas First. Bloom put ideas so high on the pedestal that he all but negated the reality of historical suffering, as well as the need for political action—a clear example of how bad Straussian methodology can wreak havoc on sound historical and political thinking. This is of course probably true about most academics to a degree and is a trope about philosophers reaching back to antiquity. But some American Straussians take it to a whole new level, and even at times as a point of pride.

The connections here between Straussian hermeneutics (or interpretive methods) and conspiratorial thinking are also plain to see. The problem that travels alongside Straussian thought is this: Once you rub the lamp of esotericism, the world becomes your oyster. If there are hidden meanings everywhere, then you are sure to find what you're looking for somewhere, and too often the belief in esoteric writing devolves into partisan and self-interested readings of philosophical texts (or formulaic "Straussian" ones).[53] At the Claremont Institute in the Trump era, Straussian-adjacent ideas devolved into rank conspiracism, from Great Replacement rhetoric to full-on election denialism. Sometimes, as we will see in the coming pages, Straussians end up squarely in the "just asking questions" corner of the far-right "race science" club, or worse.

And so too with the idea of "noble lies." If you believe, as some Straussians do, that public life is best preserved by salutary fabrications about the past, then you'll probably want to be the one telling those tales. It is no coincidence that the Claremonters were heavily involved in Trump's push for so-called patriotic education.

The good news for Straussians is that the core problems at stake here long predate Leo Strauss, exist in every corner of the intellectual landscape, and probably always will. After all, it was not Strauss but Plato who introduced the concept of the "noble lie." And most human beings are eager to be part of secret cliques and esoteric clubs that help them unearth the hidden causes of things—especially those that cause us suffering and discomfort, or that challenge given norms and are risqué. Straussian intellectuals have no monopoly on abstruse, clubby, and vaguely conspiratorial explanations of the world.[54]

That said, the Straussians, and especially the Claremonters, can help us understand the motives and styles of thinking that took over the upper echelons of the GOP under Donald Trump. As we will see in the next chapter, these are often hyper-online young men who have earned epithets like "galaxy-brained," and who understand themselves to be engaged in an epic, world-historical, culture war. And maybe they have it right.

3

The Journal of American Greatness

IF YOU WERE TO drive down West Foothill Boulevard, along US Route 66 in Upland, California, you probably wouldn't notice the office building that, from 2015 to 2024, housed the Claremont Institute. Nestled next to an after-school program, a gym, and a Domino's pizza, and across the freeway from a Big Lots and a Walmart, the place looks as nondescript as any building, in any strip mall, in any suburb in America.

Perhaps, in this way, it's a bit like Ancient Sparta.

There's an eerie passage toward the beginning of *The History of the Peloponnesian War* where the Athenian historian Thucydides predicts how, generations hence, all physical evidence of Sparta will be lost to the dust of time. Thucydides anticipated that the monuments of ancient Athens would stand tall through many generations, whereas Sparta's modest edifices would fade to nothing, giving false historical testimony to the relative significance of the two city-states. And he was right. Today, we can still behold the Athenian acropolis, whereas whatever remains of Sparta is unimpressive to behold. That fact tells us little about its historical significance. So too with that humble office suite next to Route 66.

I suspect that the denizens of the Claremont Institute would rally to my likening. They are eager to see themselves as the brave defenders of true, rough-and-tumble republicanism. To them, as to the Spartans, nothing rates higher on the hierarchy of virtues than toughness. And they, too, clearly hope to achieve an impact in the world that outstrips their humble origins.

I have some sympathy with those old-fashioned, Spartan longings. I remember being moved as an undergraduate by an essay by Nietzsche called "On the Uses and Abuses of History for Life." Early in the essay, he talks about "monumental history"—an approach to looking at the past that emphasizes high human exemplars. Nietzsche argued that a salutary, poetical glorification of the rarest lives from the past was important for the "man of the present" because:

> He learns from it that the greatness that once existed was in any event once *possible* and may thus be possible again; he goes his way with more cheerful step, for the doubt which assailed him in weaker moments, whether he was not perhaps desiring the impossible, has now been banished. Supposing someone believed that it would require no more than a hundred men educated and actively working in a new spirit to do away with the bogus form of culture which has just now become the fashion in Germany, how greatly it would strengthen him to realize that the culture of the Renaissance was raised on the shoulders of just such a band of a hundred men.[1]

The passage captures some powerful hopes—for dramatic personal achievement, deep camaraderie, radical cultural change, and human greatness. Perhaps above all else, there is a promise here of action against a background of fusty intellectualism. It is the type of grandiose, ambitious thinking that one encounters in many Straussian circles, especially among the young. With only a hundred individuals acting in concert, you might change the course of history! You might "do away with the bogus form of culture which has just now become the fashion"!

To their credit, though perhaps also in infamy, the Claremonter crowd has, since 2016, achieved something that could be interpreted in just such a way, as the vanguard of an illiberal renaissance. After the publication of the Flight 93 essay and the 2016 election of Donald

Trump, the Claremont Institute went from being a peripheral group of academics to playing a major role in national politics. The Claremonters made it to the White House. And they did so intentionally, with a plan.

As Ryan Williams, the president of the institute since 2017, explained in the *2018–2019 Biennial Report*, the Claremont Institute took a highly deliberate turn toward direct political activism after the 2016 election and declared war on multiculturalism. The institute's obsession with the "administrative state" would become a focus of the new administration.[2] Trump chose the former president of Claremont, Michael Pack—a filmmaker who had worked on films with Steve Bannon—to lead the Broadcasting Board of Governors (he was ousted in a corruption scandal within a year).[3] Bannon had been brought on to manage the final months of the 2016 campaign and served as Trump's chief of staff through the first seven months of the administration.[4] At the Conservative Political Action Conference (CPAC) that year, he said that the "deconstruction of the administrative state" would be one of the core objectives of the new administration.[5] And it was Bannon who brought Michael Anton into the White House, the connection having been forged by the PayPal billionaire (and fellow Straussophile) Peter Thiel.[6] According to reporting at the time by Rosie Gray, Bannon was a "huge admirer" of Anton. "I think Michael is one of the most significant intellects in this nationalist movement," he said. Two months into the second Trump administration, over thirty alumni of the Claremont fellowship programs, including Anton, had been hired on as staff.[7]

The Claremont Institute's gradual emergence as the beating heart of the New Right will be covered in greater detail in later chapters. Here we consider some of the people involved in the earliest intellectual defenses of Trumpism. What is the trajectory from student of American political thought and history to Bannon sympathizer and co-conspiracist?

As a window into New Right psychology, Michael Anton offers an especially useful case study because he is both bookish and online, and because he is uniquely obsessed with ideas about women and masculinity. I have a lot to say in this chapter about Anton's thinking as it relates to my own experiences in the Straussian world, and with the men who

populate it. But as concerns Trumpism Anton was not some lone opera-
tor. Before there was "The Flight 93 Election," there was a blog called the
Journal of American Greatness, written by pseudonymous authors who
took their pen names from the ancient Romans, and whose ideas were
largely reminiscent of the Old Right. They were quoting from authors
like Sam Francis (and the white supremacist Peter Brimelow) and calling themselves "Paleo-Straussians." They understood what so many
other early observers of Trumpism failed to see—namely, that it was an
expression of older right-wing forces and ideas that had perennial appeal. As the writer and scholar Timothy Shenk wrote at the time in an
article that referenced the blog, "Trump is a unique character, but the
principles he defends and the passions he inflames have been part of
the modern American right since its formation in the aftermath of the
second world war."[8] The *Journal of American Greatness* was, however,
novel for its hysterical alarmism and early flirtation with the remedy of
strongman politics (or Caesarism) as a possible solution for America's
ailments (and especially for Republicans' electoral challenges).

The blog proved that intellectualized Trumpism could find an
audience—a discovery that each of the blog's writers would exploit in
their own way. In addition to Anton, two other authors would break
their anonymity. Considering how their paths diverged can help us
begin to track the alternative trajectories of New Right thinking.

Michael Anton in Full

The historical Publius Decius Mus was a Roman consul who, according
to the historian Livy, died a glorious death in a *devotio*, or ritual self-
sacrifice, at the Battle of Vesuvius, the first battle of the Latin War of
340–338 BCE. Livy says that Decius sacrificed himself when the Roman
troops began to falter. He made a formal oath to the gods (including the
"divine Manes" or chthonic gods of the underworld) and then, "vault-
ing, armed, upon his horse, plunged into the thick of the enemy." Decius's action was so dramatic and inspiring ("every terror and dread attended him, and throwing the Latin front into disarray, spread afterwards
throughout their entire host") that it allowed the other Roman general,

Titus Manlius Torquatus, to close ranks and defeat the enemy. Later in his history, Livy recounts how Decius's son of the same name performed a *devotio*, too, in 295 BCE.[9]

In our story of the New Right, "Publius Decius Mus" was Michael Anton, and when "The Flight 93 Election" was published, Anton was a managing director with the financial asset firm BlackRock.[10] BlackRock is the largest asset management firm in the world and very much an anchor of the "Davoisie" world that Anton disparaged in the Flight 93 essay (referencing the class of international elites who attend the World Economic Forum in Davos, Switzerland). BlackRock's website reads: "Our nearly 16,000 colleagues work from 89 offices in 38 countries, help-ing people from all walks of life around the world to reach their invest-ing goals."[11] By using the pseudonym Decius, but unlike the historical Decius, Anton hedged his bets. Perhaps *The Journal of American Great-ness* began as a lark, but he kept the pseudonym for the much more seri-ous *Claremont Review of Books*, choosing not to risk his name, reputa-tion, wealth, job, or anything really until the consequences of his actions were more settled.[12]

BlackRock clearly didn't define Anton, whose fuller resume is rather unusual. Prior to his job in finance, he had worked as a communications director for Citigroup, as a speechwriter for Rupert Murdoch, Rudy Giuliani, and Condoleezza Rice, and in a midlevel position in George W. Bush's National Security Council.[13]

In addition, he had been a perennial student. Anton grew up in Northern California and studied at UC Berkeley as an undergraduate, which is where he became a right-winger ("it took the shock of being plunged into the deep end of the loony-left cauldron that is Berkeley, California, in the fall of 1987").[14] He earned an MA degree at St. John's College, the "Great Books" college in Annapolis, Maryland. In 1994, on the advice of a fellow student at St. John's, Anton participated in one of the Claremont Institute's summer "Publius" fellowship programs. And at Claremont he would remain, for the next three years, pursuing a doc-torate under Charles Kesler, a faculty member at Claremont McKenna College, editor of the *Claremont Review of Books*, and a former student of Harvey Mansfield's. Eventually, acting on advice from Larry Arnn, then president of the Claremont Institute, Anton left his doctoral program to work as a speechwriter in the California state house, which would launch his subsequent career.[15]

That brief resume does not exhaust Anton's pre-Trump undertakings, during which period he was also a prolific writer, self-professed "dandy" and connoisseur of men's style, husband and father, and classically trained chef and Francophile.[16] In his writings, and in the many interviews since his time in the White House, Anton often professes his deep attachment to Niccolò Machiavelli. In getting to know Anton and his backstory, we get a good taste of the sort of person who populates the New Right.

———

Anton came to know Jaffa in the late 1990s. Jaffa had, at that point, already retired from the Claremont Institute but was still a major presence there.[17] As Anton wrote in a tribute published in the *Claremont Review* shortly after Jaffa's death in 2015, "I stayed in Claremont for three years. Jaffa was always around." He described spending hours at a time down in the basement of the library, where Jaffa took to working post-retirement. Along with his fellow graduate students, Anton would seek Jaffa out—asking questions, listening to stories, wrestling with arguments, and occasionally being rebuked. He described Jaffa as something like an oracle: "Jaffa knew everything, or at least everything important. Much of what will be written about him in the coming days will focus on Lincoln, American politics, and modern conservatism, which is absolutely fitting. But his mind was a museum stuffed to the rafters with masterworks." Anton went on: "Jaffa in his lair was slightly different from Jaffa above ground. Down there, he would tell you things. Esoteric things." The tenor of Anton's tribute to Jaffa—full of unabashed gratitude and deeply solicitous—is characteristic of his writing about Strauss, Allan Bloom, Machiavelli, and his other intellectual heroes.[18]

The essay concluded with a comparison between Jaffa and Socrates that captures the spirit of the Claremonters. Anton explained that in contrast to Socrates, "so far was Jaffa from disbelieving in the God of his city that, if it is possible for a man to rescue from oblivion and resuscitate God, then Harry Jaffa did it." He described how Jaffa was not a corruptor but a converter, convincer, and fortifier for the young. Jaffa wanted "to persuade—and, when necessary, bludgeon—the ignorant and misguided into knowledge." Anton wrote that "to be formed in one's formative years by Professor Jaffa was an unalloyed blessing." Again, this was not a man who corrupted the youth:

> No better use could be made of one's life than to live it in strict adherence to his teachings, and all who have done so have prospered in body and soul. . . . Before I discovered Claremont and what it stands for, I had no faith and few friends, in the highest sense of souls sharing a love of the good. Because of Claremont—because of Harry V. Jaffa and the people he taught, inspired, and influenced—I have had both in abundance for 20 years and counting.
>
> Jaffa liked to quote Lincoln's remark that the idea of equality enshrined in the Declaration of Independence is the "father of all moral principle" among us. For us Claremonsters—always happy, no longer quite so few—the love of wisdom animating Harry Jaffa's soul was, remains, and will always be the father of all intellectual principle among us. Thank you, Professor Jaffa.[19]

The extreme contrast between the benevolence Anton bestows on his philosophic mentors and friends and the misanthropy with which he speaks of his political opponents and compatriots is remarkable. But there is no denying that, at his best, Anton is a terrific stylist and polemicist, and the unalloyed enthusiasm on display in this passage is, from a certain perspective, the most refreshing thing about the Straussian world.

———

It is unusual in the first decades of the twenty-first century to find people speaking openly and earnestly about virtue, "souls sharing a love of the good," and Lincoln's ideas about equality. One of the things I genuinely appreciate about (some) Straussian circles is how—unlike much of academia, which can be excessively critical or even downright clinical when it comes to most classic literature or philosophy—they make room for old-fashioned moral and ethical concerns, and old-fashioned bookish enthusiasms. Many of the books that Straussians read so closely are genuinely profound and can be transformative.

Anton's way of life, at least as it appears in his tribute to Jaffa, is infused with the confidence and breadth and happiness that sometimes accompany a rich humanities education. Having a sense of the broad sweep of history, the beauties and subtleties of literature and the arts, and the saving power of friendship can serve as a buttress against the vicissitudes of fortune, the conventional judgments of others, and the meanness of the world. This is no small thing.

But it is also easy for such an education to curdle. There is an amusing passage in *The Closing of the American Mind* where Allan Bloom lists some standard objections "to the Great Books cult." (Bloom was likely referring here in part to the "Great Books of the Western World" publications of Mortimer Adler in the 1950s, but also to the dozens of educational programs in the United States that focus on "Core Texts," or the "Western Canon.")[20] Bloom agreed with these criticisms:

> It is amateurish; it encourages an autodidact's self-assurance without competence; one cannot read all of the Great Books carefully; if one only reads Great Books, one can never know what a great, as opposed to an ordinary, book is; there is no way of determining who is to decide what a Great Book or what the canon is; books are made the ends and not the means; the whole movement has a certain coarse evangelistic tone that is the opposite of good taste; it engenders a spurious intimacy with greatness; and so forth.[21]

Bloom went on to argue that, despite these real problems, Great Books education was still better than the alternative—no education in the Great Books at all. I tend to agree, supposing an expansive and dynamic conception of what constitutes the canon. (As we will see, in recent years the New Right has exploited Americans' failure to foster and sustain this kind of formative educative project in the liberal arts and humanities.)

What Bloom doesn't say much about, at least in that passage, is when a Great Books education goes *really* wrong—when an education in philosophy, say, becomes instead an education in sophistry or rank power-seeking. One of the key thematics of the Platonic corpus is philo-sophic miseducation and corruption, which is often encapsulated among Straussians by shorthand formulations like "the problem of Al-cibiades" or "the lure of Syracuse."

Alcibiades was a young Athenian citizen who rose to the heights of political life—eventually taking the role of general—and played a con-troversial role throughout the Peloponnesian War. In the ancient sources, Alcibiades is portrayed as a friend or associate of Socrates, but also as someone who was politically questionable because his talents made his ambitions hard to contain. The question that lurks here is whether Alcibiades was one of the youths whom Socrates had "cor-rupted." Did Alcibiades—this towering, impressive, gorgeous but also questionable man—represent the natural culmination of a corrosive Socratic education? Or was he more an example of the enduring limits of political philosophy and humanism—a haunting uncertainty at the heart of political life? Similar questions are asked of Critias, an associate of Socrates who would become one of the Thirty Tyrants that ruled over Athens after the city's defeat by the Spartans.

The "lure of Syracuse" refers to Plato's own political temptations and his several trips to visit Dion and Dionysus the Younger to influence politics in Sicily, which are recounted in the "Seventh Letter."[22] When Heidegger returned to teaching after his time collaborating with the Nazi regime, a friend purportedly quipped, "Back from Syracuse?"[23]

These problems are exacerbated in our time, thanks in part to the idiosyncratic character of our educational forms and our fragmented public life. Someone like Anton can talk a big talk about Publius Decius Mus, Harry Jaffa, and Socrates. He can study great works and easily feel himself to be better educated than most of the people around him, in-cluding many intellectuals. He can sound impressive to many people and face little informed pushback—partly because the other side simply isn't paying attention to what he cares about and so wouldn't know where to begin with a response. After all, who were Publius Decius Mus and Alcibiades anyway? And why on earth should anyone care?

I do not mean to compare Michael Anton to Alcibiades—which would make no more sense than Anton comparing himself to Publius

Decius Mus. But the problems that come with sophisticated, philosophical forms of higher education—with educational forms that take big, "meaning-of-life" questions seriously and as though they might lead to answers—are nothing new. Liberalism was designed to defray and defuse some of these questions—the kinds of questions that Socrates's life put front and center. The world of right-wing intellectualism in our time is forcing modern liberals to confront them anew.

One of these problems concerns what to do with ambitious young people—and especially ambitious young men.

———

My education bears some similarities to Anton's. But my teachers—especially at the University of Alberta, where I studied when I was younger—made it clear that what they cared about most was that their students learn to think for themselves. In *The Closing of the American Mind*, Allan Bloom puts it like this: "The essence of philosophy is the abandonment of all authority in favor of individual human reason." Bloom was referring to Aristotle, but that's how I understood the activity of philosophy as an undergraduate studying with Straussians. It was about the relentless questioning of authority, including that of our teachers. You might pick up some lessons in decency and nobility along the way, but ultimately the point was to escape from the cave of conventional authority and learn to think for oneself. In this sense, it was a truly liberal and liberating activity.

There was plenty to disagree about with Dr. Craig, my first professor of political philosophy, especially looking back with hindsight. The limits of his way of thinking were perhaps clearest when it came to what Nietzsche called "the eternal war between the sexes." If I recall correctly, there was a passage in Craig's syllabi decrying all "isms," including feminism, as fundamentally unserious, so to some extent his mind was settled from the start. One year he decided to run an entire seminar course on Book V of Plato's *Republic*. The *Republic* is about the meaning of justice, and Book V is in some ways the heart of the dialogue. It is famous because it is where Socrates introduces the idea that in a truly just city, the best citizens would procreate together, men and women would be educated together, children would be raised in common, and philosophers would rule as kings. In other words, Socrates's ideal city involves eugenics, radical gender equality within each class, the abolishment of the nuclear family for the sake of communal child-rearing, and philosophic rule. It is about as radical an arrangement as I can imagine. We were pretty excited about the course.

Straussians, though, are known for arguing that Book V is intended as a comic interlude, reminiscent of the playwright Aristophanes's several comedies about women in politics. There is some real merit to the argument—Book V does seem to show that pure justice would require a grotesque and totalizing government system that controls family life, which would be destructive to human well-being (and to philosophy), and so, in the end, also to justice. Though designed to be something like a perfect meritocracy, the city in speech turns out to be both impractical and vicious. Hence the idea that the proposals are not meant seriously.

The problem is that if you dismiss the whole thing as just a joke, you'll miss a fascinating world of questions, including basically all of feminism, many questions having to do with real-world justice, and others having to do with the nature of philosophy. You'll also jettison the possibility of any kind of meliorative politics. Pure or ideal justice might not be reasonable or possible, but the questions raised in Book V—about human nature and what it would take to allow people to live in accordance with their inborn potential—are hardly a waste of time for anyone who cares about politics.

We spent a lot of time that semester talking about the reasonableness of Book V's ideas about gender. Socrates's suggestion at one point (455b–c) is that men are better than women at pretty much everything that matters, while some women are better than some men at some things (and this has implications for how the city should be organized). That was the line that Craig took, and he suggested that all true geniuses in history had been men. Women could study philosophy but could never be philosophers, he implied, with some in the room stifling their guffaws.

To his credit, Craig also took care to emphasize that these abstractions had very few implications for our own lives: Even if we took this theory of male excellence to be true, it had no statistical bearing, for example, on the relative intelligence of the various students in the room that day, especially since none of us were likely to be geniuses. Craig drove the point home: No one in that room should let Plato's ideas about the gender hierarchy of virtue go to their heads. The most obvious feminist rebuttal to this whole line of thinking is that for millennia, thanks to child-rearing and patriarchal power, women had been systematically denied the opportunities afforded by quality education, public life, and leisure. That hard historical reality probably affected the historical expression (and measure) of genius. Our objections never seemed to go anywhere in class.

Craig perhaps imagined that his argument about the statistical odds of genius would be enough to temper his young male students' irrational self-regard. But given the extent to which the Straussian reading of Book V does little but flatter conservative male prejudice—all that gender equality stuff is just a big joke! Nothing to see here, boys!—that was a miscalculation. In hindsight, the seminar taught me less about the inherent limits of political life, which have, after all, become quite nicely derailed in the modern age, or about the impossibility of greater gender equality, and a lot about the stubborn limits of the Straussian (and conservative male) imagination.[24]

Consider. When I got my PhD in political theory in the government department at the University of Texas in 2011, there wasn't a single woman philosopher or work of feminism on our core reading list (nor was there any person of color, except St. Augustine). It was still that way when I checked again in early 2025. That choice both reflects and reinforces the narrow and insular cultural expectations that govern conservative intellectual spaces.

Another illustrative case is Harvard's Harvey Mansfield, perhaps the most famous conservative professor in the United States, and one of Michael Anton's favorite men. A Straussian scholar of Tocqueville and Machiavelli, Mansfield made his mark in the academy back in 1986 by being the single faculty voice (and vote) against the creation of a Women's Studies program at Harvard, based on the idea that it was fundamentally biased (he had a lot to say about the "shameless" and "pathetic" reading list for the main course in the major), and the notion that women were not a proper object of study because they always lived in community with men.[25] For many years he served as something like the antifeminist gadfly of the Ivies. Then, in 2006—just as I was starting graduate school in Texas—he published a widely reviewed book entitled *Manliness*, which was in large part an antifeminist defense of traditional gender roles, including a celebration of manly spiritedness, mettle, and assertiveness (or *thymos* in ancient Greek). Mansfield opened the book with a passage that resonates with Anton's Flight 93. He wrote: "Manliness brings change or restores order . . . when the plan fails, when the whole idea of rational control by modern science develops leaks. Manliness is the next-to-last resort, before resignation and prayer."[26]

Manliness contained a lot of food for thought. It took aim at the "gender-neutral society" that supposes that full parity between the sexes is the goal of liberal society and was quick to point out that men have disdain for women and so will not submit to equality—that is just the way of the world. Mansfield treated this as a settled matter and relied on scientific literature to defend the eternal truth of sex difference—truths like "women do not tell jokes"—before launching into a somewhat more complicated story about the glories and pitfalls of manly courage.[27] He acknowledged that there are outliers to the patterns established by nature—he references Margaret Thatcher again and again—but the book generally works as a blunt instrument of gender-binary reification. In the course of twenty years, Mansfield had gone from a staunch refusal to acknowledge gender as a matter of serious scholarly pursuit (let alone a serious matter of justice) to publishing his own book-length defense of manly virtue that was determined to confirm all his priors. There was some real absurdity in all this, and a whole lot of preaching to the choir. But for many in the Straussian world, *Manliness* was an exercise in philosophical courage: an important act of countercultural bravado in the face of feminism's totalizing and irreversible ascendance within the academy and society at large.

These are not men who have ever learned how to be reasonable about women, and they self-selected into the corners of academia where that was acceptable. They have, in the main, and from a formative age, taken their cues from bad readings of Plato, and from the worst of Harvey Mansfield, and so have echoed and fomented an increasingly narrow-minded conservative grievance culture.

———

Michael Anton's pre–Flight 93 oeuvre is like a bad Straussian seminar on gender gone berserk. A survey of his earlier writing shows a man obsessed with women and gender, who was even for a time highly attentive to the online "pick-up artist" or PUA community.

The PUA world, exposed in the 2005 bestseller *The Game*, was a network of online groups that taught men to seduce and manipulate women. The writer Laura Bates, in her book *Men Who Hate Women* (2020), describes the PUA community as "an industry that exploits men's worst fears, preys on their vulnerabilities, and literally trains them in harassment, stalking, and even sexual assault."[28]

In the spring 2015 issue of the *Claremont Review of Books*, Anton published a little essay called "A Woman in Full."[29] It was about Tom Wolfe's insights into women, but it reveals a lot, in turn, about Anton, who revels in Wolfe's ability to disclose politically incorrect "truths" about women's nature. The essay contains a long series of such titillating discoveries, including the idea that women adore male attention; that they seek out "only the best" men and ubiquitously try to "marry up"; that they are fickle and overly choosy; that they are drawn to "bad boys" and don't give enough attention to nice guys; and that (gasp!) they are instinctively attracted to strength and protectiveness. (According to Anton, Wolfe's women fall into a few main types, like the wronged woman, the trophy wife, the gold-digger, and the serpentine co-ed who sleeps with a superstar and then cries "rape." Somehow in the course of all this Anton forgot the shrew!)

In the Wolfe piece, Anton refers to the insights of the PUA community five times. Around the same time, he published an academic paper entitled "Socrates as Pickup Artist: An Interpretation of Xenophon's Memorabilia III.11" in the peer-reviewed journal *Perspectives on Political Science*.

The purpose of that article was to show that Xenophon's Socrates, just like Tom Wolfe and Michael Anton, anticipated the powerful precepts (and methods) of the PUA community. It was, wrote an enthusiastic Anton, "at the very least an extraordinary coincidence of independent, parallel discovery (or assertion) across millennia."[30]

It is not a coincidence that the first person to publish a full-throated defense of Donald Trump also happens to have a thick written record of casual misogyny. As we will see in subsequent chapters, Anton is also friendly with some of the more extreme and misogynist characters who have since come to dominate the Straussian and New Right underworlds.

The Journal of American Greatness and the "Paleo-Straussians"

PUA sites were not the only online spaces that Anton was frequenting in the 2000s and 2010s. He was also a well-known men's style enthusiast and, in addition to writing a playful book on the subject called *The Suit* in 2005, was also a popular member of the online Styleforum community, where he posted around forty thousand messages between 2002 and 2016.[31] Then, in early 2016, as the primary season started to heat up, Anton and several like-minded colleagues started the *Journal of American Greatness* (*JAG*). This is where he worked out the ideas of Publius Decius Mus, alongside other contributors like "Plautus," "Manlius Capitolinus," "Lucullus," and "Cato the Elder." The blog ran from February through June 2016 and racked up 125 posts.

Under the blog's original "Who are we?" tab, the contributors wrote: "We are American patriots aghast at the stupidity and corruption of American politics, particularly in the Republican Party, and above all in what passes for the 'conservative' intellectual movement." The blog's authors decided to write pseudonymously for fear of professional reprisal ("Because the times are so corrupt that simply stating certain truths is enough to make one unemployable for life").[32] The primary purpose of the blog was to disrupt "conservatism's intellectual stagnation" by providing an intellectualized defense of Trumpism. Trump had taken the conservative world by storm, but no one had been able to explain how or why.

At its peak, the blog was attracting about 100,000 visits a day (this happened after Peggy Noonan wrote a column that mentioned the site, calling it "a sophisticated, rather brilliant and anonymous website that is using this Trumpian moment to break out of the enforced conservative orthodoxy of the past 15 years").[33] The authors got spooked by all the attention and scrubbed the blog from public view, but clearly there was a thirst out there for what they were doing.

It's not hard to track down original posts from the *Journal of American Greatness*, and it's not difficult to see why the authors took it down once it garnered a certain amount of attention.[34] The overall tenor of the blog is brash, ambitious, and no-holds-barred. Sometimes the posts are explicitly satirical. But there is also, from the very outset, genuine thoughtfulness in some, which belies the claim that *JAG* was intended by all of its participants to be merely "an inside joke."[35] There was clearly a serious investment of time in the blog, and the authors wrote afterward about how exhilarating the whole affair had been.[36]

Let's consider the substance of some of these posts.

Plautus/Julius Krein

Titus Maccius Plautus was an enormously popular comedic playwright who lived during the Roman Republic (254–184 BCE). Julius Krein, who chose the pseudonym Plautus for his *JAG* writings, graduated with a BA degree from Harvard College in 2008. He had been a student of Harvey Mansfield's and at one point counted Bill Kristol among his mentors.[37] Upon graduation, Krein entered a career in finance, and he was working at a hedge fund in Boston when he started writing for *JAG*.

Krein wrote the very first *JAG* post, which was called "Notes on the Origins and Future of Trumpism."[38] Its substance belied its muted title.

Krein focused his attention on one problem: the "global managerial elite." He was clearly inspired by James Burnham's book *The Managerial Revolution: What Is Happening in the World* (1941), especially as interpreted by Samuel Todd Francis.[39] Burnham (1905–1987) was a conservative thinker and editor for *National Review*; Francis (1947–2005) was a conservative writer who has also been called "the premier philosopher of white racial consciousness of our time."[40] Krein used the word "managerial" twenty-nine times in the post, which took on a relentless, mission-defining tone.

Plautus had a deep distrust of the establishment and the GOP, thanks in part to the fiasco in Afghanistan. In an interview in 2023, Krein told me that much of his disillusionment with the GOP and American politics more generally came from time he had spent in Afghanistan as a subcontractor for the Department of Defense in 2011. He said that this "was a very eye-opening experience and it revealed to me the gulf between the DC view of what was happening—the sort of standard neoconservative view of it—versus what was actually happening. Being there I saw the incompetence of the civilian effort in Afghanistan."[41] Krein's skepticism found its way into Plautus's posts and fueled his appreciation for Trump (though Plautus expressed more reservations about Trump than other *JAG* authors). For example, in a post entitled "Trump as Critic: The Need for a Greatness Agenda," Krein wrote: "When Trump tells the New York Times that Operation Iraqi Freedom 'totally destabilized the Middle East,' he is saying something that is both obvious and heresy in the Republican Party."

Krein's first post situated *JAG* writers in the broader context of American conservative intellectualism. He offered a lucid account of why they saw promise in Trump, and where they wanted to see Trumpism lead. Significantly, Krein, in this first post, takes on the mantle of paleoconservatism.

Paleoconservatism is the oppositional counterpart to American neoconservatism, which since the Vietnam War has stood mainly for conservative internationalism and democracy promotion (or adventurism). With its ideological roots in the isolationist interwar Old Right, paleoconservatism reemerged as a force at the end of the Cold War, which is when the right-wing fusionist coalition began to falter. As the historian Nicole Hemmer writes,

> With the Cold War no longer providing the motivation for a kind of conservative internationalism, or at least a conservative interventionism, suddenly there was room for the reappearance of the Old Right of the 1930s and 1940s, back when the nationalist strain in conservatism promoted protectionism and treated foreign intervention with skepticism if not alarm. The new Old Right, which would eventually be rebranded as paleoconservatism, did not fully emerge in the Bush years but was quickly coalescing as the Cold War ended.[42]

The biggest name in paleoconservatism is probably Pat Buchanan, who worked for both the Nixon and Reagan administrations and put himself forward as a presidential candidate several times in the 1990s. The columnist Ed Kilgore wrote in 2023 that Buchanan "was the living link between the nativist, isolationist, and protectionist paleoconservative tradition in GOP politics—which most observers thought had died in the 1950s—and the MAGA conservatism associated with Donald Trump."[43]

In addition to isolationism and economic protectionism, the paleoconservatives are known for their nativism in domestic affairs. In his history of American conservatism, Matthew Continetti described how "the paleoconservatives defended the Lost Cause of the South, despised Lincoln, and rejected the natural rights philosophy of the American founding." He went on to explain how paleoconservatives typically demonstrate a "revulsion for present-day America," with its increasing diversity and global connectedness.[44] Buchanan was an ardent nativist along precisely such "blood and soil" lines. In 2008 he published a book called *Churchill, Hitler, and the Unnecessary War* in which he endorsed the 1938 Munich Agreement, claimed that the West never should have declared war on Nazi Germany, and minimized Nazi war crimes. In other contexts, he has engaged in Holocaust revisionism, and in 2012 he was fired from MSNBC because of the arguments in his book *Suicide of a Superpower* (especially in the chapter called "The End of White America," which prefigured contemporary Great Replacement ideology).

Buchanan was perhaps the most obvious precursor to Trump, but Krein located the intellectual source code for Trumpism in the writings of the paleoconservative white supremacist thinker Sam Francis.[45] The late Charles Krauthammer wrote in 1992 that "With communism defeated, Buchanan emerges, like a woolly mammoth frozen in Siberian ice, as a perfectly preserved specimen of 1930s isolationism and nativism."[46] Sam Francis watched these forces at work and saw something hopeful: "The torch [Buchanan] carries illuminates new social forces that only now are forming a common political consciousness," he wrote in a famous (relatively speaking) essay called "From Household to Nation." Francis praised Buchanan for grasping that "elites themselves are the real enemy," while supporting "Middle American" interests, and for embracing "social and cultural" nationalism. "The nation," Francis wrote, "is fundamentally a social and cultural unit, not the creation of the state and its policies, but a continuing, organic body that transcends individuals and gives identity to itself through a common way of life and a common people." His only major critique of Buchanan was that he had eventually chosen to compromise his principles and endorse Bob Dole (there are echoes here of Gottfried's critique of Goldwater).[47]

Krein's language throughout his post is fervent, revolutionary, and conspiratorial. The thrust of the argument is that the global managerial elite is exploitative, actively seeks to dominate, and so is ruthlessly destroying the American way of life and must be stopped. As Krein acknowledges, Francis's approach contains a strong element of Neo-Marxism. "The managerial class," he writes, "is inevitably impelled by its internal logic to seek the destruction of any intermediating institutions, ultimately and especially the family, the homogenization, delegitimization, and eradication of culture, and the levelling, regimentation, and dehumanizing of all society." The true task of Trumpism, according to Krein, is the "destruction of the soulless managerial class, a task inseparable from the assertion of a healthier culture and a stronger elite in its place." His programmatic recommendation reads: "The political project of supreme importance is therefore the transformation of passive Middle Americans into a new ruling elite, while the ideological project of supreme significance is the formulation of a new nationalism which will justify that political project."[48] This is heady stuff.

This first post by Plautus also involved an extended critique of Lincoln's liberal universalism (or Declarationism). Krein approvingly cited Sam Francis's critique of Lincoln's myth of a "creedal" or propositional nation. Francis argued that Lincoln's civil religion was drawn from a "universalist natural rights egalitarianism" that ultimately undermined the *particularity* of the American nation.[49] There is a latent yearning throughout his work for something more grounded and particularistic. According to Krein, "the great failure of the American right has been the failure to define an American nationalism at once grounded in binding, necessarily particularist, traditions and institutions while at the same time leavened by a creed worthy of the name."[50]

Given the extent to which Krein relies on Sam Francis and sides with the paleoconservatives and against Abraham Lincoln, it is important to note that the "particularist" nationalism that Francis defended was white nationalism. Krein downplays this side of Francis's outlook; he offers a brief disclaimer, arguing that just because Francis had some disreputable views, his thought should not be disregarded entirely. But the legacy of white nationalism among the paleoconservatives is hardly peripheral to their worldview, and it is not, as Krein suggested in his post, an invention of the Southern Poverty Law Center. In the aforementioned column, Krauthammer delineated the ways in which Buchanan was fascistic, as well as an unrepentant nativist.[51] It was Dinesh D'Souza—a far less reputable conservative thinker—who would, in 1995, write the exposé of Sam Francis's racism.[52] In the first post for *JAG*, Krein tried to disentangle Francis's nationalism from white nationalism as part of his rationalization of Trumpism. But both movements—the old paleoconservatism and the New Right—are bound up with old-fashioned racism. To Krein's credit, as we will later see, he would admit as much within a year of Trump's first inauguration.

Decius/Michael Anton

One would hardly call Julius Krein's Plautus posts moderate, but taken together, they were far more restrained than those written by Michael Anton, and judging from what remained visible in the online archives, Anton posted a lot more than anyone else.

Anton was clearly the most pessimistic of the *JAG* posters (and he acknowledged this in the Flight 93 essay). His writings were the gloomiest about current conditions, the most conspiratorial about political realities, and the most radical in their prognostications for the future. Krein talked of replacing the elite within the current system; Anton did this, too, but then he also offered apologetics for Caesarism (which, tut tut, is not to be confused with tyranny).[53] Krein closed out his first post with the following claim: "Those presently occupying the commanding heights of culture, the economy, and politics clearly have no idea what to do with them. For the right, the question is, do we?"[54] Anton's version of the question was: "If we *must* have Caesar, who do you want him to be? One of theirs? Or one of yours (ours)?" There are posts where Anton suggests that corruption is so bad that America more or less deserves a Caesar ("Would an incorrupt republic have elected Barack Obama? Twice?"), and that "the country is more divided—fractured— than it has ever been, and yes, that includes the run-up to the Civil War."[55] Anton's crisis-mongering in *JAG* is as extreme as in Flight 93, or worse. There is much talk of degeneracy, and of friends and enemies; there is a post where he likens the current crop of elites to the pre–Civil War "slave power" thanks to their support for mass immigration. He saves some of his worst for Muslims.[56]

If Plautus stood for dramatic top-down cultural transformation and a new kind of nationalism, Anton, more than any other *JAG* author, stood against immigration—especially post-1965, egalitarian immigration, and his reasons for this were consistent with paleoconservatism, including Great Replacement conspiracism.[57] As with Krein, part of Anton's argument was that neoconservatives had been too attached to abstract principle, to the neglect of particular attachments and connections—the older, ancestral "love of one's own"—that the Paleos explicitly embraced. At one point he referred to all the *JAG* authors as "Paleo-Straussians."[58] He claimed not to side entirely with the Paleos, but his collection of *JAG* posts suggests that he was shifting away from a more Jaffaesque outlook—and away from an outlook that prized the Lincolnian creed of abstract human equality—and toward the much more pessimistic "paleo" outlook. He quoted well-known racists— Steve Sailer, Peter Brimelow, and John Derbyshire—approvingly and mocked anyone—especially establishment conservatives—who might be squeamish about nativism and racism. Anton went out of his way to praise Trump's "America First" sloganeering, calling it the "heart of Trumpism" and suggesting that the original America First Committee was "unfairly maligned."[59]

Anton's most blatant departure from the universe of Jaffa and Lincoln occurred during "Toward a Sensible, Coherent Trumpism" (a post that prefigured the Flight 93 essay, and that the Claremont Institute refused to publish), in a discussion of the Declaration of Independence.[60] Anton appealed to Lincoln to justify the idea that people from different places and backgrounds are rightly understood to be unequal. To make his point, he cherry-picked from Lincoln's speech responding to the *Dred Scott v. Sandford* decision (the infamous decision from 1857 wherein the United States Supreme Court declared that African Americans were not entitled to civil rights).[61] "Yes, it is true that 'all men are created equal,'" wrote Anton. "But Lincoln adds the crucial caveat: all men are not 'equal in *all* respects' . . . They are not 'equal in color, size, intellect, moral developments or social capacity.'" Lincoln, Anton implied, would have recognized that some people are ill-suited to the republican way of life and so would have objected to mass immigration.

If you know this speech, you will recognize how Anton manipulates it.[62] Lincoln did discuss the nature of human equality there and used the words Anton ascribes to him. But Lincoln also drew a clear distinction between the unjust real world and the ideal, between the descriptive and the prescriptive. He explained that, while the writers of the Declaration of Independence were not in a position to bestow equality on all people ("they could not confer such a boon"), the founders nevertheless defined "with tolerable distinctness in what respects they did consider all men created equal." They were, he explained, equal with respect to "certain inalienable rights, among which are life, liberty, and the pursuit of happiness." And he said that the Declaration was—contra the Dred Scott ruling—intended by the founders to be a beacon of hope for a more equal future. It is a memorable passage:

They meant simply to declare the *right*, so that the *enforcement* of it might follow as fast as circumstances should permit. They meant to set up a standard maxim for free society which should be familiar to all: constantly looked to, constantly labored for, and even, though never perfectly attained, constantly approximated, and thereby constantly spreading and deepening its influence and augmenting the happiness and value of life to all people, of all colors, everywhere.[63]

In "Toward a Sensible, Coherent Trumpism," Anton, like a sophist, took Lincoln's description of the empirical (but, in Lincoln's view, very bad) reality of inequality and used it to defend the normative ideals of inequality and exclusion (or what he liked to call "the historic American nation").[64] Lincoln consistently did the opposite.

Manlius/Gladden Pappin

Marcus Manlius Capitolinus was also a hero of the early Roman Republic. He is known for defending and saving the Roman citadel when the city was under attack by the Gauls in 390 BCE, and for taking up the cause of the plebians in the wake of the siege. He was subsequently accused of aspiring to monarchic rule and condemned to death by the Senate (he was thrown from the Tarpeian Rock in 384 BCE).[65] In other words, Manlius was a proto-Caesar populist sort.

Of the three most prolific *JAG* authors, "Manlius Capitolinus" was the most lucid and temperate. His real name was Gladden Pappin. Unlike Anton and Krein, Pappin had not worked in finance, and he had completed a doctoral degree in political theory.

Pappin was born in St. Louis, Missouri, and grew up in an itinerant Catholic household—both of his parents were academics. He is, from his father's side, a member of the Osage Nation, and he graduated with a BA degree from Harvard University in 2004, where he gained some notoriety for his extreme position on homosexuality. Pappin earned his PhD from Harvard in 2012, working under Harvey Mansfield, after which he spent time at the University of Notre Dame's Institute for Advanced Studies and the de Nicola Center for Ethics and Culture.[66]

He joined the faculty of the University of Dallas in 2017 and received tenure there in 2021. He is a Hungarian citizen via his wife.[67]

Pappin's main preoccupation in *JAG* concerned economics, though he also demonstrated an interest in the social sciences more generally. One of the through lines of the Manlius posts is a spirit of triumph over the liberal and technocratic presuppositions of the past, both in economics and in political science. For Pappin, Trump represented a reassertion of the properly political, over and against a stagnant and deterministic technocratic liberalism. He praised Trump for breaking the old mold of Weberian charisma, for demonstrating the failure of Obama-style "Big Data" in campaigns and elections, and for seeing a way forward in economics that broke with the presuppositions of technocracy and managerialism.[68] At the heart of these pieces is the belief that politics has ceded too much authority to the experts—that the properly political space has shrunk down in modernity, becoming pallid and stale. There are echoes here of both Leo Strauss and Carl Schmitt. Pappin wanted to bring the spirit of politics and human judgment back in. He wrote, "The political realm requires personal judgment. Where there is no judgment there is no politics. Where there is no politics there is no judgment."[69]

For Pappin, as for Krein, nowhere was judgment needed more desperately than in the realm of economics. Krein wrote of how neoliberal economics had taken on a life of its own: "Around the time of the Vietnam War, and on through the later stages of the Cold War, policy makers began to see economics as a realm with an authority and logic all its own, no longer subjugated to state power." In terms that echoed Sam Francis directly, Pappin explained that the old conservative fusionism was a marriage of convenience that had now become obsolete and destructive. Fusionism caused the GOP to overlook the "deteriorating structural and economic forms which condition family structure." Only Trump was willing to admit the deep failures of the fusionist compromise with neoliberal economics, and once again to seize the reins of the American economy. To put it in Aristotelian terms, Trump promised to return politics to its proper "architectonic" role—to actively shape the future of the American economy rather than simply submit to laissez-faire, libertarian dogma.

For Pappin, that meant new trade protectionism, keen attention to the problems of automation, and new thinking about production and value. Latent in his posts was a genuine respect for employment, manufacturing, and real production value—and disdain for commodification and financialization.

But Pappin's posts also betrayed some delusions. For example, toward the end of a post about the end of "Big Data" (meaning technocratic political science and campaign strategy) and the renewal of real political judgment and rhetoric, Pappin argued that Trump was "a statesman who knew that the basis of real political deeds, even in 2016, lay in love of real community." If you say so, Gladden.[70]

After JAG

After they shut down the blog in June 2016, the three main *JAG* writers pursued very different paths. Anton helped to create a highly sensationalized and propagandistic new website called *American Greatness*, connected to *Winston84.com*, a clearinghouse of alt-right "censored content."[71] After Trump's election, he joined the White House staff, but he resigned after the ouster of H. R. McMaster and the appointment of John Bolton to the National Security Agency. At that point, Anton returned to the Claremont and Hillsdale fold, taking up a position at Hillsdale's Kirby Center for Constitutional Studies and Citizenship in Washington, DC. He was a regular speaker in the National Conservative circuit and continued to represent the Claremont Institute wing of the New Right. We will encounter him again in chapter 6, on the alt-right and Hard Right dissident fringe, and in chapter 7 where I discuss how, in the lead-up to the 2020 election, he and other leaders from the Claremont Institute spread conspiracies about a "Biden Coup." He was one of the first appointees to the second Trump administration in early 2025.

Rather than join Anton when *JAG* closed, Krein, with the help of Pappin, began a much more wonkish quarterly journal with the generic title *American Affairs*. As Krein explained to *Politico* at the time, their goal was "to provide a forum for people who believe that the conventional ideological categories and policy prescriptions of recent decades are no longer relevant to the most pressing problems and debates facing our country."[72] Krein was determined to include voices from the right and left. The first issue included an essay by Adam Adatto Sandel, the son of Michael Sandel, the famous Harvard communitarian. The third issue offered a pointed review essay by Anne-Marie Slaughter (CEO of New America, a liberal think tank) taking the journal to task for, among other things, the maleness and whiteness of its work to that point ("It is as if the editors, funders, and contributors still believe we are living in eighteenth-century America, when the founders and framers were all propertied white men," she wrote, asking, "How can we quilt our wonderfully diverse nation together with squares that are all the same?").[73]

The problems Slaughter identified persisted. But in August 2017 Krein retracted his support for Trump, publicly and definitively. He did so in an opinion piece for *The New York Times*, published on August 17, 2017, five days after the Unite the Right white supremacist rally in Charlottesville, Virginia, where Heather Heyer was killed and over two dozen others injured. Krein was unequivocal. He explained the hopes that he had brought to Trumpism and then stated plainly that "it is now clear that my optimism was unfounded." He called the administration disgraceful and urged others to stop defending Trump. He also admitted to having been completely wrong about the question of Trump's racism. "From the very start of his run," wrote Krein, "one of the most serious charges against Mr. Trump was that he panders to racists." He contended that he and many others had convinced themselves that Trump's more outrageous comments were just gaffes. But then he said: "It is now clear that we were deluding ourselves. Either Mr. Trump is genuinely sympathetic to the David Duke types, or he is so obtuse as to be utterly incapable of learning from his worst mistakes. Either way, he continues to prove his harshest critics right."[74] Krein continued to call himself a nationalist in interviews, and he, like Anton, would later participate in the National Conservatism movement. But he deserves credit for stepping away from Trump so forcefully when he did.

Gladden Pappin did not follow Krein's lead after Charlottesville. As we will see, Pappin's push for Trumpism went well beyond *JAG*, and while he was writing as Manlius for the blog, Pappin was also pushing for

Trumpism within the small but influential new Catholic integralist movement. Adrian Vermeule, who is the main subject of chapter 10, is the most sophisticated New Right intellectual from this camp. Rather than make a break with Trumpism, then, Pappin rose through the ranks of the Catholic/Postliberal faction of the New Right and became one of its core constituents—one of its most prolific writers, most popular speakers, and an eager participant in pro-Hungary propagandizing.

One way to distinguish Krein's trajectory from that of Anton and Pappin is to say that only Krein had the good sense not to continue down anything like the Schmittian path. Carl Schmitt was a reactionary thinker and legal scholar with a Catholic background who was prominent during the turbulent Weimar period in Germany that preceded the takeover of the country by Hitler and the National Socialists. When the Nazis did gain power, he joined the Party and had significant influence, for a time, in Hitler's regime. He has been called the "the crown jurist of the Third Reich," and his work justified limitless emergency powers. The connections between his thought and the Holocaust are obvious and undeniable, and he never recanted or apologized. Schmitt was a serious antisemite.[75] He was also what we might call a radical political realist insofar as he believed in the supreme (and ultimately even metaphysical) importance of raw power and force.

A ruthless critic of liberalism, Schmitt believed in a hardened, all-or-nothing politics in which the people take sides against their enemies—and, should the need arise, are represented by a strongman who becomes a law unto himself. ("Sovereign is he who decides on the exception" is Schmitt's famous formulation from 1922.)[76] When Michael Anton wrote that "a Hillary presidency will be pedal-to-the-metal on the entire Progressive-left agenda, plus items few of us have yet imagined in our darkest moments," he was writing in a Schmittian key. When Gladden Pappin proclaimed that "where there is no judgment there is no politics," he was channeling Schmitt. (So was Donald Trump when, in early 2025, he posted on Truth Social that "He who saves his Country does not violate any Law.")[77] As we will see in chapter 10, Schmitt was also a major influence for Pappin's comrade in Postliberalism, Adrian Vermeule.

Schmittian claims like those we see so frequently on the New Right prepare the ground for extremist, unlimited politics. When Krein decided after Charlottesville that things had gone too far, he stood for a different kind of political engagement—the kind that believes in reason as a relevant part of politics, and in standards of basic human equality and decency.

In 2023, Pappin accepted an appointment as the president of the Hungarian Institute of International Affairs, an institute devoted to providing support for Viktor Orbán in foreign policy.[78] This signaled an altogether new level of commitment to right-wing populism. But before he journeyed to Hungary, and before the official *Postliberal Order*, there was Patrick Deneen and his 2018 bestseller, *Why Liberalism Failed*. In the next chapter I turn to Deneen, modern liberalism's most successful critic.

4

Postliberalism

THE FIRST TIME I heard of Patrick Deneen was when I was hired to be one of his temporary replacements, at Georgetown University in Washington, DC. It was 2013. Deneen had left Georgetown for the University of Notre Dame in South Bend, Indiana, in 2012. Another Georgetown colleague of his had been teaching abroad, so they needed some theorists to fill in for these courses.

When I got the Georgetown job, I was thrilled. The market for political theory PhDs is always bad, and this was not long after the financial crisis of 2008, so things were worse than usual. When my husband and I drove up from Memphis (where I had held a postdoc) that summer, it was my first time setting foot in DC. I can still remember waking up in the heart of the Smoky Mountains, driving through lush Virginia, and then finally crossing the Arlington Memorial Bridge. This bridge has the feel of a Parisian promenade, wide and studded with streetlights. It lines up with Arlington Cemetery on the Virginia side, but takes you straight toward the Lincoln Memorial, which, temple-like, defines the west end of the National Mall. From there we drove past the Kennedy Center and the famous Watergate buildings, before heading up the long, winding road of Rock Creek Park—joggers all around, high bridges overhead. I remember wondering why no one had ever told me how gorgeous this place was.

In fairness, though, Patrick Deneen *had* said something about the beauties of Washington, DC, in a blog post about his decision to leave for Notre Dame. I came across this post while researching the visiting position at Georgetown. Here is what he had to say in October 2012:

> [I] will admit that moving to South Bend has not been without moments of second-guessing about leaving all the cultural, culinary, and aesthetic bounties of a place like Washington, DC. These are beautiful and wealthy places, filled with interesting people leading interesting lives, places overbrimming with so much prosperity that one inevitably benefits even if one is not among the super-wealthy. Living in such places, one actually does experience a kind of "trickle-down" wealth . . . in the ancillary benefits of good schools, a constantly upgraded infrastructure, well-maintained private homes, well-stocked libraries and manicured public parks, interesting intellectual discourse, an atmosphere where personal health, personal growth, and well-being are stressed and therefore contagious.[1]

This may be the nicest thing Patrick Deneen has ever said about life in any modern city, let alone "The Swamp," and the nicest thing he has ever said about cultural elites.

But it was also just a small digression in a post that was otherwise highly critical of life in the nation's capital and of all the mainstream conservatives who flock there. Deneen called them out for the hypocrisy of their politics—Republicans kept talking about small government, but they never came close to achieving it, even when they were in power! Deneen's farewell post also spoke to a persistent theme of his writing, which is that today's cultural elites are all of a piece, and they are corrupt. Whether they reside in DC or some other "super-zip," and whether they are Republicans or Democrats, they are all subject to a kind of idolatry. Not only are they all superficially the same—eating at the same restaurants, shopping at the same stores—they also share a fundamental worldview, which involves an overwhelming preference for national and international concerns over the local and domestic. The effects of this are perceptible on the spiritual plane. Deneen wrote that today's best-educated leaders "are deeply bound by a shared perspective that what matters is the big and the expansive."[2]

Deneen framed his departure from DC as a rejection of this mainstream outlook and a retreat to somewhere smaller—somewhere more settled and contained, more connected, and more spiritually true. He drew a comparison to St. Augustine's return from Rome to Thagaste—and to his disillusionment with the "people drawn by common vices in the pursuit of earthly power." Referencing Augustine's *City of God*, Deneen wrote: "We are more apt to see the lights of that better city from locations less bright, less distracting, less self-important."[3]

In many respects, the 2012 farewell post demonstrates the consistency of Deneen's philosophical interests and political concerns and anticipates themes that were central to his breakthrough book *Why Liberalism Failed* (2018). In other respects, however, his thinking underwent dramatic shifts after he left DC, and after *Why Liberalism Failed* landed with tremendous national success. Whereas in 2012, in addition to disdain and skepticism, Deneen showed some sensitivity to the attractions of elite modern urban life, ten years later he was naming the American elite "one of the worst of its kind produced in history," calling to "replace" them, and advocating for "regime change."[4] In 2012 he was keen to identify modern idols; by 2022 he was, along with some friends, smashing them down and casting about, around the world, for something new. The latter included jaunts to illiberal Poland and Hungary.

This chapter is about Patrick Deneen's political thought and actions, the transformations these underwent during the first Trump administration, and the early days of Postliberalism and American Catholic integralism (also sometimes called neo-integralism).

Deneen is a key leader of the Postliberals—the second group of conservative intellectuals, who, after the Claremonters, got behind Trumpism. And Deneenism is the most palatable, sanitized version of Trumpy populism that one is likely to encounter. His writing combines a stern social conservatism and republicanism with strident antiliberalism and anti-elitism. It is likely to be alienating to economic liberals (so to both neoliberals and neoconservatives) but appealing to anyone who cares about culture and community, or about the environment, or who has suffered the vicissitudes of late modern capitalism in their own lives. It was appealing to JD Vance, who converted to Catholicism in 2019 and had been friendly with Deneen (and his "crunchy conservative" friend Rod Dreher) since 2016.[5] Vance has cited Deneen as a major intellectual influence and has self-identified as a member of the "postliberal right" that "tacks right on culture and left on economics."[6]

Deneen, Front Porch Republic, and Limits

When Deneen departed Georgetown and the nation's capital, he had the perfect platform from which to announce his decision: a blog he had cofounded in 2009, called *Front Porch Republic*. Deneen and a few like-minded colleagues founded the site in the aftermath of the 2008 economic crisis and Barack Obama's presidential victory (and his administration's neoliberal response to the economic crisis). Deneen had been anticipating a crisis of liberalism for many years (he was once a proponent of "peak oil" theory), and the economic collapse of 2008 seemed to ratify his contention that modern neoliberal economics—based on ceaseless competition and growth and a profit-motive detached from real value—was unsustainable in the long term.[7] *Front Porch Republic* was inspired in part by the work of Wendell Berry, a nationally renowned writer and poet who is beloved across the political spectrum for his commitment to localism. (The food writer Mark Bittman calls Berry "the soul of the real food movement.")[8] Deneen shares Berry's broad interest in the relationship between nature and culture.[9] So do I.

The tagline for the *Front Porch Republic* site is "Place, Limits, and Liberty," each of which are major themes in Berry's writing. That writing reveals a classical sensibility—by which I mean it shows a deep appreciation for the formative, positive dimensions of culture that liberals tend not to acknowledge or speak about. Berry cares about all the ways in which art, writing, and the other artifacts around us shape our souls, give texture to our relationships and lives, and prepare us to act well in the world. "Humans differ most from other creatures," wrote Berry in his classic essay "Preserving Wildness," "in the extent to which they must be *made* what they are—that is, in the extent to which they are artifacts of their culture."[10]

Berry is also a writer who cares deeply about the economy. His oeuvre might be described as a one-man crusade against the modern mindset: against, for example, excess consumption, mass modern forms of economic production, and bureaucratized education. He is a thoughtful but radical critic of capitalism, with its cutthroat competitiveness and rejection of humane limits, and its inability to recognize true value, which Berry says is always grounded in love and affection.[11] He seeks a new kind of economy that would be part of a "double recovery" of both nature and culture.

The *Front Porch Republic* writings are more political, and more conservative, than Wendell Berry's, but more "liberal" than the work, say, of paleoconservatives like Paul Gottfried. The writing, like Berry's, is ecologically grounded and earthy: something like Little House meets Thoreau meets Pope Francis's *Laudato Si*. These are writers who, like Berry, have studied the Tocquevillian art of association and various Christian traditions and want to foster those older forms and revive that older world. They are not thinkers who, like Gottfried, are overtly reactionary or nativist in their sociological thinking.

After 2013, Deneen published much less on the *Front Porch Republic* site. He turned increasingly to bigger national outlets like *The American Conservative, First Things,* and *Public Discourse.* And it is during this period, too, that he wrote *Why Liberalism Failed,* which went to press in 2018.

Wendell Berry is a writer who stubbornly rejects abstractions and theorizing—as well as most partisan politics and polemics. In *Why Liberalism Failed,* Patrick Deneen embraced an opposite sensibility. This was a book enamored of general ideas.[12] And though the work included a strong critique of the conservative establishment for its neoliberal economics, some of Deneen's choices gave the book a strong partisan inflection. By choosing to attack "liberalism" and the so-called liberalocracy—words that in an American context point left—Deneen's partisanship shone right through.

Deneen, Bloom, and Closing American Minds

Rush Limbaugh catalyzed Michael Anton's moment in the national spotlight when he read from the Flight 93 essay on air in September 2016. President Obama played a similar role for Patrick Deneen when he put *Why Liberalism Failed* on his list of favorite reads for 2018.[13]

When it was published in January 2018, the book struck a nerve because it offered a clear general explanation of all that had recently gone so wrong. For liberals shocked by Trump's success, the book was eerily prescient and appropriately catastrophizing; for the right, it offered "liberalism" as a convenient scapegoat while also calling neoliberal economics to account. For Deneen, Trumpism—or something like it—was the culminating, and inevitable, outcome of the inner logic of liberal democracy and proof of his book's central thesis. Trump was the strongman brought to bring liberalism to heel. By the time *Why Liberalism Failed* was published, Michael Anton was working as a spokesman for Trump's National Security Council. But Trumpism, as it were, had become an opportunity for Deneen, too.

Deneen's core argument in *Why Liberalism Failed* is that liberal democracy is doomed from the start because it is based on the destabilizing philosophical premises of individual autonomy and the conquest of nature, which together act as solvents on the social fabric and culture at large. According to Deneen (and many other conservatives), liberal democracy has survived as long as it has only by leaning hard on older forms of social cohesion—old religious beliefs, cultural norms and traditions, and forms of education. He holds that, thanks to mistaken early modern ideas, there is only one direction for modern liberal constitutionalism to go. Indeed, Deneen's title suggested that the failure has already happened, and he argues throughout the book that liberal elites, in truth, already constitute a despotic class: the liberalocracy.

Though these conclusions are dramatic, Deneen's book had more in common with the work of the late Allan Bloom than it did with the sensationalism of Anton's "Flight 93 Election." Deneen is not himself a Straussian, but he was influenced by Strauss, and in particular by Strauss's idea that there was an essential similarity to American liberalism and conservatism.[14] His critique of liberalism follows conceptually on the heels of Bloom's critique of higher education (itself derivative of Strauss's critique of modernity). Deneen had once been a student of Bloom's. He attended Rutgers University in New Jersey and then enrolled at the University of Chicago as a PhD student in 1986, with the prestigious Committee on Social Thought where Bloom was teaching.[15]

But soon he became "disillusioned by the program and put off by Bloom's circle of students." He must have felt strongly about this, because he made the dramatic decision to leave and complete his degree back at Rutgers, under the supervision of his former professor, Wilson Carey McWilliams, who would become a longtime mentor and close friend. Despite his departure from Chicago, Deneen spoke highly of Bloom and *Closing* in his review: "I loved the book and credit it, at least in part, for my eventual return to the academy and a career as a professor of political philosophy." There was nothing here of the vulgar cruelty vis-à-vis Bloom that we saw with Jaffa.[16]

Bloom's influence on Deneen's thinking is evident throughout *Why Liberalism Failed*, and there are substantive and stylistic parallels between the two best-selling books. Stated simply, Bloom was concerned with the (alleged) failures of liberal education in America, and Deneen with the (alleged) failure of the liberal order as such. On the most fundamental level, both authors were interested in "big idea" questions about the role of morality and values in the contemporary world, and both made weighty arguments about the paradoxes and tensions that come with modern moral openness and liberal freedoms. But both men also offered extreme, even dystopian, accounts of their respective contemporary milieus; their writing is soaked in nostalgia for bygone eras, and both books engage in overheated polemics (and sloppy scholarship) that sparked cascades of reviews and criticism.

The guiding argument of *The Closing of the American Mind* was that the contemporary American virtue of "openness" threatened to bring about America's downfall.[17] Bloom argued that, for Americans, a belief in equality goes hand-in-hand with moral relativism and a faith in "openness" that together outstrip any other value. Such a configuration of beliefs and priorities means that there is no room left in the American mind for serious moral and political thinking—for serious thinking about better and worse, right and wrong, and good and bad ways of life. It also leads to a hatred for absolutist thinking, but then this gets combined with an absolute (and so contradictory and irrational) commitment to specific democratic values like equality and human rights. Bloom traced these habits and tendencies through the history of the social sciences and philosophy, attempting a genealogy of American relativism and intellectual narrowness, with mixed results. In some respects, *Closing* was the book-length version of two conservative "gotcha" quips: "So you think all morality is relative, but is that claim relative too?" and "So you believe in toleration, but what about the intolerant?" Thoughtful liberals and philosophers have responses to these questions. But as with so many things liberal-adjacent, the answers are complex, academic, and not very quippy.[18]

One thing that Bloom does convey effectively—and which strikes me as still true today—is how people in modern democracies are confused about the role that moral evaluations play in democratic life and politics. In the universities, this often means either that ethical and moral questions are avoided entirely or that the answers are presumed and righteously taken for granted. In a chapter called "The Sixties," Bloom argues that this moral thoughtlessness and taken-for-grantedness was "an almost inevitable result of generations of teaching that the most instinctive of all questions—What is good?—has no place in the university."[19] In other words, Bloom argued, there was hardly any place on modern campuses for genuine exploration of conflicting ethical, religious, or political outlooks—for modes of thinking that did not already presume clear normative answers, and yet which also took seriously the possibility that one might be able to discover the truth.

For Bloom, this made real disagreement and discussion (as well as true philosophy, which is what he cared about most deeply) impossible and left modern citizens ill-equipped for political life. If no one in the university is really investigating how best to live, or what constitutes a good life, or what justice means and how to get it, then why would we ever expect politics to be deep or interesting? If everyone already knows what to believe and how to be an activist for progress, then what did that mean for the university? Bloom went on to connect this argument to the campus unrest of the era, posing the rhetorical question, "If the university's teachers cannot teach about the good, why should the students not teach it?"[20] He did not like his citadels being upset by students who thought they knew something about justice.

Bloom experienced some of the campus turmoil of the 1960s personally, but his response to it in *Closing* was that of a cloistered snob, or worse: He refused to take the moral claims of the activists seriously and clung tightly to a conception of the university as strictly intellectual and activism-free—as though ideas and truths never compel one to action. As the late Christopher Hitchens put it, "Chaos, most especially the chaos identified with pissed-off African Americans, was the whole motif of the *Closing of the American Mind*."[21] It is true, I think, that some institutions in society—and perhaps the university above all—should be insulated from day-to-day politics. But Bloom's assessment of civil rights activism in the late 1960s was overweening given realities the protestors were working to confront.

It is a familiar story.

That said, there was something to Bloom's argument about the normative confusion at the heart of the modern university. Leo Strauss put it memorably in his book *Natural Right and History* (1953): "We are then in the position of beings who are sane and sober when engaged in trivial business and who gamble like madmen when confronted with serious issues—retail sanity and wholesale madness."[22] The modern liberal academy was good at science and business but had become awfully squeamish about deep investigation of matters of right and principle and at the same time moralizing and unquestioning. This often resulted in a stifling and spiritless intellectual climate—a bad brew of triviality, orthodoxy, and denialism—where too much was predictable and not enough was up for real debate.

The upshot of Bloom's book was a call for more rigorous philosophizing in schools and universities, and for richer humanities and religious education. He worried that absent such a development in America's intellectual and cultural spaces, nihilism and/or authoritarianism would swoop in to fill the void. Modern liberal peoples would continue their descent into rootlessness and meaninglessness; they would eventually become desperate and scramble for a despot (or perhaps a Jordan Peterson) to give shape to their lives. Openness would lead to tyranny.

———

In *Why Liberalism Failed*, Deneen follows the basic contours of Bloom's argument about liberal education and openness, now applied to liberal society at large. But Deneen, unlike Bloom, is not on the side of openness and liberality. The grand, mantralike thesis of the book—repeated ad nauseam by Deneen throughout and in many subsequent interviews—is that liberalism failed by virtue of its own success. Just as, according to Bloom, liberal education risks choking on the virtue of openness, collapsing into relativism and emotivism, liberalism has already failed, thanks to its openness and wholesale abandonment of limits.[23] Deneen writes: "As liberalism has 'become more fully itself,' as its inner logic has become more evident and its self-contradictions manifest, it has generated pathologies that are at once deformations of its claims yet realizations of liberal ideology."[24] Liberalism, by his account, has been marvelously successful in shaping the modern world, but this paradoxically means it has also succeeded in tearing apart webs of human sociality, convention, and community.

Liberalism's latent individualism has destroyed political life and ransacked the natural order. Eventually, Deneen argues, the liberal desire for freedom leads, through paths of "deracination," "depredation," and "disintegration," to despotism. It's a vicious circle of individualism and statism, of political atomism that fuels state tyranny. And whereas Bloom presents his story as a warning, Deneen offers his as an inevitability.[25] This is pure Ideas First determinism: We are doomed because of the ideas that have shaped our lives (and since, for Deneen, liberalism has a static definition, it cannot be ameliorated).

It is easy to see how a person could become captivated by Deneen's sweeping explanation of modern life. There is a good deal of truth to his idea that liberalism—which originated as a mode of politics meant to mediate between conflicting worldviews, and to protect individuals' rights and dignity—has had disintegrative effects on some dimensions of modern social life and community, especially if one considers liberal economic policies as part of the ledger. But Deneen overstates the extent of atomism, social decline, and state tyranny—and quite dramatically, much as Bloom had overstated and misunderstood the problems of the modern campus. Bloom saw decline, but the era he discussed also witnessed the most dramatic expansion of higher education in American history. Deneen's book similarly views the dizzying social, political, and technological changes of recent decades, and all he can see is chaos and instability. Meanwhile, many of us—especially those whose lives have benefited from progressive social changes—see reconfiguration rather than destruction and wonder when things have actually been better. I often look around today and compare it to the world my grandmothers inhabited, and I can't help but shake my head at men like Bloom and Deneen.

But there are also essential differences between the two thinkers. Whereas Bloom critiqued higher education in the United States out of a sense of concern both for the life of the mind and for modern liberal democracy, in *Why Liberalism Failed* Deneen is working toward quite a different telos. He does not think liberalism salvageable, and so his purpose is far more radical and closed. Bloom, like Strauss, wrote as a friend of liberal education and liberal democracy, who wanted to deepen them and so sustain them; Deneen writes as their highly critical undertaker, or even their cheery embalmer. For Deneen, the pathologies that modern liberalism unleashes are much more concerning and destructive than Bloom lets on; so it's time to forgo liberal freedoms and work toward wholly different political ends. He titled his 2023 book *Regime Change*; when he calls himself Postliberal, he really means it.

It's also fair to say, I think, that Deneen is more earnest about politics than Bloom ever was (he is more like Jaffa and the Claremonters in this regard). Bloom is quite explicit in *Closing* that he cares about higher education and liberal democracy mainly because they provide a haven for the activity of philosophy, which he held to be the highest sort of life (and, in effect, the meaning of life). While I find Bloom's outlook a tad too rarefied (there are many other good reasons to care about politics and higher education), one of the refreshing features of *Closing* is how it provides an unabashed defense of the humanizing potential of liberal education—as something deeply rewarding, of tremendous inherent worth, and even self-constitutive. His defense of liberalism is thinner, but it is nevertheless characterized by a grudging hopefulness.

Deneen cares much more than Bloom about the things that constitute everyday political life for most people—things like elections, community associations, and school board meetings. His more earnest and idealistic interest in democratic politics vis-à-vis Bloom means, it seems to me, that he has a higher bar for what politics should mean, and more room, too, for serious disappointment. Deneen's own conservative Catholicism arguably also makes him more deeply resistant to the particular kind of society that liberalism creates. He is presumably upset not just about the problems created by free markets and consumption, but also by what he views as libertinism and moral disorder. Both Deneen and Bloom present growing moral pluralism as something that invites antimoral relativism and nihilism. But for Deneen, liberalism is unsalvageable. Only a small slice of the population—the elites—can do well under liberalism, which corrupts everything else and destroys the traditional ways in which most people (according to Deneen) are able to thrive. He has said that he was formerly a man of the left, and his populist concerns come across as sincere.[26] But whereas other critics of contemporary liberalism argue for a reorientation from within, Deneen wants something more dramatic.

The divergences between Bloom and Deneen are clearest in Deneen's account of education, which is closely tied to his understanding of human freedom. In *Why Liberalism Failed*, the early modern philosophers were made into major culprits, thanks to their emphasis on individual freedom, and Deneen presented the true great books as those that foster virtue and moral obedience, as opposed to those that challenge authority. When he imagines a new curricular reading list, Plato and the biblical authors are included; the founders and other modern authors—not to mention the postmodern ones—are not. To account for this, he explained that such an education was better because it "reinforced a basic teaching embedded deeply within its own cultural tradition, namely an education in limits."[27] He had been making these argument for quite some time. In a 2013 speech called "Against the Great Books," he criticized modern thinkers for being so critical of ancient authorities and values, and heaped praise on older forms of education, noting that "the aim of such an education is not critical thinking, but the achievement of liberty governed by the discipline—even *dictatorship*—of virtue."[28]

Deneen's mode of thought presupposes that there are specific truths and ways of seeing the world that must be left unchallenged; he wants to protect and cordon off moral and political living, even if that means sealing off critical thinking. It's an all-cave-no-light account of liberal education, and one that should be deeply unsettling to anyone who cares about free thinking. And as far as politics goes, Deneen tends to obscure the fact that the modern liberal political project, going back to Locke or earlier, was conceived as something that imposed strict limits *on government*—in order, especially, to secure space for individual freedom, including the free moral conscience.

Deneen's Antiliberalism

I first read *Why Liberalism Failed* in 2019. At the time, we were living with my in-laws in Wichita, Kansas. We were there for our own recuperative Augustinian retreat from life in Washington, DC. I had just given birth to my second son and had resigned my faculty position at American University, where I had gone to work after my year at Georgetown. I resigned because I was burnt out, unsettled in the academy, and thinking about doing something new. By then, I was more or less out of conservative academia, but it was also at around this time that I really started paying attention to conservative intellectualism. And that's when I first read Deneen's best-selling book. I found it frustrating and slightly bewildering.

One of the reasons I disliked it was what Deneen said about liberals and elites, which to me seemed silly and conspiratorial. I readily concede that liberals and elites do tend to be more cosmopolitan and rootless than their conservative counterparts, and that they are sometimes plagued by hypocrisy and self-righteousness. But, like Bloom and so many Straussians, Deneen spoke as though anyone who did not share his particular values was an amoral nihilist or relativist, rather than someone with real and fundamental moral disagreements. And Deneen's cynicism went much further. He accused liberal elites of being wholly without genuine affection, feeling, or meaning in their own lives. He suggested that their marriages were mercenary, they did not truly care for their own children, and they did not put down real roots or have a sense of home.[29] Reading this from my in-laws' basement in Wichita, with my newborn and a three-year-old underfoot, I could only laugh. Did Deneen truly believe that people like me don't understand the inherent limits of life? That we don't care about home and family, about our kids and communities and friendships? There are people out there who fit his description of unencumbered jetsetters. But as a general description of professional people, it was a caricature, cynical and distorted. As Ezra Klein put it in an interview with Deneen, "Everybody I know is tangled up in complex family, loving, critical, difficult, beautiful family relationships."[30]

The most glaring flaw of *Why Liberalism Failed* was its account of liberalism. To tell his abstract story of inevitable decline, Deneen offered a highly idiosyncratic and hyperabstract conceptualization of liberal democracy—a strawman definition that at best was radically incomplete, and at worst an unthinking import from far-right Europeans who had been complaining about "the suicidal nature of liberalism" for many decades.[31]

On the very first page of the book, Deneen offered a standard definition of what he meant by the term "liberalism": a "political philosophy conceived some 500 years ago" that "conceived humans as rights-bearing individuals who could fashion and pursue for themselves their own version of the good life." He went on: "Limited but effective government, rule of law, an independent judiciary, responsive public officials, and free and fair elections" were some of the hallmarks of liberalism.[32] This was a reasonable definition that captured the basic political and institutional features of modern liberal democracy.

But by the end of the introduction, Deneen had swerved to his much more reductive and essentialist definition that focused on individualism and the idea of the conquest of nature; liberalism, he said, imposed an "ideological remaking of the world in the image of a false anthropology."[33] With this, Deneen took two important themes within liberalism and reduced them to an essence.[34] By reducing liberalism in such a way, he avoided engagement with liberalism's political forms, the limits it imposes on government, the importance it places on freedom and self-government, and its connections to Christianity and the Protestant Reformation. He treated liberal democracy as a rigid ideological program, but what we call liberalism today is a highly variable historical phenomenon.[35] Deneen's reductive portrait left too much out—and cast it all aside too hastily.

I am highly sympathetic to Deneen's love of localism and community, and his critique of modern atomism and materialism. But when I read his book in Wichita, it left me cold. Part of it was personal—as I've said, his account of liberals and elites was just so silly and off-base—and part of it was philosophical—his account of liberalism was so ham-fisted and ahistorical. But it was also political.

For one thing, Deneen sneered at modern feminism. The early Trump years were a period of heightened feminist consciousness across the country. Several women had accused Trump of sexual assault, and shortly before the 2016 election the *Access Hollywood* recording was released where Trump bragged about assaulting women. ("I moved on her like a bitch," he said of one acquaintance. "When you're a star, they let you do it. You can do anything. . . . Grab 'em by the pussy. You can do anything.") Many people perceived Trump's victory over Hillary Clinton in the election as a betrayal of women; on the day after his inauguration, millions of people attended Women's Marches across the country. The year 2017 was also the start of the #MeToo movement. By the time I read Deneen's book, the country was in the thick of the Brett Kavanaugh hearings, transfixed by Christine Blasey Ford's testimony against Trump's choice for the Supreme Court.

For a brief interlude it seemed like the hearings might affect Kavanaugh's nomination. They didn't. But that was the context in which I read *Why Liberalism Failed*, and Deneen's approach to feminism in that book struck me as woefully inadequate: "The main practical achievement of this liberation of women has been to move many of them into the workforce of market capitalism," wrote Deneen, calling this "a highly dubious form of liberation." He continued:

Today, we consider the paramount sign of the liberation of women to be their growing emancipation from their biology, which frees them to serve a different, disembodied body—"corporate" America—and participate in an economic order that effectively obviates any actual political liberty. Liberalism posits that freeing women from the household is tantamount to liberation, but it effectively puts women and men alike into a far more encompassing bondage.[36]

I did not buy it. As Jennifer Szalai wrote in her review of the book, "You don't have to be a raging neoliberal to find this a highly dubious form of generalization."[37]

Deneen also seemed to believe that the Republican Party was becoming genuinely working-class under Trump. That seemed implausible to me, since Democrats continued to have a strong working-class constituency, including a sizable majority of minority voters; it seemed to me that GOP populism made sense only if you excluded nonwhites. Further, the Democratic platform was much more consistent with the kind of working-class initiatives that Deneen seemed to favor.[38] In hindsight, he may have understood Trump's potential here better than I.

Vermeule, Ahmari, and "Against the Dead Consensus"

As a book of academic political theory, *Why Liberalism Failed* was something of a barn-burner, but in the end Deneen still exercised a degree of restraint in his conclusions and recommendations. The final pages have a prudent and even quaint quality (especially when compared to a collection of essays that he published in November 2016, where his introduction concluded with a flourish about "refounding" America in explicit departure from "the philosophic principles that animated its liberal founding"; he recommended "appropriating those structures and even the language of liberty and rights to build a new a civilization worthy of preservation").[39] In the 2018 book, Deneen eschewed grand new theoretical or revolutionary programs, recommending instead grassroots experiments in community building and localism. He acknowledged the possibility of illiberal or local authoritarian radicalism but evaded any clear delimitation of governmental powers. Would individual rights be respected by the new localism or not? Would traditional liberal ideals governing limits on governmental power stay in place or gradually be dissolved? On such questions, in the original edition of *Why Liberalism Failed*, Deneen demurred.

In some ways, Deneen's evasive ambiguity signaled a capitulation to ongoing liberal domination, an observation that was first articulated in an early review of his book by the Harvard Law professor Adrian Vermeule, published in Julius Krein and Gladden Pappin's *American Affairs* journal in Spring 2018. The review was called "Integration from Within."[40] The title of the review was revealing. Integralism is the Catholic intellectual movement in which Vermeule has been a vocal participant since his conversion to Catholicism in 2016, and it is adjacent to Postliberalism. It rejects the traditional liberal separation of church and state and posits that the state should be subject to (or integrated with) Catholic norms and spiritual authority; it is one of the main subjects of chapter 10.

In "Integration from Within," Vermeule offered high praise for Deneen's book but also contended that it ultimately lacked ambition. "An outstanding work," he wrote, "might have been a masterpiece." Vermeule's argument was that, by concluding with an open-ended and explicit retreat from theory and ideology, and by petitioning for a return to localism in the style of Rod Dreher's *Benedict Option*, Deneen relapsed into dependence on the pluralistic liberal order. Just as liberals worried that Deneen's localist communities would infringe on hard-earned rights and liberties, Vermeule was concerned that "localist communities after Deneen's fashion must tremble indefinitely under the [liberal] axe." In other words, the local communities that Deneen favored might still be subject to liberal norms; Vermeule was explicit about the need to undermine liberal democracy more dramatically. His review included a reimagining of the ending of *Why Liberalism Failed* whereby, rather than a retreat into localism, antiliberals co-opt the power of the state to undo liberal freedoms, very much in keeping with what Vermeule, as an integralist, calls "strategic Ralliement." The thing to do would be "to co-opt and transform the decaying regime from within its own core." He suggested that the vast bureaucracy created by liberalism might "by the invisible hand of Providence, be turned to new ends, becoming the great instrument with which to restore a substantive politics of the good."

Vermeule concluded the review with a frank plea for the takeover and final destruction of liberalism. He dismissed liberal-minded concerns about excess coercion and instead insisted on the need for a strong strategic position "from which to sear the liberal faith with hot irons." The idea would be to "defeat and capture the hearts and minds of liberal agents," to take over the old regime and then turn it to the service of Vermeulean ends. "In my view, only in this way will liberalism well and truly fall victim to its own success," he wrote, "and this line of approach would make straight the crooked turn at the end of Deneen's near-masterpiece." Where Deneen remained cautious and hedging, Vermeule was excitable and, from the perspective of mainstream American conservatism or liberalism, highly unorthodox.[41] Vermeule was a good student of Carl Schmitt, who was a fierce critic of liberalism and defended an existential version of politics characterized by a hard distinction between "friends" and "enemies."

It did not take long for Deneen to come around to Vermeule's point of view.[42] In a new preface written for the paperback edition of *Why Liberalism Failed* in February 2019, Deneen explained that the time for "epic theory" (as opposed to normal theory and grassroots localism) had come much sooner than he had thought. He now believed he "was wrong to think that this project would take generations." The conclusion of his new preface read:

> Augustine's *City of God* was made necessary by the sudden and unexpected overturning of the "eternal" Roman order in A.D. 410. It seems more apparent every day that a comparable epoch-defining book will arise from our age, and I hope some young reader of this book will be the person to write it. And while I also hope to follow this book with one that offers a way out and a way forward, for now the book in your hands aspires to explain why this new departure in the epic form is not only necessary but inescapable.[43]

Deneen gave a few reasons for his change of heart in this new preface, including the upset of the 2016 election and the "accelerating demolition of the liberal order in Europe." The change in circumstances had clearly given him hope that dramatic change might be possible now rather than at some point in the distant future. He did not shy away from extremist, apocalyptic language, writing as though there were never any signs of peace and stability in the modern world. It was a strange mode of expression for a self-professed conservative with a prestigious job at one of America's top universities and a best-selling book promoted by Barack Obama.

Deneen was soon at work on his next book, and in March 2019 he took a step toward more overtly partisan public intellectualism when he signed an open letter published in *First Things* magazine called "Against the Dead Consensus."

First Things is the foremost Christian periodical on the American Right.[44] It was founded by the Richard John Neuhaus (1936–2009), an influential clergyman and writer, and its original mission was to "advance a religiously informed public philosophy for the ordering of society."[45] R. R. Reno eventually became editor-in-chief of the journal after Neuhaus's death, and though *First Things* had typically defended Catholic fusionism, that began to change under Reno's leadership.[46] By the time "Against the Dead Consensus" was published, Reno had overseen a major controversy at the magazine concerning the publication of a book review by the theologian Romanus Cessario that defended the 1858 kidnapping of Edgardo Mortara—a position that clashed with contemporary civic norms liberties, and was highly controversial according to church doctrine.[47] (Mortara was a Jewish boy who had been secretly baptized by his nanny in the 1850s and so taken by Catholic authorities and raised by Pope Pius IX; this caused a tremendous uproar across Europe and the United States at the time.)[48]

"Against the Dead Consensus" had few signatories, but it garnered a lot of attention because several, like Sohrab Ahmari, Rod Dreher, and Patrick Deneen, had public profiles, and because they were breaking decisively with the old Reagan/Buckley style of conservatism. This was something different from the pseudonymous scribbling of Anton, Krein, and Pappin, though the letter also brought the religiously oriented *First Things* crowd together with James Poulos and Matthew Peterson, both leaders at the Claremont Institute.[49] As Sohrab Ahmari would later explain, most of the signatories to the "manifesto" were young Roman Catholics.[50] In 2019 very few conservative intellectuals still defended Trump publicly. "Against the Dead Consensus" did not endorse him but did celebrate the end of the old order, and so it marked a turn.

The letter reads as a religiously inflected version of Michael Anton's defense of Trumpism, and, as its title indicates, the authors took a strong stance against the old "fusionist" GOP consensus, which it characterized as a morally corrupt handmaiden of liberal tyranny. Abortion came up repeatedly (the right to abortion was presented as a result of the fetishizing of autonomy and a prime example of liberal cruelty). The letter writers continued in this dramatic and moralizing vein: "The old conservative consensus paid lip service to traditional values. But it failed to retard, much less reverse, the eclipse of permanent truths, family stability, communal solidarity, and much else. It surrendered to the pornographization of daily life, to the culture of death, to the cult of competitiveness. It too often bowed to a poisonous and censorious multiculturalism."

A key impetus behind "Against the Dead Consensus" was clearly a sense of moral opportunism—a sense that Trumpism had opened a way forward toward a more morally upright, and far more monolithic, future. The writers were especially excited about the ways in which new kinds of conservative moral and political thought might reclaim oversight over liberal economics and technology. "Consensus conservatism," they wrote, "long ago ceased to inquire into the first things. But we will not." They concluded their piece with a list of six propositions that sound relatively innocuous. They opposed "the society of individual affluence," "attempts to compromise on human dignity," and "tyrannical liberalism," stood for "the American citizen" and "a country that works for workers," and believed that "home matters." But when the writers elaborated on each point, they dabbled in replacement theory ("We oppose attempts to displace American citizens"), credited Trump with heeding "the cries of the working class as much as the demand of capital," and embraced "the new nationalism." The signatories took aim at the old fusionist compromise with neoliberal economics, but with a distinctive and hopeful emphasis on the reactionary moral landscape that might be forged by postconsensus right-wing populism.

———

Sohrab Ahmari, at the time editor of the editorial pages at the *New York Post*, would soon become the most vocal proponent of this emergent—and radical—strain of reactionary conservative intellectualism on the New Right. Several months after publication of "Against the Dead Consensus," he wrote a follow-up piece entitled "Against David Frenchism." This attack gave Ahmari instant notoriety because of his choice of target: David French had genuine conservative bona fides. A lawyer by training (French graduated from Harvard Law School), French was also a veteran of the Iraq War. He built his career fighting for the conservative cause of religious liberty.[51]

Targeting the staunch anti-Trump conservative in aggressive and personal terms, Ahmari took issue with everything tolerant, compromising, and politically liberal about French. Sounding like a pious version of Anton, he criticized French for a politeness and civility that is "unsuitable to the depth of the present crisis facing religious conservatives." He instead recommended that conservatives "fight the culture war with the aim of defeating the enemy and enjoying the spoils in the form of a public square re-ordered to the common good and ultimately the Highest Good."[52] Then, echoing Vermeule's critique of Deneen, Ahmari spoke more plainly still, in archaic terms of totalizing religious fervor. And, intentionally or not, he too was echoing the thought of Carl Schmitt.

Ahmari delineated his core disagreement with French as one of political theology. Whereas French was a traditional social conservative, he was also a political liberal, which meant he was an accommodationist who believed that American institutions can "accommodate both traditional Christianity and the libertine ways of paganized ideology of the other side." French was part of the old Reagan/Buckley establishment and Ahmari disagreed with this way of thinking. With disarming honesty, he instead embraced "politics as war and enmity."

Traditional Christians needed to conquer the public sphere and "defeat" the enemy—meaning, presumably, that they should cease to accommodate the "libertine and the pagan" in the public square. It was time to use "the public power to advance the common good, including in the realm of public morality." Like Pappin before him, Ahmari saw Trump as a genuine force for community: "His instinct has been to shift the cultural and political mix, ever so slightly, away from autonomy-above-all toward order, continuity, and social cohesion."[53]

Ahmari's piece was infused with an overheated moral horror of everything he perceived to be decadent and decaying about liberal society. He plainly felt that the infidels were not only winning, but severely oppressing their "enemies" in the process.

There was also a more serious side to Ahmari's outlook—a more serious argument, the truth of which should be acknowledged by liberals. Ahmari's deepest critique was that David Frenchism refused to contend honestly with the rising tides of progressive norms and cultural demands and refused to admit that, for all its pretensions to neutrality, liberal, pluralistic, modern constitutionalism has normative tendencies and implicit preferences and inevitably shapes the liberal democratic psyche in specific ways. In my view, Ahmari was not wrong in this basic observation—though I favor the virtues, including autonomy and freedom, that he condemned—nor is French wrong to hope for an accommodationist dispensation from a liberal politics. But the latter must be fought for and cultivated; unlike the impulse to freedom—or for domination—the liberal spirit of toleration and civility does not come easily. Ahmari and the Postliberals can help us see why these liberal virtues are so necessary, if only because the alternative world that they wish for would be so violent and inhospitable.

The latent violence of the Postliberal movement is evident not only in the Schmittian language that they so readily deploy—the language of war and enmity, of friends and enemies and brutal choices.[54] It is also visible in their totalizing beliefs about the monolithic nature of the Common Good, and their failure to speak openly about what they would propose to do with the massive plurality of people in modern liberal societies—libertines and pagans alike—who do not see the world as they do. There is a real sense in which the Postliberals seem determined to reignite the moral and religious conflagrations that inspired the birth of liberalism in the first place.

This problem is hardly limited to the Postliberal wing of the New Right. Chapter 5 introduces the National Conservatives, or NatCons—the broadest group of New Right intellectuals, who are under the leadership of Yoram Hazony, and united around a highly monolithic idea of the American nation. As the liberal writer William Galston has observed, both Deneen and Hazony "have mounted a frontal attack on the entire individualist, rights-based liberal political tradition that they trace back to John Locke." In so doing, they reject the core of the American political project.[55]

5

National Conservatism

THE FIRST AMERICAN NATIONAL CONSERVATISM conference took place in Washington, DC, in July 2019. The keynote speaker was a man with deep and long-standing connections to the conservative intellectual world. As a sophomore at Stanford in 1987, he had cofounded the right-wing newspaper *The Stanford Review*. This was the same year that Bloom published *The Closing of the American Mind* (and around the time that Michael Anton was being radicalized at nearby Berkeley). Right-wing campus grievance was one of the new paper's core themes.

The speaker was Peter Thiel. Thiel had been a lifelong student of Carl Schmitt, Leo Strauss, and the French Catholic thinker René Girard. He supported the Iraq War and liked to speak and write in gauzy apocalyptic terms about the End of Civilization and preserving the West.[1] He had reportedly met Michael Anton at a reading group on Strauss, helped to fund his sensational website, *American Greatness* (as well as Krein and Pappin's *American Affairs*), and also facilitated his hiring in the Trump White House.[2] As Thiel spoke at NatCon, I believe Anton was in the audience, near the front, with two colleagues, David Azerrad of Hillsdale College and Arthur Milikh of the Claremont Institute.[3] Thiel is also, of course, a billionaire, thanks to his cofounding of PayPal alongside Elon Musk and massively successful subsequent investments.

Thiel is a fascinating American character, who also happens to be a lover of all things Straussian, esoteric, and right-wing avant-garde.[4] He is better known to the public for his controversial libertarian politics, his statement in 2009 that "I no longer believe that freedom and democracy are compatible," his creation of a foundation that gets promising undergraduates to drop out of college, his sinking of the Gawker website, and his support for populist political candidates like Donald Trump and Blake Masters and JD Vance, his protégés.[5]

At the NatCon conference in 2019, Thiel's speech was called "The Star Trek Computer Is Not Enough." The speech took aim at his Silicon Valley compatriots—the people trying, and failing, to build the "Star Trek Computer"—and at America's educated elites.[6]

Thiel got off to a decent rhetorical start, comparing the famous 1972 image of Earth as seen by the moon astronauts to the realities of nation-states and borders here on Earth. The standard liberal move would be to use the image to appeal to universal humanity; Thiel instead suggested that the view from space "sort of excludes the middle—that excludes the city and excludes the nation and excludes the political." Overall, it was a meandering speech, as is typical for him. He railed against Google (suggesting that its senior management had been infiltrated by Chinese intelligence and should be investigated by the FBI and CIA "in a not excessively gentle manner") and expressed his deep disappointment about the supposed plateau in innovation, a Thiel hobbyhorse for decades now.[7] He took some swipes at Michelle and Barack Obama, suggesting that their efforts to promote non–Ivy League schools constituted "the biggest lie told in the last decade, the most pernicious lie." Thiel proclaimed that, if it's not a "fancy name brand school," then "the diploma is just a dunce hat in disguise." He then asserted that even the best universities are effectively worse than useless. "We need to start criminal investigations into these places, into what's going on," he remarked.

Thiel got a standing ovation for his weird speech, by a fawning, nearly all-male crowd. He went on Tucker Carlson's show the next day and made more accusations against China.[8] As Max Chafkin chronicles in his book *The Contrarian*, President Trump tweeted about Thiel the next morning. Thiel was a direct competitor with Google at the time. Within a few years he had landed several new contracts with the federal government, worth many millions of dollars, through his company Palantir.[9] At the next American NatCon conference, Thiel was listed as a "special honoree" donor, for having contributed $50,000 or more to the Edmund Burke Foundation.[10]

The Burke Foundation is the group that organizes the National Conservatism conferences. It was founded in 2019 by an Israeli American political theorist and conservative activist, Yoram Hazony. Having recently published a book called *The Virtue of Nationalism*, as chairman of the Edmund Burke Foundation, and with donors like Thiel and others, Hazony became the leading organizer for the New Right intellectual movement. He launched a series of conferences around the theme of National Conservatism, and the NatCon group soon became the big-tent home of the emerging New Right coalition. In 2019 Michael Anton wrote an article suggesting that Hazony's "wonderful book" formed the backbone of Trump's foreign policy.[11]

In this chapter we visit the world of National Conservatism, focusing on Yoram Hazony, his book—which won the Intercollegiate Studies Institute's "Conservative Book of the Year" Award for 2019—and the early NatCon conferences.[12] Claremonters flocked to these conferences, as did Postliberals. Schisms would eventually occur, and some Postliberals would step back from the NatCon group. But through those early years, the various factions of the New Right came together at the conferences that Hazony organized. These also featured an impressive array of GOP politicians, as well as, over time, a less and less impressive array of New Right influencers and outright conspiracists and racists. In the early days, Hazony tried to maintain a cordon sanitaire around the budding institution, but that effort proved a failure within a few years. In his inaugural speech, Thiel talked about the need to widen the "Overton window for discourse." That did work, and by 2022 formerly more mainstream conservative institutions like the Heritage Foundation had migrated decisively over to the radical NatCon outlook. National Conservatism also helped set the stage for the explicit Christian nationalism that was growing throughout the United States.

Yoram Hazony and The Virtue of Nationalism

Yoram Hazony's biography is rich. Born in Rehovot, Israel, he moved with his parents to the United States when he was young. He attended Princeton University as an undergraduate, where his father was an engineering professor with a specialization in robotics, and it is here that he deepened his religious identity, met his wife Yael (born Julie), and committed to a life of conviction and community.[13]

Hazony and Yael were married on Princeton's campus in 1987, the year after his graduation and a year before hers.[14] Hazony writes movingly about his college years with her—their courtship and her eventual conversion to Judaism, as well as their decision to move back to Israel and build a family and community there.[15] While at Princeton, he and Yael, along with their friend David Polisar, founded *The Princeton Tory*. Also in 1987—the year that Thiel founded the *Stanford Review*—Hazony began graduate work in political philosophy at Rutgers University; his time there overlapped with Patrick Deneen's. Hazony describes ordinary student life at Princeton as licentious and barbaric. He also counted himself as part of an early vanguard of a conservatism revivalism that was taking place there with the rise of the Buckley/Reagan right.[16]

The depths of Hazony's religious convictions were evident in a highly sympathetic eulogy he wrote for the Jewish rabbi Meir Kahane, who was assassinated in New York on November 5, 1990. It described how Kahane's visit to Princeton in 1984 had transformed Hazony's life. Hazony describes the rabbi as something like a Socrates figure, his own Harry Jaffa. Kahane was also an ultranationalist rabbi and cofounder of the far-right Jewish Defense League (JDL). He believed that Arab people should be expelled from Israel, had advocated for violence against the enemies of Jews or of Israel, and was a convicted terrorist.[17]

In the eulogy, titled "Farewell from a Non-Kahanist," Hazony explained that before seeing Kahane he had never heard someone speak with such straightforward conviction about Judaism, Israel, and fighting for what you believe in. "Rabbi Kahane was the only Jewish leader who ever cared enough about our lives to actually come around and tell us what he thought we could do. He was the only one who seemed to understand how much we wanted a good reason to stay Jewish." This eulogy was published in *The Jerusalem Post*, where Hazony was working at the time as a member of the editorial staff. In addition to the glowing words about Kahane, he included a disclaimer about the rabbi's chosen political means: "Neither I nor any of my friends from college ever adopted Kahane's political views. We were never able to reconcile the Judaism we learned with his predilection for violent solutions to problems, nor with his abusive manner of presenting his case for these solutions."

By that point, Hazony and his young family had followed some of Kahane's advice and joined some of the first Israeli settlers in Eli, an illegal Jewish settlement in the Northern West Bank.[18] (In November 2019 the Trump administration, in a historic reversal, declared that the US government would no longer consider West Bank settlements illegal.)[19] Also in the early 1990s, Hazony was introduced to Benjamin Netanyahu, who at the time was serving as deputy foreign minister. Hazony worked as an adviser to Netanyahu from 1991 to 1995.[20]

Possibly the most important work that Hazony did during this time was cofounding in 1994 the Shalem Center, an American-style think tank that later became Israel's first liberal arts college, Shalem College. Hazony and his Princeton friends conceived of the project early in their undergraduate education, impressed by the conservative shibboleth that "ideas have consequences," and with a specific aim "to reintroduce the term 'Jewish state' into public discourse."[21] As his cofounder and friend David Polisar put it to a journalist at Princeton's alumni magazine in 2013, "It was clear to us that higher education is the leading force in shaping the way people think—certainly the most influential people in society. And therefore it shapes the future."[22] Hazony and his friends apparently shared this Ideas First conception of politics; and Hazony reportedly held on to such a conservative view of the educational purpose of the center (he wanted "to build universities that are more receptive to tradition, nationalism, and religion") that he was forced out before the college gained accreditation in 2013.[23]

In 2018 Hazony published *The Virtue of Nationalism,* a book that, alongside Anton's Flight 93 and Deneen's *Why Liberalism Failed,* galvanized American conservatives and helped them articulate what it was that they appreciated about Trumpism. The book was described as the key to Trump's Europe policy early in his first administration.[24] In addition to bringing Hazony back to his American roots, it secured him a spot in the international nationalist imagination.

————

The explicit purpose of *The Virtue of Nationalism* was a rehabilitation of the concept of nationalism—in full cognizance of the extent to which the term is used as one of opprobrium. "I have written this book so that we have a statement of the reasons for being a nationalist," Hazony wrote in the introduction.[25] He argued that, contrary to dominant elite liberal perceptions, true nationalism is actually a very great good, and that as such responsible people should be proud nationalists.

Hazony's writing is clear and straightforward, and he meant to present a strong defense of nationalism, not merely an endorsement of civic pride or patriotism. He was looking for something more and working within "a long tradition of using this term to refer to a theory of the best political order—that is, to an anti-imperialist theory that seeks to establish a world of free and independent nations."[26] Hazony means nations in the old-fashioned, tribal, and even ethnic sense—he regards a nation as a collective of tribes that comes together organically to form a political whole. He wrote that the nation is "distinguished from all of humanity in that it possesses a quite distinctive character, having its own language, laws, and religious traditions, its own past history of failure and achievement." For him, "one should be a nationalist" because the whole world benefits from the nation-state system. It's not just a matter of self-interest or power-realism. All mankind shares an interest in "a world of independent and self-determinating nations, each pursuing interests and aspirations that are uniquely its own."[27]

The major foil in Hazony's book was imperialism, in all its manifestations and variations (except, perhaps, the nationalist ones). On page 3, he defined imperialism as that which "seeks to bring peace and prosperity to the world by uniting mankind, as much as possible, under a single political regime." For him, the distinction between nationalism and imperialism is Manichean and all-or-nothing: "Either you support, in principle, the ideal of an international government or regime that imposes its will on subject nations when its officials regard this as necessary; or you believe that nations should be free to set their own course in the absence of such an international government or regime." He also made it clear throughout that he holds all versions of universalism and internationalism to be dressed-up forms of imperial domination.[28] Hazony argued for a black-and-white political sensibility where there is no room for any sacrifice of national sovereignty—a move that obliterates the distinction between violent imperial conquest and voluntary international institution building, while at the same time ignoring the real-world impacts of softer international influences and allegiances.

Hazony, for example, described the European Union (EU) as a somewhat delayed manifestation of German imperialism, now sustained and supported by the United States.[29] (In 2020 he called it a "messianic cult.")[30] As Constanze Stelzenmüller, a German international relations expert, wrote in 2019, the book is "spectacularly misinformed about the status of nation states in Europe or Germany's power over them and the EU," and it harkens back to a supposed golden age of nationalism in Europe that, in actual historical terms, is very hard to discern, let alone to recommend.[31]

Philosophically speaking, *The Virtue of Nationalism* was ambitious. Hazony sought to rewrite the history of political thought, relying almost exclusively on the Hebrew Bible (or what Christians call the Old Testament) for its philosophical foundations. He was forthright about wanting to diminish the influence of ancient Greek and Roman thought in the West, arguing that these traditions were too narrowly focused and inadequately attentive to the conditions that create and sustain political flourishing—that is, to the import of the nation-state. Throughout his work, Hazony emphasized the organic historical emergence of the nation-state around the world, but his template was the Jewish nation as articulated in the early sacred Jewish texts. What is more, he

suggested that the traditional nation-state in the Westphalian order ful-
fills a similar function, through his concept of the "Protestant Construction of the West." Through the widespread circulation of the vernacular
Bible, Hazony argued, Protestantism became a vehicle for "the unique
national traditions of peoples chafing against ideas and institutions they
regarded as foreign to them."[32] He gave the examples of several national
covenants from the early modern era (mainly the Dutch and Scottish)
showing how they were modeled on the Jewish national covenants of
the Bible. "The self-image of these Protestant peoples as rightfully
independent in the face of imperial opposition," he wrote, "was often
explicitly modeled on biblical Israel's effort to wrest its national and
religious freedom from the dictates of Egyptian and Babylonian universal empire."[33] Hazony does his reader a favor when he unearths the He-
braic influences on this history. He also embraces the appealing idea,
following John Stuart Mill, that independent nation-states are the best
preservers of genuine diversity. For him, though, pluralism must primarily be between different nations, not within them.

The Virtue of Nationalism sustained its share of criticism. For one
thing, in Hazony's telling, Protestantism becomes more about preserving parochialism and nationalism than anything spiritual or theological,
and the same is arguably true of Hazony's Judaism.[34] As the scholar
Suzanne Schneider observed in an acute article about Hazony for the
magazine Jewish Currents, "Hazony's 'tradition' presents as a particularly
emaciated one, with little to say about Judaism except as a mode of
politics."[35]

From an academic perspective, Hazony's work serves as an interesting alternative to some dominant strains of contemporary thinking, but
it indulges in far too many intellectual hijinks and oversimplifications
to make his case for nationalism persuasive. The general problem with
the book is that the theory it presented was untethered from the history
of the real world. As Stelzenmüller observed, Hazony glossed over all
manner of real problems and complex present-day challenges in favor
of what she calls his "cold-philosophical" approach. The historian Israel
Bartal noted that "there is no theory in the study of nationalism, beginning 100 years ago and until yesterday, that fits Hazony's method."[36]

Park MacDougald rightly noted in his review that Hazony's deployment of a simplistic dichotomous typology gave his arguments "a sense of unreality."[37]

Most egregiously from the perspective of political theory, Hazony, much like Deneen, flattened and misrepresented modern liberal theory, in ways that at times bordered on the absurd. Hazony presented early modern thinkers like John Locke (1632–1704) as hyperrationalists who cared only about reason and consent in politics. But in so doing he wrenched Locke's work from its historical milieu and rendered it nearly unrecognizable. The context that mattered for Locke, of course, was the sectarian political conflict surrounding the English Civil War and the Glorious Revolution. Hazony evaded this reality and interpreted Locke as though he had been writing from a theoretical mountaintop, and even then he reads Locke badly.[38]

Conservatives like to talk about how traditions represent history's solutions to long-standing problems and so should be revered because of the trouble they spare us in sorting things through anew. But this is true of the liberal tradition, too. When Hazony turns the early modern thinkers' works into mere abstractions, he evades the problems that they encountered so forcefully and robs the contemporary world of the solutions they devised.

———

The incoherence of Hazony's work on nationalism came to the fore when Russia went to war against Ukraine in 2022. When the conflict first arose, I remember wondering whether Hazony would side with the extreme and imperialist expression of Russian nationalism, or with the liberal internationalists supporting Ukraine and the Ukrainian people. To the apparent consternation of some of his fellow travelers, he sided with Ukraine, which he claimed was something very different from siding with liberal internationalism, explaining how Russia was not a nation, as Putin claimed, but an empire. He interpreted the attack on Ukraine as a warning to European liberals, who had forgotten how to defend themselves and become excessively dependent on the United States.[39] That was perhaps fair, but Hazony also reverted to his all-or-nothing thinking about liberals, arguing that those who defended Ukraine were doing so for the wrong reasons. They did not care about Ukrainian sovereignty or the Ukrainian people—all they cared about was maintaining liberal hegemony.

Others on the New Right were more resistant to providing support for Ukraine. The American journalist Kathryn Joyce called the overall movement on the New Right vis-à-vis Russia a "dizzying ideological switchback."[40]

I did not ever wonder where Hazony would side on the Israel-Palestine conflict. Even before Hamas's grotesque attack on Israel on October 7, 2023, and Israel's brutal ultranationalist response, it was impossible to read Hazony's work and not recognize his failure to address the plight of the Palestinian people. Again and again in his discussions of the Jewish State and Israel's history, the Palestinians go unacknowledged.[41] Hazony says as an abstract matter that "what is needed for the establishment of a stable and free state is a majority nation whose cultural dominance is plain and unquestioned, and against which resistance appears to be futile."[42] So when it comes to the question of Palestinian self-determination, his answer is forcefully implied: They are not robust enough of a nation to deserve it, and/or imperial aggression against them does not count. If you spend enough time with Hazony's work, the entire intellectual artifice of *The Virtue of Nationalism* comes into focus as little more than a reason-giving exercise in the denial of human rights, or worse, to the Palestinians.

Which makes it an extremely worrisome model for the rest of the world. As Schneider writes:

> What Hazony offers as a global template is none other than the blueprints for the Jewish state in its most reactionary and exclusionary form. The reason his prescriptions feel at odds with actually existing conservatism in either the US or the UK is that they were cast from the mold of religious Zionism, and thus reflect everything from its belief that the state is obligated to uphold and enforce the religious norms of the nation, to its insistence on the innate cohesiveness of the national community.

She continues, piercingly: "[Hazony] understands better than most that international support for Israel's status quo cannot be secured other than by contesting the virtues of liberal democracy itself. National Conservatism is one of the engines behind this global project of social and political engineering."[43] Far-right leaders like Javier Milei of Argentina have reciprocated with outspoken support for Zionism.[44] Geert Wilders of the Netherlands has been talking about creating "a Zionism for the nations of Europe" since at least 2013.[45]

Let us consider how National Conservatism took root in the United States.

Christopher DeMuth
and the Early NatCon Conferences

The Virtue of Nationalism was published in September 2018 and became something of a sensation on the American right. Not only was it selected as the Conservative Book of the Year by the Intercollegiate Studies Institute (or ISI, an organization founded in 1953 by Buckley and Frank Chodorov dedicated to promoting "foundational principles" on college campuses), it was also widely reviewed and has since been translated into a dozen languages. Very soon after the book appeared, party leaders began speaking in terms of nationalism and continued to abandon America's "creedal" self-understanding; Christian nationalism was in ascendance in these circles, too.

On October 22, 2018, perhaps just by coincidence but tellingly nonetheless, President Trump, at a rally for Senator Ted Cruz in Houston, made headlines by embracing the term "nationalism"—in contrast with the "corrupt, power-hungry globalists"—more directly than ever before: "You know, they have a word, it sort of became old-fashioned. It's called a nationalist. And I say really, we're not supposed to use that word. You know what I am? I'm a nationalist. OK? I'm a nationalist."[46] As the crowd erupted, Trump continued: "Nationalist. Nothing wrong. Use that word. Use that word." Chants broke out: "USA! USA! USA! USA!" Steve Bannon was reportedly pleased.[47]

Shortly after the publication of his book, Hazony was approached by some interested donors and, together with some colleagues, created the Edmund Burke Foundation. From here, they set out to organize the first National Conservatism conference.[48] Hazony became chairman of the foundation; the role of president would go to David Brog, a graduate of Princeton University and Harvard Law. Brog, like Hazony, was an Israeli nationalist with a long background in politics (he had been executive director of Christians United for Israel, or CUFI, the largest pro-Israel organization in the United States).[49]

Hazony and Brog were also joined by Christopher DeMuth, who became chairman of the National Conservatism conference. DeMuth's onboarding was significant because of his mainstream experience in the conservative think-tank world. He was president of the American Enterprise Institute for over twenty years, between 1986 and 2008, and was a longtime distinguished fellow at the Hudson Institute until he moved over to the Heritage Foundation in 2023. A Harvard graduate who then trained as a lawyer at the University of Chicago Law School, he had worked in both the Nixon and Reagan administrations (he is sometimes referred to as Reagan's "deregulation czar"). It is hard to imagine a person who could better signal National Conservatism's mainstream aspirations than DeMuth.

But DeMuth was no mere figurehead. His writings and contributions to the movement show us someone who is clearly a true believer in the new Nationalism, but who at the same time hoped for a more moderate and capacious version of it than what we see in Hazony's work. DeMuth made his position clear in an essay published in the Winter 2019 issue of the *Claremont Review of Books* titled "Trumpism, Nationalism, and Conservatism" (Hazony would later call it a "watershed essay" for the movement).[50] The essay began: "Trumpism has an essence, and that essence is nationalism. It is the American version of the revival of the spirit of nationhood in the rich democracies of the North Atlantic. It is bigger than President Trump's personality and program, and is certain to outlast the drama and fate of his tenure in office."

The whole essay was infused with this same cheery, if blinkered, hopefulness. The "spirit of nationhood" that DeMuth refers to across the

Atlantic is, as he acknowledges, the spirit of the far-right movements of Britain, Poland, Hungary, Italy, and the "neo-nationalist parties of Germany and France." DeMuth vouched for these groups' insurgent efforts to oppose "an international elite with its own, self-serving agenda." He— like Deneen and Vance before him—would side with the local "Somewhere" people over the internationalist "Anywheres."[51] DeMuth took on the whole mantle of nationalism unapologetically and within a few years was on record denying the "creedal" character of America.[52] As Bill Galston observed at the time, this was a "bluntly anti-Lincolnian move."[53]

DeMuth's prescriptive solutions exposed some of the internal inconsistencies in an ideology whose proponents claimed it to be based on eternal truths. He recommended the revitalization of Congress, forging a "New Nationalism" to "counter our tribal politics," and more financial transparency and accountability about the costs of the welfare state. This turn to financial responsibility at the end of the essay, in particular, prefigured schisms that would later affect the movement. The lingering question would be whether American conservatives—so long enamored of "Reaganomics" and highly dependent on an elite and wealthy donor base— could reassert themselves on a different set of economic presuppositions.

To many that seemed to be what Trump promised. But DeMuth, like so much of the New Right, seemed to be talking out of both sides of his mouth. He recognized the need for something new—and rejected whole swaths of the American political tradition going back to Lincoln—while also insisting on neoliberal mantras from the past. Nowhere did he acknowledge how Reagan, Clinton, and the austerity programs of the 1980s and 1990s fostered the circumstances under which so many "Somewheres" were struggling.

So much New Right ideology obfuscated these more complicated political realities.

———

The first major American National Conservatism conference ("NatCon 1"), where Thiel took the stage as keynote speaker, created a buzz and was covered by national news outlets and magazines from *The New York Times* to *Reason* magazine. Most of the main characters discussed in the early chapters of this book were there, as were others who will figure in the chapters to come. There was a strong showing from the Claremont Institute and Hillsdale College. Michael Anton gave a talk about imperialism.[54] On a plenary panel about "Identity Politics vs. National Conservatism," Charles Kesler gave a good talk ("Nationalism, Creed, and Culture") about the relationship between nationalism and the American creed.[55] These Claremont types were joined by folks from other cohorts and conservative traditions, and clear intellectual patterns and tensions emerged. The major tension would be between those who prioritized culture war issues and those who were serious about economic reforms. The Claremont group were clearly some of the most dedicated culture warriors.

Among the more serious speakers at NatCon 1 was Patrick Deneen, who appeared on the same panel as Anton.[56] In his speech, and in a sign perhaps of schisms to come, Deneen voiced several reservations about taking up nationalism as a guiding principle, as well as about the problem of statism or big government. (He did not return as a speaker at a NatCon conference in subsequent years, but he became both more nationalistic in his rhetoric and more open to big-state interventions in public life.)[57]

Other participants also seemed sincere in their economic populism from the get-go. Julius Krein—the *JAG* author Plautus who had repudiated Trump after Charlottesville—was there making a pitch for the old-fashioned idea of "national development" (following Michael Lind).[58] Krein's powerful speech began with a scathing critique of twentieth-century conservative economic policy. He stated plainly that Americans have "constructed an economy increasingly geared toward producing financial wealth for narrower segments of the population, rather than growing through productivity gains, innovation, and widespread improvements in real economic conditions." Krein also, refreshingly, acknowledged that the American conservative movement "bears special responsibility for this." He delineated how destructive conservative laissez-faire economics had been, effectively arguing that none of the financial beneficiaries of corporate profits had ever decided to reinvest their earnings in the American economy. When he turned to the question of what should be done, the first thing he suggested was that it was time to leave behind "moralistic debates about the free market versus socialism or whatever."[59]

On the second day of the event, Oren Cass, author of the book *The Once and Future Worker: A Vision for the Renewal of Work in America* (2018), debated libertarian Richard Reinsch on the resolution, "America should adopt an industrial policy." After a formal debate, the resolution passed with 99 votes in favor and 55 against.[60]

There were a few additional American celebrities in attendance besides Thiel. Tucker Carlson was there eagerly straddling the culture-warrior/economic-populism divide, praising Elizabeth Warren (as had Krein), raging against monopoly powers and the threat that corporations posed to American liberty (a precursor to attacks on so-called woke capitalism), claiming that all progressive thinking is mere projection (especially on questions of race), and that the left is "not interested in peaceful coexistence."[61] His Q&A was moderated by *First Things* editor Rusty Reno, who took his big moment onstage to echo Thiel's complaints about higher education ("the fish rots from the head down"). JD Vance gave a speech called "Getting Beyond Libertarianism" that was very much in line with the economic vision put forward by Krein, Cass, and Lind.[62]

The culminating speech of the three-day event came from Senator Josh Hawley, who at the time was the youngest member of the Senate. He delivered a speech chock-full of New Right catchphrases and seemed positively intoxicated with its own sense of poetry and purpose.[63] The American "middle" was mentioned a dozen times at least, as was the word "Republic," but his main bogeyman was the "cosmopolitan class."

Hawley concluded his speech by telling the story of Horatius, a noble defender of Rome during the early Republic. Hawley spoke of courage, asking, "How can man die better, than by facing fearful odds for the ashes of his fathers and the temples of his gods?" His finale was rousing: "So let us stand together. Let us stand for love of country and hearth and home. Let us stand with the conviction of Horatius." Then he quoted Thomas Babington Macaulay poem, "Horatius at the Bridge": "For in yon straight path a thousand men may well be stopped by three. Now who will stand on either hand, and keep this bridge with me?"

The audience stood for Hawley, just as they had for Thiel.[64] Hazony was delighted ("That made me happy . . . I love the words and music"). But he did take a moment in his concluding remarks to correct Hawley's approach to history. Better to reach back even further in history for the true foundations of politics, Hazony suggested; better to talk of Abraham and Israel than of Horatius and Rome.[65]

National Conservatism in American Context

The question of the NatCon movement's proximity to racism and various ethnic nationalisms was on everyone's mind at that conference, in large part because President Trump made it so. Early in the morning on Sunday, July 14, 2019, the day the conference began, Trump tweeted out an incendiary message about several "'Progressive' Democrat Congresswomen" (i.e., the so-called Squad: Representatives Alexandria Ocasio-Cortez, Ayanna Pressley, Ilhan Omar, and Rashida Tlaib).[66] He said that these women came from "countries whose governments are a complete and total catastrophe, the worst, most corrupt and inept anywhere in the world (if they even have a functioning government at all)," and that they should "go back and help fix the totally broken and crime infested places from which they came." These comments informed the media's coverage of NatCon: What did the nationalists have to say about *that*?

The conference organizers had tried to head off this problem. Hazony attempted to preserve the old establishment cordon sanitaire, rejecting the registration of Peter Brimelow and his wife Lydia in early June. Peter Brimelow is the founding editor of the white nationalist anti-immigration site VDARE, and Lydia was an editor there.[67] Brimelow wrote an illuminating essay in the wake of this rebuff, expressing shock and surprise at having been excluded, and noting that he felt himself to be a true ally of Hazony's. He cited a passage from *The Virtue of Nationalism* and exclaimed, "Of course, I think this is wonderful. It sounds exactly like positions we have argued for years."[68]

Whether prompted by Trump's attacks or to head off other critiques that they viewed as inevitable, the NatCon organizers began the conference with some stern words about the relationship between nationalism and racism. During the first plenary panel, on the morning of July 15, David Brog gave a speech full of winsome bromides, in which he made it clear that, in his mind at least, nationalism need not be racist. Brog was emphatic. After celebrating the fact that the president had declared himself a nationalist, he said:

> Critics have rushed in to define this concept in the most negative ways possible. Rather than merely ignore their slanders, let's reject them in the clearest possible terms. Number one: We are nationalists not white nationalists. We have received multiple requests to attend this conference from people who define our American nation in terms of race. We have rejected every single one. But no screening system is perfect, so if there is anyone here tonight who believes being an American has anything whatsoever to do with the color of someone's skin there is the door. Please leave. Your ideas are not welcome here.[69]

This is a strong statement of the leaders' intentions. It did not stop the creeping controversy.

For one thing, the incendiary law scholar Amy Wax had been invited to speak at the conference, and true to form she made controversial claims about the racial effects of cultural immigration preferences. Wax's NatCon speech—one of only a few that are not publicly available on the NatCon YouTube channel—was covered by the Vox journalist Zack Beauchamp, who called out the racist character of her claims.[70] Hazony defended Wax at the time—at length, on Twitter—though she has not appeared on the list of NatCon speakers since.[71]

Wax had been a guest speaker in 2018 at the white nationalist–friendly HL Mencken Club's conference, which is organized by the paleoconservative thinker Paul Gottfried, and where Brimelow had also been a regular speaker. It appears that she returned to that conference in November 2019, just a few months after NatCon 1.[72] In his presidential address to the Mencken Conference, Gottfried, presumably referring to Wax, made strange hay of the controversy:

> This past summer a well-publicized conference on "conservative nationalism" took place in Washington thanks to a Zionist philanthropist,

David Brog, and to an Israeli nationalist Yoram Hazony. This conference may best be remembered by whom it declined to invite or by whom it took pains to disinvite. Memories of this gathering will also be kept alive by a speech given by an academic luminary who happens to be in this room and who said what speakers were not supposed to mention.[73]

But the National Conservatives' problems did not end with Wax and her transgressions. In 2020, in the thick of renewed criticisms concerning a subsequent conference in Rome, Hazony defended his organization's decisions once more: "The Edmund Burke Foundation has itself been bitterly attacked by white racialists and anti-Semites. Why? For excluding them and their views from our events. In Rome we pursued the same policies."[74]

The guest of honor at the Rome conference was Prime Minister Viktor Orbán of Hungary, who gave a long interview with Christopher DeMuth. DeMuth is fawning and friendly as an interviewer, which makes Orbán come across as even more ruthless and savvy than usual.[75] DeMuth shows no curiosity about or understanding of the manipulations that Orbán undertook over the course of over a decade to, as the Hungarian Prime Minister put it in the interview, "get the power and keep the power."[76]

But the most chilling moment in the interview came when DeMuth inquired about the "immigration crisis of 2015"—in other words, the Syrian refugee crisis, in which millions of Syrians were displaced by civil war—and asked Orbán what this has meant for Hungary. Orbán (who once referred to the refugees as "Muslim invaders") began: "First of all, just as a description: In Hungary, we have *this* number of Muslim migrants"—and here he gestured "zero" with his right hand—"so zero, so we don't have [any]."[77] Before he could continue, the crowd erupted in applause.

———

For someone who is so attentive to the supposed withering effects of liberal ideas on society's social bonds, Yoram Hazony is awfully rigid in his denialism about the dangerous, and often racist or Islamophobic, entanglements that travel alongside nationalist tribalism. And as Hazony's big tent grew, space was made for increasingly "controversial" figures and ideas. We will encounter some of them again in the coming chapters—people like Paul Gottfried, Darren Beattie, Jason Richwine, and Nathan Pinkoski.

In a speech at the third NatCon conference in Miami in 2022, Hazony gave a talk called "After the Revolution—What Happens Next?," which offered a justification for further radicalization on the right.[78] Looking back from the vantage point of 2022, he argued that 2020 was a "watershed year in the history of the United States" and "of the democratic world." According to him, 2020 had brought with it a transformation and paradigm shift in the "basic framework that guides public life in the United States and in Britain and across Europe." The public philosophy of these places had been liberal, but in 2020 "hegemonic liberalism came to an end." A "completely new America" was coming into being, subject now to "woke Neo-Marxism"—a neo-McCarthyist phrase that Hazony and others increasingly used to describe the antiracist left (including, for example, groups like Black Lives Matter). Hazony pleaded with the audience, "Please do not be mistaken, this country is on the brink." He did not define woke Neo-Marxism with any specificity.

The year 2020 was one of political turmoil in the United States. It was the first year of the Covid-19 pandemic, and the presidential election that year was followed by two months of election denialism that culminated in the sorry events of January 6, 2021. But Hazony was not referencing any of that. For him, the paradigm shift was precipitated by what the New Right likes to call the George Floyd Riots.

George Floyd, a Black man, was murdered on May 26, 2020, by a white police officer named Derek Chauvin, in the presence of several colleagues and bystanders. The murder was filmed by a young woman, Darnella Frazier, and her video went viral. Millions of people watched it, all around the world, and it became a galvanizing moment for the Black Lives Matter movement. Polls suggested that between fifteen and twenty-five million people participated in the subsequent protests in the United States, making the George Floyd protests the largest in American history.[79] A small percentage of these protests turned violent.[80] Twenty-five people were killed in the course of the summer, around fifteen thousand were arrested, and estimates put the property damage from the protests at $2 billion—also the highest in history, ahead of the Los Angeles riots of 1992, which were much more regionally contained.[81] Police violence also continued throughout the summer of protests.[82] And for the duration of the protests, President Trump pined for "Law and Order," as did Senator Tom Cotton, who on June 3, 2021, wrote an op-ed that was published in *The New York Times* under the headline "Send in the Troops."[83] Cotton thought it would be good to invoke the Insurrection Act (a notoriously vague and controversial piece of legislation) to quell the riots.[84] At the time, the country felt like a tinder box—with distrust in the police growing, racial tensions mounting, a consequential election looming, and the pandemic heightening everything. Republicans were focused on rioting, looting, and civil unrest; Democrats worried that Trump would use the crisis as a pretext to further expand executive power and oppress people.

When Yoram Hazony referred to 2020 being a watershed year that signified the new dominance of woke neo-Marxism, he did not discuss the murder of George Floyd or the national fallout from that crime. Instead, he ignored that broader context and took issue with liberal pundits and the firing of the *Times* editor who green-lighted Cotton's op-ed.[85] And he used the events of 2020 to double down on his vociferous nationalist ideology. In his telling, 2020 brought a revolution and the beginning of a "completely new America," in which liberalism had been "replaced by this woke neo-Marxism as the dominant ideology." He asserted that "there's really only one question: What force is strong enough to be able to stop that?" His answer was straightforward. "The only thing that is strong enough to stop the religion of woke neo-Marxism is the religion of biblical Christianity. That's the only thing." Hazony then exhorted his audience to move forward confidently and proclaim that "this was a Christian nation, historically and according to its laws, and it's going to be a Christian nation again."

The George Floyd summer was just violent and ideological enough to justify his own movement's slip into white supremacy and explicit Christian nationalism. The words that Dr. Martin Luther King Jr. spoke about Barry Goldwater some sixty years ago—that his philosophy gave "aid and comfort to the racist" and would serve as "an umbrella under which extremists of all stripes would stand"—had proven true, in a concrete way, of Hazony and the National Conservative movement in the United States in the first parts of the twenty-first century.[86]

———

When Martin Luther King Jr. was assassinated, on April 4, 1968, in Memphis, then-senator Robert F. Kennedy was campaigning for the Democratic presidential nomination and was due to give a campaign speech that evening in the heart of the Black community in Indianapolis. He learned of MLK Jr.'s death only upon arriving in Indiana, at which point—and against the advice of the city's police chief and mayor, who were worried about the senator's safety—he proceeded as scheduled.[87] Many if not most of the people in the crowd, which was mostly Black and included many radicals and activists, had not yet heard the awful news, so that became the first purpose of his speech. The words Bobby Kennedy chose that night, though, would form one of the great speeches of the twentieth century. It was said to have been mostly extemporaneous.[88]

The speech was brief. It began with the announcement that King had been shot and killed. Kennedy framed this news as "sad news for you, for all our fellow citizens, and people who love peace all over the world," because Martin Luther King Jr. had dedicated his life to "love and to justice between his fellow human beings," and "he died in the cause of that effort." Kennedy then spoke of all that was at stake: "In this difficult day, in this difficult time for the United States, it is perhaps well to ask what kind of a nation we are and what direction we want to move in." Briefly, he spoke of race, and of the desire for vengeance. He held up MLK Jr.'s way as an alternative, speaking of how we might, through his example, "replace that violence, that stain of bloodshed that has spread across our land, with an effort to understand with compassion and love."

Then, for the first time since 1963, he spoke of his brother's assassination: "For those of you who are black and are tempted to be filled with hatred and distrust at the injustice of such an act, against all white people, I can only say that I feel in my own heart the same kind of feeling. I had a member of my family killed, but he was killed by a white man. But we have to make an effort in the United States, we have to make an effort to understand, to go beyond these rather difficult times."[89]

At this moment Kennedy did not say more about race, and he did not turn to Christianity. Instead, he drew on the ancient Greeks.[90] He spoke very simply: "My favorite poet was Aeschylus. He wrote: "In our sleep, pain which cannot forget falls drop by drop upon the heart until, in our own despair, against our will, comes wisdom through the awful grace of God." Then he continued:

> What we need in the United States is not division; what we need in the United States is not hatred; what we need in the United States is not violence or lawlessness; but love and wisdom, and compassion toward one another, and a feeling of justice toward those who still suffer within our country, whether they be white or whether they be black.
>
> We can do well in this country. We will have difficult times; we've had difficult times in the past; we will have difficult times in the future. It is not the end of violence; it is not the end of lawlessness; it is not the end of disorder.
>
> But the vast majority of white people and the vast majority of black people in this country want to live together, want to improve the quality of our life, and want justice for all human beings who abide in our land.
>
> Let us dedicate ourselves to what the Greeks wrote so many years ago: to tame the savageness of man and make gentle the life of this world. Let us dedicate ourselves to that and say a prayer for our country and for our people.

———

The night that Martin Luther King Jr. was assassinated, riots erupted in cities all over the United States. Thousands of people were arrested, and more than forty lost their lives over the course of the following week.[91] That didn't happen in Indianapolis, and Bobby Kennedy's speech has been cited as one of the reasons why. If you watch video footage of the speech, you will see that there is some plausibility to that claim.[92] RFK was himself assassinated just two months later, on June 5, 1968. As the classicist and writer Daniel Mendelsohn observed in an article from 2013, the murder of Bobby Kennedy so soon on the heels of these other events seemed to demonstrate, with dreadful irony, "that the savageness could not be tamed."[93]

Bobby Kennedy's record on civil rights is complex, and his words resonate differently more than half a century later.[94] But his speech also offers a useful mirror and foil to Hazony's speech at NatCon 2022, and to National Conservatism more broadly.

The Aeschylus quote that RFK chose came from a play called *Agamemnon*, which is part of the *Oresteia* trilogy, the only complete set of tragedies that have been preserved from the ancient world. The plays are also a marvel of classical humanism and have inspired poets and artists all over the world for many generations (Aeschylus was also a favorite of Karl Marx). Taken together, the *Oresteia* plays dramatize a historical shift in Athenian society and consciousness. The move is away from a primitive justice system of retributive blood vengeance (framed as feminine and irrational, and personified by Clytemnestra and the chorus of Furies), and toward a more complex form of democratic constitutionalism that elevates political bonds over tribal ones and celebrates equal dignity before the law (this is presented as masculine and rational). Aeschylus puts the sobering heartbreak of political reality onstage, and then, over the course of three plays, tentatively considers the possibility of reconciliation, and maybe even of progress. The reforms are liberal in the highest sense, meant to enlarge the commonweal, protect individual citizens, and prepare the way for peace.

National Conservatism offers nothing along these lines. It stands for a reversion to particularism, tribalism, and closed-mindedness. And it is entirely comfortable with illiberal forms of politics that stamp on individual rights and instead embrace raw exertions of majoritarian (or, if necessary, minoritarian) power. The predominant national group calls the shots. Case closed.

The next chapter is about those members of the National Conservatism group and the New Right more generally who are also part of (or leading) the racist or fascist constituencies of the movement. I have, with a few exceptions, limited myself to a discussion of individuals who have received PhDs from prestigious institutions of higher education.

6

From Alt-right to Hard Right

STEVE BANNON IS FAMOUS FOR, among other things, his love of Thucydides.

Bannon is a former naval officer with an Irish Roman Catholic working-class background. He attended a private military Catholic high school in Virginia, and then went to Virginia Tech for college. He also has master's degrees from Georgetown's School of Foreign Service and Harvard University. And during his time in the Trump administration, which spanned November through August 2017, there was much talk of his "obsession" with the ancient Greek historian. He reportedly spoke about Thucydides all the time, used "Sparta" as a computer password, and, in a 2016 article, compared the Breitbart-Fox media contest to a "modern-day version of the epic Peloponnesian War." Breitbart was more like hardcore Sparta; Fox like the tired Athenian imperialists.[1]

In the early Trump White House, Bannon's affection for Thucydides was apparently matched only by that of General James Mattis and then-national security advisor H. R. McMaster.[2] In 2017 the Harvard scholar Graham Allison was invited to speak to the National Security Council about his new book, *The Thucydides Trap*. Kori Schake, writing for the *Atlantic*, dubbed the summer of 2017 the "Summer of Misreading Thucydides," noting with irony that it is generally the populists "who wreak damage on the body politic" in Thucydides' *History of the Peloponnesian War*.[3] That summer was about other things too, though, and Bannon had a reputation beyond militarism and populism. He was also known to be a fixture of what was then called the "alt-right"—another group with a thing for Sparta and its symbols.[4]

Bannon's association with the alt-right was his own doing. In an interview with the investigative journalist Sarah Posner in July 2016, he—who was at the time the executive chairman of Breitbart News—proclaimed, "We're the platform for the alt-right."[5] Hillary Clinton would echo the claim in a lucid campaign speech on Thursday, August 25, in Reno, Nevada. Secretary Clinton accused Trump of promoting racist lies and pushing conspiracy theories. She said he was "taking hate groups mainstream." The "paranoid fringe" had always existed in politics, she explained, but "it's never had the nominee of a major party stoking it, encouraging it and giving it a national megaphone, until now."[6]

Bannon was appointed to be Donald Trump's chief strategist and senior counselor in the White House in November 2016, after having served as the chief executive of his campaign since August. It was a controversial move, precisely because of Bannon's ties to the alt-right. At the time, Julie Davis, a reporter for *The New York Times*, confronted Trump about the decision:

> DAVIS: You hired Steve Bannon to be the chief strategist for you in the White House. He is a hero of the alt-right. He's been described by some as racist and anti-Semitic. I wonder what message you think you have sent by elevating him to that position and what you would say to those who feel like that indicates something about the kind of country you prefer and the government you'll run.

> TRUMP: Um, I've known Steve Bannon a long time. If I thought he was a racist, or alt-right, or any of the things that we can, you know, the terms we can use, I wouldn't even think about hiring him.[7]

Bannon, too, objected to charges of racism and antisemitism, preferring the label "economic nationalist." But he and senior advisor Stephen Miller would, as their first acts in the administration, play a crucial role in the enactment of the Trump travel bans targeting Muslims.[8] By the summer of 2017, and in the wake of a deadly clash between the alt-right and counterprotestors in Charlottesville, Virginia, Bannon's alt-right

Breitbart self would clash sufficiently with his spruced-up White House self that he would be forced out of the administration. Throughout this period, Bannon was one of a few alt-right figures working for Trump and also part of a thick network of such personalities, several of whom have PhDs from distinguished institutions.

This chapter is about this ugly underbelly of the New Right, which was formed in large part by a group of men who profess passionate admiration for all things Spartan, "Bronze Age," and Homeric, and who were cultivated in manly lairs like the Claremont Institute. They used to be fringe characters on the right but began making serious inroads into the mainstream after Trump's victory in 2016. Under Trump, the far-right American underworld came up for air.

Sparta had an ugly—nay, grotesque—underbelly, too. The worst of it concerned its slave population. Slavery was part of ancient Greek life everywhere, but it is thought to have been especially brutal and pervasive in Sparta, where the Helots (the Spartan slave class) formed an enduring underclass. There is evidence that the Spartans treated the Helots with calculating violence. The Spartans may have been manly "exemplars," but they also lived in a state of constant fear and, possibly, subject to premeditated cruelty. There is a famous passage in Thucydides where the Spartans are said to have selected two thousand of the most impressive Helots for freedom—at which point they executed them instead.[9] In the great contest between Athens and Sparta, it says something about people when, like Steve Bannon, they idolize the latter.

To meet some of the others who constitute Bannon's underworld, and to understand these networks, we must enter a confounding swirl of characters and controversies. The underbelly is ugly, but it is also exciting and risqué. The personalities we encounter here are adept at weaving tantalizing conspiracies about, for example, the dark female forces that ruthlessly dominate the commanding heights of politics and culture in America today. They have a knack for being deeply aggrieved by the most basic institutions and norms of liberal government, deeming them evil and plotting revenge, in a way that far surpasses anything on the left. And while the alt-right lost some of its momentum during this period, the ideas it promoted were being mainstreamed through places like the Claremont Institute.

Right Turn in Charlottesville

Before he worked for Trump, Stephen Miller worked for Alabama senator Jeff Sessions, whom Trump would appoint as US attorney general in February 2017. Miller joined Trump's campaign staff early in 2016. He was an important member of the transition team before being made senior advisor in the administration. Miller and Bannon reportedly wrote Trump's inaugural speech, which struck a dramatic "America First" tone and was dubbed the "American carnage" speech.[10] The most memorable part went: "The crime, and the gangs, and the drugs that have stolen too many lives and robbed our country of so much unrealized potential. This American carnage stops right here and stops right now." Trump promised to "reinforce old alliances and form new ones, and unite the civilized world against radical Islamic terrorism, which we will eradicate completely from the face of the Earth."[11]

Miller served Trump during the full four years of the administration. He was mainly responsible for immigration policy during his tenure— from the travel ban to the vicious child separation policy that the administration pursued at the southern border, where more than five thousand children were forcibly separated from their parents.[12] He was a longtime collaborator with Bannon, having written regularly for Breitbart. Miller has contested the idea that he is or was part of the alt-right rather than merely adjacent to it. But regardless of his actual status within the movement, his life and career offer a way into the origins and scope of the movement, both within the administration and in the New Right more broadly.

———

Born and raised in Southern California, Miller became a right-wing pundit and personality at a very young age. He was an early protégé of the right-wing activist and pundit David Horowitz and, from the start, was opposed to immigration and multiculturalism.[13] He did his undergraduate degree at Duke University, graduating in 2007 with a degree in political science. Miller would gain notoriety at Duke for bullheadedly, and rightly, defending the men's lacrosse team from rape allegations and charges that would collapse under scrutiny over the course of the subsequent year. The scandal, which took place in 2006–2007, has been cited as one episode, still years before Gamergate, that seeded the alt-right.[14] It is also what brought Miller together with Richard Spencer.

At the time, Spencer was a PhD student in the Duke history department (he had earned a BA from the University of Virginia in 2001 and an MA from the Humanities program at the University of Chicago in 2003).[15] Both Spencer and Miller were part of the Duke Conservative Union, a small student group led by Miller. Though he was older, Spencer speaks of that time as one in which he learned from Miller by watching him defend the lacrosse team. "I was, philosophically speaking, more or less the person I am today," Spencer explained in a 2017 interview, "but the Duke lacrosse case catalyzed me to be a pugilist for my views. I'm more combative and come out of the gate taking stands in a way that I wasn't then."[16]

Spencer's philosophy at the time was white nationalist—"identitarian" in the far-right European tradition of the French New Right writer Alain de Benoist, but with a more explicit emphasis on race and white supremacy.[17] Spencer studied music history and English at UVA, where he says he was "red-pilled by Nietzsche."[18] The idea of "red-pilling" was originally borrowed from the movie *The Matrix*; in alt-right meme-speak, it describes the shattering but also exhilarating moment where you discover that the conventional cave-world is not what it seems, but rather illusory and full of lies (as in "I was red-pilled by Plato-loving Straussians in Alberta"). Spencer says that it was at Chicago that he discovered the white supremacist thinker Jared Taylor.[19] He also lists Leo Strauss and Carl Schmitt among his influences.[20]

Spencer left the PhD program at Duke in 2007 and turned single-mindedly to political activism. He wrote for the extremist Taki's magazine for a period and then left in 2009 to found a site called AlternativeRight.com.[21] George Hawley, an expert on the American far right, notes, "The site's section dedicated to human biodiversity (HBD) contained endless discussions about the heritability of IQ."[22]

In a 2013 conference attended by Benoist, Spencer explained how "our dream is a new society, an ethno-state that would be a gathering point for all Europeans. It would be a new society based on very different ideals than, say, the Declaration of Independence."[23] Spencer has been called a neo-Nazi and white nationalist but has rejected these labels because he does not support extra-parliamentary violence or colonialism; he instead supports "right-wing Gramscianism"—which is to say, culture-warriorism; he has advocated for "peaceful ethnic cleansing."[24]

Graeme Wood, in a profile of Spencer, helpfully summarized the meaning of the alt-right as "white European cultural and racial supremacy, with a deep contempt for democracy." Spencer is often credited with coining the term 'alt-right,' but he attributes the idea to Amy Wax's friend Paul Gottfried.[25]

———

Paul Gottfried is Jewish (his parents left Germany in the 1930s), but he has been a stalwart figure in far-right groups for decades. To get a sense of his tenure in these circles: Gottfried is also credited with having coined the term "paleoconservative."[26] He earned his PhD in 1967 at Yale under the leftist thinker Herbert Marcuse.[27] He was an advisor to Pat Buchanan in the 1990s, has published dozens of academic books, and is also active in far-right circles abroad.

In 2008 Gottfried founded the HL Mencken Club, which for over a decade hosted small conferences featuring prominent white nationalists like VDare founder Peter Brimelow and former *National Review* writer John Derbyshire (i.e., people who existed outside of the old GOP's cordon sanitaire).[28] In 2013 Derbyshire delivered a speech to the club called "Politics and Intelligence," where he questioned whether "some people should be considered too dumb to vote." At the start he said: "A lot of people are too dumb to vote. I don't think that can be doubted. Democrats and a lot of Republicans. The number of Democrats who are too dumb to vote is likely greater because the Democrats are the party of racial minorities with low statistical profiles on IQ."[29]

For reasons that we will come to, the HL Mencken Club website is now defunct, but the old site is preserved on the Internet Archive. Gottfried likes to distance himself from Nazism and overt racist nationalism, but he was a pioneer for high-brow American white nationalism and fascism, and his club was a hub for extremist anti-Black voices as of its inception. In 2021 Gottfried was appointed editor-in-chief of the extremist paleoconservative magazine *Chronicles*.

Richard Spencer was a featured speaker at each of the HL Mencken Club conferences from its inception in 2008 through 2014 (these conferences are small and feature just a dozen speakers or so). Throughout this period his notoriety was growing. In 2009 he launched AlternativeRight.com, and in 2011 he was invited to lead the National Policy Institute (NPI), a white nationalist group funded by William Regnery II, heir to the conservative publishing house Regnery. (William Regnery II had been bankrolling prominent white nationalist initiatives—including the Charles Martel Foundation, Jared Taylor's New Century Foundation, the *Occidental Quarterly*, and *The Occidental Observer*—since 2001. In 2017 he told Buzzfeed news: "My support has produced a much greater bang for the buck than by the brothers Koch or Soros Inc.")[30] Under Spencer's leadership, the NPI group and the AlternativeRight.com site grew in prominence.[31] The historian Joshua Tait writes that Spencer "saw their project as the creation of a genuine—if revolutionary—alternative to the conservative movement that refocused the right's energy on racial consciousness."[32]

The NPI gained brief notoriety in the immediate aftermath of Trump's win in 2016, when, at their annual conference in Washington, DC, Spencer gave an exuberant speech that included the words "Hail Trump, hail our people, hail victory!" This moment led to spontaneous "Hail Hitler!" salutes in the audience. Other clips of the speech contain pro-Nazi references, dehumanizing rhetoric, and calls for the renewal of white America under Trump.[33]

There is no evidence that Gottfried attended the conference, but he and the Mencken Club had staged a dress rehearsal of sorts for the event just prior to the election. That conference was called "The Right

Revisited." Peter Brimelow spoke, as did John Derbyshire, along with a man named Darren Beattie.[34]

———

In 2016 Darren Beattie was a visiting faculty member at Duke University. He had graduated from Duke with a PhD in political science earlier that year, having written a dissertation called "Martin Heidegger's Mathematical Dialectic: Uncovering the Structure of Modernity." Beattie gained some attention at Duke for having signed on to the scholars' endorsement of Trump for the presidency and predicting Trump's victory.[35] He was also connected to the Claremont Institute, having been a Publius Scholar there in 2008; he responded eagerly to a Claremont email from right-wing provocateur Charles Johnson about whether to support Trump early in 2016 ("I'm graduating this May and would very much like to get involved," he wrote).[36]

Beattie's speech at the HL Mencken Club was called "The Right and the Intelligentsia," which, according to a publicly available version of the speech, was about the emergence of a new antiglobalist intelligentsia.[37] Beattie was also a staunch defender of Trump's travel ban. By 2018 he was working as a speech writer and aide in the White House.[38]

During his time in the first Trump administration, it appears that Beattie became close with Steve Bannon (as well as with Michael Anton). In a book about Bannon, *War for Eternity* (2020), Benjamin Teitelbaum (a musicologist at the University of Colorado) wrote about a dinner he attended with Bannon at a Tucson smokehouse in 2019, where Beattie was in attendance. Teitelbaum describes how at the time Beattie was enthusiastic about a scholar named Michael Millerman.[39]

———

Millerman is a University of Toronto PhD who writes apologetics for the neo-fascist Russian thinker Aleksandr Dugin. He received his degree in 2018; the title of his dissertation was "Beginning with Heidegger:

Strauss, Rorty, Derrida, Dugin and the Philosophical Constitution of the Political."

Millerman's graduation from Toronto was controversial, and two faculty members, Ronald Beiner and Clifford Orwin, resigned from supervisory roles on his dissertation committee early on. Beiner told me that this was due to Millerman's obvious and disturbing devotion to Dugin's fascist philosophy and his having allowed his translations of Dugin to be published with Arktos, the largest far-right publishing house in the world.[40] As a Canadian journalist put it in 2018, "Over the course of his studies, Millerman emerged as the world's leading conduit into the English language for the work of Aleksandr Dugin, a Russian neo-fascist who is under sanctions by Canada for his role in the annexation of Ukraine."[41] In his book, Teitelbaum reports that after Beattie mentioned Millerman, he (Teitelbaum) immediately brought up the name of the then–chief editor at Arktos, Jason Jorjani. In Teitelbaum's telling, that got the attention of Bannon, who jumped in eagerly, surprised to hear Jorjani's name mentioned.[42]

———

Jason Jorjani is a bizarre figure. He received his PhD in philosophy from SUNY Stony Brook in 2013, having written a dissertation titled "Prometheus & Atlas: An Inquiry Into the Spectral Essence of Technoscience," and was subsequently hired at the New Jersey Institute of Technology. He is an Iranian American, whose deepest aspiration is for the revival of "Indo-European world order" based in a de-Islamicized Iran.[43] Jorjani and Spencer met for the first time at the 2016 NPI "Hail Trump" meeting in DC. Shortly after the 2016 election, Jorjani told Carol Schaeffer of *The Intercept* that "what happened is that a hyperintellectual, vanguardist movement used a U.S. presidential election to advance its agenda."[44] In January 2017 Jorjani began a new collaboration with Richard Spencer called the AltRight Corporation. *The Atlantic*'s Rosie Gray reported on their efforts to create a "one-stop-shop" for the alt-right.[45]

Less than a year into the Trump presidency, though, during Thucydides summer, the alt-right began to fracture and fail.

———

In May 2017 Richard Spencer led rallies in Charlottesville to protest the removal of a statue of the Confederate general Robert E. Lee. There were chants of "Russia is our friend!" and "You will not replace us." Spencer told one crowd: "We will not be replaced from this park. We will not be replaced from this world. Whites have a future. We have a future of power, of beauty, of expression."[46] In August 2017 one of these rallies turned deadly.

The "Unite the Right" rally that took place in Charlottesville that August was organized in part by Spencer and featured him as a speaker and leader of the tiki-torch march. The event faced opposition and counterprotests. This led to violent clashes, including the murder of Heather Heyer by James Alex Fields Jr. of Ohio. Fields intentionally drove his car into a crowd of protestors on August 12, killing Heyer and injuring nineteen others.[47] Fields would plead guilty in 2019 to twenty-nine federal hate crimes and negotiate a life sentence.[48]

In the immediate aftermath of Charlottesville, Bannon was ousted from the White House.[49] He was already scheduled to leave the administration, but after Charlottesville Trump's new chief of staff, John Kelly, insisted that he leave immediately. Jason Jorjani was the next alt-right personality to face consequences for his views.[50] He was suspended from his job at the New Jersey Institute of Technology after a *New York Times* exposé of his extremism was published in September 2017.[51] He and Spencer also had a falling out, and soon he was no longer chief editor at Arktos.[52] Michael Anton left the Trump White House in April 2018. He had been brought in by Michael Flynn but had worked mainly under H. R. McMaster. When McMaster was replaced by John Bolton, Anton was ousted, too. Darren Beattie was forced out in August 2018, when CNN uncovered his participation at the 2016 HL Mencken Club meeting.[53] He was then hired by Matt Gaetz, which led to further controversies.[54] Later he would start a conspiratorial website called *Revolver News*, where he would become an ideological innovator for "Stop the Steal."

In many respects, Charlottesville marked the decline of the alt-right and the holding to account of some of its key figures. But it also marked the early ascendance of something new and different, and more mainstream. Some of its key figures merely migrated to, or invented, other platforms; others worked their ideas into more conventional-seeming outlets. Bannon was out, but Miller would remain in the White House. The "alt-right" was on the way out, but the "dissident" Hard Right was rising.

Curtis Yarvin, Costin Alamariu, and the Bronze Age Mindset

Sometime around when Darren Beattie was fired from the White House, the editors of the *Claremont Review of Books* decided it would be a good idea to publish a piece about the alt-right, and to have Michael Anton write it. The piece appeared in the summer 2019 issue, under the cute title "Are the Kids Al(t)-Right?"[55]

Anton opens his essay with characteristic coyness, suggesting that he hesitated to take the project on because he didn't really know what the "alt-right" was (he made no effort to trace the origins of the term), and because the movement had "immolated itself in Charlottesville in August 2017." He begged off until a friend of his named Curtis Yarvin brought him a book called *Bronze Age Mindset* (*BAM*) by someone named "Bronze Age Pervert" (BAP). *BAM* was self-published in June 2018 and quickly became a bestseller on Amazon. Anton admits even after receiving the gift from Yarvin, he had a hard time taking it seriously. Then, he says, his "young friend and former White House colleague, Darren Beattie," urged him to "try again and persevere." Anton continues: "The book, [Beattie] said, has struck a chord with younger people—especially men—who are dissatisfied with the way the world is going and have no faith in mainstream conservatism's efforts to arrest, much less reverse, the rot."[56]

As for Yarvin, Anton refers to him as a "tech entrepreneur and anti-democracy blogger," which is true, but Yarvin is better described as one of the founders of the neoreactionary movement (or NRx, also known as the Dark Enlightenment, a term coined by the "accelerationist" philosopher Nick Land). Yarvin went to Brown University as an undergraduate and then dropped out of a computer science PhD program at UC Berkeley. He was involved in the early internet and, beginning in the 2000s, took to blogging under the pseudonym Mencius Moldbug. The name of his original blog was *Unqualified Reservations*. Moldbug was prolific and gained an underground following in Silicon Valley, where he became a pioneer of nerdy avant-garde and right-wing brospeak. As an outsider, it is hard to understand how that was possible: Yarvin's writing is very bad, and the reasoning is worse; come for the edgelord conspiracism ("Did Barack Obama Go to Columbia?" pondered Moldbug in 2008), stay for the non sequiturs and slapdash pseudohistorical bricolage.[57] There may be nothing on the New Right more depressing than the rise of Curtis Yarvin.

Yarvin's thinking began as an outgrowth of the libertarianism of Silicon Valley. He was influenced by Murray Rothbard and is a longtime friend of Peter Thiel (he purportedly watched the 2016 election results come in at Thiel's house), as well as an acquaintance of JD Vance.[58] Yarvin is thought to have been the earliest popularizer of the "red pill" meme, and his libertarianism eventually morphed into a preference for strict authoritarian rule, styled on the self-actualizing tech startup CEO.[59] He believes in "turbocapitalism" and has written, for example, about how President Nayib Bukele might repurpose El Salvador as a "startup state."[60] Joshua Tait described him as "a new type of radical Right activist at odds with the conservative mainstream: young, coastal, anonymous, secular, male, and adept at manipulating digital technologies to advance an anti-progressive agenda."[61] While the neoreactionary movement is often associated with the alt-right, it is more radically elitist. Yarvin is full of contempt for the democratic hoi polloi, including its white denizens, which puts him somewhat at odds with the populist GOP.[62] His explicit political preference is for a new technocratic absolute monarchy, and his blogging is full of appeals to strongmen and

Caesarism, which has had an impact on Thiel and many others across the New Right (in 2024 he recommended Elon Musk for the role of American Caesar).[63] As Suzanne Schneider has written, "it takes a special kind of delusion to look at the present political and economic order and say, 'Well, it could be great if only the tech bros, financiers, and consultants had a bit *more* power.'"[64]

With all that said, the differences between neoreaction and the alt-right should not be overstated. As concerns white nationalism and racism, Yarvin once famously said that he's "not exactly allergic to the stuff." And though he has a snobbish preference for techno-monarchy over populist demagoguery, his criticisms of the modern liberal democratic order are entirely of a piece with the Hard Right populists and paleoconservatives.

One of Yarvin's most celebrated idea is that of "the Cathedral," the provocative name he gives to the supposedly all-powerful institutions most beloved by the liberal bourgeoisie—namely, the media, government, and academia.[65] Yarvin claims that these institutions exert a monolithic and hegemonic power over modern minds. The idea of the Cathedral is catchy and taps nicely into the right's perpetual concern about liberalism's failure to live up to its supposed promise of moral neutrality: "Look—they aren't really liberals! It's like a religion to them!"[66] But it is also a rebundling of older conservative tropes and bogeymen, from Burnham's managerial elite, to the administrative state, to Anton's Davoisie. There is not much to differentiate the Cathedral from Plato's original notion of the Cave, now with a modern inflection, or from Nietzsche's worries about the Last Man, or plotlines from *The Matrix*.

It is a special trick of the American conservative intellectual class to turn the existence of basic political structures, norms, and hierarchies into some kind of eternal "own" of liberals and liberal democracy. But unlike some on the right, Yarvin clearly favors dramatic action. He has been writing about purging the Cathedral since 2008—a notion that is tidily summarized in his popular acronym RAGE, or "Retire All Government Employees."[67] Yarvin's thinking is also spiked with a thirst for violence and domination. In one of his Substack posts on the Cathedral, he offers a jokey line about what might happen to elite institutions from the vantage of an imagined future: "They were simply *liquidated*— rounded up, shot, dumped in a ditch, soaked with gas and *burned*."[68]

What Yarvin termed the Cathedral, Bronze Age Pervert would render, more or less, as "the Longhouse." His solution was not Caesarism, but the *Bronze Age Mindset*.

———

In his article for the *Claremont Review of Books* on Bronze Age Pervert, Anton did a good job summarizing *Bronze Age Mindset*.[69] BAM is divided into four parts, plus a prologue, and in this and other respects it is a mimicry of Nietzsche's popular work, *Thus Spoke Zarathustra*. Anton notes that the fourth section, which BAP calls "A Few Arrows," is a reference to Nietzsche's *Twilight of the Idols* and suggests that this means "the heart of his book is really Parts One through Three." This interpretation has the handy effect of minimizing the aggressive programmatic recommendations of the final part and elevating the more theoretical portions of the book. It is one of the ways Anton defangs and euphemizes BAPism. Anton also kept mum about BAP's real identity in his 2019 review, either out of solidarity or because he was left in the dark. BAP's real name is Costin Alamariu.

Alamariu was born in Romania and immigrated to the United States with his parents as a child. He grew up in Newton, Massachusetts, did an undergraduate degree at MIT, and earned a doctoral degree in Straussian political philosophy from Yale University in 2015. His dissertation was titled "The Problem of Tyranny and Philosophy in the Thought of Plato and Nietzsche."[70] Alamariu went to Emory University as a postdoc, but his contract was not renewed. Soon after his de facto departure from academia, he published *Bronze Age Mindset*—though, as Rosie Gray has shown, he had already been cultivating the far-right personality online for some time.[71]

Part of that persona is a hammed-up, thick Romanian accent, which translates in writing to a style that ignores grammatical conventions. As Anton observes, "Words are often misspelled or dropped, verbs mis-conjugated, punctuation rules ignored. For example, a prototypical BAP sentence reads "Wat means?'"[72]

BAP's persona and writing style are effective because they are both humorous and sharp. Peak *BAM* is probably a long passage in part 3 where he analogizes between Mitt Romney and the ancient Athenian Alcibiades. Anton is right when he says the passage is hilarious; it makes you sad about the overall trajectory of Alamariu's life and work.

That trajectory isn't nice. BAP's on-again-off-again Twitter/X feed alternates between racist spewings, photographs of white muscle men posing on beaches around the world, and prowar propaganda. His life's goal appears to be to inspire bodily and military strength among young white men, to weaken or destroy everyone else, especially women, and to be worshiped as a god himself for having the courage to speak openly in such terms.

Before proceeding, though, it is worth acknowledging a problem that comes with writing about BAP, which has to do with his rhetorical "excesses." As Anton notes, "The strongest and easiest objections to make to *Bronze Age Mindset* are that it is 'racist,' 'anti-Semitic,' 'anti-democratic,' 'misogynistic,' and "homophobic.'"[73] Anton tries to resolve this problem by acknowledging that BAP is very hierarchical, and that much of the outrageousness serves to provide "air cover for the outrageous things he means in deadly earnest." Graeme Wood, writing for *The Atlantic*, put it like this: "BAP's vile utterances, whether sincere or not, serve a purpose: to keep whiny leftists so busy cataloging his petty thought crimes that they overlook his more serious heresies. Meanwhile, those capable of reading him without being rage-blinded quietly learn from him and heed his advice to bond, network, and plot."[74]

This is true, but there is a parallel danger that comes with not cataloging BAP's "petty thought crimes," as well as with presuming that there is something "earnest" and "serious" undergirding Alamariu's work that can somehow be disentangled from his rhetorical faux pas. The danger there is that, to look cool, you whitewash and elevate the genocidal writings of a maniac. In what follows, I try to keep both problems in mind.

In *BAM*, BAP tells a counterintuitive story about man's history. For him, the Bronze Age was a golden age of human history because it represented the hard suppression of what supposedly came before—which was the womanly, proto-socialist age of the communal "longhouse" (BAP was referencing the communal dwelling style found all over the world historically). Bronze Age man, in BAP's telling, revolted against the feminine tyranny of the Iron Age, exerted his power, and invented political order and rule, and this was exceptional and great. Sadly, in the West today, mankind has succumbed once more to something like the older natural state of "gynocracy." So it is time for the manly men to rise up and take action.

Action includes sensational rhetoric. Though Alamariu has the benefit of hindsight that, say, Nietzsche lacked, and so he cannot profess ignorance, say, about the Holocaust or Stalinism, he spews violent rhetoric everywhere. Whether this is meant to alienate the soft-hearted or entice and inspire the manly men, BAP talks of purges, purification, and destruction right from the start of *BAM*. In the prologue, he speaks of how nature exerts "divine justice" through its "violence against the surfeit of populations." He glories in nature's destruction of "the feeble designs of reason, the pointless words of man." The prologue concludes with a paean to the Bronze Age men of "life and force," and a promise that he sees such a spirit returning "in our time." He makes appeals to "Piratical bands and brotherhoods," and the final line of the prologue is "May they inhabit us again and give us strength to purify this world of refuse!" Throughout his work, BAP refers to the "refuse" sorts as "bugmen"—another echo of Nietzsche.

BAP's recommendation of a life of piracy is part of a more general rejection of modernity and what he calls "owned space." This is one of the main points of part 1 of *Bronze Age Mindset*. BAP is referring to the idea that there is no real wilderness left, nothing untouched or undiscovered or unowned by mankind; we could relate it to the Anthropocene (or maybe to something like the inverse of *Lebensraum*). He draws connections between the absence of wildernesses and the decline of masculinity: The fact that boys are not allowed to play in the wild and experience rough-and-tumble nature is a betrayal of their essence and their freedom, and some boys perceive and resent the artificiality of the world ("Such boy perceives . . . the conditional and entirely *dependent* character of life in our age"; this is also, according to BAP, the cause of the supposed rise in homosexuality in the modern world).[75]

In BAP's telling, contemporary masculinity is just performance art for women and has nothing to do with the real thing. True manliness "develops into the will to actually dominate space around oneself . . . this domination is not possible when space is already owned." It is hard to see why exactly that would be the case, but throughout the book, BAP compares modern "owned space" to a prison.

And, metaphorically at least, according to BAP, the world's spaces are all dominated and owned by women, and by gay men.[76] This is the theme of part 2 of the book, "Parable of Iron Prison." The "iron prison" is also "the longhouse"—"the sallow night of matriarchy"—which means the return of Iron Age socialism and feminism. BAP warns that the world's domination by women is taking place psychologically, too: "The higher instincts of the spirit are being overtaken physiologically by the retrograde and prehistoric."

In the next two parts of the book, BAP turns more positive and practical. Part 3, "Men of Power and the Ascent of Youth," involves a series of character sketches (including the passage about Romney), and part 4, "A Few Arrows, Programmatic," offers advice to young readers. Among other things, they should lift weights, join the military, prepare for a takeover of the world, sow great chaos, and discredit the system. They might also, in preparation, undertake something that Alamariu calls "the great down-going," which involves visiting marginal communities—slums and dives, in effect; because these are still relatively unowned and free, you can act with impunity, and you can stir up disorder that undermines the security of the liberal state.[77] BAP is adamant throughout his work that only a fool would talk openly about their love of BAP.

By way of concluding my own unloving discussion of BAP, I want to note that what we find in *Bronze Age Mindset* is tame compared to what BAP is willing to say on his podcast or other livestream events, where he speaks in a manner that is more fully unhinged. So as to avoid whitewashing BAP, I want to say something about one of his brief monologues, on the subject of the Longhouse, which was re-posted, in three parts, on Twitter by "Bronze Age Aesthetics," @pro-teinpilled, on February 16, 2022.[78] The voice is unmistakable. I have kept a recording.

Alamariu described the Longhouse as a "type of absolutist herdism" that, much like Nietzsche's Last Man, but with a singularly sexist inflec-tion, "has put safety as its highest promise." He claimed that Covid-19 had proven his account of the Longhouse to be totally true: "You live already in a post-political post-state gynocratic order." At the same time, he disavowed conspiracism. The Longhouse gynocracy is not under the control of a secret cabal or executive planner; rather, "you are just enslaved by the desires of 40-something femme-cels who haven't been fucked in years, or by the husbands of the occasionally married femme-cels who bully their house-bounds." If Alamariu was clear about one thing in this clip, it was that the gynocracy is not lethar-gic or enervated; rather, it is subhuman and dangerous, subject to the "dark yoke of female and deviant tyranny, which is darker, more hope-less and brutal than any that has existed." The future, BAP warned, is "a tyranny that promises horrors even worse than what Bolshevism or communism delivered."

From here, Alamariu went on to explain his deployment of irony and humor. He admitted that he uses humor to break free of the "lame narcissistic self-important style that is now favored by intellectuals," and because it is the best way to reach people, and to give people cover ("you can say 'BAP is a buffoon!'"). Then his voice took on a fierce militancy. He said that his humor also represents his "attempts as a humble internet poster to DECLARE WAR ON ALL MANKIND." He went on, and as music started to play, he reiterated the point, declaring war on "the bug creature who is bored and lives in fear of death and wants to make a world a surveilled padded nursing MADHOUSE." He called for "TOTAL WAR" three or four times, against the meek, the scurrying, and the safety-obsessed, and then just "on mankind." The clip con-cluded with these words: "I come with tablets of hatred, and destruc-tions for the SPLEEN of mankind. In hundreds of years they will say he came on a donkey with tablets of hatred for all mankind. He was a Moses to the frogs. He was a Moses to the redeemers of the world in FIRE."

We will see more of Alamariu in chapter 11.

———

Darren Beattie concluded his 2016 speech to the HL Mencken society—the little speech about the possibility of a new right intelligentsia—by referencing a beautiful line from the poem "Patmos," by the German writer Hölderlin. The line is famous because it also concludes Heidegger's essay, "The Question Concerning Technology." It reads: "Wo aber Gefahr ist, wächst das Rettende auch" ("Where, however, there is danger, salvation also grows"). In Hölderlin's poem, the line references the salvation that Christ brings even in the wake of the greatest devastations. In his essay, as I understand it, Heidegger takes the line in a different direction, attributing the "saving power" to the thoughts and conceptualizations that serve as something like Aristotelian first causes in the human world's unfolding (and so also, potentially, as sources of repair in the world). I always think, in connection with this line, of a phrase from Nietzsche's *Thus Spoke Zarathustra*: "Die stillsten Worte sind es, welche den Sturm bringen, Gedanken, die mit Taubenfüssen kommen, lenken die Welt" ("It is the stillest words that bring the storm. Thoughts that come on doves' feet guide the world").[79]

At the HL Mencken conference for white supremacists, Beattie put his own twist on the line, reversing the meaning from hopeful to cautious: "In light of the possibility of political and cultural success, but continued philosophical and spiritual darkness, I close with the following modification: 'Hinter das Rettende [*sic*] liegt auch das [*sic*] Gefahr'" (Behind salvation, the danger also lies)."[80] Beattie's concern was that right-wing political victories might not translate into "something of real philosophic significance." He was right to be concerned.

It is hard not to speculate about what Nietzsche would have thought of these twenty-first-century men and aspiring Übermenschen. My sense is that he would diagnose them straightforwardly as late modern decadents under the sway of vengeful Pauline morality and aesthetics, desperate for meaning, lashing out in anger and resentment, small-souled and sterile. In my sweeter moods, I think of the soothsayer who haunts Zarathustra in part 4 of *Thus Spoke Zarathustra*, who is suffering in a state of nihilistic despair, grasping for something to live for. To him, Zarathustra responds, "No! No! Three times no! *That* I know better! There are still Isles of the Blest! Be quiet about *that*, you sighing set of mourning-pipes! Stop babbling about *that*, you raincloud in the fore-noon!"[81] Another character who comes to mind is the Sorcerer of part 4, whom Zarathustra calls a "wicked counterfeiter" who "harvested disgust" as his single truth.[82]

The great thinkers whom BAP, Beattie, and others profess to admire offer their readers more than the stink of hatred, disgust, and cruelty. Nietzsche's work, for all its destructive hatred of Pauline Christianity, contains praise for Jesus the man, and in his *Nachlass* he famously wrote that his style of *Übermensch* would resemble a "Roman Caesar with Christ's soul."[83] In "Patmos," Hölderlin speaks of how Jesus always, even in his final days, "Had words of kindness to speak, / ... To soften the violence and wildness of the world." Even Homer—whose *Iliad* must be taken as nothing less than the apex of Bronze Age literature, and which consists, in effect, of twenty-four books of bloodshed and gore, spurred on by a most wretched bout of existential furor—nevertheless reserves places in his poetry to celebrate the sweet gentleness of the world at peace. While Achilles rages for his lost friend, he carries a shield fashioned by the craftsman god Hephaestus and covered in pas-toral scenes of simple humanity—scenes of war, yes, but also of animals being tended, of young people dancing, of a marriage festival, maybe a longhouse or two.

Homer never lets nihilistic anger or hate consume his world. Such rage and ugliness have threatened the New Right, which, as a move-ment, has proven either eager to embrace the extremists with a wink and a nod, incapable of keeping them out, or shamefully weak in its protestations. Signs of the extremist underbelly of the New Right—and of extremist normalization—have popped up everywhere.

The Normalization of Violent Extremism

In November 2019, two years after Charlottesville and the same year that Anton published his BAP article, trouble brewed for Anton's former White House colleague, Stephen Miller. Hundreds of his emails had been leaked to the SPLC's Hatewatch group by a former Breitbart staffer, Katie McHugh. These emails demonstrated Miller's connections not only to Breitbart, but also to white nationalist ideology. In some, Miller promoted *The Camp of the Saints*, a novel by Jean Raspail.[84]

The Camp of the Saints is dystopian fiction about the mass invasion of France by migrants (the first wave comes from Calcutta). It is deeply racist. This is not a book that worries about the challenges of cultural adaptation and integration, but a dehumanizing and fear-mongering tract about the future subjugation of Europe by nonwhite foreigners. As the journalist Cathy Young wrote in reporting about Viktor Orbán's embrace of the novel:

> Throughout the book, the migrants are presented as a repulsive, seething mass of dark bodies; the only identifiable person among them, a leader of sorts, is a man known as "the turd eater," a black giant with his gruesomely deformed son perched atop his shoulders as a "hideous totem." . . . Predictably, Raspail's racist horror show often takes the form of grotesque porn. The Indian refugees aboard the ships spend most of their voyage in indiscriminate pansexual orgies—"a mass of hands and mouths, of phalluses and rumps"—in which even young children are fair game.[85]

In another of Miller's emails, he promoted the work of Jason Richwine, a Harvard PhD who wrote his dissertation on "IQ and Immigration Policy."[86] Richwine resigned from the Heritage Foundation in 2013 after the extent of his Harvard-backed racism was exposed, but he was being rehabilitated on the New Right. He and Amy Wax published an article in Krein and Pappin's *American Affairs* in Winter 2017.[87]

When these connections to the far right were exposed in 2019, there were petitions to oust Miller from the White House. By that time Sessions, Bannon, Anton, and Beattie were all gone. But when it came to

Miller, nothing changed. On November 13, 2020, the Trump administration appointed Beattie to the Commission for the Preservation of America's Heritage Abroad. That same day, it also appointed Jason Richwine to a senior position at the National Institute of Standards and Technology.[88]

The normalization of extremism is most vivid with the Claremont crowd, especially since their decision to publish Anton's sympathetic piece on BAP. In March 2020 Ryan Williams, the president of the Claremont Institute, went on a podcast called *Jack Murphy Live* to explain "why they engaged with Bronze Age Pervert, Curtis Yarvin, and Jack Posobiec." As the founder of a man's group called The Liminal Order, Murphy was himself a growing influence on the far right, and over the years he interviewed numerous Claremont Institute fellows like Michael Anton, Christopher Caldwell, Glenn Ellmers, and Thomas West, extremists like Beattie, Dugin, Millerman, and Posobiec, and other familiar figures like Sohrab Ahmari, Christopher Rufo, and JD Vance (the interview with Vance took place in 2021; this was all before Murphy's own colorful past was discovered).[89]

The interview with Williams was revealing. He alternated between being cautious and excited about BAP, but at one point he referred to *BAM* as a piece of philosophical art and admitted that they published Anton's piece in part "to stir things up." He conceded that Claremont had something to prove—namely, that they "weren't just fusionist Reagan Republicans" but were instead "open to new ideas" and "*not . . . afraid* of the arguments that are gaining some traction on the right." Then Williams took a more evangelizing turn. He talked about how important it was to bring eclectic and heterodox thinkers like Yarvin to new readers, to "continue the conversation." He and Murphy gloated about how these sorts of thinkers had influence in Trump's White House. Williams said that the very online landscape of the New Right was an "increasingly huge thing" that was quickly replacing and delegitimizing the old media. At the end of the interview, Murphy commended Williams for "the direction you're taking the organization. . . . If the Bronze Age Pervert thing was meant to be a bat-signal to the young and new right and the internet right—well, we heard it, we saw it, here we are." Williams chuckled. The Claremont Institute would accept Murphy as a Lincoln Fellow the following year.

It was not just the Claremont Institute that was radicalizing. So many of the people affiliated with the institute, after all, were participants in the National Conservatism group. And though Hazony made efforts to keep out white nationalists like Brimelow from their conferences, others trickled in over time. Within a few years of the Wax controversy, Gottfried would be welcomed as a speaker at NatCon. So would Darren Beattie, whose racism and role in fomenting the conditions for the January 6 attack on the US Capitol are considered in the next chapter.

7

Stopping the Steal

THERE IS A FAMOUS CHAPTER in Tocqueville's *Democracy in America* where the Frenchman defends, of all the people in the world, America's lawyerly class: "Men who have made the laws their special study have drawn from their work the habits of order, a certain taste for forms, a sort of instinctive love for the regular sequence of ideas, which naturally render them strongly opposed to the revolutionary spirit and unreflective passions of democracy."[1]

Tocqueville would have been awfully disappointed in John C. Eastman.

Just before 11 o'clock on the morning of January 6, 2021—an hour before President Donald Trump would appear onstage in front of the White House, and two and a half hours before the US Capitol would be overrun—Rudy Giuliani spoke to the "Save America" rallygoers. John Eastman stood by his side.

Eastman was the founding director of the Claremont Institute's Center for Constitutional Jurisprudence, a senior fellow at the institute, and a member of its board of directors.[2] At the time he was also a law professor at Chapman University and a visiting scholar at the Benson Center for the Study of Western Civilization at the University of Colorado Boulder. Eastman went to the University of Chicago Law School and clerked for Justice Clarence Thomas and Judge J. Michael Luttig. He was also chairman of the board of the National Organization of Marriage (NOM, a lobby group dedicated to fighting same-sex marriage that was chaired for a time by Princeton's Robert P. George) and a prominent member of the Federalist Society.[3] Eastman ran as a tough-on-crime candidate in the Republican primary for California's attorney general in 2010.[4] Steve Cooley won the GOP primary; Kamala Harris got the job.

But on January 6, 2021, John Eastman was virtually unknown beyond conservative circles. Onstage, wearing a dark suit, paisley scarf, camel overcoat, and brown-brimmed hat, he cut a suave figure next to the grimacing man who, two decades and a lifetime ago, had been dubbed America's Mayor.

Professor Eastman's job that day was to explain how the Democrats had perpetuated voter fraud, both in Georgia's run-off election the day before (on January 5, 2021) and on November 3, 2020. Eastman took to his task with gusto. Gesturing emphatically, he asserted that dead people had voted and that election officials had ignored or violated state law. According to Eastman, the "old way" of doing fraud "was to have a bunch of ballots sittin' in a box under the floor," but now "they put those ballots in a secret folder in the machines."[5] From here, his theory went like this: When 99 percent of the vote was in, the Democrats pulled an elaborate trick. By that point they knew who had and hadn't voted, and they knew how many more votes would be needed to take the lead in the count. So they paused the counting, took out their stash of electronic ballots, matched each of "those unvoted ballots with an unvoted voter," and "put them together in the machine" marked as Democratic votes. "Voila!" Eastman explained, "We have enough votes to barely get over the finish line. We saw it happen in real time last night, and it happened on November 3rd as well!" At one point he said: "You don't see this on Fox or any of the other stations" but you can see it in "the data."

The crowd was thrilled.

Within a year, Eastman's name would resonate in households across the country, because he did more than spread conspiracy theories on that January 6 stage. He was also the author of the notorious "coup memos," which outlined various avenues through which the Trump campaign might postpone the peaceful transfer of power, on dubious grounds, and/or overturn the election.[6] Subpoenaed documents would prove that Eastman had been involved with the president's efforts as of early December 2020.[7] He spent January 4 and 5 in the Oval Office making the case to Vice President Mike Pence that Pence had the authority to intervene in the counting of the Electoral College vote. Eastman's name would appear over five hundred times in the January 6th Committee's Final Report.[8]

There is language in both of Eastman's memos describing how the act of postponing or overturning the election results was necessary to maintaining the legitimacy of the American republic.[9] At the rally, Eastman concluded with the same message, offering an impassioned plea for Pence to allow state legislators to investigate these matters, so that "we get to the bottom of it, and the American people know whether we have control of the direction of our government or not." Eastman became very animated, pumping his fists and yelling: "We no longer live in a self-governing republic if we can't get the answer to this question! This is bigger than President Trump! It is the very essence of our republican form of government, and it has to be done!" As wild as this presentation was—with a tenured law professor arguing that the only way to preserve the American system of government was for Congress to heed the calls of conspiracists—Eastman's moment was one of the tamer parts of the day. Everyone knows what followed.

The Eastman memos provided Trump with something invaluable: a veneer of legal legitimacy with which to cover up a plan that was flagrantly unconstitutional and antidemocratic. Vice President Pence recognized the problem and refused to cooperate, so that plan failed. But Eastman's legalistic efforts were part of something much broader and more dangerous, other dimensions of which were promoted by others at the Claremont Institute. In the lead-up to January 6, the institute's leadership peddled the "Big Lie" about the 2020 election and a false narrative about a "Biden coup." They gave cover to Eastman in the aftermath of January 6, and some figures affiliated with the Claremont Institute—including its main donor and board chairman, Thomas Klingenstein (also one of NatCon's biggest funders), continued to peddle conspiratorial lies about a stolen election, and about racial politics and the overall decay of the country, through 2024.[10] So did Donald Trump and his 2024 running mate, JD Vance.[11]

This chapter moves chronologically through the New Right's involvement in and response to the 2020 election and January 6, 2021. I examine the words and actions of men like Michael Anton, Darren Beattie, Ryan Williams, John Eastman, and Charles Kesler, as well as others like Patrick Deneen and Adrian Vermeule, during this fraught period. Some of these men forged and fomented the ideas that led to violence on January 6, others egged things on, while some stayed silent or played dumb. But as a general matter, the events of January 6 represent a massive failure of prudence and judgment on the part of the New Right. It was also a moment of jarring partisan hypocrisy. Those who had the most extreme reactions to the George Floyd protests in 2020 were the most blasé about January 6, 2021. In the end, what started as a startling conspiracy about a stolen election became, as the writer David A. Graham observed, conservatives' "New Lost Cause" and loyalty test. The neo-Confederate Lost Cause myth sought to reframe the South's role in the Civil War as heroic and just. As Graham wrote in October 2021, "the New Lost Cause, like the old one, [sought] to convert a shameful catastrophe into a celebration of the valor and honor of the culprits and portray those who attacked the country as the true patriots."[12]

The 2020 Election and the Lead-Up to January 6

In 2020 everyone was worried about the election. Covid-19 was ransacking the country, which had led many states, both red and blue, to expand mail-in voting. Summer 2020 was also made more volatile by the George Floyd protests and riots. And President Trump was an extremely polarizing figure. Like many others across the country, several affiliates of the Claremont Institute were concerned about the election well before it took place.

John Eastman and others took part in a project called the "79 Days Report," which was organized by the Claremont Institute and a group called the Texas Public Policy Foundation and published on October 20, 2020. The report was presented as a right-wing counter to the Transition Integrity Project (TIP), a bipartisan effort that brought together experts from both parties to game out several possible election scenarios. The 79 Days Report was not bipartisan in any sense. Other participants included Ryan Williams (president of the Claremont

Institute), Charles Haywood (a conspiratorial blogger and far-right Christian influencer; we will meet him again in chapter 12), K. T. McFarland (the former deputy national security advisor under Michael Flynn), Kevin Roberts (at the time the director of the Texas Public Policy Foundation; he would later ascend to the presidency of the Heritage Foundation), Jeff Giesea (a tech entrepreneur, friend of Peter Thiel, and former friend to the alt-right—at least according to Richard Spencer, who claimed that Giesea had donated $5,000 to his National Policy Institute in 2016),[13] and Gladden Pappin (aka "Plautus").

The 79 Days Report authors emphasized that the TIP "intentionally did not game legal strategies in any detail," whereas the authors themselves did. Ironically, they concluded that "when employed, the legal system will be up to the task of adjudicating disputes over election results."[14] In other respects, though, the 79 Days Report was much less sanguine. As Christian Vanderbrouk noted in his analysis of the document, the authors repeatedly imagined that the left would engage in violence after the election—all the better for the state to respond with impunity. "A barely concealed bloodlust runs through the report," wrote Vanderbrouk. "This isn't a serious wargame or a policy study so much as a bowdlerized retelling of *The Turner Diaries*."[15]

Over the course of the summer and early fall of 2020, the Claremont Institute published several pieces that anticipated possible electoral challenges, including a potential "Biden coup." The authors often used others' efforts—like the Transition Integrity Project and Claremont's joint effort with the Texas Public Policy Foundation—as the launching point for their own speculative work. A relatively temperate August 2020 essay, "Sleepwalking Into Succession" by Andrew Busch, a government professor at Claremont McKenna College, involved such a prepare-for-the-worst premise; it was the exception that proved the rule that there was something rotten in Claremont.[16]

A few weeks later, in early September, the *American Mind* site published an essay by Anton called "The Coming Coup?" with the subheading "Democrats Are Laying the Groundwork for Revolution Right in Front of Our Eyes."[17] In the second half, Anton suggests that Democrats would use Covid-inspired changes in state laws to steal the election.

Ever the Machiavellian, Anton gamed out what the Democratic conniv-ers were really up to ("it *must not look like a conspiracy,*" he observed). From this point on, he became increasingly unhinged, and in the lead-up to the election proper, it became clear that for some thinkers on the right there was no world in which a Democratic win could be legitimate, no world in which the Democrats could prevail without committing a violent coup. And the week after "The Coming Coup?" ran, the *Ameri-can Mind* editors dropped all pretense of good faith. On September 12, in an editorial titled "Stop the Coup," they declared the Biden coup a reality. "It's time to unmask the revolution," they asserted, and all through the article they treated the Biden coup as a fait accompli. The election was nearly two months away.[18]

When Election Day came on November 3, any supposition that the actual election results would and should matter fell away completely. On November 4—while several states were still counting votes, and three days before the press informally called the election for Joe Biden—*American Mind* published a new Anton piece, entitled "Game on for the Coup?" Anton admitted in this article that he wasn't sure what was really going on—"The thing could (but will never) be proved"—but he was confident enough to lay out a game plan that he called "Stop the Steal."[19] Against the Biden coup, Anton recommended that Trumpists organize court challenges, rallies, disputes about elec-tors, and a massive grassroots campaign in support of their candidate. At that point, he was rehearsing a plan from an article published earlier that day on the conspiratorial news site run by Darren Beattie, *Revolver News.*[20]

Lest anyone wonder whether Anton's views on the election were merely his own or reflected Claremont's institutional position, one day later, on November 5, key leaders at the institute—including its presi-dent, Ryan P. Williams; Arthur Milikh, the executive director of its Cen-ter for the American Way of Life in Washington, DC; Matthew J. Peter-son, the institute's vice president of education and founding editor of the *American Mind*; and James Poulos, a conservative essayist and the executive editor of the *American Mind*—published an editorial called "The Fight Is Now." It read as a plan and manifesto for the delegitimization campaign that we saw unfold on the American right through to January 6. It is replete with distortions and lies. Except for one sentence at the very beginning, the editorial took as plain fact a steal/coup on the part of Joe Biden—e.g., "Republicans must aggressively investigate and prosecute any and all wrongdoing in *the attempt to steal this election*"; and "the Republican base also understands both the stakes and *the attempt to steal the election that is now well underway*."[21]

The actual plan presented in "The Fight Is Now" was mostly a rehash of Anton's article from the day before, itself a rehash of Beattie's *Revolver News* piece. Williams, Milikh, Peterson, and Poulos recommended that the GOP send "swarms of lawyers" to "demand explanation and investigation of every vote in every disputed state NOW" since the "Democratic city machines" are "churning out votes for Biden." From there, they revealed a four-part plan to "Bring Out the People." The final part of that plan was cringeworthy in its chest-thumping bluster but also alarming in its militancy:

> Finally, all weak sisters on the right must be called out. In military doctrine, psychological operations only work on a populace that is already experiencing a defeat. They backfire when conducted against resilient and confident foes. The media and the left right now are trying to defeat and demoralize half the country under the guise of "democracy" and disingenuous cries of "just count the votes!" After the last six months, the last thirty years, the last damned century—conservatives and Republicans who lack steely resolve need to be called out and cast aside for those who will fight![22]

Everything these men were arguing for was completely upside down and backward. It flew in the face of the actual election results, which went the other way. The Claremont "Biden coup" narrative, as with "Stop the Steal," was rank sophistry and counterfeit.[23] Trump was the one trying to overturn a legitimate election, not Biden. Trump spent months laying the groundwork for a challenge to the legitimacy of the election should he lose, repeatedly predicting that the election would be "rigged." All the way through to January 6, he was engaged in an effort to overturn valid election results via false claims about election fraud. Had he succeeded, he would have invalidated the legitimate votes of over eighty-one million Americans, thereby profoundly damaging the democratic foundations of the country. It almost certainly would have brought mass instability and violence.

The Claremont Institute was there the whole time, playing along and stoking the lies.

———

Though their activities were the most reckless by far, the Claremonters were not the only ones on the New Right who got caught up in conspiratorial fervor in the wake of Biden's 2020 election victory. Both Patrick Deneen and Adrian Vermeule engaged in election denialism and/or conspiracism on Twitter in the election aftermath. In December 2020, for example, Deneen quote-tweeted the well-known conspiracist and former Claremont Institute fellow Jack Posobiec, who himself was quote-tweeting a Chinese academic making a cynical argument about the American electoral system. Deneen summarized his own view as follows: "Not infrequently, the view from outside gives you better insight into what is going on inside. The U.S. today is a unique form of liberal oligarchy that was disrupted by a momentary burst of democracy. The elite made sure to roll that back—amusingly, in the name of 'democracy.'"[24]

Adrian Vermeule went further than Deneen, and his postelection activities on Twitter resulted in calls for an official rebuke from Harvard.[25] In addition to many retweets suggesting that the election outcome was illegitimate, Vermeule at one point tweeted that "Lol the election isn't over until Team Joe fixes up your ballot for you." In another he wrote: "A lot of you are upset because you woodenly imagine an 'Election Day' with 'rules.' Instead you must come to think of the election as a process, a kind of improvisational dance that expresses our commitment to make sure everyone can vote when and as they feel like it." As the student letter-writers to Harvard explained, "Prof. Vermeule may try to play off his statements as a joke, but they amount to a pattern of promoting demonstrably false conspiracy theories."[26]

John Eastman's Plan for January 6

John Eastman went further than anyone else on the New Right in his efforts on Trump's behalf, and his involvement continued way beyond the election proper and its immediate aftermath. It began in September 2020, when Cleta Mitchell was assembling a team of lawyers to help Trump with his postelection legal action (Mitchell partook in similar efforts in 2024).[27] His involvement continued after Election Day and included efforts to establish "alternative slates" of electors in various places, which was a crucial piece of the plan he articulated in the infamous "coup memos."

Eastman's memos provided a road map for the postponement or overturning of the vote during the joint session of Congress on January 6, 2021. To comply with the plan, Vice President Pence would have had to agree that the states had acted wrongly, and possibly illegally, in their respective submissions of the slates of electors, such that the official slates were invalidated. The existence of alternative slates of electors was crucial to this gambit. To be at all persuasive, those slates would have needed some legitimacy. They never had any.

In December 2020, Eastman helped try to concoct alternative slates of electors in Georgia and Pennsylvania.[28] He also filed a brief on behalf of Donald Trump in Texas in an effort to invalidate the elections in several swing states that went to Joe Biden (the court quickly tossed the suit).[29] And then, on December 24, 2020, a Trump aide reportedly asked Eastman to provide Trump with a memo about the process by which Congress certifies electoral results on January 6 after each presidential election. He did so. Two distinct versions of the memo became public: a long one that involved "War Gaming the Alternatives," and a short one, which Eastman has called "a preliminary, incomplete draft," that takes one alternative and provides a more particularized plan.[30]

It is easy to get caught up in the arcane details of these memos. But the crucial thing to understand is that Eastman's plan relied on the idea that Democrats had broken the laws in conducting the election and that, as a result and response, legitimate alternative slates of electors had been formed. These premises were false. The idea had been rebuffed in lawsuits across the country.³¹ And while it is true that, in the seven states Eastman mentions, the Republicans who would have been Trump electors (had he won) got together in mock ceremonies to cast their electoral votes for Trump, these actions had no more legitimacy than if a group of strangers had met in a bar and claimed to be the true electors.

The most interesting legal question raised by the Eastman memos concerned the scope of Pence's power during the electoral vote in the case of a dispute. Eastman argued for a vast plenary role for the vice president in such a case. On January 6 Pence released a letter explaining why he was not persuaded. He said that Eastman's plan violated the design of the Constitution: "Vesting the Vice President with unilateral authority to decide presidential contests would be entirely antithetical to that design."³²

On January 4 Eastman met with Trump and Pence in the Oval Office. Reports of what he said and did at this time conflict, but if Eastman had reservations about what he had advised in the memos, it did not stop him from standing on a dais on January 6, crying fraud, and insisting that Pence had no choice but to act.³³ That day President Trump placed enormous pressure on Pence in his public statements. Some of his supporters certainly heard the message, chanting, "Hang Mike Pence! Hang Mike Pence!"

A person does not need a law degree or a PhD in political science to see that John Eastman's memos did not amount to ordinary, professional legal counsel. Both his memos took widespread fraud and illegality in the 2020 election as premises—claims that had no merit. Both memos supposed the existence of alternative slates of electors that did not exist.

An email exchange from that day between Greg Jacob, a top lawyer for Pence at the time, and John Eastman revealed the truth. Jacob explained to Eastman that his legal framework was "a results-oriented position that you would never support if attempted by the opposition, and essentially entirely made up." He added: "Thanks to your bullshit, we are now under siege." Eastman retorted: "The 'siege' is because YOU and your boss did not do what was necessary to allow this to be aired in a public way so the American people can see for themselves what happened." To this, Jacob replied:

The advice provided has, whether intended or not, functioned as a serpent in the ear of the President of the United States, the most powerful office in the entire world. And here we are. Respectfully, it was gravely, gravely irresponsible for you to entice the President with an academic theory that had no legal viability, and that you well know we would lose before any judge who heard and decided the case. And if the courts declined to hear it, I suppose it could only be decided in the streets. The knowing amplification of that theory through numerous surrogates, whipping large numbers of people into a frenzy over something with no chance of ever attaining legal force through actual process of law, has led us to where we are.[34]

One White House lawyer said that on January 7, 2021, he spoke with Eastman and told him, "I'm going to give you the best free legal advice you're ever getting in your life: Get a great f-ing criminal defense lawyer. You're going to need it."[35] Eastman knew he was in legal trouble. Four days later, he requested a pardon from Trump.[36]

Over the course of subsequent years, a chorus of lawyerly opprobrium against Eastman took shape.[37] One judge would call the pressure campaign against Pence "a coup in search of a legal theory . . . the illegality of the plan was obvious." Attorney General Bill Barr told the House January 6th Committee that Trump's claims about widespread voter fraud were "bullshit."[38] During the committee hearings, Judge Luttig called the plan "the product of the most reckless, insidious, and calamitous failures in both legal and political judgment in American history."[39] After the attack of January 6, Eastman, under pressure, resigned from his faculty position at Chapman University. During the summer of 2023 he was indicted by a Fulton County, Georgia, grand jury, for participating in efforts to overturn the election results there. He was also thought to be one of the six coconspirators discussed in the August 1, 2023, indictment of Trump that came from the district court in Washington, DC.[40] Eastman was recommended for disbarment in California in March 2024.[41]

None of these judgments or accusations would deter him, as he kept peddling election lies in a series of glossy interviews produced in 2023 by the Claremont Institute's Thomas Klingenstein.[42] These interviews were notable because of the lies they contained, and because they were clearly a fundraising mechanism to help with Eastman's growing legal fees.

Extremists and Apologists

I'm persuaded that John was wrong in the advice he gave Trump. . . .
Whether his actions will hurt us [at the Claremont Institute] or not,
I'm not sure. It's awkward and it raises some questions.[43]

—CHARLES R. KESLER

Thomas Klingenstein was not the only one who stood by Eastman. During the January 6 attack, Darren Beattie, the Duke PhD and founder of *Revolver News*, sent out a series of vile tweets that reveled in what was going on at the Capitol. These tweets each named a Black public figure, including Republican senator Tim Scott, then-president of the Heritage Foundation Kay Cole James, and the best-selling antiracist author Ibram X. Kendi. Beattie wrote that they must "learn their place" and "take a knee to MAGA."[44]

Michael Anton also continued to hype the election fraud narrative in the pages of the *Claremont Review of Books*.[45] The New Lost Cause of an ongoing election crisis was not so different from the original Flight 93 crisis. Once you begin understanding our national politics as a matter of emergencies, corruption, and lies reparable only by figures of exceptional heroism, there is no returning to a politics of the everyday, of democratic choice and representation, and of disagreement, contestation, and compromise. As Jonathan Chait observed in February 2021, "the future of conservatism is Flight 93 Elections forever."[46]

Glenn Ellmers, another Claremont senior fellow (and visiting research scholar at Hillsdale College), fell into this dystopian trap, too. In March 2021 he wrote a bizarre article for *American Mind* called "'Conservatism' is No Longer Enough," offering a crystallization of the relentless divisiveness and delusional self-regard that fueled Eastman's actions. The essay—topped by a stock-art photo of a boxer wrapping his hands for a fight—began by characterizing the enemy, which, it turns out, consisted of most of the country: "Most people living in the United

States today—certainly more than half—are not Americans in any meaningful sense of the term." The people he had in mind were those who voted for Joe Biden ("the senile figurehead of a party that stands for mob violence, ruthless censorship, and racial grievances, not to mention bureaucratic despotism"). The real and "authentic" Americans were, by and large, the seventy-four million people who voted for Trump—"the vast numbers of heartland voters who still call themselves Americans." As John Ganz wrote at the time, "Its themes of pervading national corruption and decadence, and the need for a counter-revolution and a national rebirth put this text firmly in the radical reactionary or fascist ballpark."[47]

Another person who was all-in with Eastman was one of the original founders of the Claremont Institute, Christopher Flannery. In August 2022 Flannery wrote a piece for Anton's *American Greatness* under the headline, "John Eastman Is an American Hero: He Put His Life on the Line to Stop an Unconstitutional Election."[48]

The dramatic turn to militancy at the Claremont Institute that began with Anton's Flight 93 essay and culminated in Eastman's corrupt legal advice to Trump was not limited to financiers like Klingenstein, or staff like Williams, or extremists like Beattie, Anton, Ellmers, and Flannery. It also involved people like Roger Kimball, the well-known conservative editor. In September 2021 Kimball argued in the pages of Hillsdale College's journal *Imprimis* that, "As the years go by, historians, if the censors allow them access to the documents and give them leave to publish their findings, may well count the 2016 presidential election as the last fair and open democratic election in U.S. history."[49]

The turn also involved another prominent scholar at the Claremont Institute, Charles R. Kesler, who remained defensive of John Eastman. After January 6 Kesler became the institute's hedger-and-apologist-in-chief. A student of Harvey Mansfield, he graduated with a PhD in government from Harvard in 1985. He later became the Dengler-Dykema Distinguished Professor of Government at Claremont McKenna College. Kesler is also a senior fellow of the Claremont Institute and the founding editor of the *Claremont Review of Books*. On his faculty profile, he lists American constitutionalism and constitutional law among his areas of expertise.[50] Shep Melnick, a professor at Boston College, wrote in 2021 that "Kesler is, without a doubt, the brains of the outfit."[51] When Eastman resigned from Chapman University in early 2021, he defended himself in the *American Mind*, a Claremont web magazine. In *Claremont Review of Books*, Kesler, who perhaps more than anyone else on the New Right channels the genteel spirit of Buckley, defended him in turn.[52]

Kesler had Eastman's back—but intelligently, with sophistication and verve. When Kesler published his initial defense of Eastman, he was bullish but careful. He expressed disapproval of the violence of January 6, critiqued the Trump administration for being unprepared for what had unfolded, and evinced mild skepticism about Eastman's theory of vice-presidential powers. But as a general matter, Kesler's essay was an exercise in apologetics for Trump, and so, indirectly, for Eastman. Memorably, Kesler kept the door wide open to the possibility that Eastman and Trump's claims of a stolen election were justified, even though no evidence had been found at the time (despite plenty of looking, and sixty-plus lawsuits lost).[53] He went so far as to imply that empirical claims can never truly be refuted: "Truth is, of course, that claims are 'baseless' only until such time as a base of evidence appears for them."

Kesler went on at length, playing up counterfactuals, provisionally granting Trump and Eastman's premises to explore the esoteric implications of their arguments, and so forth—a sophisticate's version of Bannonesque "flooding the zone with shit"[54]—but he eventually conceded that "there is persuasive evidence of a more normal sort" that Trump simply lost the election. He also quietly conceded the only thing that has ever really mattered: "In any event, none of the state legislatures in question had actually filed a formal request to withdraw and reexamine their state's electoral votes." In other words, the whole thing—the entire justificatory schema that played an obvious role in the violence that unfolded on January 6—was bogus from the start.

The closest that the Claremont organization came to criticizing Eastman was through the publication of a long exchange between him and a conservative critic, Joseph M. Bessette, in the fall 2021 issue of the

CRB. Bessette's counter to Eastman was powerful.[55] But the *CRB* endeavor lent Eastman unwarranted credibility by treating his position as merely controversial rather than simply unhinged.

In early 2022 Kesler appeared on Steve Hayward's *Power Line* podcast to address "The Claremont Question." By that point, revelations about Eastman had put the Claremont Institute in the national spotlight. Kesler's contribution to the podcast consisted primarily of his self-satisfaction over his magazine's handling of the Eastman issue: He was proud of having published a critique of Eastman in the *CRB*. In Kesler's view, using the magazine to present both sides constituted "service to the community," since the issues involved were "very complicated."[56]

A few months later, in the summer of 2022, after the Eastman-related hearings by the January 6th Committee, Kesler was singing a slightly modulated tune. In remarks made to *The Washington Post* and *The New York Times*, he admitted that he had been persuaded that Eastman was wrong, that he has "always thought that Trump lost" the 2020 election, and that it was "awkward and it raises some questions" for the institute.[57] Even in this context, however, Kesler obscured the connection between Eastman and Trump's ideas about election fraud, on the one hand, and the furor that drove January 6 rioters into the Capitol, on the other. In the interviews, Kesler spoke as though Eastman's theoretical ideas, and his own indulgence of those ideas, were entirely separable from what transpired on January 6.

Kesler's evasiveness seemed to serve him rather well. He did as much as he could early on to preserve Trump's reputation and protect John Eastman while also offering understated concessions to truth: The evidence of fraud didn't exist; Eastman's theory had no sound basis in electoral reality; Trump had lost the election. These admissions he framed as matters of opinion and relatively inconsequential detail. The overall effect was that he never had to grapple publicly with the implications of these truths and appeared accountable to no one on either side.

In the aftermath of the 2020 election and January 6, the Claremont Institute became an important nexus for election conspiracies and denialism, as well as a haven for figures and arguments from the hard (fascist) right, like Glenn Ellmers and Raw Egg Nationalist (whom we will encounter again in chapter 11).[58] Kesler treated all this as an amiable dispute among friends, rather than a matter of basic intellectual and moral integrity with considerable effects on the future of American democracy and constitutionalism. Some ideas, I guess, are consequence-free.

The Claremont Way

Kesler's motives and reasoning are surely mixed, but it isn't hard to guess why he played a long, coy minimization game. The basic, straightforward explanation—and one that is serviceable for all the thinkers I discuss in this book—is that (1) it has been enormously advantageous, in some respects, for Kesler to stand behind Trump; and (2) he believes in it. Kesler expressed disagreement with John Eastman about the specific question of 2020 election fraud, but in more than a few ways, he is ideologically simpatico with New Right extremism.

The parallels between the Kesler worldview and that of Anton and other Claremonters were evident in his book *Crisis of the Two Constitutions: The Rise, Decline, and Recovery of American Greatness*.

The book was released very shortly after January 6, in February 2021, which was bad timing for Kesler, for it is not difficult to see how his thinking could fuel political zeal. The book conveys a Manichean and abstract conception of history (and of constitutionalism) that evades historical realities and challenges. It demands rigid adherence to one narrow conception of constitutionalism and suggests that anything less is grounds for revolt.

Kesler's title referenced Harry Jaffa's *Crisis of the House Divided*, which alluded to Lincoln's House Divided speech from 1858—which is to say that Kesler's title alone involved him in a hyperbolic, dystopian analogy between today's partisan struggles and the shattering conflict over slavery.[59] His argument in *Crisis of the Two Constitutions* was that there are two main ways of understanding constitutionalism in America: the Founders' Constitution (the good one), and the Progressive Constitution (catastrophic). Kesler argued that the latter had all but replaced the original, which meant that America was close to wrecked. His vitriol for contemporary liberalism was in places on par with that of Anton and the shock-jock right. The book supported the idea of a "new founding" and "counterrevolution" on the part of American conservatives. He began his final chapter, called "Thinking About Trump," by coyly mocking those who saw something "dangerous" in Michael Anton's Flight 93 rhetoric. Kesler defended Anton's work as merely "galvanizing" and metaphorical; after all, he wrote, "almost any spirited political appeal involves an element of exaggeration for effect."[60]

These were strange words to stand by after January 6. As Shep Melnick put it in his review of Kesler's book, "The arguments of Kesler's book can easily be read as a justification for storming the corrupted seat of power in hopes of restoring American greatness."[61] Rich Lowry, editor of the *National Review*, also saw the connections.[62] In a response to Melnick, Kesler denied that his thought provided cover for extremist action.[63] If that was his genuine view, then it does raise questions about why he continued to be so involved with the Claremont Institute.

Whatever Charles Kesler's personal aversion to political violence, lying conspiracism, and extremism might be, the Claremont Institute has certainly benefited from its populist pivot. Its profile rose sharply, in some quarters, since its turn to Trumpism, and its donor base expanded.[64] And to speak out against the institute would doubtless have been costly for Kesler. It would have put him in flagrant contradiction with the people in charge and cost him friendships, as well as his standing on the New Right. Further, criticizing Eastman's anticonstitutional extremism would have meant admitting complicity in something extreme and dishonest and destructive—a tough psychological proposition for anyone, especially someone purportedly committed to the cultivation of virtue and high statesmanship. Much easier to embrace—tentatively—the Big Lie and New Lost Cause.

———

When George Floyd was murdered in 2020, leading to mass protests and riots, Charles Kesler wrote an opinion piece in the *New York Post* with the headline "Call Them the 1619 Riots." The headline referenced the 1619 Project, *The New York Times*' special issue magazine, published in 2019, which sought to center slavery and racism in the telling of American history. With this op-ed, Kesler implied that there was a direct Ideas First causal connection between the 1619 Project and the violence that broke out in connection to the George Floyd protests. (The Claremont Institute had made similar claims in its leadership "salvos" in the summer of 2020.)[65] As we have seen, Kesler was not so eager to indict himself, or Anton, or Eastman, for any part in what happened on January 6, 2021—even though their involvement was far more immediate than anything that contributors to the 1619 Project did in relation to the George Floyd protests.

When Kesler published his opinion piece, the *Post* was under the editorial guidance of Sohrab Ahmari.[66] Soon a clear pattern emerged in which the people who were the most adamant about the extremism of the 2020 summer were also the most dismissive of the January 6 attacks.[67] Kimball later wrote a nasty editorial about George Floyd—calling him "St. George Floyd" and parroting a Tucker Carlson conspiracy that the "the whole George Floyd story was a lie."[68] Kimball argued, among other things, that "the Black Lives Matter hooligans . . . released a mesmerizing, racially fortified toxin into the atmosphere that addled the minds and hearts of all the beautiful people who run the country and from which we have yet to recover fully."[69] When it came to January 6, 2021, he was not concerned about the New Right's mesmerizing toxins, released in pieces like "The Coming Coup?," "Stop the Coup," "Game on for the Coup," and "The Fight Is Now." His aforementioned article for Hillsdale College's *Imprimis* maximally downplayed the violence of that day and ran under the headline "The January 6 Insurrection Hoax."

During the summer of 2020, in addition to Kesler's op-ed, Ahmari published his own piece titled "Worse than War: My Night Besieged by Looters and Thugs in NYC."[70] Then, on the anniversary of January 6 in 2022, he wrote an opinion essay for *The New York Times* with the heading, "Jan. 6 Looks Different Through the Lens of 'American Carnage,'" in which he called the event the "cornpone intifada" and argued that it was the result of populist economic disappointment with Trump.[71] Patrick Deneen and Gladden Pappin each tweeted out Ahmari's article. Deneen called it "a superb essay . . . challenging the lazy understanding of 1/6. Trump wasn't radical enough, and the events of a year ago were a manifestation of his failure to advance a genuinely populist revolution." It would not be the last time Deneen invoked the language of revolution, though in subsequent years his rhetoric became even more extreme. Pappin called Ahmari's essay "essential reading."[72]

I tend to agree with Postliberals like Ahmari, Deneen, and Pappin—as well as with many liberals and progressives—that America is long overdue for serious economic innovation and reform, and I have appreciated some of their ideas about how to make it happen. That said, it was tendentious to see January 6 as the result of worker dissatisfaction rather than the outcome of an elite-manufactured "stolen election" story hyped enthusiastically by the sitting president, and levied ferociously across right-wing media, including by many New Right intellectuals, as well as by the Christian right (a matter I explore in chapter 12).

To be clear, there was never a parallel story of liberals and leftists hyping up a "Big Lie" to get people into the streets after George Floyd's murder; they went out—I went out—to protest a gross injustice. Whether you agree with the protestors or not, they were not trying to overturn a presidential election or risking a constitutional crisis based on a fraudulent lie.

The New Right, though, would tell you a different story—about the 1619 Project, the meaning of American history, the "lies" of so-called wokeness, and the motivations behind January 6, 2021. In the next chapter I explore the New Right's thinking—and activism—surrounding "Patriotic Education" in the lead-up to and immediate aftermath of January 6, as a way into some of these other themes. This involves digging deeper into the 1619 Project and the New Right's reaction to it. It also brings another right-wing institution that flourished under Trump—Hillsdale College—into our story and introduces two characters who played a growing role in the post–January 6 New Right landscape as it concerns education: Christopher Rufo and Larry P. Arnn.

8

"Patriotic Education"

Fondly do we hope—fervently do we pray—that this mighty scourge
of war may speedily pass away. Yet, if God wills that it continue until
all the wealth piled by the bondsman's two hundred and fifty years
of unrequited toil shall be sunk and until every drop of blood drawn
with the lash shall be paid by another drawn with the sword as was
said three thousand years ago so still it must be said "the judgments
of the Lord are true and righteous altogether."

—ABRAHAM LINCOLN,
SECOND INAUGURAL ADDRESS, MARCH 4, 1865

ON SEPTEMBER 1, 2020, Christopher Rufo made an appearance on Fox
News' *Tucker Carlson Tonight*. In the three-minute segment, Rufo made
a few bold claims. He began: "It's absolutely astonishing how critical
race theory has pervaded every institution in the federal government.
And what I've discovered is that critical race theory has become, in essence, the default ideology of the federal bureaucracy, and is now being
weaponized against the American people."[1]

Rufo provided some evidence for his claims: The Treasury Department had hired a diversity trainer named Howard Ross to conduct
a seminar on antiracism and critical race theory; the FBI was holding
"weekly seminars on intersectionality" (Rufo's evidence for this was
an announcement that they were holding voluntary meetings on

intersectionality in August 2020); and Sandia National Laboratories (a privately run but nationally owned research lab that, according to Rufo, "designs America's nuclear weapons") had conducted diversity and inclusion training seminars for its staff.[2] Rufo concluded with an appeal to President Trump:

> The president at the White House, it's within their authority and power to immediately issue an executive order abolishing critical race theory trainings from the federal government. And I call on the President to immediately issue this executive order and stamp out this destructive, divisive, pseudo-scientific ideology at its root. And I think . . . that he's denounced this kind of Black Lives Matter and Neo-Marxist rhetoric in places like Portland and Seattle, but it's time to take action and destroy it within his own administration.

Rufo's segment struck a nerve. The next day, according to subsequent reporting, he received a phone call from Mark Meadows, who was President Trump's chief of staff. "He saw your segment on 'Tucker' last night," Meadows said, "and he's instructed me to take action."[3] The secretary of education at the time was Betsy DeVos. In a subsequent memoir, DeVos revealed that during that summer of 2020—which was already fraught because of Covid-19 and the George Floyd protests—Trump had been thinking a lot about *The New York Times Magazine*'s 1619 Project. She recounts how he called her one weekend that summer to "rant" about the project and floated the idea of banning it from classrooms. DeVos resisted: "I had to remind him that the United States does not have a national curriculum, and for good reason."[4] When Rufo appeared on Carlson's show on September 1, he tapped into one of Trump's, and the New Right's, main fixations.

At the time, Rufo was not well-known, though he had made his way around a variety of conservative intellectual institutions, like the Discovery Institute, the Heritage Foundation, and the Manhattan Institute.[5] Graduating with a degree from Georgetown University's School of Foreign Service in 2006, Rufo had previously worked as a documentary filmmaker, and in 2017 he participated in one of the Claremont Institute's summer institutes as a Lincoln Fellow. Shortly after his call with

Mark Meadows, Rufo flew out to Washington to help draft an executive order along the lines of what he had proposed on TV.[6] And on September 22, 2020, President Trump issued an "Executive Order Combating Race and Sex Stereotyping." It banned any teaching or training in "divisive concepts" within the federal government and among its contractors.[7] "Divisive concepts" were defined broadly to include not only claims about the superiority or inferiority of a given identity-based group, but also any other form of "race or sex stereotyping," including "any claim that, consciously or unconsciously," members of some race or sex are inherently racist or sexist or oppressive of others.

The problem with the order was not that it forbade the government or related entities from teaching certain kinds of racially essentialist concepts as dogma. Contra Rufo's claims, there was scarce evidence that that was happening.[8] Rufo consistently distorted and exaggerated what was being discussed and taught.[9] So the order, in effect, forbade something that was not happening. In another sense, though, it was a big deal because of potential chilling effects. Its vague, all-encompassing language arguably made it harder to engage in honest, good-faith discussions about how race and sex matter historically and continue to impact Americans, since it is pretty much impossible to talk about contemporary or historical racism or sexism without wading into "divisive" territory. The new executive order came with steep penalties, as well as a tip hotline for noncompliance.[10] Thus the New Right launched a fresh attack on free speech in the United States.

The New Right surely believed that voluntary antiracism seminars and diversity trainings had chilling effects of their own. And this belief, in my view, was not entirely unfounded.[11] But chilling effects are something very different from coercive oppression and the force of the law (even if progressives' language of safe spaces and "silence is violence" suggested otherwise). And the New Right's solution—using the law as a cudgel to micromanage and surveil federal workplaces—was paranoid, overweening, and vastly worse.

With the signing of Executive Order 13950, Rufo proved his effectiveness within the New Right ecosystem—and reaffirmed the ongoing salience of right-wing culture wars stemming from the problems of race and racism in the United States. Rufo was a relative newcomer to this scene, but together with others, like Larry Arnn and folks at the Claremont Institute, he presided over a forward push of culture-warrior activism, especially in the realm of education, that would occupy the American right in the chaotic months and years following January 6, 2021.

This chapter is about the first major volley in that battle: the creation of President Trump's 1776 Commission Report, which was the culminating—and disappointing—result of his first-term efforts at "patriotic" educational reform in the United States. In what follows, I introduce Larry Arnn, who oversaw the commission, and consider the origins and aims of the report, which involves a brief discussion of the 1619 Project. I also dig deeper into the motives behind the New Right's response to that project, both because some of those same motives drove the push for "Patriotic Education" and because, in the abstract at least, I agree with some of their concerns. If I squint a little, I do not have trouble understanding why the New Right says we are at a point of civilizational crisis as concerns education in this country. Some of the problems are real. That said, the final report of President Trump's commission was an absurd response to the real issues at hand.

The 1619 Project and New Right Reaction

Launched in the summer of 2019, the 1619 Project was a special edition of *The New York Times Magazine* commemorating the first known arrival of enslaved Africans at Point Comfort, Virginia. It was a piece of collaborative journalism conceived by the journalist Nikole Hannah-Jones that was clearly aimed at shaking up the national discourse on race against a presumed background of ongoing public ignorance and historical whitewashing. The authors were journalists and scholars, and they covered a wide variety of themes—from electoral politics and medicine to music, mass incarceration, and economics.[12] The original project contained powerful stories and research. It also included controversial passages and, in my view, some misleading assertions. It led to pushback among some mainstream liberals and centrists, including several respected historians, followed by several rounds of robust (but sometimes charged and accusatory) public debates. The project's organizers also produced curricular material with the Pulitzer Center to accompany the project, and Hannah-Jones published a book-length elaboration of the original in 2021. To be clear, there was never any national 1619 Project curriculum; it was always a curricular supplement.[13]

The 1619 Project was met with downright fury and hysteria on the right.[14] It played a dramatic and outsized role in the national discourse, as well as in the right-wing imagination, in the final years of the first Trump administration.

Some of the loudest critics of the project came from a familiar chorus. "The ambitious goal of the project," wrote leaders at the Claremont Institute, "is nothing less than the alienation of Americans from their country's true philosophical and political founding in 1776—and its replacement with a new founding narrative about the struggle of groups to secure their rights against American hypocrisy, cruelty, and indifference."[15] Similarly, the editorial board of the right-wing literary journal *The New Criterion*, edited by Roger Kimball, argued that one purpose of the 1619 Project was to justify "the endless whining of black radicals." They said that the project's "ultimate aim" was "to deliver another blow in the campaign to besmirch and diminish the political and moral achievement that is the United States of America. It is as despicable as it is mendacious."[16]

In a critique for *City Journal*, Allen Guelzo argued that the project authors showed insufficient gratitude for the fact that Black people have, in such a meager time, advanced to such positions of high authority in the United States. "It is the bitterest of ironies," Guelzo wrote, "that the 1619 Project dispenses this malediction from the chair of ultimate cultural privilege in America, because in no human society has an enslaved people suddenly found itself vaulted into positions of such privilege, and with the consent—even the approbation—of those who were once the enslavers."[17] Guelzo went on to argue that "the 156 years since emancipation are less than a second on human history's long clock, so that such a transformation is more in the nature of a miracle to be celebrated than a failure to be deplored for any seeming slowness." He asserted that "it is a miracle Frederick Douglass celebrated," a gross distortion of

Douglass's views (which are explained at length in a speech about Lincoln and emancipation that he delivered on April 14, 1876).[18]

———

What was it about the 1619 Project that upset the New Right so deeply and made them respond so irrationally? Was it all just pent-up racism and white supremacy? I am sympathetic to the idea that a good deal of it was. For all its inroads with minority groups, the Republican Party is still overwhelmingly white, and I am persuaded that racial dynamics are a significant factor in these discussions and reactions, perhaps an overwhelming one. One thing that I found disturbing about events during this period was the right's inability to see and comprehend the problem of police violence and immunity, and to consider the racial dynamics at play here.

But I also want to consider these issues from a different angle. It seems clear that for the New Right intellectuals (and many other conservatives, too), the 1619 Project was a lightning rod because it came to represent, for them, everything that is wrong with higher education—and perhaps even all mainstream public education—in the United States. And there is a lot wrong with education in the United States. Indeed, when I try to understand why the 1619 Project touched such a nerve—apart from race—I am brought back to questions that I care about, and concerns about education and higher education that I share. The New Right framed the problems in terms of patriotism and love lost for America's noble past, but there are other related concerns lurking here.

It is difficult to get a synoptic view of American education, which, in addition to being constituted by both public and private programs, includes a good deal of regional complexity. By my lights, the single worst problem with K–12 education is that public schools are funded in large part by local property taxes, which has created an unjust system that sustains inequality.[19] But I know the world of higher education much better. I worked and taught at four excellent institutions between 2010 and 2018—UT Austin, Rhodes College in Memphis, Georgetown University, and American University (AU)—and I generally think that right-wing attacks on higher education are badly misplaced. But that does not mean that there are not big problems on university campuses—there clearly are.

One moment stands out in my mind as symbolic of the complexity of the problem. While I was at AU, I worked with a committee of faculty in the School of International Service concerned with undergraduate affairs. These were some of the most thoughtful people I have ever worked with, and they cared enormously about undergraduate education. It must have been sometime in 2017, because Trump had recently won the election. One day in our meeting we were talking about a curricular problem having to do with core requirements in the university. The details do not matter, but the suggestion was that a required course in American politics be dropped. Students could still take it, but it would no longer be a requirement for the BA degree in international studies. For my colleagues, who cared most about international affairs, this was not a big deal. Perhaps they believed that everyone got the basics of American politics in high school. But I remember thinking at the time: Have you all lost your minds? This country has just elected a demagogue, civic morale seems to be at an all-time low, and you want to get rid of *which* course?

The other thing I remember thinking was: Laura, do you really want to fight this battle? Because the truth was that I had almost zero influence and no real job security. I was part of the so-called academic precariat, subject to the so-called adjunctification that had shaped higher education for decades. I was lucky to have an academic job at all, but I was still pretty low in the system, and even though I was friends with these colleagues, I imagined that to a few of them I would sound like a reactionary weirdo. I thought to myself: Is it really worth it? In the end I registered my concerns. I said that I objected, that I thought the change sounded short-sighted and misguided. I may have said something to the effect of "there has to be room in this country—even in a school of international affairs!—for some kind of education in American politics!" They were unpersuaded, and the change went into effect.

This was such a small thing, but the problems on American campuses are not small. They are big. And there is no single culprit: We are talking about complicated, internecine dynamics, whether it be in state systems, at small liberal arts colleges, or in the Ivy League. They have to do with academic specialization, and an obsession with research, publication, and "quantification" so severe that it stymies free-thinking. They have to do with sensationalized and nationalized media and a failure to report on or acknowledge what ordinarily goes on college campuses—especially those outside the Ivy League. They have to do with the political gulf between the professoriate and the students who come to learn from them, especially in the liberal arts.[20] They also have to do with small-minded right-wing attacks on higher education that go back decades, as well as with massive (and related) funding failures on the part of state legislatures, especially in red states.[21]

Perhaps above all, from my perspective, the problems are associated with a lack of vision and understanding when it comes to the purposes of higher education—on the part of university presidents and administrators, university boards, and sometimes even faculty themselves. Much too often, university leaders do not seem to know how to articulate—and so to protect—what it is universities seek to do (and in many, if not most, instances are already doing!). This is especially true, again, when it comes to liberal education and the humanities—the disciplines where people get to ask big questions, learn concretely about their own past, think deeply about what it means to be human, and expand their souls. When politicians and university presidents talk about the meaning of higher education in strictly utilitarian terms, or speak of students as clients, customers, and stakeholders, they are missing the things that matter most. And it means that they fail to protect what matters. Enrollments shift, disciplines die, and academic job markets collapse.[22]

The New Right has its own list of complaints against higher education, and when the 1619 Project came along they used it as a vehicle for their grievances, which were not that different from what Allan Bloom disliked in the 1980s. In brief, the New Right tends to skip the socioeconomic arguments I have just described and go right for the Ideas First jugular, which has to do with concepts like identity, critique, and deconstruction.

If I were to ventriloquize the New Right's assessment of contemporary higher education, it would go something like this:

Contemporary education is based on simplistic and ahistorical claims (about, for example, "power," "neoliberalism," or binaries of oppressors and oppressed) that are promoted by people who—as a professional class—tend to be snobbish, aloof, and full of disdain for ordinary people. It is borderline antiphilosophical: consumed by vapid methodological approaches, and/or focused on divisive identity groupings grounded in negative grievance rather than positive affirmation or belief.[23] It is happy to debunk the past but disrespects cherished traditions and refuses to celebrate or be inspired. And because it is so overly critical, this kind of education is also inadequate to the sustenance of human souls. It is an approach that shows deference to concepts like critique, "the hermeneutics of suspicion," complexity, skepticism, subjectivity, and specialization but has nothing properly constructive to say. You can't build or preserve a life, a community, or a country on those kinds of ideas. As Deneen might say, it is no way to discipline the virtues and teach real liberty.

To put this in more Straussian (or Platonic, or Aristophanic) language: There are reasons why Socrates was seen as a destabilizing force in ancient Athens; too much critical thinking threatens to corrupt the youth and destroy the city.

Now, all these hypothetical critics forget to ask: The sustenance of whose souls? What is critical and destructive to one person or community might be positively restorative to another. I will come back to that.

But I also want to note that it is not just conservatives and Straussians who make these kinds of arguments. We find parallel concerns articulated—more carefully and quietly, and in full recognition of how their words will be perceived as reactionary—by mainstream sources in the academy. Rita Felski, a professor of English at the University of Virginia, published a book in 2015 called *The Limits of Critique* that delineated some of the issues that are relevant here. Felski worried about what she calls the "relentless grip" of an "antinormative normativity," or "skepticism as dogma." She observed: "There is a growing sense that our intellectual life is out of kilter, that scholars in the humanities are far more fluent in nay-saying than in yay-saying, and that eternal vigilance,

unchecked by alternatives, can easily lapse into the complacent ca-
dences of autopilot argument." As she assessed it, critical approaches
were crowding out other legitimate forms of intellectual life; she likened the problem to invasive kudzu. In her conclusion, she argued that
"a persuasive defense of the humanities is hindered rather than helped
by an ethos of critique that encourages scholars to pride themselves
on their vanguard role and to equate serious thought with a reflex
negativity."[24]

More recently, Roosevelt Montás of Columbia University has offered
a powerful defense of liberal education in classical and Socratic terms
(and along the lines of what Allan Bloom called "the Great Books cult").
In his book *Rescuing Socrates: How the Great Books Changed My Life and
Why They Matter for a New Generation* (2021), Montás writes: "Liberal
education concerns the human yearning to go beyond questions of survival to questions of existence." He cites Aristotle, who described this
kind of education as one "given not because it is useful or necessary but
because it is noble and suitable for a free person." And he writes movingly of Socrates, whose profound and earnest questions about what it
means to live well "are the lifeblood of the humanist profession." The
humanities, Montás writes, are "bound to be feeble and anemic, inau-
thentic and ham-fisted, unless they take these questions seriously and
place them at the center of their practice." Speaking from personal experience, he defends the democratizing potential of Great Books
programs.[25]

The work of Felski and Montás is scholarly, reasonable, and self-
critical. The New Right took an altogether different approach, and
they used their old-fashioned "classical" language to pretend that no
one else cares about the good. Frustrated with the critical excesses of
the reigning intellectual class, and filled with fervor, they saw themselves more as culture warriors and spiritual saviors—or perhaps like
Nietzsche's monumental historians, pushing back against a terrible
critical unravelling.[26] The alternative they sought for America's would-
be patriots would teach confidence, moralism, simplicity, objectivity,
and affirmation against the status quo of critique. In other words, they
would offer indoctrination. They were out to save the country and

preserve Western Civilization. As you will hear so often on the New Right, it was time to look again to the Good, the True, and the Beautiful.[27]

Larry Arnn and Hillsdale College

On Constitution Day, September 17, 2020—close to the time that he wrote the Rufo-inspired executive order—President Trump announced the creation of the 1776 Commission. He did so at the White House Conference on American History at the National Archives, which was presided over by Larry P. Arnn.[28] We first met Arnn in chapter 1 because he was a student of Harry Jaffa's and one of the original founders of the Claremont Institute, in 1979.

Arnn was born in Pocahontas, Arkansas, and attended Arkansas State University as an undergraduate, graduating in 1974. He then earned an MA degree in government from Claremont Graduate School in 1976, spent some time studying at the London School of Economics and Oxford (where he worked as a researcher for Martin Gilbert, Winston Churchill's biographer), married in 1979, and returned to California shortly thereafter. In 1985 he earned his PhD in government, again from Claremont Graduate School—and several years after having founded the Claremont Institute. His dissertation was completed under the supervision of Jaffa and titled "Churchill as Minister of Munitions: A Study of Domestic Decision-making in War Time." Arnn served as the president of the institute from 1985 to 2000. In his early years as president, he was one of the three main initiators and authors of the California Civil Rights Initiative, or California Proposition 209, which passed in November 1996. This was the law that effectively ended affirmative action in California public institutions. In 2000 Arnn was appointed the twelfth president of Hillsdale College, in Hillsdale, Michigan. He was a natural choice to lead Trump's 1776 Commission. Patriotic conservative education had been Hillsdale's brand for many years under his leadership.[29]

At the White House Conference on American History, Arnn was joined onstage by the historian Wilfred (Bill) McClay, then a professor at the University of Oklahoma but soon to be the Victor Davis Hanson Professor of History at Hillsdale College; and Allen Guelzo, a senior research scholar at the James Madison Program in American Ideals and Institutions at Princeton University.[30] Several other writers and activists were there, as well as Ben Carson, who at the time was Trump's Department of Housing and Urban Development secretary.

Two of the panelists—Arnn and Peter Wood, president of the National Association of Scholars (a conservative advocacy group)—spoke at length about the George Floyd protests and riots that previous summer. Arnn traced them back to the thinking of Howard Zinn, a left-wing historian who has been a punching bag for conservatives since his popularizing *People's History of the United States* was published in 1980. Wood asserted that the riots were "staged events managed by well-trained experts," and that the scripts for these events were campus activists, including some faculty and students "who have spent years immersed in anti-liberal ideology, identity, indignation and the study of Maoist tactics."

Trump announced the 1776 Commission after the panel discussion, in terms that might as well have come straight out of the Claremont Institute's *American Mind.* "Our mission is to defend the legacy of America's founding, the virtue of America's heroes, and the nobility of the American character," Trump began. "We must clear away the twisted web of lies in our schools and classrooms and teach our children the magnificent truth about our country." Later, he named names: "Critical race theory, the 1619 Project, and the crusade against American history is toxic propaganda, ideological poison that, if not removed, will dissolve the civic bonds that tie us together. It will destroy our country." And he repeated Arnn and Wood's claim about the origins of the recent racial justice movement: "As many of you testified today, the left-wing rioting and mayhem are the direct result of decades of left-wing indoctrination in our schools." The 1776 Commission was created to push back against the alleged indoctrination. It aimed to protect "America's Founding Ideals by Promoting Patriotic Education."

Trump issued the executive order establishing the commission on November 2, 2020, the day before the election. Later that month, the

White House tapped Matthew Spalding to serve as executive director of the commission.[31] A professor at Hillsdale College, Spalding was also vice president of operations for Hillsdale's Washington, DC, campus and dean of its graduate program in government in DC. (He had been Charles Kesler's student at the Claremont Graduate University, where he wrote a dissertation on Washington's Farewell Address; Jaffa was on his committee, too.)[32] According to subsequent reporting, Trump's aides had been in talks with Spalding about educational matters for some time prior to the request, and it was Spalding who solicited other commissioners—including Arnn—and wrote much of the report.[33] When Trump formally established the commission, he seemed to be channeling Jaffa: "We will state the truth in full, without apology: We declare that the United States of America is the most just and exceptional Nation ever to exist on Earth."[34] It was Hillsdale's moment to shine, and the Claremonters had written the script.

———

Hillsdale College was founded in 1844 by a group of Free Will Baptists. From the outset, though, it was a nondenominational college, and it has a history of free-thinking and independence. Hillsdale was the first college in the country to prohibit discrimination based on race, sex, or religion in its charter.[35] It has always admitted women and Black students and was the second college in the country to grant four-year degrees to women.[36] Some of Hillsdale's earliest leaders, like Edmund Fairfield and Ransom Dunn, were figures in the antislavery movement and played an important part in the founding of the Republican Party.

In the 1970s, under the presidency of George Roche III, the college made national headlines for its refusals to identify students according to race, as required by federal loans programs. This began a decade of litigation, which ended with a Supreme Court ruling against Hillsdale in 1984. By this point the college had declared financial independence from the federal government. It refused to take federal assistance and instead funded student tuition aid through private funds, one of just a handful of American colleges to chart this course—a course that would transform Hillsdale into a darling of the conservative movement. Ronald Reagan spoke at Hillsdale in 1977, giving a speech called "Whatever Happened to Free Enterprise?" and Russell Kirk was a Distinguished Visiting Professor of Humanities there toward the end of his life.[37] The library contains the personal collection of the libertarian economist Ludwig Von Mises.[38] Hillsdale's reputation did falter in 1999, when George Roche III resigned amid scandalous and tragic circumstances, but Larry Arnn stepped in to take his place and has been a beloved leader there ever since.[39]

If you speak to people who know Hillsdale well—students who have gone there or faculty who have taught there—they will tell you that there are, in effect, two Hillsdales. One includes the public-facing political machine operated by Arnn and sustained by faculty in the (all-male) politics department, the Van Andel Graduate School of Statesmanship, and the campus in Washington, DC; the other comprises the traditional Christian liberal arts college in Michigan, where students and faculty, though conservative compared to other colleges, are not especially political. Arnn bridges this divide.

Hillsdale has grown as a beacon of conservativism under Arnn's leadership. The college's monthly publication, *Imprimis*, grew from around a million subscribers in 2000 to over six million in 2024, possibly one of the most widely distributed publications in the country.[40] The college began investing in the charter school movement in 2010, about a decade into Arnn's tenure, developing a program that supported new classical charter schools.[41] The first schools affiliated with the program opened in 2012, and the group has added schools almost every year since then.

Hillsdale was also a pioneer of online education. In 2011 it launched its online courses program, which aimed to extend the mission of the college and "teach the core subjects of a Hillsdale education free of charge." As of 2024 it offered more than forty such courses, on topics ranging from Exodus to Dante to Jane Austen to "The American Left: From Liberalism to Despotism" (the latter course was taught by Kevin Slack, a graduate of the University of Dallas, whom we will meet again).[42] Hillsdale claims that millions of people have participated in these courses, which are regularly advertised on conservative radio and media, as well as on social media.[43] As of 2024, only one of the forty-plus online courses—the one on *Northanger Abbey*—was taught in its entirety by a woman.[44]

Hillsdale's footprint in DC has expanded exponentially under Arnn's leadership, beginning with the creation of the Allan P. Kirby, Jr. Center for Constitutional Studies and Citizenship, which opened its doors on Massachusetts Avenue in 2010. Arnn would in turn become a powerful political actor, sitting on a variety of significant governing boards—like the Claremont Institute, the Henry Salvatori Center at Claremont McKenna College, the Heritage Foundation (he was offered the foundation's presidency in 2012 but declined), Landmark Legal Foundation,[45] the Center for Individual Rights,[46] and the Intercollegiate Studies Institute (or ISI).[47] He was outed as a member of the powerful and secretive Council for National Policy in 2014.[48]

Along with his Claremont Institute brethren, Arnn was an early supporter of Trump for president in 2016.[49] He was considered for secretary of education, the job that went to Betsy DeVos.[50]

Larry Arnn gained increased right-wing recognition for Hillsdale and its programs through his support for Trump. In 2019 he oversaw an expansion of the Kirby Center on Capitol Hill to include the Van Andel Graduate School of Government. The new school offered a Master of Arts degree in government as well as a "James Madison Fellowship Program" reminiscent of the Claremont Institute's programs.[51] Hillsdale has long been a major pipeline to GOP jobs and influence; that has only accelerated since 2016. The choice of Arnn and Spalding to lead the 1776 Commission was unsurprising.

The 1776 Commission Report

The 1776 Commission brought together eighteen conservative academics, politicians, and activists. It met twice before publishing the final report—once on January 5, 2021, the day before the Capitol attack, and again on January 15.[52] During that second meeting, the commissioners seemed uncertain about the status of the draft materials.[53] Arnn concluded the meeting by saying, "I think this is great. And I think we might get a superb report out of it. So we've got some work still to do. But thank you all for being so timely about this thing." The final report was published three days later. It contained an introduction, four substantive sections, a conclusion, and several appendices. The document's purpose, explained on page 1, was to summarize the animating principles of the founding, offer a record of the men and women involved, and resolve deep divisions among Americans about the meaning of the country. "The facts of our founding are not partisan," they wrote. They used the opening ten pages or so—the first two substantive sections—to describe the purpose and meaning of the Declaration and the Constitution, relying on lessons from the *Federalist* for the latter. The tone was highly jingoistic, but the document certainly contained valuable information for Americans.

It is easy to imagine a report in which these crucial, history-defining documents are introduced with both enthusiasm and care—where the processes through which the documents came into being are explored, their complex and at times contentious meanings considered, and the debates they inspired acknowledged. To be sure, one essential part of such a report would be to provide an account of the core principles and ideas that the Declaration and Constitution expressed, which include the fundamental liberty and equality of all men, the rule of law, and the institutional arrangements of a free government.

But it should be possible to acknowledge the ways in which the founding documents, while inspiring in some respects, were also inadequate or faulty or even shameful. And it should be possible to admit, in plain language, how the original constitutional documents permitted the institution of slavery. Some of the men who wrote those documents anticipated a time when slavery would be abolished. But these questions were contentious at the time, the founders were a diverse group of men whose opinions and interests varied, and historians continue to debate their intentions.

Any adequate report on the American founding would also have to devote considerable time to the fact that abolition did not come quickly. It would have to discuss, instead, the tremendous growth and expansion of slavery, and of racism, in the early 1800s (there were an estimated four million enslaved persons by midcentury, or roughly 20 percent of the population), and to acknowledge, as Lincoln saw so clearly, how it threatened, especially after the Dred Scott ruling in 1857, to extend throughout the rest of the country. It would have to discuss that the end of slavery came at the cost of war and over half a million deaths. An adequate report on the founding would also have to offer some discussion of America's indigenous peoples.

Trump's 1776 Commission Final Report does not do much of this. The discussion of the Declaration of Independence and the Constitution, which spans pages 1–10 of the document, does not mention slavery. Instead, the opening sections rest on gauzy abstractions and point away from historical realities. Here, for example, is how the commissioners put it on page 1:

> Comprising actions by imperfect human beings, the American story has its share of missteps, errors, contradictions, and wrongs. These wrongs have always met resistance from the clear principles of the nation, and therefore our history is far more one of self-sacrifice, courage, and nobility. America's principles are named at the outset to be both universal—applying to everyone—and eternal: existing for all time. The remarkable American story unfolds under and because of these great principles.

The idea that America's historical wrongs were "always" met by resistance from "the clear principles of the nation" and that "the American story unfolds under and because of these great principles" barely rises to the level of a Platonic noble lie. Rather, the nation's worst historic wrongs also found, in addition to resistance, a great deal of support—from citizens, activists, governors, presidents, and Supreme Court justices, many of whom relied on different and wrongheaded, but hardly insane, interpretations of the Declaration of Independence and Constitution. That was because at the time of the founding the principles were in stark contradiction with late-eighteenth-century realities. As the Englishman Samuel Johnson famously put it in 1775, "How is it that we hear the loudest yelps for liberty among the drivers of Negroes?" Or, as Nikole Hannah-Jones said in an interview in 2019, "What I'm arguing is that our founding ideals were great and powerful. Had we in fact built a country based on those founding ideals, then we would have the most amazing country the earth has ever seen."[54]

The authors of the 1776 Report do take up the question of the founders' hypocrisy in the third substantive section of the document, entitled "Challenges to America's Principles." The challenges enumerated in this section are slavery, progressivism, fascism, communism, and "racism and identity politics." As many others have observed, this is an unserious list; the inclusion of progressivism and identity politics is a sign of the commissioners' extraordinary and unthinking partisanship. Even Charles Kesler later expressed regret about how progressivism was treated in the final report.[55]

As concerns slavery, the report authors begin the slavery subsection by denying the hypocrisy of the founders and the idea (reminiscent of the 1619 Project) that "the country they built rests on a lie."[56] Oddly, they later say that "the Declaration's unqualified proclamation of human equality flatly contradicted the existence of human bondage." They say this as though it somehow erased the actual existence of slavery—as though you could redefine hypocrisy so that it had only to do with intentionally, and not the clash between beliefs and deeds. But you can't.

———

The silliest arguments to be found in the 1776 Commission Report concerned so-called identity politics, and the claim that the civil rights era and subsequent progressive identity politics have led to run-amok group rights, "reverse racism," and rampant new forms of injustice. The argument was that measures taken to compensate for historical injustices—like school busing, affirmative action, or same-sex marriage legislation—in fact constitute "reverse racism" and other forms of prejudice against white people and heterosexuals. It is an argument that exploits formal similarities between affirmative action and racism—i.e., the fact that both affirmative action and racist actions discriminate according to racial categories—and ignores the broader historical context that shapes such choices. In one instance discrimination harms a marginalized population and exacerbates historic injustices, while in the other it is a countermeasure that aims to mitigate against historical inequalities and level the playing field. These are two very different types of scenarios—with opposite intents and disparate impacts—but context collapse erases the difference.

The authors of Trump's commission reached peak sophistry when they likened contemporary identity politics to the thinking of John C. Calhoun in a manner that, again—and perversely—equated identity-based fights against identity-based oppression with the Calhounian fight *for* identity-based oppression. From the report:

> The Civil Rights Movement was almost immediately turned to programs that ran counter to the lofty ideals of the founders. . . . Among the distortions was the abandonment of nondiscrimination and equal opportunity in favor of "group rights" not unlike those advanced by Calhoun and his followers. The justification for reversing the promise of color-blind civil rights was that past discrimination requires present effort, or affirmative action in the form of preferential treatment, to overcome long-accrued inequalities. Those forms of preferential treatment built up in our system over time, first in administrative rulings, then executive orders, later in congressionally passed laws, and finally were sanctified by the Supreme Court.[57]

John C. Calhoun was famous for his elaborate defenses of the white majorities within the slave-holding South; when the 1776 Report authors liken proponents of identity politics to Calhoun, they are likening those who have worked against inequality to those who worked for Southern white people's right to hold slaves (which Calhoun deemed to be a "positive good" for both enslavers and enslaved).

But beyond this, what world are these authors of this passage living in? The Civil Rights Act was passed just over fifty-five years prior to the 1776 Report. At what point during this time frame, one wonders, did matters tip first from the entrenched inequalities of the Jim Crow South, redlining, and segregation, first to a system of relative equality, and then to the purported contemporary system of "reverse racism"? When precisely did Black people and other minorities gain so much power? And if such a shift happened, why are inequalities still so pronounced?[58] (The Hard Right, of course, has some answers ready-to-hand.) Finally, why are the Report's authors so confident that the core justification for preferential treatment that they articulate—namely, the overcoming of "long-accrued inequalities"—runs counter to the lofty ideals of the founders? Why do they assume that the founders would take as blinkered a view of the public interest as they do?

In an appendix to the report that has even more to say about identity politics, we find this claim: "While not as barbaric or dehumanizing, this new creed creates new *hierarchies as unjust as the old hierarchies of the antebellum South,* making a mockery of equality with an ever-changing scale of special privileges on the basis of racial and sexual identities."[59]

Diversity, equity, and inclusion has its problems; there are people whose identity politics are unthinking and dogmatic; and (shocker!) there are young people who take things in bad directions or go too far. The 1776 Commission Report made a mockery of sound thinking on these issues.

New Right Intellectualism (The Claremont Way 2.0)

A person would be hard pressed to find a better testament to the insular, intellectually bizarre world of conservative academia in America than the 1776 Commission Report of 2021. It was not good, true, or beautiful. And not merely because it was put out too soon. The report was rushed and badly done, but it also reflected the instincts of the conservative intellectuals who were gaining influence at the time, and who have a perennial habit of glossing over the hard parts of American history. Along with many others, I share some abstract concerns about excessively critical education. But there are parts of history that scream for serious critical analysis. The conservative mind has made a habit of resisting that kind of thinking, and the 1776 Report is the kind of intellectual infrastructure that results. This is one of several obvious reasons that no civics program should remain in the exclusive hands of the right.

You can see conservative scholars' failure to contend with questions of racial justice when you listen to their public commentary or read their books. From Charles Kesler and Christopher Caldwell to Patrick Deneen, even the foremost intellectuals of the New Right get it wrong. It's not so much that they aren't "woke." It is that, judging from their work, they have not given even basic consideration to the problems that fester here.

Take Charles Kesler, for example. Kesler acknowledges the brutality of slavery in *Crisis of the Two Constitutions*, but he also, in many instances, abstracts away from its gruesomeness in ways that elevate and celebrate the founders unthinkingly. In the book's most thorough discussion of slavery, he claims that "considerable progress had been made" on the matter in the years leading up to the Civil War—a claim that completely sidesteps the dramatic growth of slavery during that same period.[60] It's an argument that takes a series of positive legal changes to be weightier than growing on-the-ground barbarity. At another point, Kesler praises the early United States for its civilizational superiority to France and Germany. He heaps scorn on the French Revolution ("the unforgettable modern example of citizenship's self-destruction") and credits America's reverence for law and its founding myths as "the sort of things that kept and continue to keep the United States from going the way of Weimar Germany."[61] His basic point—that early America had distinctive traditions that contributed to civic virtue—is not original (cue Tocqueville); what is original is that Kesler somehow does not feel it necessary to account for the practice of slavery in his grand historical ledger (in sharp contrast to Tocqueville, and certainly to Harry Jaffa, who once wrote that "American slavery was as much an institutionalized denial of the moral claims of the Ten Commandments as Hitler's concentration camps or the Gulag Archipelago").[62] At the conclusion of a chapter about civility and the greatness of George Washington, Kesler bizarrely describes the start of the Civil War as a moment when "civility and citizenship were rent in two by the controversy over slavery."[63] Hadn't slavery already rent "civility" in two?

Again and again in the conversations and writings coming from the New Right, euphemistic abstractions and gauzy generalities are used to cover up grave historic injustices against Black people.

I am not the first to notice how Kesler and other Claremonters dodge America's racial history, or otherwise ignore or gloss over the ways in which other historical developments were responses to genuine challenges. As Shep Melnick observes in his review of *Crisis of the Two Constitutions*, Claremont's "best regime" narrative deflects attention away from actual historical problems and glosses over the conflicts that often arise between American principles and American practices. They will readily decry Reconstruction, affirmative action, the New Deal, the War on Poverty, or even the civil rights movement, but are, in Melnick's words, "reluctant to address the deeply rooted problems that those flawed measures [sought] to address."[64] When the folks at the Claremont Institute or Hillsdale condemn the "woke" present, they are usually also dodging swaths of the past.

The strangest example of the problem might be Christopher Caldwell's treatise *The Age of Entitlement: America Since the 1960s.*[65] Caldwell, a well-regarded conservative public intellectual, is a senior fellow at the Claremont Institute and a regular contributor to *The New York Times* opinion section. His book, published in 2020, made an argument that had a lot in common with Charles Kesler's "two constitutions" thesis—except that where Kesler traced the progressives' (supposed) anticonstitutional break to the New Deal, Caldwell traced the bad progressive constitution back to the Civil Rights Act. The book is not without empirical evidence showing the growth of bureaucracy and the proliferation of rights protections since the 1960s, but it is written in a mocking tone that takes hard-fought legal protections for minority groups as an obvious step toward decline because it involved governmental growth. Not only does he fail to contend with the most obvious problem here—that *not* having basic civil rights protections was a much graver violation of the Constitution than the expansion of the federal government—he similarly offers no sensible way forward that would not reignite those older injustices. As Jonathan Rauch observed in a scorching review, "The real heart of Caldwell's story is race and civil rights. A more descriptive subtitle might be: 'How the Civil Rights Revolution Overturned the Constitution, Divided America and Victimized Whites.'"[66]

It may be the case that Caldwell simply favors the older ways. Caldwell's commitment to white identity politics and whitewashed historical sentimentality was on full display in an essay published in the spring 2021 edition of the *CRB*. It was an essay about Robert E. Lee, and Caldwell reverted to cloying romanticism and "Lost Cause" hagiography on behalf of the Confederate general. At the essay's low point, he spoke of the "mayhem" involved in the George Floyd protests of the prior year. He brought it back to the Lee statues, describing how "the urgent, invective-filled attacks on Lee that are beginning to appear would have seemed overheated even if the Civil War were still going on."[67] The fact is, of course, that millions of Union soldiers risked their lives trying to kill Lee and his army—a simple truth that reveals the perversion of Caldwell's thinking.

It isn't just Claremont Institute types that struggle in this way. *First Things* editor-in-chief R. R. Reno sounded a lot like Caldwell when, in the introduction to *The Return of the Strong Gods*, he argued that events of 2020 indicated that "the strong gods are returning on the left as well." He proceeded to argue that the rise of the term "equity" on the left pointed to a wholly new form of leftist radicalism. "Diversity is a feel-good word," he wrote. "Equity," on the other hand, "topples statues."[68]

Patrick Deneen, to his credit, acknowledged racism in his book *Regime Change* (2023), but the result is nearly as conspiratorial and intellectually tenuous as what we find in the 1776 Commission Report. Deneen argues that critical race theory and other, related ideas like "intersectionality" arose precisely at a time when the living conditions of white working-class Americans began to crater (in the 1990s). He calls this a "remarkable coincidence" and continues in breathless terms to explain how "*just as the conditions for working-class solidarity across racial lines became increasingly possible*, the ruling class changed the narrative." His argument was that elites—and white elites in particular—used critical narratives to divide and conquer the working class and preserve their own status.[69] There are some interesting, non-conspiratorial versions of this argument out there, but this isn't one of them.[70]

The New Right mode of understanding puts a theoretical vice grip on the past. It looks back at historical reality—which, like the present, is always fluid, dynamic, and difficult to navigate—and allows there, post-hoc, to only be one "right" way through. Anything else—from the New Deal, to the civil rights movement, to Obamacare, to "wokeism"—is taken as a source of instability and grave injustice. For the Claremonters, almost everything is also taken as a grave departure from the founders' intentions. It's a matter of applying impossible abstract standards, and discounting the real-world problems that historical figures were contending with. It's like a child who cries "Jimmy broke my toy car" without also noting that Jimmy used the car to prop open the door, to save the garage, which had, at the time, been flooded in a storm.

The New Right scholars succeed with these kinds of arguments, to the extent that they do, because of the growing insularity of the conservative intellectual world. This is a world (not the only one, to be sure) that is self-sealing and self-congratulatory, constituted by people who long ago gave up on the idea of engaging seriously with mainstream scholarship, and whose work suffers as a result. This is most obvious when it comes to their approach to America's racial history, which is decidedly unwoke, and worse as a result.

———

After the 1776 Report came out, just two days before President Biden's inauguration, it was widely panned, and it soon slunk out of the public imagination. But Hillsdale was just getting started.

Within months, leaders at Hillsdale were working on a new project called the 1776 Curriculum, a thorough set of lessons devoted to American history and civics, for K–12 educators.[71] This project was launched in July 2021 and coincided with the ongoing expansion of Hillsdale's charter school and K–12 initiatives.

Dr. Katie O'Toole (Larry Arnn's daughter) is the director of K–12 education at Hillsdale.[72] O'Toole has insisted that the 1776 Curriculum was not a response to the 1619 Project, and that it was not ideologically motivated: "We're not telling students this is what you ought to believe," she told a reporter in July 2021. "We're telling them, here are the facts, here's the information. Here are some big questions to ask about it. Let's think it through together based on the information that we have, the documents that we have."[73] This would be a more persuasive claim if it were possible to believe that there is no ideological or evaluative component involved in figuring out which facts get included and which don't. Too often claims like these give cover to a particular ideological story.

The introduction to the 1776 Curriculum includes a "Letter to Teachers" from O'Toole that illustrates the point. The letter is a near-perfect distillation of what we might call Hillsdale's feel-good "constructive" civic education, as opposed to the left's more critical approach. It begins with an exhortation and affirmation of the nobility of the teaching profession. O'Toole then continues with an exhortation to truth and proceeds to delineate the truths that Hillsdale believes to be accessible to human reason—that is, true of all people and all times. These include ideas like "truth is objective"; the Aristotelian idea that all actions aim for the good (and "the good shows us how we ought to act, which we call right moral conduct"); the idea that "human nature itself does not fundamentally change or progress"; and the idea that people should be judged for their actions and character, not their identity.

Here is another of O'Toole's truths: "The more important thing in American history is that which has endured rather than that which has passed, that is, America's founding principles which have outlasted and extinguished from law various forms of evil, such as slavery, racism, and other violations of the equal protection of natural rights." This is a nice, patriotic idea, but is it true? Has racism been extinguished from the law by America's founding principles? Is it true that that which has endured is more important that that which has passed away? O'Toole's list concludes with the refrain that "America is an exceptionally good country." She recommends that teachers dive into their subject with these principles in mind: "Learn it, wonder at it, love it, and teach so your students will, too."

The curriculum itself mirrors the tenor of O'Toole's letter. It is, to be sure, better and more thorough than the 1776 Commission Report, and by 2024 it was running at over four thousand pages. I was glad to see that they included some lesson plans on the expansion of slavery prior to the Civil War, but it still had its weird blips and selective occlusions. As Adam Hochschild observed, "Thomas Jefferson's name appears hundreds of times, but Sally Hemings's never."[74] And there were all the same Hillsdale-style jabs about the New Deal, progressivism, and the "administrative state."

I am in favor of civic education of some kind—in grade school—though I agree with Betsy DeVos that it should not be a national program. I also agree with some of what O'Toole says in her letter, and I even like some things about the "cringey" loving spirit of Hillsdale's overall approach. The problem is that civic education in a pluralistic liberal democracy—one with some truly ugly history alongside the beautiful and astounding—should not be so self-sealing and self-assured. There is no good reason to be so jingoistic, and it does nothing to promote the virtues that are needed by free citizens. The Hillsdale 1776 Curriculum would be so much better if it were more "woke" and self-critical—if it included critiques from other quarters, maybe a supplement about that other American founding back in 1619, or deeper consideration of the "bondsman's two hundred and fifty years of unrequited toil."

Citizens deserve to experience civic love that is grounded in more than partiality and exclusion, and that does not coddle one demographic to the exclusion of the rest. There are ways to model civic education—and humanistic education—that are open and generous toward actually existing, pluralistic populations, and that invite serious, fair-minded contestation.

Such a civic rapprochement was not on the horizon in 2021. The New Right's attacks on mainstream education were about to get much more sophisticated, as Rufo took his campaign against critical race theory (CRT) up a notch (or ten).

Critical race theory originated in the 1970s and 1980s as a subset of legal analysis that explored systemic racism—including the ways in which seemingly fair laws and norms can have prejudicial and disparate effects on different groups. It's the sort of analysis that high-lights absurdities like the 1776 Report's arguments about identity politics and John C. Calhoun, but that also takes a sharp look at the ways in which laws, institutions, and norms reify the status quo and fail to deliver justice. It is sometimes explicitly activist in its orientation and has had a growing influence in American universities over the past few decades.[75]

The campaign against CRT (as with the 1776 Commission Report before) went a long way toward validating its core thesis—namely, the idea that ostensibly colorblind policies or practices could work to the detriment of some groups and not others. And it was astonishing how quickly power accrued to Christopher Rufo, the New Right's anti-CRT spokesperson. If Larry Arnn is the New Right face of the baby boomers in Washington, DC, Christopher Rufo is the public face of New Right activism writ large, and a capable conduit to the Hard Right, too.

9

Laying Siege to the Institutions

ON MARCH 19, 2021, David Sessions, a historian, was exploring a social media space called Clubhouse. Clubhouse facilitated livestream conversations and had short-lived buzz during the pandemic, and on that day Sessions happened into a Clubhouse room called "Building a New Right: Red States vs. Wokeness." Sessions told me that at the time he was mainly interested in figuring out how Clubhouse worked, but he also had an interest in the New Right. At some point, after entering the room, he decided to take notes.[1]

The panelists for the Clubhouse talk were Matthew J. Peterson, Kyle Shideler, James Poulos, David Reaboi, Christopher Rufo, Nate Fischer, and Ryan Williams. In other words, this was very much a Claremonter affair.[2] David Sessions's notes delineate with specificity a plan to use propagandistic terms to cultivate the antileft culture war. The participants openly acknowledged their intentions to launch a destructive and dishonest campaign against mainstream public institutions.

The discussion began with a presentation by Rufo, whose aims were clear: The New Right should work to turn "critical race theory" into a toxic catch-all term—so toxic that it would lead to new laws in red states. He told listeners not to worry about potential backlash against them, because claims of white supremacy and racism had lost all meaning. And he concluded by advocating for a "propaganda war against public institutions." The plan was to turn critical race theory into a toxic

brand category meant to "annex the entire range of cultural construc-
tions that are unpopular with Americans."[3]

The rest of the participants presented variations on Rufo's theme.
Reaboi emphasized that they would have to "call CRT racism, and an
attack on the American founding." He continued: "They have to hate it
and have to have the backs of politicians who will take this stuff on."
Both Reaboi and Peterson emphasized the rottenness and "savagery" of
public education, with Reaboi emphasizing that "from a comms perspective" he would go "full bore against the educational establishment"
and try to demonize teachers' unions, professors, graduate schools, and
theorists. Shideler warned that honest discussion about, for example,
the difference between equality and equity does not motivate "the average middle American" to attend a school board meeting. Instead, "this
is going to be trench warfare, this is going to be a knife fight."

There is so much bad faith here—not to mention the presumption
to speak for middle Americans. But notice, in addition to the extremism
and gross dishonesty, how the campaign plan mirrors the assumptions
of the 1776 Commission Report in its abstraction away from empirical
history and the reality of ongoing inequality in America, its perverse
claims about "reverse racism," its reductive contempt for mainstream
institutions, academic and otherwise, and its willingness to lump together all kinds of disparate people and ideas.

One of the key misdirections taken by Rufo was the choice to single
out the critical race theorists as central objects of their attacks.[4] As
noted briefly in chapter 8, critical race theory is an academic theory
that has had influence within the academy. But it is also true that, in
the early decades of the twenty-first century, the people who had the
most impact on the national discourse around race in America were
not obscure critical theorists—they were people like Michelle Alexander, a lawyer and civil rights advocate whose groundbreaking book
The New Jim Crow (2010) lucidly explained how the American legal
system, and mass incarceration in particular, worked in a systematic
way against people of color.[5] They were people like Barack Obama,
the first Black president, whom Trump and the far right welcomed to
the national stage with birther lies (and indirectly raised awareness

about American racism). And they were people like Ta-Nehisi Coates, a writer and journalist whose article "The Case for Reparations" (2014) struck a major chord in the American mainstream thanks to its vivid narrative account of the practice and legacy of redlining.[6] Then, of course, there was the Black Lives Matter movement, which did not start in an academic vacuum but in Ferguson, Missouri, after the killing of Michael Brown.[7]

The Rufo crowd prudently decided to bypass all of those ideas and events and instead focused on the 1619 Project and obscure abstractions that were much easier to distort. It's easier to lie about critical race theory than mass incarceration, birtherism, redlining, and excess police violence.

And using CRT as a cypher in this way was successful. The culture war that Rufo spearheaded worked exactly as he had hoped, and then it morphed and grew.

This chapter chronicles the New Right's efforts to seize and reclaim American institutions, starting with the anti-CRT campaign and the legal changes it effected and moving through to its takeover of organizations like the Heritage Foundation and the Intercollegiate Studies Institute.[8] Before I proceed, however, it's worth saying more about a new ideological framework within which the New Right was operating.

Longmarcherism

Beginning around 2021, New Right actors articulated—in their articles, speeches, and books—an elaborate new galaxy-brained theory about why such radical action was necessary. The basic story was this: For decades, radical leftists had been engaged in a deliberate, top-down radicalization scheme to infiltrate and conquer American institutions. They had succeeded, so it was time to mount a counterattack and siege. It was a fresh variation on a familiar "hour is late" refrain.

Rufo is the high priest of New Right propaganda, and he developed this story at length in his book *America's Cultural Revolution: How the Radical Left Conquered Everything* (2023). As evidence for the theory,

Rufo looked to European leftists of the 1960s and 1970s—the activists and theorists who first spoke of a leftist "long march through the institutions." Foremost among them was Herbert Marcuse, a German American philosopher of the New Left (and dissertation supervisor to Paul Gottfried), who described the "long march" strategy as "working against the established institutions while working from within them." In addition, Marcuse recommended a "concerted effort to build up counterinstitutions," or "counter-cadres," in nongovernmental arenas like media and education. Rufo et al. took these leftist strategy notes and hopes and argued that they described the reality of the past half-century. According to him, over the course of the prior decades, accelerating under the first Trump administration, and peaking with Biden, the "woke" leftists and Marxists had infiltrated and conquered the "commanding heights of culture" as well as elected government, the administrative state, and the corporate world.[9]

This last part—the takeover part—was not entirely novel. It is of a piece with other New Right concepts like "managerial elite," "Davoisie," "liberalocracy," "Cathedral," and "Longhouse." What was new was this particular historical yarn. And it was just that—a yarn, a tall tale, a story.[10]

The Longmarcher story simply did not line up with reality. It is true that the left won real victories like civil rights protections and *Roe v. Wade* in the last century, and a few in the first part of this one— the major one being marriage equality. And the twenty-first century did see the growth of diversity, equity, and inclusion. But there had also been plenty of losses and claw-backs (the rise of mass incarceration, *Citizens United*). On matters of race, in particular, Rufo minimized the many real factors that contributed to left-wing activism (racist police violence, Trumpism), while exaggerating the impact of left-wing agitation on "the regime." Wokeness was a response to real-world problems. It also was not especially lasting or effective. The police were not defunded, prisons were not abolished, and reparations went unpaid. None of those realities stopped the New Right from importing and retrofitting the idea of the long marcher takeover to justify their own ever-radicalizing agenda. In a review of Rufo's book, Zack Beauchamp concluded that "Rufo has serially exaggerated the phantom menace of a leftist cultural revolution because he seeks to justify its right-wing mirror: a wholesale assault on mainstream liberal institutions designed to indoctrinate the public into its preferred social vision."[11] That's right.

Rufo was direct about his intentions. In a speech at Hillsdale in 2022, he concluded that "even those of us who are temperamentally predisposed to defense must recognize that offense—laying siege to the institutions—is what is now demanded."[12] He put it like this: "The theorists of the counter-revolution must breathe new life into the American myth, and mobilize the tremendous reservoir of public sentiment toward a project of restoration." He talked about "laying siege to the institutions that have lost the public trust." The goal was not to assume control of the bureaucracy, but "to smash it."[13] The final lines of the book offered a promise:

> The American public can restore the mechanisms of democratic rule, reform the institutions that have compromised public life, and revive the principles of the revolution of 1776. And, unlike their enemies, whose promises vanish into the ether, they can make them real. They can re-secure the rights of the common citizen, allowing him to live as an equal, raise a family, participate in the Republic, and pursue the good, the true, and the beautiful.[14]

Let's take a closer look at what all this meant in practice.

The Anti-CRT Campaign and Beyond

In February 2021 the Conservative Political Action Conference (CPAC) held its annual conference in Orlando, Florida. CPAC is the major organizing conference for American conservative politicians and activists. Donald Trump's speech referred to "left-wing lunacy" but not to critical race theory, which was not yet a unifying cause.[15] But it would be soon. Rufo's Clubhouse presentation took place the following month, and anti-CRT rhetoric exploded. In a "War Room" podcast from May 2021, Steve Bannon put the matter simply: "The path to save the nation is very simple—it's going to go through the school boards."[16] In July 2021 CPAC held another conference, this time in Dallas. Trump's speech there referred twice to critical race theory. "With the help of everyone here today, we will defeat the radical left, the socialists, Marxists, and the critical race theorists," Trump explained. He added, "Whoever thought [we] would be even using that term?"[17] Who indeed.

Legislation

Use of the term CRT moved into the mainstream quickly. Parents across the country were showing up to advocate against CRT and antiracist teaching in schools, and school board meetings became a site of intense political conflict. *NBC News* reported in June 2021 that over 165 local and national groups had popped up, aiming "to disrupt lessons on race and gender." These groups were being supported and reinforced by conservative think tanks, law firms, and other activist groups. The Manhattan Institute, a New York think tank where Rufo was a fellow, released a "toolkit for concerned parents" about "Woke Schooling" that included a primer on "critical pedagogy" and extensive advice about how to respond, ranging from "polite and conciliatory" engagement, to "getting angry," to "getting organized."[18] Hillsdale was spearheading efforts to provide a substantive countercurriculum for schools across the country.[19]

Lawmakers also jumped to action. Between January and June 2021, Republicans introduced bills to limit instruction in critical race theory or "divisive concepts" in almost every state and passed them in over a dozen, all across the South (excepting only North Carolina and Louisiana), as well as Montana, Idaho, the Dakotas, and New Hampshire.[20] Sometimes the laws read as innocuous, since they replicate the (false) assumption of Rufo and others that critical race theory indoctrination was widespread in schools. Most of the laws sounded as though they were simply banning teaching about the inherent superiority or inferiority of one group or another. The problem, again, was that the laws were written vaguely, they created confusion for teachers, and it was obvious that the problems only went one way: It was fine to teach one version of American history—the one that says America was not racist; introducing more complicated ideas could get you fired.[21]

In the summer of 2021 parents' concerns about curricula were buoyed by their frustrations about Covid-19 restrictions. Protests against masking, critical race theory, and gender identity merged, and schools became a major flashpoint for this trifecta of political disagreement and frustration.[22]

Feedback from Hungary

As these debates played out, the New Right rallied behind the anti-CRT campaign, which they viewed as both important and highly successful. During a trip to Hungary in the summer of 2021—the summer when Tucker Carlson had also decamped to Hungary for a week or so—Patrick Deneen spoke highly of the American campaign against CRT and gender-related education in the schools. Deneen was interviewed alongside Rod Dreher by Boris Kalnoky, a professor at Mathias Corvinus Collegium (MCC) in Budapest.

The setting for this conversation was appropriate because MCC is the largest private college in Hungary and had recently been granted an enormous sum by Orbán—1.7 billion dollars—in the name of patriotic, nationalist education, and the creation of a new conservative elite.[23] Orbán had long had his eye on educational institutions. In 2018 he banned gender studies programs, and by 2019 he had forced the Central European University (founded by the Jewish Hungarian American billionaire George Soros) out of Budapest.[24] The revamping of MCC was, in a way, Orbán's response to CEU, and many conservatives on the New Right see MCC as an example of how patriotic nationalist education might be achieved. An appreciation for Orbán's "illiberal democracy"— and his willingness to use the law to legislate morality—is one thing that unites the New Right.

Kalnoky was struck by Dreher and Deneen's deep pessimism about the United States: "This 'the end is nigh' atmosphere and much of what you write contrasts with, well, if I compare our history with your history, then nothing bad ever happened to America and yet, you guys are so pessimistic! Whereas we lost to the Turks in 1526, didn't even have a state for hundreds of years, suffered Communism, and, yet here we are, have not lost courage and keep on going. So is that something that may be an inspiration for Americans?"

Dreher responded to Kalnoky's question first, by reciting still more reasons for pessimism—including the loss of Christianity and "the acceleration of the dismemberment of American society by the left" over the prior four years. Dreher had imbibed Rufo's propaganda wholesale. He exclaimed, "I don't want to see my country descend into low level civil war, or even actual shooting!" And he asked how the country is going to defend itself when "something like critical race theory" had been taken up "not only by every institution in America, but even by the CIA and the US military."

Deneen's response was more restrained, but he too saw very hopeful signs in the anti-CRT campaign. "It's been striking," he began, "even over the last several weeks and months to see the numbers of parents who are suddenly showing up to school board meetings all around the country." Deneen lauded those who protested "critical race theory in the schools, and also transgender teaching in the schools."[25] After vouching for the anti-CRT campaign, as well as the anti-trans campaign that was taking shape around this same time, Deneen did, to his credit, make a point of addressing Kalnoky's blithe comment that "nothing bad ever happened to America," taking note of the American Civil War.

Beyond CRT: Anti-LGBTQ and Anti-ESG

At the National Conservatism Conference in 2021 (NatCon 2), Rufo's impact on the New Right scene was obvious. He opened the second day of talks with a speech called "Critical Race Theory and Its Enemies." Balázs Orbán, one of Viktor Orbán's key employees (no relation) and the main person responsible for organizing the funding of Mathias Corvinus Collegium, gave a talk on a panel called the "International Nationalist Alliance." The conference concluded with a keynote by the writer, activist, and soon-to-be senator JD Vance. Vance's talk echoed Thiel's in 2019. It was called "The Universities Are the Enemy."[26]

The big story from the 2021 election (which took place right after NatCon 2) was the victory of Republican Glenn Youngkin over Democrat Terry McAuliffe in the Virginia governor's race. Loudoun County in Virginia had been a site of major school board drama, and Youngkin had campaigned in part on parent's frustrations with schools' pandemic closures and on an anti-CRT message, promising to ban critical race theory on the first day of his governorship.[27] (He had some help from McAuliffe, who in his second debate with Youngkin foolishly declared, "I don't think parents should be telling schools what they should teach.")[28]

It was not clear whether anti-CRT messaging was definitive for tipping the race, but Rufo took a victory lap. "Glenn Youngkin made critical race theory the closing argument to his campaign and dominated in blue Virginia," he tweeted. "We are building the most sophisticated political movement in America," he continued, "and we have just begun."[29]

And that was true. Anti-CRT and "antiwoke" legislation kept moving through the states. Often these efforts included an ugly parallel push against sexual minorities and transgender people. Much of the new legislation included bans of racially relevant books and other material being taught in public schools. The contentious Youngkin-McAuliffe contest, for example, included an episode where Youngkin produced an ad that featured a mother (and Republican activist) who had worked to remove Toni Morrison's *Beloved* from her son's senior Advanced Placement English high school curriculum.[30] Much of the new legislation also targeted books featuring homosexual characters or exploring issues of gender identity. Later these efforts would move beyond schools to target public libraries.

Subsequent legislation would be far more aggressive against LGBTQ people, particularly transgender people. It included laws banning lessons on sexuality and gender identity for grade school students, restricting bathroom usage and signage, banning transgender women from competing in school sports, and, most significantly, prohibiting gender-affirming care for minors and restricting it for adults.[31] In June 2022 the Supreme Court overturned *Roe v. Wade*, the 1973 ruling that entrenched, for half a century, a woman's right to abortion. The New Right seemed to think they could use anti-trans activism to fill the organizing void left by Roe, while also working to pass more restrictive abortion bans.

Just as Rufo and peers took a peripheral academic theory and exaggerated its threat to a generation of students, the New Right cynically acted as if transgender people—who account for less than half a percent of the population—posed a grave threat to "the nation."

Enter Ron DeSantis

Leading the charge on "antiwoke" legislation was Ron DeSantis, who was elected as Florida's governor in 2018 and took office in 2019. DeSantis was a Trump ally who hoped to build national recognition as an aggressive New Right populist. He moved to ban CRT in Florida's public schools in June 2021. In December 2021 he announced a proposal for the Stop Wrongs to Our Kids and Employees Act, or the "Stop WOKE Act," which was made into law in June 2022, and which, in addition to further limiting CRT "indoctrination," prohibited diversity training in Florida workplaces. The major tension in the law was that it forbade lessons from being "used to indoctrinate or persuade students to a particular point of view," while at the same time insisting on a particular antiwoke, "patriotic" point of view.[32]

In March 2022 DeSantis's government passed the controversial Florida Parental Rights in Education bill, otherwise known as the "Don't Say Gay" bill, which prohibited teachers from discussing sexuality or gender identity with students in pre-K to third grade. Once again, this is the sort of bill that sounds innocuous, since presumably there is very little time devoted to these subjects in those grades. The problem was that, practically speaking, the law had a disparate impact. Could a lesbian second grade teacher mention her wife or girlfriend to her students, or would that be a violation of the law? Nothing had changed for heterosexual couples in terms of talking about family life freely. In April 2022 the Florida legislature moved to expand this law, with some exceptions for pre-existing curricular material, to grades 4–12.[33] The Disney Corporation, one of Florida's major employers, objected strongly to the

Don't Say Gay bill, which led, as we will see shortly, to a major dispute between Disney and DeSantis.

In 2021 and 2022 DeSantis also introduced efforts to "fund the police," tightened public disorder laws, and revived the Florida State Guard, a group that had been dormant since 1947.[34] In September 2022 he made a cruel spectacle of America's immigration problems when he chartered two planes to fly some Venezuelan asylum seekers from San Antonio, Texas, to the notoriously liberal Martha's Vineyard in Massachusetts.

In addition to the controversial new laws, DeSantis sought to transform public education by creating new institutions that over time would usurp existing structures. He pushed to expand the charter school system to accommodate Hillsdale-style schools. Hillsdale already had a few affiliated charter schools in Florida, and DeSantis was eager to work with them on an expansion.[35] As was Tennessee's governor, Mike Lee, who hoped to open a hundred new Hillsdale-affiliated charter schools in his state and met with Arnn to make it happen (these plans were scuttled when Arnn made controversial remarks about how teachers today are trained "in the dumbest parts of the dumbest colleges in the country").[36] Red state efforts to expand charter school access dovetailed with long-standing right-wing skepticism about public schooling and their belief that charters, which in most states do not have unionized teachers, can deliver a better education. On the left, the projects were viewed with alarm as efforts to defund public education.[37]

DeSantis's work to expand Hillsdale-style charter school education was bold and served a radical long-term purpose, but his move to overhaul New College, a public liberal arts and honors college in Sarasota, was more akin to Rufo's "smashing." DeSantis removed six of the college's thirteen trustees and replaced them with loyal conservatives and activists, including Christopher Rufo, Matthew Spalding, and Charles Kesler. DeSantis's chief of staff expressed the hope that New College would become "Florida's classical college, more along the lines of a Hillsdale of the South."[38] Rufo published an opinion piece in *The New York Times* declaring that it was time to recover "the purpose of a university." What was that singular purpose? "For most of the classical liberal tradition," Rufo asserted, "the purpose of the university was to produce scholarship in pursuit of the true, the good and the beautiful." Today, though, "many universities have consciously or unconsciously abandoned that mission and replaced it with the pursuit of diversity, equity and inclusion."[39]

The revamped board fired the college's president, Patricia Okker, dismantled the DEI office, changed procedures governing hiring practices and training, denied a whole round of early tenure applications, and moved to dismantle the gender studies program.[40] It also requested nearly half a billion dollars from state taxpayers. By the start of the 2023–2024 school year, nearly 40 percent of the New College faculty had resigned.[41] DeSantis's actions at New College resembled Orbán's project at MCC, and observers saw a more general convergence between DeSantis's new laws and those that Orbán had enacted in Hungary.[42] Rufo had spent time in Hungary as a visiting fellow at the Danube Institute, was impressed with what he saw there, and was paid well by Hungary for his time.[43]

Unsurprisingly, these initiatives were popular among New Right intellectuals. The NatCons hosted their third annual conference in Miami in September 2022. DeSantis gave the keynote speech, "Florida is a Model for the Nation."[44] Months later, the Claremont Institute announced that Scott Yenor, a professor at Idaho's Boise State University, would move to Tallahassee and become the think tank's "inaugural senior director of state coalitions," where he would help to fight "woke policies." (Yenor was by then a controversial figure because, at NatCon 2, he had called professional women "medicated, meddlesome and quarrelsome," and referred to universities as "citadels of our gynocracy" that undermine traditional family life.)[45]

Woke Capitalism and Disney

Rufo's culture war initiatives worked. The efforts he spearheaded got the public into the school board meetings and served as a relevant talking point for GOP candidates in 2021 and 2022; they led to Republican governors enacting legislation; they pumped new energy into the classical charter school movement as championed by Larry Arnn and Betsy

DeVos; and they paved the way for radical initiatives like the overhaul-
ing of New College.

The next front in the war was the entire American economy, which
had been conquered by "woke capitalism." If even the free market was
being threatened by wokeness, then no one was safe from tyrannical
progressivism. The New Right continued to presume that the woke
takeover of corporations was exclusively the work of elites who had
been brainwashed to care about things like diversity and gender equality and were determined to impose these ideologies on the public, including through supposedly woke financial initiatives like Environment,
Social, and Governance (ESG) standards. In other words, it had nothing to do with demographic shifts and changing consumer tastes and
demands. No one, by their reckoning, actually cared about things like
Black Lives Matter or LGBTQ rights or environmental sustainability—
it was all being imposed from above.

With the "woke capitalism" turn, the New Right recycled the thinking of the anti-CRT craze. And just as the new antiwoke laws were in
tension with everything that conservatives had been saying for decades,
and continued to say, about the importance of free speech and the First
Amendment, these attacks on "woke capitalism" contradicted long-
established right-wing talking points—and Supreme Court rulings—
about the relationship between money, politics, and speech. It was fine,
according to *Citizens United*, for corporations to fund political campaigns, even secretly. Now the New Right was saying that it was, at the
same time, not fine for corporations to take political stances openly.

The highest-profile case related to "woke capitalism" involved the
Disney Corporation and DeSantis. Disney's then-CEO Bob Chapek
had spoken out against DeSantis's Don't Say Gay bill, and shortly thereafter, in an undeniable action of retribution, DeSantis took control of
the governing body that oversees the district in Florida where Disney
World properties are and transformed the company's tax status.[46]

The situation between Disney and the GOP signaled growing com-
bativeness between New Right conservatives and big business. It wasn't
just that DeSantis disagreed with Disney, and vice versa. It was that
DeSantis and others had become convinced that businesses should not

speak out at all about politics or take political stances. There was an overwhelming sense on the right, especially in the aftermath of the George Floyd protests, that corporate entities had overstepped the rightful bounds of civil society by taking positions on public matters.

Conservatives were not upset about nothing. There was, beginning in the early 2000s, a noticeable growth in marketing that was infused with progressive messaging. Dove's "Real Beauty" campaign is often credited as being the first of its kind, bucking the status quo with body-positive messaging and diverse actors.[47] Trump's election supercharged this trend, and corporations increasingly started taking official or implied stances on matters like the immigration ban, #MeToo, and George Floyd, and by making advertisements and products that were clearly aimed at more progressive audiences. Nike made an ad with Colin Kaepernick; Target started selling merchandise celebrating the LGBTQ community; Miller Lite celebrated Women's History Month; and even the NFL had ads with social justice messaging. Some Americans were displeased with these changes, which to them felt like an unwelcome and unnecessary intrusion of politics into their private lives and leisure. With others, the new approach seemed long overdue: After all, the older status quo—with ads and shows dominated by skinny, straight white people—never felt "neutral" to them. Hobby Lobby and Chick-fil-A had long engaged in identity politics, and it was about time that the market started to reflect a changing population. (Others saw these new marketing styles as the social justice equivalent of greenwashing. Corporations could rewrite their ads and talk up their commitments to social justice without doing anything meaningful—or worse, while providing cover to an exploitative economic system.)

The New Right doubled down on behalf of those offended by the progressive advertising, in a manner that was analogous to how they doubled down on DEI, on CRT, and on LGBTQ people. They hyped up the alleged dangers, using vague or abstract language that served as a catch-all for all kinds of disparate things. They promoted boycotts and tried to delegitimize "woke" institutions (in this case, banks and mainstream financial practices). In some states they passed laws to try to thwart "woke" interests. And they worked to build counterprograms that could better represent conservative values.

The Anti-ESG Campaign

In the financial world, Environmental, Social, and Governance metrics have been around for nearly two decades. In the world of asset management, ESG is a way of assessing a company based on how it contends with environmental risks, social considerations (treatment of its workforce, for example, or the diversity of its board), and its internal practices. Some aspects, such as equity across gender and race, fit squarely in the target of the New Right, while other dimensions, such as adequacy of cybersecurity defenses (part of the "Governance" metric), have no connection to hot-button social issues.[48]

The ESG controversy is complicated. Broadly speaking, corporate America's concern with the pillars of ESG has increased exponentially over the past two decades, reflected most prominently in the emergence of DEI initiatives, increased focus on equitable representation of women and minorities among executives and board members, and myriad efforts to measure and lessen corporate contributions to climate change. As businesses increasingly focused on improving ESG components for their own reasons—often simply the self-interest of being able to benefit from, for example, a diverse workforce, higher employee morale, or marketing claims to customers (e.g., "100% recycled materials")—an increasing number of investors decided they wanted to take ESG metrics into account when deciding where to invest. Increasingly, investors wanted to support companies that operated in line with their values, and ESG provided one avenue through which to do this. Most often this manifests as prohibitions against investing in certain types of companies that score poorly on ESG—including most obviously fossil fuel companies and weapons manufacturers.

The impact of ESG metrics—with respect to either furthering social values or protecting shareholders' investments—remains to be seen, but the right considers its rise as a threat. If more investors base their decisions on ESG scores, more companies will focus on improving their scores, creating a self-propelling cycle. So it was that attacking ESG-based investing became a component of the broader New Right culture war.

ESG was growing quickly in popularity in the early 2020s and soon came to constitute one-third of US assets that were professionally managed.[49] In 2021 Larry Fink, CEO of BlackRock—the largest asset management firm in the world (where Michael Anton had worked)—published a letter in which he signaled strong support for ESG investing. This caused a minor uproar in the financial world, and Fink was accused of going "woke."

The New Right saw an opportunity. They could combat the underlying corporate trends, while at the same time proving their antiwoke bona fides and riling up supporters through exaggeration and misinformation. Instead of taking their case to investors, who enjoyed the freedom to choose where to invest, the New Right went to their allies in red state legislatures. For example, in 2021 Texas passed a law that forbade state and municipal entities from doing business with banks and firms that had restrictions on investments in the state's oil and gas industry, including through the ESG investment mechanism. It was, effectively, a tit-for-tat move that penalized banks that had judged certain oil and gas investments to be overly risky. Here is how Texas's comptroller, Glenn Hager, justified the ban: "The environmental, social and corporate governance (ESG) movement has produced an opaque and perverse system in which some financial companies no longer make decisions in the best interest of their shareholders or their clients, but instead use their financial clout to push a social and political agenda shrouded in secrecy."[50] The reality is that publicly traded companies are obligated by law and long-standing norms to operate in the service of their shareholders' interests, and—despite what opponents asserted, falsely—considering ESG elements does not eliminate this requirement. Financial actors warned that these limits would hurt earnings and violated free market principles, but red states continued to pass these laws. Other such efforts failed.[51]

In a manner that paralleled the launch of the 1776 Curriculum in schools, members of the New Right established alternative venture firms that would present an alternative to ESG. Matthew Peterson and Nathan Fischer began a venture capital and media company, New Founding, after the 2020 election to fight wokeness (and ESG and DEI) and to promote a vitalist, Christian, pro-technology counter to the "left's totalitarian agenda."[52] With support from Peter Thiel, Bill Ackman, and JD Vance, Vivek Ramaswamy started a group to counter behemoth investment groups like BlackRock, StateStreet, and Vanguard.[53] By September 2023 it had raised over a billion dollars.[54] Another firm, called 2nd Vote Value Investments, was formed in 2021 by Andy Puzder (a senior fellow at the Heritage Foundation) and Mike Edelson.[55] Their efforts appear to have been less successful.[56]

At the annual National Conservatism conference in 2022 in Miami, where DeSantis gave his keynote, Rufo and CRT were no longer front and center on the agenda, but ESG and the "Woke World Order" were. There was a panel devoted to that topic, featuring luminaries like Darren Beattie. It also featured Balázs Orbán, who by that point had become Prime Minister Orbán's political director and chairman of the board at MCC. His talk was called "The EU Is a Woke Leviathan." Another panel was titled "ESG: Evil, Stupidity, or Grift?" Andy Puzder gave a speech calling ESG "socialism in sheep's clothing" and a "neo-Marxist form of investing" that was also a "total rejection of our founding principles."[57]

In May 2022 Mike Pence, the former vice president, took the fight to a broader audience, writing in an op-ed in *The Wall Street Journal* that "the next Republican president and GOP Congress should work to end the use of ESG principles nationwide. For the free market to thrive, it must be truly free."[58]

There was something confounding about all this. As was typical, the anti-ESG movement dramatically overestimated the "wokeness" of ESG (and, arguably, its real-world effectiveness on woke issues), while at the same time underestimating the extent to which ESG investing took off because of market demand. The focus on the underlying components of ESG metrics arguably made strong business sense for companies, which is why the growth of DEI, climate consciousness, cybersecurity defenses, diverse boardrooms, and the like all started long before ESG investing became popular, and would continue—mostly but not totally undeterred—through the anti-ESG campaigns.

Other problems were more obvious. The New Right had positioned itself as a populist bulwark *against* predatory globalism, but now it was asserting itself as the vanguard of pure financial interests and competition—and arguing that no mechanism except for unfettered, red-blooded, free-market greed had any economic legitimacy. Except, of course, if the interested parties were antiwoke. Then, efforts to shape the moral ecosystem of the economy were legitimate. There was something crudely contradictory about the New Right's claims that anti-ESG supported freedom. As with the anti-CRT campaign, the anti-trans campaign, and the anti-abortion campaign, the anti-ESG movement was about narrowing the playing field, limiting freedom, and taking choices off the table.

The good news is that, since the anti-ESG campaign targeted corporations and financial groups rather than, say, trans kids, high school teachers, and sociology professors, its success was, at least at first, more limited. In March 2023 the US Congress, led by Republicans, passed an anti-ESG measure. President Biden used the first veto of his presidency to block it.[59]

Seizing GOP Institutions

As the New Right worked on its seizure of mainstream institutions—school boards, higher education, and the economy at large—they were also succeeding at their (further) takeover of the commanding heights of the GOP.

The 2022 NatCon conference in Miami featured a significant moment of establishment GOP capitulation to the New Right, and even to the Hard Right. The most significant moment of the 2022 conference was when Kevin Roberts took the stage. Roberts had been named the new president of the Heritage Foundation in October 2021. He came from the Texas Public Policy Foundation, where he had been president since 2016 and had worked with Ryan Williams and others on the 79 Days Report. Roberts replaced Kay Cole James, whom Darren Beattie, on January 6, 2021, had said "needed to learn her place and take a knee to MAGA."[60]

At the opening of his speech, Roberts effectively announced that the old establishment conservatism had submitted to the New Right and National Conservatism (and not vice versa). He began by thanking Yoram Hazony for his wise counsel in his early days at the Heritage Foundation and credited Chris DeMuth for first suggesting that he "give National Conservatism a chance." Then he pledged allegiance:

> I come to this convention as president of the Heritage Foundation to extend my gratitude for the ideas and energy National Conservatives have injected into the national debate and my fellowship with the principles you advanced to rescue America from the barbarians inside the gates of our very own institutions. I come not to invite the National conservatives to join our conservative movement but to acknowledge the plain truth that Heritage is already part of yours.[61]

Halfway through the speech, Roberts recounted how as a high schooler he had volunteered for Pat Buchanan's 1992 presidential run. "You might say," he related, "that my people knew what time it was in America before most even knew the clock was ticking."

To understand the significance of what Roberts had said, it's useful to know a bit more about Heritage. The foundation was established in 1973 and had served as the flagship policy group on the right for decades—much of Ronald Reagan's policy platform was based on Heritage's publication, "Mandate for Leadership I" (1981), which inaugurated the organization's tradition of publishing policy recommendations for incoming administrations. In 2013 the institution took a distinctively activist and ideological turn under the leadership of Jim DeMint, who became president that year (as one trustee put it, "DeMint has not only politicized Heritage, he's also trivialized it").[62] The organization still had some harsh words for Trump prior to the 2016 election, but in the end it helped with the transition and with staffing the new administration. By 2018 Trump (like Reagan) had "embraced nearly two-thirds of the policy recommendations from the Heritage Foundation's 'Mandate for Leadership.'"[63]

Behind the scenes, though, Heritage was in disarray during the early Trump years. In early 2017 DeMint was forced out, to be replaced by Kay

Cole James, the first African American and first woman to hold the position. James was much more moderate than DeMint, and in 2018 she was joined in leadership by Kim Holmes, a traditional Reagan-era conservative, who took on the role of executive vice president.[64] Holmes was decidedly anti-Trump and antinationalist.[65] Kay Cole James published an op-ed decrying American racism in the wake of the George Floyd protests.[66] This "return to normalcy" approach led to some departures among the think tank's more radical staff (including by Matthew Spalding, David Azerrad, Arthur Milikh, and Ryan T. Anderson).[67] But ironically, the "normalcy" did not last long after Trump's defeat in 2020. James and Holmes retired at the same time, in March 2021, and Kevin Roberts took the helm. The choice of Roberts meant, in effect, that the board of trustees at Heritage believed Trump-style right-wing populism to be the future of American Conservatism. The New Right's "Lost Cause" narrative around January 6, 2021, far from waning, was only gaining force.[68]

Roberts's 2022 speech at NatCon 3 in Miami symbolized the extent to which the New Right had taken over. Traditional conservative institutions like Heritage and the Intercollegiate Studies Institute had clearly made the shift. The Libertarian Party collapsed into full-on Trumpism under the leadership of the radical and hyper-online "Mises Caucus"—signs of both the shallowness of the new GOP economic populism and the intense pull of the culture wars.

With the libertarian movement at large, matters were more complicated. Shikha Dalmia, a libertarian writer who was ousted from her job at *Reason* magazine in 2020, explained in 2024 how the mainstream of the libertarian movement had simply "settled into a heterodox, right wing–inflected bothsidesism" and had "abdicated [the libertarian cause] just when they were most needed."[69] But it would be a mistake to suggest that the entire libertarianism movement had joined the New Right. *Reason* still published occasional criticism of Trump and the New Right, and various Koch-affiliated groups like the Cato Institute, the Institute for Humane Studies, and the Mercatus Center kept their distance from Trump and Trumpism.

As for mainstream conservatism, the American Enterprise Institute generally kept Trumpism at arms length. The editors at *National Review* had been staunchly anti-Trump in 2016 but were excited about Ron De-Santis.[70] In 2024 Michael Brendon Dougherty, one of the *Review*'s senior writers, supported Trump.[71] But he was a lone voice. The more important contrast is between the Reaganite/fusionist *National Review* and the proliferation of New Right publications (like *American Greatness*, *The American Mind*, *American Affairs*, and *Compact*, which were often headed by young people) seeking to replace the old guard.[72]

Conservative funding was also migrating over to the New Right in a serious way. After he was ousted from Heritage, DeMint founded a lobbying group called the Conservative Partnership Institute (CPI), and the organization grew exponentially in 2021 after a major donation from Trump's Save America PAC. As Jason Wilson of *The Guardian* wrote in 2024, "That donation was part of a $45.7m cash haul that year, followed by nearly $36.4m the following year according to CPI's IRS filings." The organization was committed to cultivating talent and incubating new organizations and groups seen as supporting the New Right populist vision. These included Greta Mitchell's "election integrity" organization, the opposition research group American Accountability Foundation, a group called American Moment (led by Saurabh Sharma and "on a mission to recruit and train the next generation of Republican elites"), and America First Legal (AFL), a legal office directed by Stephen Miller.[73]

This period also saw the creation of the America First Policy Institute (AFPI), a new think tank aiming to promote the former president's policy agenda, and which served as something like a holding ground for former members of his administration, including eight former cabinet members.[74] The AFPI also had close ties to extremist Christian groups that were close to Trump, including Charlie Kirk, founder of Turning Point USA.

———

Within a few years, AFPI and many of these other organizations were cooperating with the newest iteration of Heritage's Mandate for Leadership, entitled "Project 2025." This version was different. As the historian

Thomas Zimmer wrote at the time, Roberts's introduction to the nine-hundred-plus page document "oozes the siege mentality, self-victimization, and grievance-driven lust for revenge that is fueling the Right and animating the plans for a second Trump administration." It contained signature elements of the New Right: catastrophism and Ideas First culture warriorism on behalf of a monolithic and antiliberal moralism. Roberts wrote of how the "long march of cultural Marxism through our institutions" had already come to pass and called "The Great Awokening" a totalitarian cult. The task at hand now was to "reverse this tide and restore our Republic to its original moorings." This would require collective action. "We have two years and one chance to get it right."[75]

But Project 2025 promised more than just Flight 93 anger and rage: It offered a comprehensive blueprint for how to dismantle segments of the government—while at the same time mobilizing the state, wherever possible, in favor of conservative moral purposes.[76] The dismantling part would include eliminating the federal Department of Education, installing a "conservative" Environmental Protection Agency, and limiting the capacity of the Center for Disease Control (CDC) to make recommendations. A major part of the plan involved removing job protections for civil servants and replacing them with political appointees and loyalists. The mobilization part would include using the CDC to collect abortion data at the state level, as part of efforts to end "abortion tourism." As Zimmer showed in his analysis of the document, Project 2025 channels the New Right's Flight 93 spirit into a concrete policy agenda that appeases disparate elements of the movement—the side that wants to dismantle government, and the part that wants to harness and use it. As he observed, Project 2025 was organized around the true principle motivating the New Right: "This was always, at its core, an anti-left project, an attempt to prevent any leveling of established discriminatory hierarchies."

———

While mainstream conservatism continued its rightward journey, the New Right kept welcoming the Hard Right in, too. At NatCon 3, that looked like welcoming Darren Beattie as a speaker, as well as "IQ and Immigration" specialist Jason Richwine.

NatCon 3 also included a speech by a man named Nathan Pinkoski. Pinkoski was a political theorist who, like me, attended the University of Alberta as an undergraduate. He then went on to do his PhD at Oxford. In 2022 he was a research fellow and director of academic programs at the Zephyr Institute, a conservative humanities institute set up to serve the students of Stanford. Prior to that he had been a postdoctoral fellow at Robert P. George's James Madison Program in American Ideals and Institutions at Princeton, which is part of the same conservative network.[77] Pinkoski's NatCon talk was called "Catholicism and the Necessity of Nationalism." It began with high praise for Raspail's *Camp of the Saints* and strongly implied that liberals (perhaps including Pope Francis) were satanic. He used the book to connect Catholic teachings to a Hazony-like preference for particularism and in so doing quoted selectively from papal sources with a level of dishonesty reminiscent of Michael Anton's use of Lincoln in *JAG*.[78] Pinkoski spoke hurriedly, and his demeanor was anxious and scholarly, so it would be easy enough, lacking context, to miss the ugly fanaticism of his argument, which, despite its Catholic inflection, was not too far off from dressed-up BAPism.[79] He was clearly a Carl Schmitt enthusiast, and his speech also featured a quote from Charles Maurras, an ideologue for the far-right Action Française.

Within months of giving his first NatCon talk, Pinkoski was brought on as a senior fellow with Hazony's Edmund Burke group. In May 2023 he published an analysis of *Camp of the Saints* with *First Things*, which had published a pseudonymous explainer of the Longhouse, by "L0m3z," that same year.[80] Patrick Deneen took offense at the Longhouse article and fired off a strongly worded (and since-deleted) tweet: "Disappointed doesn't quite capture my response to First Things publishing a Nietzsche-lite article by a Twitter anon. The justified opposition to Wokeism increasingly dominating the mainstream right is in danger of descending into very dark places."[81] Such was the immediate opposition to the rising tide of far-right extremism among people like Hazony and Deneen, the most conscientious of New Right intellectuals.

L0m3z would later be identified as Jonathan Keeperman, a lecturer at the University of California Irvine behind the far-right publishing house Passage Press, which published many works by Curtis Yarvin. He too would eventually be welcomed as a speaker at NatCon, as would Paul Gottfried.[82] In 2023–2024 Pinkoski became a visiting faculty member at the University of Florida's new Hamilton Center for Classical and Civic Education (another GOP-led initiative, this one designed to promote the Western canon and civil discourse; Pinkoski's appointment ended after one year).[83]

Schism

A lot changed in the world between NatCon 2 in Orlando in 2021 and the one that took place in Miami in the fall of 2022. Most significant was Russia's invasion of Ukraine in February 2022, which started a full-scale war that galvanized Western powers and contributed to some schisms on the New Right. Suddenly—and more obviously than before—Vladimir Putin's destructive and violent nationalistic ambitions were plain for all to see, as was his hatred for Europe and the West.

In his first term as president, Donald Trump expressed admiration for Putin, as did many New Right intellectuals, who admired Putin's manly bravado, his revival of Russian culture and nationalism, and his contempt for Western liberal norms—especially the openness to LGBTQ people. Foremost among these figures were Tucker Carlson and the journalist and Claremont Institute fellow Christopher Caldwell.[84] David Reaboi captured the general tenor of right-wing sentiment in a tweet from February 26, 2022: "I don't like Putin," he wrote, "but if you think you're going to make me hate him like I hate the left, you're way wrong."[85]

In practical terms, though, the war in Ukraine brought some confusion to the New Right movement. It forced the various members of the coalition to choose between their obvious sympathies with Putin's reactionary traditionalism and old-fashioned American liberal internationalism. Generally speaking, those on the New Right who formed the activist arm of the movement (and so also those who were more beholden to donors and the actual right-wing base) tended to side with Ukraine and the American establishment's support for it and Europe. Yoram Hazony became an uneasy Ukraine supporter, and so an indirect defender of liberal internationalism, even while Russia claimed to be acting on nationalist principles (in addition to obvious imperialist ones).[86] Those who were more intellectual and aloof tended to hold back from overt support for Ukraine and instead expressed an isolationist's skepticism about engagement abroad that seemed much truer to the original spirit of the New Right—including their burgeoning sympathies with Orbánist (and pro-Putin) Hungary. It was at around this time that the Postliberal faction of the New Right went their own way.[87]

In March 2022 Ahmari left his job at the *New York Post* to cofound a magazine called *Compact,* an endeavor in which he partnered with Matthew Schmitz of *First Things* and Edwin Aponte, a leftist. They founded the magazine as a platform for unorthodox thinking from the left and right.[88] That included a piece early in the Russia-Ukraine war in which Ahmari pointed out some of these emerging contradictions: "A calamity for the Ukrainian people," he wrote, "the war also offered a gleaming opportunity for elite ideological reconciliation in the West. As stunning as scenes of tanks rolling across Europe's borders were, something still more astonishing took place in the halls of Western power, and on Twitter, where elites talk to each other: Liberalism and nationalism embraced for the first time since their estrangement in 1945."[89] The magazine also published a letter entitled "Away from the Abyss," whose authors offered a cautionary warning against US involvement in new wars.[90] The signatories here included the most prominent Postliberals but also spanned the New Right (Anton, Rufo, and Williams signed on). It also included prominent voices from the left (like Freddie deBoer, Glenn Greenwald, and Samuel Moyn).

But the schism between the Postliberals and the rest of the New Right appeared to be real. The core Postliberal group—Ahmari, Deneen, Pappin, Vermeule—were not on the roster at NatCon 3 in Miami. And in the summer of 2022, when the National Conservatives published a "Statement of Principles," the American Postliberal cadre did not sign on.[91]

The first clause of the statement asserted NatCon's support for national independence, and the sixth principle was "Free Enterprise." This was a slight shift from some of the nationalist and populist economic rhetoric that had previously characterized the New Right. The New Right's isolationist and economic populism legs were proving wobbly—a good reason for the Postliberals to keep their distance.

Ironically, during this same period President Biden passed legislation that was much truer to the spirit of New Right economics than anything done during the first Trump administration. Biden kept some of Trump's protectionist tariffs intact and then did the New Right one better with his industrial, antitrust, and labor policies. By 2022 he had passed a major infrastructure bill, the Inflation Reduction ACT and the CHIPS and Science Act. He did so with the support of moderate Republicans, not MAGA New Right types.

Another irony of this period was the rise of Elon Musk as a New Right figure. His purchase of Twitter in June 2022 and subsequent efforts to shape America's media environment were certainly contrary to the New Right's skepticism about libertarian economics and elite "Davoisie" and oligarchic power.[92] But Musk fit in pretty conveniently with a "smash the institutions" approach.

The NatCon statement of principles was also notable for its strident social traditionalism and exclusive definition of the family ("The traditional family, built around a lifelong bond between a man and a woman, and on a lifelong bond between parents and children, is the foundation of all other achievements of our civilization"), its unconstitutional embrace of state-supported religion ("Where a Christian majority exists, public life should be rooted in Christianity and its moral vision, which should be honored by the state and other institutions both public and private"), as well as its stark opposition to immigration.[93]

I was most struck by part of the "National Government" clause (clause 3). Here, the authors expressed their skepticism about the administrative state and their belief in federalism, "which prescribes a delegation of power to the respective states or subdivisions of the nation so as to allow greater variation, experimentation, and freedom." Then, however, they explained that "in those states or subdivisions in which law and justice have been manifestly corrupted, or in which lawlessness, immorality, and dissolution reign, national government must intervene energetically to restore order." This was a clear carve-out for authoritarian action. And what counts as moral dissolution to the NatCons? BLM protests, abortion access, birth control, gay marriage, and no-fault divorce? On these questions there is no obvious schism in the New Right movement. There is a sense in which the New Right is a one-legged stool, steady as can be.

In the next chapter we spend some more time with the Harvard legal professor and Postliberal integralist Adrian Vermeule. Vermeule is not an activist like Kevin Roberts, and he has never been part of the National Conservatism group. But his work dovetails beautifully with Project 2025. It provides the most sophisticated defense out there for the part of the New Right that wants to use government for conservative moralizing ends. If Rufo is the high priest of New Right propaganda, then Vermeule is the movement's high priest, simpliciter.

10

Common Good Constitutionalism

THE INTERCOLLEGIATE studies institute WAS founded in 1953 by Frank Chodorov, who belonged to the isolationist, classically liberal "Old Right" of the early twentieth century. Inspired by William F. Buckley's *God and Man at Yale*, the institute aimed to fill the "gaping void in higher education," meaning the gaping void of conservatism. A young Buckley was its first president. ISI is a relatively small organization, but it hosts student events and "Great Books" programming, has its own in-house publishing house and journal (*Modern Age*), and supports chapters and student journalists on campuses across the country.[1]

In September, 2020, John A. Burtka IV was appointed president of ISI. Burtka went to Hillsdale for college and has a graduate degree in theology from La Faculté Jean Calvin, a Protestant (Reformed) seminary in France. He had been a Lincoln Fellow at the Claremont Institute in 2018. Under Burtka's leadership, ISI added new programming and in 2022 opened a new conference center (endowed by Linda L. Bean). Some observers perceived a dramatic turn and narrowing toward nationalism and Trumpism under Burtka; others contested that view.[2] In 2023, ISI hosted its inaugural American Politics and Government Summit, and when I saw the roster of speakers, I decided to attend.[3] I was already writing this book, so it was a good chance to see Burtka in action, observe some of the New Right's key activists, and see how their ideas traveled.

So far as I know, I was the most liberal person at the conference. It was pitched as a serious academic meeting, but it still had the tenor of a conservative activists' affair—plenty of jokes about pronouns, "the Democrat Party," assumptions about everyone being on "our side," and an 8-to-1 ratio of men to women on the program.[4] The conference took place at the Hilton Fort Lauderdale Marina hotel, Trump flags hoisted high on the yachts docked outside. John Eastman was there (his wife was a speaker). So were Yoram Hazony, Charles Kesler, Ryan Williams, and Michael Anton. But there were also many classical liberals and fusionist types in attendance, including a few friends and acquaintances.

This chapter is focused on Adrian Vermeule and other Postliberals. I begin at the Fort Lauderdale conference because one of the first things I noticed there was how, although the Postliberals were not in attendance, their ideas sure were.

For example, during a luncheon on the first big day of the conference, Henry Mack III, who at the time was a senior chancellor for the Florida Department of Education under Ron DeSantis, was asked about the meaning of democratic citizenship.[5] He answered that part of citizenship involved understanding the common good. He also noted that, to get a more definitive sense for himself of what the common good might mean, he was working through the ideas of Adrian Vermeule and his book *Common Good Constitutionalism* (2022). There were two ironies in this disclosure. First, Mack, who earned three degrees at Catholic University in Washington, DC, had recently given an interview to *City Journal* about Florida's higher education reforms, where he argued that higher education in the United States should "educate in view of the Common Good."[6] Shouldn't he have figured out the common good *before* making such big claims? The second irony was that, as we will see, Vermeule's book was not going to provide him with satisfying answers.

The final keynote speaker for the conference was Robert P. George, McCormick Professor of Jurisprudence and director of the James Madison Program in American Ideals and Institutions at Princeton University—where Nathan Pinkoski had been a fellow—and one of the country's most well-known Catholic thinkers. George is well-connected in influential conservative Catholic circles and has helped to form a network of moral and "civics" institutions adjacent to prestigious American universities all over the country (I put the word civics in scare quotes because these institutes, connected to Luis Tellez and the Foundation for Excellence in Higher Education, or FEHE, have a notable conservative valence).[7] Known in conservative circles simply as "Robby," George is recognizable for his elegant three-piece suits, his banjo-playing, and his much-hyped, bridge-building friendship with Cornel West, the Black leftist intellectual, actor, and 2024 presidential candidate.

George's talk was called "Leaders Should Be Servants," and it referenced the idea of the Common Good about thirty-five times. In many respects, however, George was shadow boxing with the New Right, and with the work of Adrian Vermeule and the Postliberals in particular.

Professor George spoke the old-fashioned language of fusionist conservatism, as well as the old-fashioned language of American Catholicism. He defended the free market and traditional constitutionalism. He defended academic tenure, intellectual freedom, and the rights of religious dissenters. He cited John Rawls's idea of "the fact of reasonable pluralism." And he defended the Catholic concept of subsidiarity—a Postliberal favorite having to do with supporting the local institutions that constitute the thick connective tissue of social life—but then used it to justify principles of limited government and liberal economics. Though he embraced the idea of the common good, his speech involved a rich account of the complexity of the concept, and he ultimately settled for a deflationary version that focused on its instrumental value to actual, living people. For George, the common good had to do with embodied human activities and with concrete human flourishing. It was not about vague abstractions.

When the audience in Fort Lauderdale pushed George on several core New Right issues, like ending tenure, banning parts of the university curriculum, or using the government to pursue substantive moral principles, he took a moderating tone. The final questioner put it to him forthrightly: "Under what circumstances may the right to revolution be exercised?" George replied: "When there is no other choice and there is genuine tyranny. And we are not there."[8]

Robby George didn't know what time it was.

George was the foremost Catholic speaker at the conference, while also being something like a haunting from the not-so-distant past. He spoke in a way that was ideologically opposed to the New Right, and to the Postliberals, but he also clearly did not want to upset the crowd. (And I do not want to overstate his liberal sensibilities; he is strident in his opposition to abortion, and, based on Facebook posts from 2024, my sense is that he probably still voted for Trump over Kamala Harris.)[9]

This chapter is about the philosophy of Adrian Vermeule and other Catholic Postliberals (like Patrick Deneen) who are some of the most intellectually radical members of the New Right, as well as the most ideologically consistent in their opposition to fusionist conservatism of the kind supported by George, and to neoliberal economics.

The philosopher Kevin Vallier wrote the first thorough consideration of this small but influential group in his book *All the Kingdoms of the World* (2023). He rightly called Vermeule's faction—the integralist (or neo-integralist) faction—"the premier radicalism on the New Right." As Vallier explains, it "offers the alienated something positive: an ultimate goal, a vision, a dream."[10] Vallier focused on integralism, which is more radical and openly religious than mere Postliberalism, and in this chapter so do I. (Not all Postliberals are Catholic integralists, but basically all integralists are Postliberals—these categories will become clearer over the course of the chapter.) My aim is to add a layer to our understanding of this important segment of the New Right, which in the American context is closely associated with Patrick Deneen. But be forewarned: Vermeule's work is sophisticated and highly abstract. This is a theory-heavy, Ideas First chapter, and it's as long as your average law review article.

Vermeule is the centerpiece here because, as a constitutional law scholar and active participant in integralism, he is the most radical of the Postliberal group, and the most interesting. His work on American constitutionalism lays the groundwork for a dramatic departure from conservatism's "originalist" past, and for a future that is defined by a particular conception of Catholic politics. Vermeule has worked to create the constitutional infrastructure for a radical New Right politics unbound from traditional legal or interpretive limits and instead governed by supposedly objective "classical" moral norms—norms, in other words, that he says aim for the (objective) common good—combined with a Schmittian conception of politics and power.

In the stultified world of originalist jurisprudence—and, conveniently, around the time when conservatives gained a solid 6–3 advantage on the Supreme Court and were set to overturn *Roe v. Wade*—the time was ripe to go on interpretive offense.

Adrian Vermeule

Adrian Vermeule is an interesting character—by all indications he is mild-mannered but also pugilistic—with an eclectic intellectual background. He is the Ralph S. Tyler, Jr. Professor of Constitutional Law at Harvard Law School and is also, in a sense, the perfect high ivory-tower analog to Trump, the common thread being a bravura that intimidates and bamboozles. But whereas Trump deploys harsh personal charisma in the service of his own interests, Vermeule's weapon is raw intellect, and he does not appear to be in it for the money.[11] He converted to Catholicism in 2016 (with support from Robby George),[12] and his political radicalism has a distinct goal: to promote the common good, as conceived by conservative Catholicism and interpreted by Adrian Vermeule.

Vermeule grew up in Cambridge, Massachusetts—an upbringing apparently as cloistered in the academy as Trump's was in the world of New York real estate. His mother, Emily, was a celebrated archaeologist and expert on the Bronze Age (and one of the first women professors at Harvard), while his father was an art curator at Boston's Museum of Fine Arts.[13] Vermeule spent his summers near archaeological sites in Europe, which left him with a strong affection for classics and the ancient world, and he attended Harvard as an undergraduate, where he studied ancient Chinese philosophy. He told Brooke Masters for a 2022 profile in the *Financial Times* that Chinese philosophy was in many respects similar to the classical tradition he knew growing up, but "different enough to give him scope for independent thinking."[14] After graduating from Harvard summa cum laude in 1990, he went on to Harvard Law, graduating in 1993 and proceeding to clerk for Devid Sentelle on the DC Circuit Court of Appeals and for Antonin Scalia on the Supreme Court in 1994–1995. He joined the faculty at the University of Chicago Law School in 1998 and returned to Harvard Law as a professor in 2006. He has been there ever since.

Harvard Law is among the most prestigious law schools in the country (the chief competitors being Yale and Stanford). Its alumni regularly work at the highest levels of government in the United States and include many members of Congress and Supreme Court justices. President Obama graduated from Harvard Law in 1991. Justices Gorsuch, Jackson, Kagan, and Roberts all graduated from Harvard Law.

In 2012, at the age of forty-three, Vermeule was admitted to the American Academy of Arts and Sciences.[15] His interests in public law are varied, and his understanding of the law and the American regime has often been, in the context of American conservatism, unconventional. If you ignore the matter of temperament, you can see commonalities between Vermeule and Harry Jaffa: in the willingness to skewer conventional approaches and take a bold stance on principle and against originalism. In other respects, however, Vermeule's work is the antithesis of the Claremonter outlook. The group at Claremont has, for decades now, advocated for a hagiographic view of the founding generation, combined with much acidic scholarship about the supposed tyranny of the unelected, and so unaccountable, administrative state. These are not concerns that Vermeule really shares.

Vermeule appreciates the American founders to an extent, but he is far more interested in abstract questions about the meaning of laws and constitutionalism than about the historical particularities of the American system. And throughout his career, he has consistently argued on behalf of governmental authority—and in defense of a strong executive and a strong administrative state. And unlike many at the Claremont Institute, Vermeule's scholarly output, which is extremely impressive by any standard (except perhaps that of traditional American norms of liberty), is not overtly partisan. Indeed, Vermeule steers clear of petty partisanship. Cass Sunstein, the University of Chicago Law School professor and famous liberal who, between 2009 and 2012, worked in the Obama White House, has been one of his regular collaborators since

2005. In 2020, Vermeule and Sunstein published a short book called *Law and Leviathan: Redeeming the Administrative State*, which defended the basic "morality of administrative law."[16] In Vermeule's extensive body of work, there is a consistent emphasis on the legitimacy of authority and significant concern about excessive constraints *on* government action. In a friendly review of a book by Sanford Levinson from 2015, for example, Vermeule approvingly recalled a remark from Alexander Hamilton at the constitutional convention that warned: "Establish a weak government and you must at times overleap the bounds. Rome was obliged to create dictators." Vermeule continued: "The ordinary law was like a straitjacket that had to be ripped apart to give the polity any freedom of action at all. Better to have a comfortable garment that allows flexibility while retaining its basic shape."[17] He later developed this idea into a more full-fledged theory that he called the "Publius Paradox."[18]

Vermeule's work consistently grants government significant leeway for prudential action. In any given context, such an outlook might make sense: Hamilton preferred a strong central government, and Lincoln suspended habeas corpus. But Vermeule's scholarly output amounts to something like a total preemptive grant of authority to the executive branch of the United States government and so opens the door wide to unaccountable rule; that problem does not seem to concern him. In this way his work is lopsided toward autocracy.

The extremism lurking in Vermeule is more evident in his collaborations with Eric A. Posner, also at the University of Chicago Law School (and son of Richard Posner, one of the most influential legal scholars of the last century). Together Posner and Vermeule have mounted repeated defenses of the ever-growing power of the American executive. They wrote a defense of John Yoo, author of the notorious "torture memos" under Bush, in *The Wall Street Journal* in 2004. In 2009 they coauthored a working paper titled "Tyrannophobia," which argued that, in an American context, fear of dictatorial power was irrational. Together, as we will see, they helped to rehabilitate the Nazi jurist Carl Schmitt, seeing him as a visionary of executive authority in the modern age. In 2015, about a decade after the defense of Yoo, Vermeule published a review with the *Northwestern University Law Review* with the title "Optimal Abuse of Power."[19]

It would be easy to see Vermeule as an unwitting purveyor of extreme antiliberal ideas were he not also so upfront about his personal commitment to far-right Catholic integralism, so open about his own antiliberal "strategies," so clear about his support for would-be European despots, and so committed to the political thought of Carl Schmitt. It is perhaps difficult to believe that Vermeule, a prominent, well-published constitutional scholar with a named chair at Harvard Law, is also an antiliberal authoritarian and advocate for Catholic moral and political domination, but based on his public record it is also difficult to conclude otherwise.

Before we turn to Vermeule's *Common Good Constitutionalism*, in which he provides a lucid legal justification for a new interpretation of the American regime, it is crucial to understand these other features of his intellectual background.

―――――

Vermeule was baptized as a child and raised in the Episcopalian and Anglican traditions but fell away from the religion in college. Then, in 2016, he converted to Catholicism very publicly. In an interview about his conversion with *First Things* on November 4, 2016, titled "Finding Stable Ground," he reported feeling disheartened by the "heterodox" changes and influences that had taken over the Episcopalian church (the Episcopal Church allowed some gay marriage in 2015).[20] He also reported that he had been persuaded by thinkers like John Henry Newman, a nineteenth-century English theologian who made a midlife conversion to Catholicism, and the Notre Dame historian Brad Gregory that "there is no stable middle ground between Catholicism and atheist materialism."[21] Vermeule's conversion was not just intellectual, though; it was also clearly personal and spiritual, perhaps even mystical. Twice in the course of the brief conversation, he reported having been influenced by the biblical Mary ("Behind and above all those who helped me along the way," he said, "there stood a great Lady"; when asked about those who had influenced him, he said "nearest to my heart, a young and fiercely courageous Jewish refugee girl who teaches inexhaustible lessons, Miriam bat Joachim"). A year later Vermeule argued in a different *First Things* article called "A Christian Strategy" that liberalism saves its "deepest enmity" for the Blessed Virgin. He went on to suggest, pointing to Genesis 3:15 and Revelation 12:1–9, that the "true identity" of liberalism is aligned with Satan.[22]

Perhaps the most striking thing about Vermeule's conversion interview was his commentary on the rule of law. At the end of the interview, he was asked which areas of the law he finds most hopeful. For a professor of American constitutionalism, his response was unusual, though it made sense given the context: "I put little stock or hope or faith in law. . . . In the long run it will be no better than the polity and culture in which it is embedded. If that culture sours and curdles, so will the law; indeed that process is well underway and its tempo is accelerating. Our hope lies elsewhere." Vermeule is one of those people whose thoughts shoot up into the stratosphere—and in this case to an apocalyptic politics—almost instinctively.

Several days after the interview was published, Trump won the election, and Vermeule would soon be making the case for a total, top-down, intellectual reconfiguration of orthodox conservative American constitutional thinking. This reorientation would be shaped by his active engagement in the burgeoning Catholic integralist movement.

Catholic Integralism

Catholic integralism is a way of thinking about religion and politics that, in opposition to the modern separation of church and state, and in opposition to dominant strains of contemporary Catholic political thought, advocates for church-state integration and unity.[23] It dates back to the antiliberal and antimodern movements of the eighteenth through twentieth centuries in Europe, which are typically associated with thinkers like Joseph de Maistre, an opponent of the Enlightenment and the French Revolution; Juan Donoso Cortés, who became an ardent defender of Catholicism and the monarchy in Spain; and Charles Maurras of the far-right, monarchist Action Française.[24] The Portuguese dictator Antonio Salazar was something like an integralist and has been praised as such by the New Right.[25] In the context of American conservatism, it is best represented by L. Brent Bozell Jr., the quixotic friend of Bill Buckley (and later his brother-in-law) who was also the ghostwriter for Goldwater's *Conscience of a Conservative*, and would eventually move to Spain and found *Triumph* magazine, a small but influential journal that promoted Francoism and Catholic theocracy.[26]

The contemporary iteration of the movement (sometimes called neo-integralism) was initiated by Father Edmund Waldstein, a Cistercian monk in Austria. In the early 2010s Waldstein became convinced—red-pilled might be an appropriate term—by the English theologian Thomas Pink's reinterpretation of the Second Vatican Council's proclamation about religious liberty, *Dignitas humanae*, from 1965. *Dignitas humanae* was concerned with how the church could continue to function politically in the modern era given the rise of secularism. Pink saw a way of reading *Dignitas humanae* in a conservative, antiliberal fashion, but without risking schism with Catholic orthodoxy.[27]

Waldstein popularized and added substance to the vision offered by Pink. As Vallier explained, Waldstein's integralist movement began with a Facebook group in 2013. Then it grew thanks to a live Slack chat, where Vermeule was a participant, and he later launched a blog called *The Josias*, to which Vermeule has contributed. Gladden Pappin, whom we know as Manlius from the *Journal of American Greatness*, was supportive of Waldstein's movement and *The Josias* blog from its first days.

According to Vallier's interviews, the early iteration of Waldstein's group consisted of people with a range of political perspectives, but in 2016 that changed. At the same time that Pappin was writing for *Journal of American Greatness*, he was also angling for the Waldstein integralists to get behind Trump, whose disruptive potential he saw so clearly. Vallier explained how almost everyone he interviewed "agreed that Pappin was critical in ensuring that the politically ambitious integralists won out." He continued: "[Pappin] began to manifest serious organizational talent, which he devoted to the cause. He also made the young community more unstable. In 2016, it shattered." *JAG* shuttered, but, by Vallier's account, Pappin was successful with the integralists; the conservative wing "converted a group of friends into a radical political faction dedicated to turning the US government into a Catholic state."[28]

In his blogging for *The Josias* site (which included three posts in 2018) as well as in his review of Patrick Deneen's book and his writings for *First Things*, Vermeule was explicit about his ultimate aims and purposes, as well as the means he would deploy on behalf of integralism. They included an infiltration of American liberal democracy, which he expected would implode soon, at which point the integralists would be ready to generate a newly Catholic state. Recall that he recommended searing the liberal faith "with hot irons," taking over liberals' hearts and minds, and facilitating the final destruction of the liberal order.[29] In "A Christian Strategy," Vermeule spoke of how Christian politics needed always to be strategic, "viewing political commitments not as articles of a sacred faith, but as tactical tools to be handled in whatever way best serves the cause of Christ." The priorities here are clear, and have significant consequences.

At bottom, Catholic integralists are in favor of the *reintegration* of church and state. Vallier offers the following helpful definition of integralism:

> Catholic integralists say that governments must secure the earthly and heavenly common good. God authorizes two powers to do so, they assert. The state governs in matters temporal, and the church in matters spiritual. Since the church has a nobler purpose than the state (salvation), it may authorize and direct the state to support it with certain policies, such as enforcing church law. At times, the church may need assistance to advance its objectives.[30]

Integralists believe that the government must serve both earthly and spiritual ends—as opposed to the liberal state, which (they hold) serves only much lower earthly purposes.[31] As Vallier's definition makes clear, it is not quite right to conflate integralism with theocracy, depending on one's definition. If by theocracy we mean the direct rule by religious authorities, then this is not it. Integralism is more subtle, or, depending on your point of view, more insidious. Catholic integralism is certainly theocratic in the sense that political rule is subsumed under that of a specific religion. But, at the outset at least, the integralist merely seeks to amplify the power of the faithful within the parameters of the institutional and cultural status quo: to staff the federal bureaucracy, to put integralists in positions of high executive authority, and to install them throughout the judiciary. The longer-term aim is for these actors to make political decisions with a view to the religious ends that they hold close, and effectuate a deeper transformation of the system—i.e., a deeper integration of religion into civic and political life. The writer Jeet Heer described it as "a state where religion is woven into the fabric of everyday common life, with the sanction of the state, in contrast to secularism's partitioning of the sacred into private life."[32]

For Vermeule and his integralist compatriots, the spiritual ends and results matter substantially more than the specific means used to attain them (and here we see a difference between Vermeule and Robby George, who cares more than Vermeule does about the liberal democratic provisions of American constitutionalism). As such, there is a latent volatility to the integralist movement, reminiscent of much older (i.e., preliberal) political-theological disputes. After all, what political means wouldn't be justified by the pursuit of the highest heavenly ends? What *in principle* stands in the way of the integralist ruler?

While the individuals who constitute the Postliberal group vary in their commitment to Catholic integralism, Vermeule does not waver, though in his legal scholarship he defaults to more secular language. But, given what Vermeule has said about the primacy of spiritual ends, it is important to understand that his recent legal work is situated within his Catholic integralism, and secondary to it. In brief—and this is the big takeaway to keep in mind with respect to Vermeulean constitutionalism—integralism supplies the deep substantive content that can be so elusive in originalist jurisprudence, and which is, according to him, so wildly indeterminate in progressive or "living" constitutionalism.[33] Integralism provides the answers, and it does so whether they happen to line up with actual American constitutional history or not.

Before turning to *Common Good Constitutionalism*, one more set of observations is in order, which concerns Vermeule's longstanding interest in the thought of Carl Schmitt. Since there are Schmittian reverberations throughout the New Right, it is worth spending some time here.

Carl Schmitt

In addition to being an unrepentant Nazi and antisemite, Schmitt is best known for his ideas about political theology, his critique of liberalism, his hard-line defense of the importance of the friends-enemies distinction in politics, and his defenses of dictatorship and the "state of exception." To this day, Schmitt enjoys a cyclical popularity in academic circles, including on the left, and there was a resurgence of Schmitt studies in the United States after the 9/11 terrorist attacks and the passing of the controversial Patriot Act. I studied Schmitt in grad school in the 2000s; Vermeule, along with Posner, has done his share to keep that cycle going. Schmitt is a thinker worth taking seriously for several reasons, but his work and life also exemplify, in pure form, the derangement that can come with a highly theoretical orientation.

Schmitt saw some of the problems with the Weimar system and wrote about them with unusual clarity and directness. The Weimar Republic was a liberal democratic constitutional order, and it was highly unstable. Schmitt, like Vermeule after him, worried about the dangers of a weak state, which contributed to his eventual support for Hitler. He was also devoted to a kind of political theology that puts theological imperatives and holy spiritual ends at the heart of political life. He was raised Catholic in Protestant Germany, and though he was not a committed Catholic later in life, his thought (especially its "decisionist" aspect) was influenced by Catholic counterrevolutionaries like de Maistre and Donoso Cortés.[34] Schmitt's critique of liberalism, like theirs, aimed at the foundations of liberal modernity, which had sought to unsettle religious assumptions and convictions and make space for alternative conceptions of freedom and the good life. According to Schmitt, liberal democratic claims to neutrality were always false and disingenuous. Liberalism, for all its pretended openness, was in fact a mask for a particular set of metaphysical claims, with its own normative implications and political imperatives.

For Schmitt—and this is a point we see rehearsed across the New Right going back to Harry Jaffa and the Ideas First mantras of Richard Weaver—liberalism represented not only the rejection of true religion but also the embrace of a totalizing relativism, and with this he saw no middle ground. People like Bloom and Strauss argued that liberalism and democracy invited relativism, but they were very far from concluding that liberal democracy necessitated nihilism or the abandonment of meaning. And while they appreciated that liberalism was not neutral, they could also see the difference between liberal openness and moral pluralism, on the one hand, and enforced dogmatic indoctrination, on the other. For Schmitt, liberal openness meant a kind of nothingness (or interminable discussion and metaphysical evasion) and ultimately amounted to something like apostasy vis-à-vis real politics.[35] Not only was there no such thing as neutral in politics; anything but totalizing commitment was an affirmative choice for meaninglessness or worse. Political decision-making necessarily had a metaphysical valence.

Schmitt's work was an outcry against the liberal crisis of the era, and on behalf of "the political." In his most well-known work, *The Concept of the Political*, he argued that, "the political," properly speaking, always involves an existential position taken by a group of "friends" against their "enemies" and is expressed in situations where people are willing to kill, and potentially die, for whatever unites them. Schmitt loathed liberal and parliamentary politics in part because it avoided true politics and decision-making. One gets the sense in reading Schmitt that politics of this kind—deadly, dangerous—was an existential necessity. You cannot be truly serious about something unless you are willing to fight and die for it. And if you are willing to do so, that means it is real, for you.[36]

Vermeule's appreciation for Schmitt spans more than a decade, including a long *Harvard Law Review* article "Our Schmittian Administrative Law" (2009).[37] Then, in 2011, he and Posner published their controversial book *The Executive Unbound: After the Madisonian Republic*, which leaned heavily on Schmitt, and in which they argued that "the legally constrained executive is now a historical curiosity" and the "Madisonian separation of powers is obsolete."[38] This was a good thing. Modern executives should be empowered to act decisively in rapidly changing modern environments, and political checks would be there to limit them should they overstep. Posner and Vermeule followed up their book with a contribution to *The Oxford Handbook of Carl Schmitt* called "Demystifying Schmitt." There they continued to make the case for a Schmittian approach to modern politics, or "governance through ex post standards, rather than ex ante rules"—i.e., an approach that acts first and asks questions later. "Schmittian commissarial dictatorship," they wrote, "is just the purposive approach to legal interpretation, writ very large and applied to the constitution as a whole."[39]

Much of this work is highly technical, and though it contains interesting insights into how modern politics operate, it also consistently minimizes the purposes to which Schmitt's work was eventually subsumed.[40] As is so common on the New Right, Vermeule's work also abstracts away from tangible realities in America. Legal scholars consistently made this critique in their reviews of the book. Mark Graber wrote that Vermeule and Posner tended "to substitute rational speculation for closer examination into historical sources." Richard Pious said that the book neglected lobbying and campaign finance, noting that "It is as if members of Congress and judges were all political theorists, immersed in the monographs of Schmitt written in the early 1920s." Chris Edelson wrote: "It is ironic for a book that begins by taking liberal legalism to task for being disconnected from reality to base so much of its discussion on abstractions."[41]

Vermeule's commitment to Schmitt is also signaled repeatedly in his more recent Catholic writings, where he discloses his radical goals and vast ambitions, often in Schmittian terms. In "A Christian Strategy," Vermeule praised Schmitt's defense of the extreme political "flexibility" of Catholic Church leaders, and as a major point in his favor. "Schmitt," he wrote, "saw that the universal jurisdiction and mission of the Church require it to be flexible in different places and times, willing to enter into coalitions that would be unthinkable for anyone with a merely political horizon." Vermeule cites the tactics of Paul the apostle ("I have become all things to all men, to save at least some. All this I do for the sake of the gospel"—1 Cor. 9:20–23). He concludes by recommending a path that is "radically dogmatic as to ends, radically flexible as to tactics and means"—a perfectly Schmittian sentiment that makes no pretense of caring for particular legal and constitutional forms.

A final example of Vermeule's Schmittian style comes from an essay called "All Human Conflict Is Ultimately Theological," which was based on a speech that Vermeule gave at George's James Madison Program in 2019 and began and ended with quotes from Schmitt. (In it, Vermeule mocked those who bridle at the use of Schmitt as "demi-intellectuals" infected by "intellectualized moral Puritanism.")[42] The subject of the talk was "sacramental liberalism," an idea about the fundamentally religious and ceremonial character of liberalism that owes something to Schmitt. The upshot was that liberals are driven by compulsive theological urges that disrupt other important goals and are revealed in moments of liberal overreach (Vermeule gives the example of *Obergefell*).[43] He concluded with a quote from Schmitt about the ultimate importance of ideas: "To the political belongs the idea, because there is no politics without authority and no authority without an ethos of belief."[44] Liberalism's theoretical incoherence would be its undoing.

There are weighty counters to Schmitt's thought—that it doesn't accurately capture the nature or essence of politics; that its celebration of mortal combat as truth-or-faith-disclosing is untrue and incoherent; that just because liberalism is not neutral, that does not mean it is totalizing; and that any all-or-nothing "political theology" amounts to a nihilistic devaluation of the regular goods of this world.[45] But my sense is that Vermeule is onboard with most of Schmitt's major insights. Vermeule sees liberals and liberalism (but not Schmitt) as the Satanic enemy. He believes in granting extraordinary power to the executive and shows few concerns about potential abuses of power. And he defends the idea of ruthless political "flexibility" in the service of divine spiritual ends, while lambasting liberals for incoherence. One ought not venture into Vermeule's constitutional thinking without a sense of this Schmittian context.

Common Good Constitutionalism

Vermeule's defense of common good constitutionalism began with an article in the *Atlantic* that made his comfort with authoritarian politics very plain. "Unlike legal liberalism," he wrote in 2020, "common-good constitutionalism does not suffer from a horror of political domination and hierarchy, because it sees that law is parental, a wise teacher and an inculcator of good habits." He described how the just law would transform subjects, against their will and coercively if necessary, and "subjects will come to thank the ruler" later for the legal strictures that transformed their lives and "better track and promote communal well-being."[46] His subsequent book, *Common Good Constitutionalism* (2022) was likewise written in the modest language of legal interpretation, rather than integralism and Schmittian existentialism, but it reached for a thorough overhaul of the American constitutional order.

The purpose of *Common Good Constitutionalism* was to reground American constitutional law on its true foundation. Written as a counter to the two reigning modes of interpretation in the contemporary American tradition (originalism and progressive "living" constitutionalism), Vermeule argued that *the* aim of legal interpretation is "to promote the common good." This approach allows for more interpretive latitude than originalism (Vermeule claims that originalists are beset by a needless "horror of judgment," meaning they are afraid to moralize and adjudicate what is right or wrong), but it is narrower in scope than liberal "living" constitutionalism. For Vermeule, the conservative originalist mode is too constrained and needs to be unbound, whereas the liberal mode is too active (and individualistic) and needs to be bound down. *Common Good Constitutionalism* is the Goldilocks of judicial interpretation since it offers both scope and traditional grounding: If you need to determine whether a law or action is legal, you ask, "Does it serve the common good?" and voila, you have your decision.[47]

Of course, if I put it like that, it raises a lot of questions: What is the common good? Who decides? Does anything limit the court's ability to impose said common good? What about individual rights? To be sure, Vermeule's account is more complex than the foregoing. But it is not complex enough. The book includes smart and sustained discussions of the interpretive problems of originalism and living/developmental constitutionalism, but the heart of the spare volume is about defending two concepts, "the common good" and the "classical legal tradition." These concepts are meant to provide answers to our questions—to give us something concrete to grasp when we think about the common good standard, and, further, to persuade us that the common good benchmark has been the true (but long forgotten) standard all along. The results of this part of Vermeule's endeavor are enormously dissatisfying. Ultimately, Vermeule is subject to a "horror of judgment," too, but he pushes it back to the metaphysical plane, where he disallows liberal democratic freedom about what is good, right, and legal, and finds his answers in tradition, as reconceptualized by him.

Before I turn to Vermeule's conceptual definitions, I want to say something about the broad philosophical context here. Typically, questions about "the good" are seen as central to political philosophy in general, and as more-or-less irresolvable in modern political philosophy, if only for "the fact of pluralism" referenced by Robby George, and a modern liberal commitment to intellectual humility—i.e., not because they do not believe in goodness. In Aristotle and Plato, for example, abstract questions like "What is the good?" are treated as multifarious and difficult. Abstract answers (happiness, flourishing, virtue, social cohesion) are offered but never settled, and tensions between the good of individual persons and the collective are always kept alive (think of Athens vs. Sparta). Modern political thinkers have tended to punt on these sorts of questions, offering new respect to the individual while creating political edifices that allow for a wide variety of collective and individual answers. Adrian Vermeule treats the good differently: namely, as a matter of straightforward and uncontroversial dogma. The common good is, "for the purposes of the constitutional lawyer, the flourishing of a well-ordered political community."[48] He does get more specific, but just barely.

When it comes down to it, the common good consists of what he calls the "famous trinity" or classical "triptych" of *justice, peace*, and *abundance*. Later he supplements these with the "modern triptych" of health, safety, and security.[49] Throughout the book, Vermeule treats these six abstract ends—justice, peace, abundance, health, safety, and security—as the straightforward and objective aims of all healthy political life. Strangely, he also insists that this sixfold common good is "unitary and indivisible" rather than something that could be understood in the aggregate (which I take to be his quasi-mystical way of minimizing the importance of individual freedom and of the material dimensions of our common political life). Vermeule's strange composite-unitary list includes some very good and important things, but it is simply too abstract to provide much guidance. It also actively excludes other goods, the most important being freedom, which Vermeule carefully subsumes as a secondary good in his schema.[50]

Vermeule writes as though the common good is a well-established, universally recognized concept in some readily accessible canonical library.[51] But it is not. It is a concept that Vermeule has fashioned himself, out of various threads of numerous traditions, and based on his own idiosyncratic theoretical and spiritual affinities. The legal scholars Micah Schwartzman and Richard Schragger suggested that Vermeule's vagaries were symptomatic of a reticence to disclose the religious basis of his outlook, and I concur. As they note, Vermeule cites the *ragion di stato* or "reason of state" tradition as the source of his original triptych and claims merely to provide a framework for thinking about the common good, not a blueprint. But as Schwartzman and Schragger further observe, he insists that some specific policy outcomes follow from his theory, including "a constitutional right to life for 'unborn children,' most likely a prohibition on gay marriage, bans on pornography and perhaps blasphemy, and restrictions on various forms of dangerous or false speech."[52] Those specifics only follow if you accept Vermeule's legal sources as infallible.

The name that Vermeule gives for his fuller framework is the "classical legal tradition." According to him, this tradition is a set of background assumptions, unwritten norms, modes of interpretation, and aims that were assumed by the best jurists of the past and informed the American founders. Vermeule appeals to Blackstone and the English Common Law, to the Roman Civil law and the Continental system, to natural rights and natural laws, to Aristotle and Aquinas. And while he is quick to point out that the classical legal tradition is not a monolith, he nevertheless insists that all these strands amount to a singular "matrix in which American law grew." Crucially, the various parts of his classical legal matrix all "afforded broad scope for public authorities to act in service of the common good." The law should be interpreted according to the common good standard, as embedded in the classical legal tradition.[53]

Vermeule is not the first to argue that legal interpretation takes place against a field of background assumptions, inheritances, thick principles, and unwritten rules. Abraham Lincoln argued for a version of this understanding, as have Harry Jaffa, Lon L. Fuller, Ronald Dworkin, and, more recently, George Thomas and Jonathan Gienapp. But Vermeule goes much further in his brazen insistence that both the common good and the classical legal tradition amount to a single, unified matrix of meaning.

All of which is fine. Vermeule is free to believe whatever he wants about the deep superstructure of the American constitutional order. His story becomes factually dubious, however, when he further argues that the classical legal tradition has always, with a singular voice, undergirded American jurisprudence. He presents *Common Good Constitutionalism* as a project of radical recovery, against a background of what he calls "our legal culture's amnesia."[54] He claims that American legal actors used to abide by common good constitutionalism and the classical legal tradition, just as he understands them, but over time that tradition was forgotten and replaced with the imposter theories of originalism and living constitutionalism. "The fundamental teleological aims of government identified by the classical tradition," he writes, "are also the aims of our constitutional order."[55] This is blatant historical retrofitting and is impossible to reconcile with the historical record.

Vermeule's demotion of liberty in the pantheon of American goods and values suffices to demonstrate the point. He argues that freedom not only should be but traditionally *has been* better understood as a secondary value in the American tradition.[56] It simply isn't so. Individual liberty has always, obviously, been core to the American project, including its legal traditions. If we were to go looking for the agreed-upon goods and values that inform the American psyche, we could do worse than the Declaration of Independence and the Preamble to the Constitution. The second sentence of the Declaration of Independence, of course, declares "Life, Liberty and the pursuit of Happiness" to be unalienable rights. Neither liberty nor happiness makes it onto Vermeule's sixfold list. The Preamble states that the Constitution was established "to form a more perfect Union, establish Justice, insure domestic Tranquility, provide for the common defense, promote the general Welfare, and secure the

Blessings of Liberty to ourselves and our Posterity." Vermeule's list covers all of these *except* the "Blessings of Liberty." He addresses this point directly in the book, channeling Patrick Deneen's conception of virtue, and arguing that "On the classical conception, 'liberty' is no mere power of arbitrary choice, but the faculty of choosing the common good." Liberty consists in our capacity to aim for those other goods teleologically and "in exactly the same way as the classical tradition of *ragion di stato*."[57] This is, at best, a fudge. It erases the fact that modern liberty has to do with self-government and setting limits on the power of others: it's not just the "faculty of choosing the common good," it's actually getting to choose the good, for yourself and your community.

And, of course, it is not just the Declaration and Preamble that celebrate this kind of freedom. So does the Bill of Rights. In the Gettysburg Address, Lincoln described America as a nation "conceived in Liberty" and resolved that "this nation, under God, shall have a new birth of freedom." He was talking about the end of slavery, not a renewal of virtue ethics. The Reconstruction Amendments, the Nineteenth Amendment, and, much later, the Civil Rights Act all served and aimed for liberty conceived in this emancipatory mode.

To his credit, Deneen is more honest about the liberal character of the American founding, and the ways that it departs from anything that could be called the classical legal tradition. In *Why Liberalism Failed*, he called the Constitution the "applied technology of liberal theory" and "the embodiment of a set of modern principles that sought to overturn ancient teachings and shape a distinctly different modern human." It was obvious to Deneen that the founders hoped to expand "the sphere of individual liberty."[58] The good, as conceived of by the American legal tradition, is simply not as objective as Adrian Vermeule thinks.

Popularizing Common Good Constitutionalism

Common Good Constitutionalism struck a nerve. Upon its publication, Vermeule became something of a cult figure in the upper echelons of the Catholic New Right—with the magazine profiles, conferences, and panels that attend such acclaim—and suddenly everyone was talking in terms of the "common good." It became evident that the Vermeulean "common good" was as flexible a concept as any good Schmittian could hope for. Other actors on the New Right proceeded, along with Patrick Deneen, to provide variations on the theme.

The *Postliberal Order* Substack was founded just prior to the publication of Vermeule's book in February 2022. The first post by Deneen was entitled "A Good That Is Common," but Deneen emphasized the "commonness" of common goodness and eschewed philosophical abstractions. He wanted to talk about "those needs and concerns that are identified in the ordinary requirements of ordinary people."[59]

A man named Josh Hammer was probably the most prolific lover of the new common goodness. An early National Conservatism enthusiast, research fellow with the Edmund Burke group, and editor at *Newsweek*, Hammer had earned an undergraduate degree from Duke University and a JD degree from the University of Chicago Law School. Shortly after the publication of Vermeule's original *Atlantic* article, Hammer raised the notion of a tweaked—and less radical—alternative to Vermeule's thought. He did so in the Claremont Institute's *American Mind*, in an article called "Common Good Originalism," and in later essays and "salvos" like "Undoing the Court's Supreme Transgression," "Who's Afraid of the Common Good," "A Better Originalism," and "The Telos of the American Regime."[60]

If one reads these articles, it becomes obvious that, like Vermeule, Hammer and others on the New Right were deeply offended by Justice Neil Gorsuch's ruling in *Bostock v. Clayton County, Georgia* (2020), a case in which the Supreme Court ruled in favor of federal laws prohibiting employer discrimination against LGBTQ people. As Hammer, echoing Josh Hawley, put it at the time:

> There is no escaping the takeaway of *Bostock v. Clayton County, Georgia*, in which Federalist Society-vetted "originalist" golden boy Neil Gorsuch became the latest member of the ignominious list of Republican nominees at the Court to cave on a civilization-defining cultural issue. That conclusion is both stark and depressing: The conservative

legal movement, with all its attendant institutions, theories, and pedagogies, *has failed conservatism.*[61]

Like Vermeule, Hammer was eager to recover the broad, high, moral ideals of the American founding as something that ought to guide constitutional interpretation.[62] And like Vermeule, he insisted that these true ideals were much more communitarian than was commonly believed. But unlike Vermeule, whose approach was abstract and "continental" (Hammer's words), Hammer sought to situate his approach within originalism, broadly conceived—more in the tradition of Aristotelians and Straussians like Harry Jaffa and natural law theorists like Hadley Arkes.[63] Sometimes Hammer referred to his outlook as "moral originalism," or "Manly Originalism."[64]

In the summer of 2021, Hammer published a longer essay explicating his outlook in the *Harvard Journal of Law & Public Policy*, which describes itself as "one of the top five most widely circulated law reviews and the nation's leading forum for conservative and libertarian legal scholarship." Hammer's essay was fiery and struck an urgent, Claremont-style tone, claiming that, despite some appearances to the contrary, "the state of conservative jurisprudence in America has reached a crisis point." He again took issue with positivistic and libertarian interpretations of the Constitution, preferring a much more moralizing and communitarian mode. He claimed to share "Professor Vermeule's belief that solipsistic citizens' 'own perceptions of what is best for them' are, for all intents and purposes, constitutionally irrelevant." Like Vermeule, Hammer wanted to demote individual liberty in the American pantheon of values.[65]

Hammer helped to keep the New Right movement active and growing, and the new constitutional conservatism continued to flourish. Roger Kimball's cultural journal *The New Criterion* published a special symposium devoted to the theme in January 2022.[66] Hammer accused various critics—but especially the former vice president of the Heritage Foundation, Kim R. Holmes—of "not knowing what time it is" in America. He expressed hope that Roberts would have a "shrewder understanding of what time it is in these late-stage United States." He also

explicitly emphasized "the connection between common-good originalism and national conservatism, which is more willing to prudentially
wield state power to pursue a substantive vision of the good."[67]

After Vermeule's book was published, there was another flurry of activity, with many searing reviews of the book in mainstream legal jour-
nals and other media.[68] But it created a stir in conservative quarters
because it seemed to promise something richer and more concrete—
something more fully "good"—than originalism ever had. *Common
Good Constitutionalism* opened a prospect for bringing the Highest
Good (back) into politics.

In October 2022 Sohrab Ahmari organized a conference around Ver-
meule's book called "Restoring a Nation: The Common Good in the
American Tradition."[69] This small gathering in Steubenville, Ohio, in-
cluded the crème de la crème of the Catholic contingent of the New
Right scene. In addition to Ahmari, all the writers for the *Postliberal
Order*—Vermeule, Deneen, Pappin, and Pecknold—were on the
agenda. R. R. Reno, the editor of *First Things*, was there. So was Matthew
Schmitz, who had formerly worked as an editor at *First Things* and was
Ahmari's collaborator on *Compact* magazine.

It was also a crossover crowd. John A. Burtka IV, the new president
of the Intercollegiate Studies Institute, was in attendance. So was JD
Vance, a recent convert to Catholicism who would be elected senator
from Ohio the following month. Josh Hammer gave a talk. Michael
Lind, a professor at the Lyndon B. Johnson School of Public Policy at
the University of Texas—and a hard-to-categorize critic of libertarianism, defender of the working class, and thoughtful regular contributor
to *Compact*—spoke too, just as he had done at the National Conservatism conference in Miami a month prior.[70] Rachel Bovard was also a
speaker in Steubenville. She struck a culture-warring tone ("Nothing in
the last thirty years suggests that the left's fascist orgy is somehow going
to abate") and generally exemplified how the posh ideas of the Postliberal crowd (in her case, Postliberal ideas about freedom) get translated
into the rest of the movement.[71]

At around this same time, Harvard University also hosted a conference on the book.[72] And in fall 2023 the *Harvard Journal of Law &*

Public Policy devoted an entire issue to *Common Good Constitutionalism*. Refreshingly, some of the contributors to that symposium were liberals, and they pointed out that liberals believe in the common good, too. Linda C. McClain and James E. Fleming wrote a powerful article called "Toward a Liberal Common Good Constitutionalism for Polarized Times" that acknowledged points of agreement with Vermeule. As they argued, "A common good constitutionalism will be the only constitutionalism that has a chance against challenges like climate change, rolling pandemics, economic injustice, racial and gender injustice, uncontrolled technological change, advancing oligarchy, and recrudescing white Christian nationalism in the United States."[73] They also made plain the extent to which Vermeule's book relied on mysteries and vagaries about the actual substance of the good. As much as Vermeule would like to be the sole supplier of that substance, the good is a highly contested category—it is *the* contested category—especially in a pluralistic modern liberal democracy. To deny that, as the Postliberals are keenly aware, is to deny the core of liberal democratic ideals and practices. It is to replace toleration, pluralism, and democratic contestation with their own monolithic and hierarchical conception of what is true and meaningful.

––––––––

In April 2023 I had a chance to witness the impact that Vermeulean thinking had on Patrick Deneen, at an AEI event in DC called "Religion's Refusal to Die."[74] Nathan Pinkoski was there, and so was Robby George. But the highlight of the conference was a panel on the first day called "Religion and American Liberalism," which involved a conversation between Deneen and Meir Soloveichik. Soloveichik is a prominent Orthodox rabbi and professor at Yeshiva University in New York City. He is very conservative, and a former student of George's. Like George, he is more sympathetic to liberal democracy and the American founding than Deneen.

By the time the AEI event had happened, Deneen had radicalized significantly beyond what he wrote in *Why Liberalism Failed*. There he had defended something along the lines of Rod Dreher's *Benedict Option*—the idea that people of faith should isolate themselves from the broader liberal culture, at least as a preliminary step, if they wanted to preserve their communities against modern decadence and decay. By 2023 he was arguing forcefully against "defensive crouch conservatism" and on behalf of something much more radical.

In the conversation with Soloveichik, the question of how best to contend with the encroachment of contemporary liberal culture came up. Soloveichik and Deneen agreed that the *Benedict Option* response was dissatisfying, because conservatives and religious people needed to be able to engage in public life. Soloveichik argued that conservatives should look beyond mere religious liberty and seek to have a cultural impact—to build parallel cultures, or rival cultures, to liberalism. But Deneen went much further, deploying all-or-nothing Schmittian language to prove his point. He strongly objected to Soloveichik's idea of a "parallel" culture, because "you either have a culture or you don't." He said he could accept the idea of "rival" culture because, as he put it, "a rival wants to win." He became more adamant: "I think we really have to adopt the mentality and the view that we have to win. We don't just want to coexist. We have to win."

Deneen's next book, published just a few months later, reflected this new militancy (Vance, now a senator, spoke at the book launch). With *Regime Change*, Deneen joined Vermeule more explicitly in the constructive project of "integration from within." The title alone implied a total repudiation of liberal democracy. On the common good, Deneen followed Vermeule, but with a few twists. He argued for "common-good conservatism," which involves a revival of Aristotelian "mixed constitutionalism," and something he called "Aristopopulism," which means rule by a new and better class of elites. The final chapter was titled "Toward Integration." One of the Postliberal changes that Deneen advocated in this vein was the embrace of an overtly Christian state, with holy holidays and tax-funded religious public works.

Regime Change was slightly fantastical in its Manichean embrace of hard populist dualities. Deneen insisted on reinvigorating a supposedly long-lost classical distinction between "the many" and "the few," and he took it on himself to speak for the long-neglected masses (presumably from the vantage point of one of the few worthy aristocrats). To Deneen, the working-class masses are naturally conservative, at least in their cultural tastes and moral sentiments (which seemed here to matter more to him than economics). He wrote, for example, that "what is needed—and what most ordinary people *instinctively seek*—is stability, order, continuity, and a sense of gratitude for the past and obligation toward the future. What they want, without knowing the word for it, is a conservatism that conserves."[75] As others have observed, many liberal social policies—like abortion rights and birth control, marriage equality, and no-fault divorce—are significantly more popular with the general public than are the conservative ones that came before.[76] And even on economics, as Becca Rothfeld wrote in a memorable review of the book, "This facile taxonomy is not class analysis; it is astrology for the bow-tie set."[77]

In *Regime Change*, Deneen also embraced Schmittian all-or-nothing language, albeit with typical hedging and coyness.[78] He advocated for the transformation or "replacement" of today's elites with a new and more virtuous kind of "genuine aristoi." As Jennifer Szalai wrote in her review, "After spending 150 pages disparaging the 'elite,' Deneen goes on, in the last third of the book, to try to reclaim the word for a 'self-conscious *aristoi*' who would dispense with all the liberal niceties about equality and freedom and instead serve as the vanguard of a muscular 'aristopopulism. . . . The raw assertion of political power by a new generation of political actors inspired by an ethos of common-good conservatism.'"[79] *Regime Change* contained some interesting theoretical observations about the Aristotelian idea of a mixed constitution, and some good recommendations about policy changes that could help revitalize American life. But Deneen also repeatedly justified the deployment of "Machiavellian means to achieve Aristotelian ends" as a central part of his new vision, at one point approvingly citing a particularly dramatic passage from Machiavelli that refers to mobs in the senate and the streets with "shops boarded up."[80] Deneen suggested that "existing political forms" could remain the same so long as, à la integralism, "a fundamentally different ethos informs those institutions and the personnel who populate key offices and positions," but it is hard to read his citation of Machiavelli as anything other than a flirt with violent revolt.[81] *Regime Change* had nothing to say about the violence of January 6, 2021.

Economics, Orbánism, and the Hard Right

The Postliberals depart from the rest of the New Right in crucial respects. While they share with the rest a univocal and reactionary social conservatism—and a willingness to use the government to shape morality in traditionalist directions—they are more serious about moving beyond neoliberal economics in ways that would help the working class. They are also at once more skeptical of the New Right's crude nativism and more free-thinking when it comes to international affairs. The Postliberals' status as the intellectual Brahmins of the New Right allows them to be more ideologically pure. They are far less interested in day-to-day movement politics than the National Conservatives, or the Claremont group, or Robby George. They are not beholden to GOP donors, or to the GOP base.

Which also means that, with the exception of their influence on JD Vance, they have been the least influential thinkers of the New Right. Julius Krein started articulating the problem as early as 2020 ("For all the talk of Trump as a tribune of the working class—including from the president himself," he wrote, "his administration never really strayed from Republican orthodoxy on conventional labor issues").[82] And this ineffectiveness was conceded by the more public-facing Postliberals in the course of 2023. In the spring edition of *American Affairs*, Gladden Pappin wrote an article titled "Requiem for the Realignment." He argued that the conservative turn toward genuine economic populism was something of a mirage, unlikely to come to fruition.[83] Trump had basically followed the standard GOP model of massive tax breaks for the rich, and apart from measures taken in the wake of the Covid-19 pandemic, Trump's GOP had not passed any major, lasting socioeconomic legislation that would help the working class. President Biden, on the other hand, had.[84] The Postliberals recognized these inconsistencies—on Ukraine, and on the economy—and kept distancing themselves from parts of the New Right.

Sohrab Ahmari—whom by that time I had taken to calling the "Where's Waldo" of the New Right—was even more forthcoming, which was whiplash-inducing at the time. Indeed, it was hard at first to take Ahmari's retreat from strident New Rightism seriously because he had been such a forceful advocate for culture warriorism in his writings on "David Frenchism" (where, recall, he had said that the way forward was to "fight the culture war with the aim of defeating the enemy and enjoying the spoils in the form of a public square re-ordered to the common good and ultimately the Highest Good"). And as late as September 2022, Ahmari was defending Donald Trump (in a *Compact* essay titled "He's Still the One").[85] Over time, however, Ahmari's views about social democratic economics and the priority of economics over culture-warring began to gain some credibility.

In August 2023 Ahmari published an op-ed in *Newsweek* in which he declared: "I was wrong. The GOP will never be the party of the working class." The substance of the article was forthright and compelling. Ahmari began by acknowledging his role in peddling GOP populism and hoping that Trump could deliver, helping working people "attain lives of security and dignity." Then he pivoted: "Now I'm faced with the realization that he couldn't—no one could, because the Republican Party remains, incorrigibly, a vehicle for the wealthy." He went on to explain that, while he was "ferociously conservative" on cultural issues, he was increasingly drawn to the economic policies of the left—and to figures like Senators Elizabeth Warren or Bernie Sanders. For Ahmari, these two stood out against "the vast majority of leaders in American politics, and especially those on the right" who were unwilling to tackle the "corporate hegemony and Wall Street domination" that makes daily life "all but unlivable" for the working class. He went even further: "Indeed, I increasingly despair of the whole Right, now almost completely lost to a mindless politics that reduces *every* problem to 'wokeness.'[86] Ahmari's anticorporate arguments were much smarter than the anti-ESG and "woke capitalism" lines coming from Claremont and the NatCons.

Ahmari's book *Tyranny, Inc.* was also published in August 2023, and it was generally well-received on the left.[87] The book avoided the culture wars and stayed tethered to real working-class issues, support for unionization, and achievements of the progressive past like the New Deal.[88] Perhaps Ahmari's background as a journalist and immigrant has kept him more bound to the real world. Sometimes, not having a PhD can be a boon to clear thinking.

———

If the Postliberals have some real independence of mind vis-à-vis American politics, their international allegiances still make their theoretical extremism plain enough. And, except for Ahmari, these appear mainly to be with far-right leaders in Europe.[89] Vermeule, Deneen, and Pappin have consistently hyped the leaders of Europe's far-right while sanitizing their illiberal and antidemocratic tendencies. On this front, there is no daylight between the Postliberals and the rest of the New Right.

Adrian Vermeule, for example, has been an outspoken supporter of Nigel Farage, the controversial right-wing Brexit politician and major Trump backer, whom he called in 2018 "the defining mind of our era."[90] He is also an admirer of the arch-conservative Polish intellectual and politician Ryszard Legutko (who is also a regular participant at NatCon conferences).[91] Legutko is a prominent intellectual leader in Poland's far right Law and Justice Party, and was elected to the European Parliament in 2009. Vermeule has defended some of the controversial Polish judicial reforms through which that party achieved power.[92] In 2022 Vermeule praised Legutko's embrace of "the European tradition in the broadest sense. . . . Which stands upon the three pillars of Greek philosophy, Roman law, and Catholic faith." This way of putting it erases the Protestant and Enlightenment parts of the European tradition. At this same time, Vermeule expressed excitement about the revival of "the European tradition" in the United States, praising the (American) New Right movement for being "unafraid to use public authority in the service of the common good where necessary."[93] Deneen offered a similar sentiment during his visit to Hungary in 2021.[94]

The Postliberals' admiration for Viktor Orbán's Hungary is also well documented. In August 2022 Deneen and Pappin published a "Dispatch from Budapest" that entailed their "Notes on a Conversation with

Hungary's Viktor Orbán."[95] They wrote of Orbán's "remarkable candor," his "remarkable analytic and even philosophical depth." They claimed to have witnessed a "genuine tour de force of political analysis and vision, a quality almost wholly absent in today's American political class." The post culminated in a description of Orbán's thoughts about how "conservative leadership can win, lead, and shape the next generation." And they claimed, "Without question, Hungary is a singular example of such success in recent years." Deneen and Pappin praised Orbán's turn away from the "liberal conception" of freedom and his return to a Christian framework for "understanding the bedrock commitments needed for good politics."[96]

Nowhere did Vermeule, Deneen, or Pappin question the illiberal measures that Polish and Hungarian far-right leaders took to gain and consolidate power. Presumably, they approved. And why would they not?[97] Such measures are entirely consistent with notions like "Common Good Constitutionalism," "Aristopopulism," and using "Machiavellian means to achieve Aristotelian ends."[98] Shortly after Pappin declared the populist realignment in the United States to be a failure, he took a job as president of the Hungarian Institute of International Affairs, the state-owned think tank advising Orbán.[99]

———

Sohrab Ahmari was the exception to the Postliberals' infatuation with illiberal European politics. Though he dedicated *Tyranny, Inc.* to "Adrian, Chad, Gladden, and Patrick," on the first page he spoke of freedom in affirming, liberal terms. He declared that freedom "is suffering a global funk" and called this a tragedy with multiple and varying causes, from the "seductive allure of populist demagogues," to the "perceived failure of liberal democracy to solve ordinary people's problems" and the "advent of social media as a tool for spreading misinformation." And then he stated the matter of despotism plainly, and in relation to American sentiments:

Whatever the causes, the sum effect is that vast multitudes now labor under the yoke of coercion, in some cases having willingly thrown in their lots with elected despots, from Poland to the Philippines, Hungary to Turkey. This is an agonizing development for Americans especially. As one group of pro-democracy advocates has written, the yearning for a noncoercive society "is the question at the center of every pivotal moment of American history."

In this last clause, Ahmari was quoting a Freedom House report cited by William Galston in *The Wall Street Journal*.[100] Here, both by calling out people like Orbán as "elected despots" and in his defense of freedom as noncoercion, Ahmari broke with his integralist colleagues.[101] He published an essay in the Spring 2024 edition of *Liberties,* a liberal literary journal, where he concluded with a declaration that "American democracy is itself a most precious common good."[102]

Furthermore, Ahmari was the only New Right commentator I know of who came out strongly, in writing, against the Hard Right around this time. To his credit, Deneen did warn against Bronze Age Pervert in public talks.[103] But Ahmari really went for it. In the pages of the *New Statesman* in 2023, he dubbed them the "Unabomber Right," naming figures like Raw Egg Nationalist, Bronze Age Pervert, and L0m3z.[104] He was also a strong and regular critic of Elon Musk's antiworker policies, as well as his takeover of Twitter (calling X a "cesspool").[105] He would write that DeSantis's campaign in the GOP presidential primary failed because it was too online, too rigid, and too weird; DeSantis, he wrote, was too much "the darling of the intellectual right."[106] Ahmari would continue this campaign against the "barbarian right" through 2024, as the power and visibility of the Hard Right continued to grow. It was lonely work.[107]

11

The End of Men

THE DOCUMENTARY BEGINS WITH footage of President John F. Kennedy's remarks at the fiftieth anniversary of the creation of the Children's Bureau, an administrative unit within the federal Department of Health and Human Resources, in 1962: "I welcome this opportunity to speak to the American people about a subject which I believe to be most important, and that is the subject of physical fitness."[1]

The camera cuts to an image of a very muscular man, at dawn, throwing a spear. That shot splices to a space rocket, and then we have a scene of young men exercising outside together, hard, perhaps sometime in the 1950s. Superimposed across these images, we get some grandiose words:

IN AGES PAST

A CYCLE BEGAN

HARD TIMES MADE

STRONG MEN.

The president continues: "A country is, in a way, as strong as its citizens and I think that mental and physical health go hand in hand."

Again, the grandiose overlay:

STRONG MEN

MADE GOOD TIMES.

Here, the tenor of the images starts to shift. There is a clip of President Biden stumbling on an airplane stairway on the tarmac. We see an irrigation wheel dispensing what look like chemical fertilizers. President Kennedy continues: "There is nothing, I think, more unfortunate than to have soft, chubby, fat looking children. . . . I hope that all of you will join the United States to make sure that our children participate fully in a vigorous and adventurous life, which is possible for them in this very rich country of ours."

Now we are shown stock footage of a shirtless heavyset Black man; and then of a heavyset white man. We see an image of polluted wastewater, a sea of garbage, and a wash of dead fish.

GOOD TIMES

MADE WEAK MEN.

Then we see a photo of a group of Democratic senators, masked and kneeling. It is of Senators Tim Kaine, Chris Van Hollen, Martin Heinrich, and Michael Bennet, taken on June 4, 2020, in Emancipation Hall of the United States Capitol, during a moment of silence held by Senate Democrats in honor of George Floyd.[2]

WEAK MEN

MADE HARD TIMES.

The final image of the sequence is of a mangled (white, male) body lying, possibly dead, on the pavement, during a protest.

The montage lasts about a minute. It marks the beginning of a thirty-four-minute-long feature for the Fox News series *Tucker Carlson Originals* called "The End of Men."

———

The tagline for the episode was "Testosterone levels in American men are collapsing. Fertility is in decline. Is this the end of men?" And it came with a trigger warning: "This program contains high levels of toxic masculinity, high levels of testosterone, bro science and testicle tanning, which may be triggering to some viewers. Discretion is advised."

Once it aired, on October 5, 2022, "The End of Men" was roundly mocked in the mainstream media. In fact, it was mocked even before it aired. There was much ado, in particular, about a scene in which a man stood on a hill at dawn, in front of some kind of machine, doing, as *Rolling Stone* magazine put it, "infrared ball tanning."[3]

But there was more to that documentary than indiscreet red-light therapy. Carlson's video offered a snapshot of a moment in American history where several dramatic developments converged, and the New Right reached a tipping point.

What we saw in the video was an overt embrace of various forms of extremism, which signaled an extraordinary hardening of parts of the movement beyond the former parameters of respectable politics. The more extremist, illiberal elements of the New Right had become more mainstream and dominant among GOP leadership. These included elements of the so-called Manosphere, as well as conspiratorial elements like the Great Replacement theory and 2020 election denialism. New alliances had been formed between Hard Right extremists and the hard left. This convergence also included the dramatic growth of overt Christian nationalism, discussed in chapter 12, and best evidenced by the ascension of Mike Johnson to the role of Speaker of the House.

In this chapter, I survey the hard edges of the New Right movement as they materialized during the final years of the Biden administration, from Tucker Carlson's embrace of the Manosphere to the nomination of Donald Trump as the 2024 presidential nominee for the GOP. Due to Trump's innumerable personal liabilities and ninety-one criminal indictments, he was not necessarily the New Right's first choice for 2024. But after failing in various efforts to raise Ron DeSantis to preeminence—a sign, it seemed, of the limits of their strange movement—they rallied. By this point, the New Right was all-in with some of the most brazenly destructive and delusional forces in the country.

"The End of Men"

I had low expectations for "The End of Men," since Tucker Carlson had, over the course of the first Trump administration, descended into racism, conspiracism, and mania. Those expectations were thwarted somewhat by the documentary. To be sure, it did contain absurdities like ball tanning and raw egg chugging, scenes that were apparently filmed on one of Alex Jones's properties just outside of Austin, Texas, and featured a group of weight-lifting "bros."[4] But it also had some substance. It featured, for example, clips from a well-regarded environmental scientist, who clearly explained the problem of endocrine inhibitors and other toxins in the environment. Dr. Linda Birnbaum, a microbiologist and former director of the National Institute of Environmental Health Sciences, is not a quack or a conspiracist. She has long been concerned about the harmful effects of toxins in the environment, and of regulatory failures to contain them. She has faced pushback from Republicans for her work.[5] She is not someone I would have expected to see on Carlson's show.

But there she was, talking about "chemicals in the environment that had the potential to harm human health," how statutes are structured such that "the chemical is regarded as innocent until it's proven guilty," and how huge agrochemical corporations like Monsanto played "whack-a-mole" to kill newly proposed studies that might put limits on pollutants. This was not quackery or conspiracism; these were ideas that thoughtful leftists, environmentalists, and sociologists had been concerned about since Rachel Carson's *Silent Spring*.[6] It is true that Tucker Carlson hyped up and manipulated Birnbaum's message, emphasizing testosterone and sperm counts, at one point concluding, "So the end of men has a chemical cause!" But it was still surprising—and, if I'm honest, refreshing—to hear a message like hers get airplay on Fox News.

And there were other things to like about "The End of Men." The line from President Kennedy about "soft, chubby, fat-looking children" is rude, but his and the rest of the documentary's focus on physical fitness and strength in men—as well as our society's failure to support physical fitness and activity in young people more generally—are well-taken. (Needless to say, Carlson doesn't mention Michelle Obama's "Let's Move!" campaign, or President Obama's Task Force on Childhood Obesity.) Carlson gave some airtime to Robert F. Kennedy Jr., who, in addition to much quackery, expressed more reasonable concerns about microplastics. There was a lot in the show about something called "bro science," which sounds absurd—but it was also tongue-in-cheek and just involved extreme fitness regimens and strange experimental diets.

The serious upshot of what Carlson presented was a critique of the pharmaceutical industry and the medical establishment—for being almost entirely focused on profit and out of touch with what makes for actual health and well-being. A few subjects in the show discussed how they have transformed and saved themselves from extreme unhappiness or depression through rigorous diets and exercise regimens. "Bro science" may not be scientific, but it's probably not the worst "wellness" regime out there. If you squinted a little (maybe a lot), this didn't sound so different from the idea of "Medicine 3.0," a popular concept whereby the medical industry takes a more holistic and preventative approach to health.[7] Especially considering Carlson's promotional material, some of what he presented in "The End of Men" was surprisingly reasonable.

The problem was all the other stuff that Carlson included that was inconsistent, lopsided, unreasonable, deeply misleading, outright loopy, or openly fascistic. A small example: In the original JFK speech used in the opening, the president praised the invention of vaccines and noted the need to make them more fully available. In the rest of their program, RFK Jr. and Carlson spouted antivax conspiracies. Or consider how Carlson used Birnbaum's findings in ways that were completely inconsistent with his other programming choices. He had two other "Originals" devoted to the problems with wind farms and green energy, which might as well have been sponsored content from the oil and plastics industries. There is no reason to believe that Carlson would have been talking about endocrine disruptors had it not allowed him to use that science to stir up a panic about testosterone levels, declining manliness, and the end of human civilization. And stir up a panic he did.

————

The best way to get a sense of the extremism that "The End of Men" peddled is to consider one of its star characters, a man who goes by the pseudonym "Raw Egg Nationalist" (REN).

When I first saw "The End of Men," Raw Egg Nationalist was not new to me. But it was astonishing to see him platformed on Fox News. I had written about him for *The Bulwark* in April 2022, after he had published an article called "The Decline Is Real" in the Claremont Institute's *American Mind.* That article made many of the same arguments about testosterone levels that Carlson would make in his show.[8]

Carlson introduced Raw Egg Nationalist as the "spiritual leader" of the "bro scientists." Then he cut to a long segment where REN expounded on his message with a monologue. First, he described the enemy. The words "The Great Reset" flash over shots of masked people, people isolated during the pandemic, factory belts covered in Covid-19 tests, and so forth. The music is ominous. Then REN speaks:

> The enemy today is what I like to call soy globalism. The globalist aim is to destroy nations and local communities. And they do this by isolating communities and sickening them through food, and also through so-called medicine, and all the dreadful chemicals we're exposed to on a daily basis. The globalists want you to be fat, sick, depressed and isolated, the better to control you and to milk you for as much economic value as they can before they kill you. That's soy globalism in a nutshell. Own nothing, live in the pod, eat the soy.

Succinct and simple, and funny. At the same time, the message here, flagged by "The Great Reset" tagline, is conspiratorial and fantastical. "The Great Reset" was the name of an initiative launched by Klaus Schwab, the chief executive of the World Economic Forum, which sought to articulate an ambitious economic recovery plan in the wake of the Covid-19 pandemic. As Raw Egg Nationalist illustrates, the Great Reset plan immediately became fodder for bizarre conspiracies.

The idea that the hellscape that REN describes is the result of secret plots and projects on the part of a globalist cabal determined to weaken and destroy the populace, rather than the predictable outcomes of human greed, capitalism, technology, and even some good intentions, is deranged. In its desperation to find something— someone!—to blame for human suffering, it wildly overestimates the power of individual human actors in the world and seriously misunderstands ordinary human motivation. There is something slightly pathetic about this. (Ironically, the sort of thinking that Carlson and REN engage in is precisely the kind of thinking that Nietzsche attributes to slave morality—i.e., to the morality of the naturally weak who suffer from life. Like the weak types in Nietzsche's analysis, REN and other conspiracists see dark forces operating where ordinary motivations make more sense.)[9]

After this brief introduction to "the enemy," the music turns cheerful, and the camera shows beautiful young men "slonking" their eggs in the morning light. Raw Egg Nationalist continues, declaring that "The best response to this is a strong politics of nationalism. The nation is only as strong as the individuals who make it up, and that's where all the eggs come in." REN proceeds to explain the superfood status of eggs, and how they are the "absolute opposite of the disgusting rubbish that the globalists want you to eat." They are cheap, he says, and can't be patented. "By making the individual strong you make the nation strong," he proclaims, and the segment culminates with a theatrical affirmation of self: "I'm Raw Egg Nationalist. I'm an anon right-wing bodybuilder and I dispense Red Pill fitness and health information to the masses. Why should somebody believe me? Well, I'm just channeling the wisdom of the ancients really. I'm a vessel." REN keeps making the case for eating a lot of raw eggs, as the soundtrack shifts to Richard Strauss's *Thus Spoke Zarathustra* (aka the main theme track to *2001: A Space Odyssey*).

Though it did not make it into Carlson's documentary, one of REN's favorite topics from the alternative lifestyle zone is "Russian household gardening." In 2022 he published a book called the *Eggs Benedict Option*—a play on Rod Dreher's *The Benedict Option*—in which he explains how Russian household plots (the countryside gardens near the famous dacha cottages/summer homes) play a central role in food production, combatting all the problems that come with corporate food production, including dependence on global supply chains.[10] He also wrote about it for the *American Mind*.[11] Over 50 percent of food production happens at this very localized level, according to REN, citing an unconventional dissertation passed in May 2008 at the University of Missouri.[12] If you have any taste for community gardening, this will all sound very nice. If you dig into REN's figures, though, you will find that they are a myth.[13] You shouldn't believe everything you read in people's dissertations.

From here it gets much, much worse. If you glance at the *Eggs Benedict Option*, you will discover that REN not only believes in the "Great

Reset" conspiracy but also subscribes to the thinking of Aleksandr Dugin. In the book, dacha gardening is largely presented as a countermeasure to the "Planetary Health Diet" promoted by "our globalist overlords."[14] If you look still further, you will discover that REN is tightly ensconced in the world of white supremacy, ethnic nationalism, and neo-fascism.[15]

What Tucker Carlson's program fails to tell you, and Raw Egg Nationalist's *American Mind* byline doesn't mention either (but which I included in my article about REN and the Claremont Institute) is that REN published some of his work with a group called Antelope Hill Publishing. Antelope Hill is a small fascist publishing house in Allentown, Pennsylvania (the town where Billy Joel set his blue-collar lament and anthem of the same name in 1982).[16] It publishes books like Dr. Joseph Goebbels's novel *Michael*, as well as titles like *Testament of a Russian Fascist* and Richard Walther Darré's *A New Nobility of Blood and Soil*, which is described on the Antelope Hill website as follows: "Richard Walther Darré, an Obergruppenführer in the SS, was the leading 'Blood and Soil' ideologist of Germany and served his people as Reich Minister of Food and Agriculture. This book, *A New Nobility of Blood and Soil*, was massively popular in the Third Reich and led to a strengthening of the agrarian and agriculturalist movements. Highly influential on Hitler, the principles in this book are foundational to the National Socialist worldview."[17]

A *Daily Beast* article from January 2022 referred to Antelope Hill as "openly fascist"; a blog that tracks reactionary racism labeled it "a white supremacist publishing company." To celebrate Hitler's birthday on April 20, 2022, it offered a discount on all its books, and an even bigger discount on a collection of Hitler's speeches, with the cutesy discount code "birthday boy."[18]

That is who Tucker Carlson featured in "The End of Men." Toward the end of the video, Carlson warns that "no one in Washington seems interested at all in why testosterone levels are dropping, it's a joke to them." He notes that Stephen Colbert and Joy-Ann Reid responded to the trailer for his show by laughing at its "homoeroticism" and "pretty blatant fascist posturing." He concludes: "So if men want to stay male, they must be fascists, and also gay. That's what the media tells you. If you care about your health, if you want to stay fit, you must be a right-wing extremist because good people are fat and passive." It took some real cojones on Carlson's part to dismiss these critiques while at the same time failing to disclose Raw Egg Nationalist's connections to actual fascists and Nazis, presuming he is not one himself (and I have no reason to suppose that).[19] This is the easygoing sort of context collapse and selective disclosure that makes "plausible deniability" so easy for the far right, and the normalization of genuine extremism difficult to expose.

Around when "The End of Men" was being advertised—in the summer of 2022—Raw Egg Nationalist was a guest on Bronze Age Pervert's podcast, "Caribbean Rhythms."[20] They were both very excited about "The End of Men," and the fact that REN had been brought on as a guest for the documentary. (BAP: "It's very exciting." REN: "This is a big deal. This is a really big deal.")

It is evident from the episode that BAP appreciates REN's work—especially his *Man's World* magazine—and that Raw Egg Nationalist is slightly in awe of BAP. At one point BAP conceded, not for the first time, that he considers himself a fascist. They also briefly discussed the so-called hit piece that I wrote against REN and the Claremont Institute for *The Bulwark*—but, like Carlson, they did not mention Antelope Hill. Maybe they understood that consorting with, or being, actual Nazis and pro-Hitlerites could still hurt them in the public eye. The mainstreaming hadn't gone quite that far yet.[21]

Mainstreaming BAPism

About a year after "The End of Men" aired, Bronze Age Pervert made his own big splash, a demonstration of his rising clout. In August 2023 he was the subject of an extended profile in *The Atlantic* magazine. The staff writer Graeme Wood had known BAP personally for a long time, and his profile named and identified BAP as Costin Alamariu. It was a detailed exposé of BAP's intellectual lineage and included comments from Alamariu's advisors at Yale, Bryan Garsten and Steven B. Smith.[22]

Smith, who was the head of Alamariu's dissertation committee, explained that he was enraged by Alamariu's work, which in his mind clearly undermined the principles of liberal democracy. He told Wood that he was "shocked that his family would escape Ceauşescu's Romania only for Costin to undermine the principles of [American] democracy. I view that as a shameful act of betrayal." (Ceauşescu was the Communist dictator of Romania from 1965 to 1989.) Smith further said that he "made his disgust known" but ultimately signed off on Alamariu's work in 2015 because he "was his dissertation adviser, not his censor." This is, in many respects, admirable. In any case, it is difficult to think of a more perfect demonstration of the natural vulnerabilities (and nobility) of liberalism than the willingness of BAP's committee to sign off on his dissertation. Other forms of political order imprison, exile, or kill their ideological opponents; the liberal "regime" gives them tassels, velvet robes, and profiles in *The Atlantic* magazine.

Alamariu had already gained a lot of attention as BAP at this point. In 2022 Nate Hochman, a rising star on the New Right, told the writer Elisabeth Zerofsky that every junior staffer in the Trump administration had read *Bronze Age Mindset*.[23] Alamariu also had a crystal-clear understanding of the power of his Yale doctorate, and of his new status as elite magazine curio. A month or so after the *Atlantic* article came out and his real identity was brought to light, he cashed in. On September 15, 2023, after a good deal of self-promotion on X (formerly Twitter; the site was purchased by Elon Musk in 2022, and the name was changed in July 2023), Alamariu self-published his dissertation as a book, now with a new preface and an offensive title: *Selective Breeding and the Birth of Philosophy*. (The dissertation was called "The Problem of Tyranny and Philosophy in the Thought of Plato and Nietzsche.") *Selective Breeding* enjoyed a brief stint on the Amazon top 100 list.[24]

In his book, Alamariu argued that the birth of philosophy was intimately connected to the idea of "breeding," which he said was coeval with the discovery of the concept of nature (*physis* in the Greek). He bundled the concepts of nature and "breeding" to aristocracy and contrasted these with convention, "taming," and "fundamental democracy" or "totalitarian democracy" (reminiscent of the Longhouse).[25] He contended that philosophy and tyranny are indelibly connected—not as antagonists as is commonly supposed, or as sharing some ironic similarities, but as truly kindred. And he asserted that virtue is straightforwardly hereditary—this being the claim that probably mattered the most for him in his role as white supremacist agitator. As Dustin Sebell, a Straussian scholar, pointed out in a harrowing review of the book, Alamariu was not consistent on this last point.[26] The book was full of muddled concepts and categories and relied overmuch on what Sebell called "Straussian lullabies" (that is to say, unquestioned dogmas).[27]

The thing I found silliest about Alamariu's dissertation was how he manipulated what he came across in the old books he was interpreting. Some of the insights he makes so much of in his effort to spook people are not as esoteric or shocking as he supposes. The kind of "breeding" programming that forms the crux of his argument is not exactly secret or esoteric: Eugenics is a key policy plank in the "best regime" in Book V of Plato's *Republic* (see 459a–460a). Alamariu repeatedly fell prey to a particularly juvenile form of cognitive bias: the supposition that every "insight" that is titillating or cruel must also be secretly true and important.[28]

Alamariu also infused some raw "race science" into the self-published version of *Selective Breeding*. A choice sample from page 45 suggests that, contrary to popular teachings, there are massive genetic differences between different "historical population groups." He said that Luigi Luca Cavalli-Sforza disproved Richard Lewontin's argument that most genetic variation was within human populations and not between them. Alamariu then singles out "Black Africans, in particular," for being "so divergent from the rest of humanity that they exceed the threshold commonly used in other species to draw sub-species boundaries. A revelation as shocking as it is by now indisputable." On this lying point, the sources that Alamariu uses do not even say what he says they do.[29]

Two days after *Selective Breeding*'s publication, someone brought renewed attention to the support that Alamariu had gleaned from his doctoral committee for his work. Someone with the X handle "TheognisOMegara" posted the records of the committee's official dissertation commentary (from 2015) on the site, including grades, for all the world to see. These sorts of records are typically kept confidential in a student's university file, so it is hard to imagine that Alamariu did not leak them to "Theognis" himself. Alamariu retweeted that post with the comments, "Quite weird, odd . . . and maybe interesting?!"[30] The commentaries left Alamariu's committee—which also included Harvard's Harvey Mansfield—exposed, because each faculty member praised Alamariu's work. To be sure, the reports also contained clear criticisms and rebuttals, but those do not resonate as much as one might like, knowing what we know now.[31]

In any case, Alamariu seems to have understood the power that those reports would have to anyone on the outside. Posting the doctoral commentaries was, in its own tiny Twitterverse way, an astonishing stunt.

More astonishing were all the people suddenly eager to openly celebrate BAPism. The online bros of the Hard Right were clearly bedazzled by Alamariu's work—as were, perhaps more surprisingly, slices of the American far left. It was reviewed on several Hard Right sites, and on some more mainstream ones.[32] Christopher Rufo congratulated Alamariu on his new book on X. Rising right-wing star Richard Hanania expressed support for it, too.[33] And so did Dasha Nekrasova. Nekrasova, who had a recurring role on *Succession* (as "Comfrey"), is, along with Anna Khachiyan, cohost of the *Red Scare* podcast, one of several left-wing podcasts that were originally inspired by the 2016 Bernie Sanders campaign (the main one being *Chapo Trap House*). Dasha celebrated Alamariu's new publication on X, and Alamariu responded in turn.[34]

If *The End of Men* revealed the spiritual overlap between the far right and the New Age, antivax left, *Selective Breeding*'s publication shone new light on the growing relationship between the Hard Right and the so-called dirtbag left.

Red Scare and the Dimes Square Scene

Political commentators sometimes use the phrase "horseshoe theory" to explain the connections between the far right and the far left, the idea being that at a certain point the extreme ideological ends of the political spectrum come together. We have already seen how some of the environmental and homeopathic sensibilities of the left came to appeal to Raw Egg Nationalist. In 2024, Naomi Klein chronicled her own uncanny experience with this phenomenon in *Doppelganger*—which tracks the transformation of Naomi Wolfe (the strident formerly left feminist who Klein affectionately refers to as "Other Naomi") into a conspiratorial crossover star of the far right.

Since so much of the New Right is at least rhetorically devoted to rejecting neoliberal economics, it is not surprising that new alliances with the left would emerge, and there is also a strong contingent on the left that is stridently opposed to left identity politics (which they see as elite posturing). Sohrab Ahmari's journal *Compact* was dedicated to this crossover crowd. In any case, the more extreme the right became, the more appealing it became to the far left—to people like Glenn Greenwald, who is friendly with the *Red Scare* duo, or the European philosopher Slavoj Žižek. As the New Right grew more mainstream and came to dominate right-wing politics, Democrats and Never-Trumpers were increasingly locked-in as the mainstream establishment, and so became even less attractive to the left.

The *Red Scare* podcasters' flirtations with Hard Right figures, and with BAP, seemed at the time like a high-water mark of the left-to-right pipeline.

Khachiyan and Nekrasova's affection for BAP became evident when they reviewed *Bronze Age Mindset* on their podcast in 2022.[35] (Christopher Rufo had been on just a few episodes prior, and Glenn Greenwald was on just before that.) They were both clearly taken with the book—with its aesthetics, humor, and transgressiveness—and Khachiyan admitted to being jealous of BAP because she wanted what he had as a writer: "When somebody's art is pure and good, you cannot help but be truly appreciative of them and celebrate their existence"—while fully acknowledging its latent fascism and hard-core racism.

Around a year later they had BAP on their show for a three-hour interview. They were excited. As one Patreon member said in the comments section for that episode, "The girls are really in turbo pick-me mode rn."[36] BAP seemed to like them, too:

You guys should know you have a gigantic audience. I talk to people from all walks of life who will listen to you at so called highest levels of American society and they love you. For example, private counsel for X company. . . . And not just one . . . love, loves you. And so your audience is you know, maybe we don't have an audience as big as Tucker, but people who listen to us are, you know, "important" so-called people, right?[37]

The heart of America's avant-garde "horseshoe" world came to be known as the Dimes Square scene in Lower Manhattan. In 2020 the area gained notoriety for its edgy countercultural writers bucking pandemic restrictions to hang out. There was a transgressive ("antiwoke") film festival in October 2021, New People's Cinema Club, that was funded by Peter Thiel and featured a *Red Scare* interview of the filmmaker John Waters.[38] Thiel's good friend Curtis Yarvin (aka Mencius Moldbug) was supposedly a fixture in this new scene, which included writers, artists, filmmakers, and podcasters—most of whom, like the *Red Scare* duo, delighted in flouting progressive cultural norms and constraints. There was room here for MAGA Republicans and for cynical left-wing aesthetes, for "canceled" heterodox thinkers, and even for radical Catholics. In August 2022 *The New York Times* published an opinion piece by *First Things* editor Julia Yost under the headline "New York's Hottest Club Is the Catholic Church," detailing the various Catholic strains in Dimes Square.[39] She included Nekrasova, who has described herself as ironically Catholic or "Catholic like Andy Warhol."[40] Honor Levy, an up-and-coming writer and recent Catholic convert, was also mentioned in this vein. On August 17, 2023, Ahmari hosted the book launch for his new book, *Tyranny Inc.*, at Sovereign House, an underground venue in Dimes Square. Bhaskar Sunkara, president of *The Nation* and founding editor of *Jacobin* magazine, cohosted the event.[41]

Like other parts of the New Right, the Dimes Square scene was soaked in contrarian irony and "wink-wink" camaraderie. The general mood seemed to be one of cool nonchalance—but there was also a taste for titillating spectacle, and even LARPing, proto-fascistic nastiness. One observer of Dimes Square became the target for a piece of performance art where he was publicly humiliated on camera, apparently in retribution for his having written critically about the scene.[42] Reading his account reminded me of Thomas Mann's short story about fascism in Italy, *Mario and the Magician*—minus the murder, and minus the hoi polloi. Curtis Yarvin was one of the key participants in this, as was Dasha Nekrasova.

The Rufo Manifesto

During his interview with *Red Scare*, Costin Alamariu disclaimed any interest in serious fascist politics, saying that it was totally unrealistic and had no future. He insisted that his project was strictly cultural: He was interested in filmmakers, artists, and other literary phenomena, not in political candidates. He also expressed disagreement with others on the New Right—like Richard Hanania and Steve Sailer—for their Podunk, shopkeeper-like interest in race science; Alamariu's racism is much more visceral and brutal.[43]

This line—this idea of caring only for culture, and not for politics—has been a favorite of elite fascist intellectuals since the 1930s. It is reminiscent of Heidegger's efforts to forge a distinction between "vulgar National Socialism" and "spiritual National Socialism," or of Alain de Benoist's "metapolitical" ideas for "total ideological saturation" and a "Gramscism of the Right" in the *Nouvelle Droite* of the 1960s through the 1980s.[44] It was also a line taken by fascist intellectuals in Alamariu's Romania.

The famous University of Chicago professor Mircea Eliade's commitment to the fascist Legionary Movement was fully exposed only after his death, thanks in large part to precisely that sort of dissembling. Throughout his life he would say that he had only ever been interested in the cultural and religious dimensions of the movement. But for Eliade, as for many others, fascism involved mystical vitality, and, in particular, the myth of a "new man."[45] Here is a sample of such rhetoric, from 1934:

Revolution? Why not? Everyone who wants to endow his life with meaning is born through revolution. But let us remember that a true revolution (not a politicianized pseudorevolution, a change of nobles and rulers) begins with a very full soul, with a sacred, biological fury against lies and hypocrisy, with a pagan thirst for a new life, a new man, a new world. The man who prepares himself for revolution is a man of mystery. He goes shouting the new spirit in the streets only after he has accomplished the revolution himself, after he has seen and tasted it. A new man! But, by God, this new man is our salvation, he is the sense of our existence! The new man is made, not awaited. Above all, the new man means a complete break with the hypocrisy and cowardice of the society in which we live. A young man unattached to anything, without fear and without stain, with eyes on the future, not the practices of the past.[46]

By 1937, Eliade was tying the myth of the "new man" inseparably to the fascist (and ruthlessly violent) Legionaries in fascist publications.[47]

Eliade's fascism was mystical and Eastern Orthodox, whereas BAP's is more pagan (though Alamariu himself is Jewish), but both rely on a mythical presentation of male vitality, and both men dissemble about the relationship between their vitalistic myth-making and hard politics. The feigned distinction between politics and culture-warring is just a mask for totalizing politics.

———

Others on the New Right, of course, do not share BAP's faux skepticism about political action. Shortly after BAP did his part to humiliate the Yale and Harvard faculty who constituted his dissertation committee, the New Right, with Christopher Rufo at the helm, found a way to call into question the legitimacy of the entire Ivy League.

It began with an embarrassing session in Congress in which the presidents of Harvard, Penn, and MIT were questioned by Representative Elise Stefanik (R) about antisemitism and failed to articulate and defend university principles and guidelines surrounding free speech and student safety. This happened in the wake of campus turmoil following the gruesome terrorist attacks against Israel of October 7, 2023, and then the brutal—critics called it genocidal—response on the part of Israel in

Gaza. The line of questioning pursued by Stefanik was clearly a setup, but the three presidents walked right in. Within weeks, Penn president Liz Magill had resigned, and recently appointed Harvard president Claudine Gay became a new target for aggressive right-wing activism. Christopher Rufo was very open about his campaign against Gay, which involved, crucially, the discovery of plagiarism in her published scholarship. Rufo posted about the allegations in coordination with others at the *Washington Free Beacon*, and additional evidence soon materialized.[48]

This was a tenuous time in campus politics. Though it is always hard to get a synoptic picture, it was rich to see some American conservatives so deeply concerned about "student safety" after years of ridiculing woke liberal snowflakes and campus safe spaces; it was jarring to see some people on college campus dismiss Jewish students' safety concerns after years of safetyism on college campuses, and after their recent, more proactive support of Black students following George Floyd's murder ("silence is violence," we were told, but not so "From the River to the Sea"); it was truly sickening to see college administrations that for many years had celebrated (and marketed) activism and diversity react so forcefully against pro-Palestine student protesters and critics of Israel's gruesome war on Gaza.[49] It was also excruciating to watch liberal and progressive academics make excuses for Claudine Gay just because the accusations against her were made in bad faith.

Gay resigned from the Harvard presidency on January 2, 2024.[50] Rufo took his victory laps.[51] And on January 4, 2024, he published his own set guidelines for the new movement, called "The New Right Activism: A Manifesto for the Counterrevolution," in a Hard Right magazine called *IM-1776*.[52] It reads as a blend of Eliade's fascism, Vermeule and Deneen's "integration from within," and the Heritage Foundation's Project 2025.

Rufo's manifesto recommended a new activism "with the courage and resolve to win back the language, recapture institutions, and reorient the state towards rightful ends." He made the case that the ends justify the means in plain, militant language, à la Claremont, arguing that today's "regime" consists of an "opaque and coercive set of psychological, cultural, and institutional patterns that has largely replaced the old constitutional way of life," and that today's status quo "requires not conservation, but reform, and even revolt."

Rufo's case for revolt borrowed justification from the Postliberal and Schmittian idea that high principles outweigh "procedural values." For Rufo, modern liberalism is clearly dissatisfying, and he wants to renew the "great political tradition of the West." He described the latter in nice Aristotelian terms of "republican self-government, shared moral standards, and the pursuit of eudaimonia or human flourishing." Like Vermeule, Rufo disavowed the idea of liberal institutional neutrality, and of liberal public reason ("political life moves on narrative, emotion, scandal, anger, hope, and faith—on irrational, or at least subrational feelings that can be channeled, but never destroyed by reason," he wrote). For Rufo—since neutrality is an illusion—the government is ultimately always in charge of cultural formation, and this should be made explicit: "The chief vectors for the transmission of values—the public school, the public university, and the state—are not marketplaces at all. They are government-run monopolies. In truth, the hand that moves culture is not an 'invisible hand,' but an iron clad in velvet— that is, political force." To be effective, the right must harness these state forces and seize the cultural levers of power, too.

Much of Rufo's manifesto consisted of a cloying faux-pious account of how the New Right must perform a reenactment of the Gospel of John. "In the beginning was the Word," he wrote, and "this is true also in politics." As such, the New Right should engage in wordy "agitprop," to control the political discourse, which will eventually result in the "elevation of . . . discourse into law." Rufo asserted that "institutions are where the word becomes flesh." This insight forces the activist to recognize the importance of subterfuge and impurity. Sometimes, "he must conceal his radicalism in the mask of respectability." Ultimately, though, all that matters is who is in charge: "The only question is who will lead [today's institutions] and by which set of values. The New Right must summon the self-confidence to say, 'We will, and by our values.'" He then recommends a path that by now should sound familiar: "We must recruit, recapture, and replace existing leadership."

Rufo concludes with the thought that all this must be done for the sake of higher-order principles, for "a telos." Here, I think, he says something interesting:

> The language of ends has almost vanished from American life, and this disappearance supplies the greatest opportunity for the New Right. Because of its religious adherence, the Right still has access to the language of ends—the language of God, or, in its more contemporary form, "Nature and Nature's God." My conviction is that ends will ultimately triumph over means; men will die for truth, liberty, and happiness, but will not die for efficiency, diversity, and inclusion.
>
> The best way to counter the degradations of American institutional life is to remind the public of the fundamental purpose of those institutions, and to communicate that purpose. What is the purpose of the university? What is the purpose of a school? What system of government will guide us toward human happiness? These questions provoke doubt and anxiety in the current regime. And no wonder. The idea of happiness, properly understood, can be revolutionary.

The rest of Rufo's essay consists of a further attack on the "regime," and one final declaration that "the fight is here."

For all his fascist buffoonery, Rufo's comments about the ends of politics and political institutions strike me as correct, at least to a degree. He exaggerates when he says that the language of ends and purposes has "almost vanished" from American public life, but he is right that the liberal American mainstream is anxious and squirrely when it comes to questions about purpose and meaning, and that these anxieties supply "the greatest opportunity for the New Right." Where Rufo and the New Right go wrong is in their understanding of the relationship between liberalism and "the language of ends," or the role of human meaning, values, and morality in the context of liberal democracy. The basic theoretical confusion is as follows: The New Right mistakes academic liberalism for the real thing. They assume that liberalism's embrace of political neutrality means a simple rejection and disavowal of all particular conceptions of the good life, and of values like "truth, liberty, and happiness" (or "the Good, the True, and the Beautiful"), in favor of an empty commitment to equality and relativism. But that is absurd. Liberalism tries to be procedurally neutral with respect to whole traditions and ways of life, but it is not neutral all the way down. It cares about happiness and liberty and truth—and it certainly does not reject "the good life," or even the fascist "new man." Rather, it is morally pluralistic. And it actively makes room for divergent accounts of what is good, which people and communities are then, within negotiated, political limits, free to make their own.

But liberalism is not intuitive, and it can be hard to understand, articulate, and appreciate. And it does not include any single, totalizing, wholesale cultural program. These are major vulnerabilities that the New Right exploits, ruthlessly. Just like fascism does.

NETTR

IM-1776 magazine, where Rufo published his manifesto, was founded in 2020. It pitches itself as more concerned with literary excellence than with politics, but its first ever post was a sparkling review of *Bronze Age Mindset* by the Dugin popularizer and Toronto PhD Michael Millerman. The chief editor of the magazine is Mike Granza, an Italian who moved to Hungary in 2022.[53] In addition to their online site, and somewhat like Raw Egg Nationalist's *Man's World* magazine, *IM-1776* publishes high-end print editions, in keeping with the Hard Right's antimodern aesthetic. Everything about *Man's World* and *IM-1776* screams fascism.

In their mission statement from September 2020, the *IM-1776* editors wrote "welcome to the end of modernity."[54] They claimed to be operating against liberalism and progress because they cared so much about education and the "necessary education for civilization—conversation, friendship, and insight." They concluded with an uplifting thought: "We will encourage friendship among our writers and readers. Love of nobility and love of wisdom will be our answers to these trying times." In 2023 the editors announced an effort to fund more writers. There they insisted: "Transgression for the sake of transgression isn't our principle. What's needed is a real vision for a better future with Truth and Beauty at its core."[55]

IM-1776 regularly publishes Millerman's work, as well as a good number of the most extreme Claremont Institute affiliates like Michael

Anton, Glenn Ellmers, and Scott Yenor.[56] It is part of a growing network of Hard Right media outlets that includes websites like *American Greatness, The American Mind, Revolver News,* and *TheBlaze,* as well as a seemingly limitless proliferation of podcasts.

The political militancy of *IM-1776* came to view in an interview that the magazine editor Daniel Miller conducted with a man named Charles Haywood in December 2022. Haywood is a lawyer and former personal care product manufacturer who turned to far-right blogging and Christian activism after he sold his company in 2020. He has close connections to the Claremont Institute and helped to found a secret Christian nationalist men's society in 2020 called the Society for American Civic Renewal (SACR).[57] Others leaders at the Claremont Institute, like Ryan Williams and Scott Yenor, and former Lincoln Fellow and venture capitalist Nathan Fischer, were also involved in SACR—a fact disclosed in 2024, when various journalists obtained Yenor's emails via public record requests through his employer, Boise State University. Later, when Williams and others from this crowd decided to "resettle across America" and form small, "aligned" right-wing enclaves, they got their own glossy write-up in *The New York Times.*[58]

The *IM-1776* interview had to do with an argument that had erupted between Haywood and the writer Rod Dreher over the subject of right-wing loyalty and the slogan "No Enemies to the Right" (or NETTR, a policy that, in effect, advocated for the complete abandonment of the old cordon sanitaire). Haywood was a hardened proponent of the tactic, whereas Dreher found it unhinged and morally corrupt. The dispute had been provoked by the discovery that Thomas Achord, who at the time was also the principal of a private Christian school in Louisiana, was a rabid white nationalist. This happened in late November 2022 and caused a minor uproar on the right, in part because Achord's podcasting partner, Stephen Wolfe, had just published his book *The Case for Christian Nationalism* earlier that month (Wolfe figures prominently in the next chapter). Rod Dreher does not think of himself as someone who likes racists, and he was aghast at the discovery about Achord, who had been operating a pseudonymous account under an alias for years, where he posted anti-Black and misogynist comments online.[59] Dreher's children had also attended the school that Achord led, so it was personal for him. He took a principled stance.

In response, Charles Haywood vented a good deal of spleen, offering a vivid glimpse, once more, of the atmosphere of this Hard Right universe. Here is an excerpt from the interview:

> What is our end? That is easy—winning. What is the winning condition? It is the total, permanent defeat of the Left, of the ideology at the heart of the Enlightenment, with its two core principles of total emancipation from all bonds not continuously chosen, and of total forced equality of all people. When this defeat is accomplished, Right principles, those based in reality and recognizing the nature of man, his limitations, and his capabilities, can again become ascendant.
>
> Winning does not mean electoral victory such that Right principles may be voted into law, and then nullified or voted out again. *It means the total, permanent elimination of all Left power, and, even more importantly, the total discrediting, both on a moral and practical basis, of all Left ideology.* What is Left should be seen for what it is, evil, and it should be seen as not only destructive in practice, but laughable, the ideology of losers and idiots, or at most something from the discredited past, viewed with vague curiosity, as the cult of Mithras is today.[60]

Later in the interview, Haywood explained, in hyper-paleoconservative, anti-Enlightenment form, how William F. Buckley was a "Judas" who "in hindsight we can see deliberately led the American Right into a box canyon, swiftly spiking any gun that seemed as if it might be effective in the war waged by the Left on decent America for over a hundred years." He was presumably referring to Buckley's efforts to purge extremists from conservative movement politics.

A year or so after *IM-1776* published that interview, on September 26, 2023, Christopher Rufo hosted a debate on Twitter Spaces on the subject of "No Enemies to the Right," which was sponsored by *IM-1776* and featured Charles Haywood and Nathan Fischer on the "pro" side, and Neil Shenvi and Michael Young ("Wokal Distance") arguing against.[61] By this point the matter had become more urgent because prominent New Right figures just kept being revealed as white supremacists or Nazi sympathizers.

In June 2023 Pedro Gonzalez, a former Claremont Institute fellow, editor for Paul Gottfried's *Chronicles*, and a pro-DeSantis influencer, was exposed by Breitbart News for antisemitic and racist text messaging. Breitbart was acting against DeSantis for the Trump campaign; DeSantis's choice to run a hyper-online, Trumpier-than-Trump campaign had not necessarily paid off.[62] (In addition to Gonzalez, the DeSantis campaign also enjoyed boosts from other former Claremonter fellows, including Josh Hammer, David Reaboi, and Jack Murphy.)[63]

In July 2023 Nate Hochman, a communications staffer on the campaign (and a 2021 Publius Fellow with Claremont), was exposed for having secretly created and shared a promotional video for DeSantis that included the Nazi sonnenrad symbol. He had previously gotten into trouble for a Twitter Spaces conversation he had with Nick Fuentes.[64] But Hochman did not seem to be that radical or fringe. As David French explained at the time, in an opinion piece called "The Lost Boys of the American Right," Hochman was once a staff writer at *National Review*.[65]

(As an aside: Nick Fuentes is a Catholic influencer and reactionary, rabid misogynist, white supremacist, and antisemite; he and BAP sometimes spar and troll each other over BAP's Jewishness. Trump had dinner with Ye/Kanye West and Fuentes at Mar-a-Lago in November 2022. The Israel-Palestine conflict that began in 2023 led to schisms within the Hard Right, with people like Fuentes and Candace Owens lining up against Israel, and BAP and many others siding with the Israeli ultranationalists.)

In August 2023 Richard Hanania, at the time a fellow at a new Salem Center for Public Policy at the University of Texas and an up-and-coming right-wing commentator, was exposed by the *Huffington Post* for having posted for years as the white supremacist "Richard Hoste," who argued for eugenics and the forcible sterilization of people with low IQ.[66]

The Twitter Spaces discussion organized by Rufo about "No Enemies to the Right" was interesting primarily because it brought some key tensions in the movement to light, and not just among fanatics like Charles Haywood and the others, but also among various Christian constituencies on the right. All five participants in the discussion were professing Christians, and so inevitably the question of the relative importance of politics versus religion came into play. Didn't faithfulness and spiritual ends matter more than political action and efficacy? Was it Christian to ally with sin and darkness? Shenvi and Young spoke eloquently, quoting scripture, about both the practical and spiritual costs of "No Enemies to the Right." Haywood and Fischer were unmoved.

On the X platform, while this conversation was streaming, beneath Rufo's tweet announcing the discussion, a man named Clifford Humphrey piped in. Humphrey has a PhD in American history from Hillsdale, was then the director of Religious Coalitions at Yoram Hazony's Edmund Burke Foundation, and in May 2023 was appointed executive vice chancellor of the Florida College System. Beneath Rufo's tweet on X, Humphrey said, presumably referring to one of the moderates (so Shenvi or Young), "Someone get this guy a watch. He has no idea what time it is."[67]

Hazony had for a time followed Buckley's lead, keeping the worst extremists out of National Conservatism. But here was his director of religious coalitions publicly declaring that nothing extremists on the right could do or say was beyond the pale. The Dimes Square scene showed how the Hard Right seduced the far left. The *IM-1776* X discussion offered a glimpse of how the Hard Right moves around in, divides, and conquers the Christian right. Contemporary far-right Christianity is the subject of chapter 12.

12

Christian Nationalism and Revival

ON OCTOBER 2, 2023, a member of the House of Representatives and vice chair of the House Republican Caucus, Mike Johnson, took part in a livestreamed prayer call organized by a group called the World Prayer Network.[1] The leader of the call, an evangelical pastor named Jim Garlow who in 2016 had likened Hillary Clinton to Jezebel, opened, as he typically does, by emphasizing the purpose of the call: "To pray for holiness and righteousness and for Biblical justice, not social justice." He continued: "We're way beyond the issue of partisanship. We're way beyond the issue of Republican versus Democrat, or right versus left. Where we *are* squarely is right versus wrong, good versus evil, light versus darkness, biblical truth as opposed to anti-scriptural constructs, the things of God as opposed to the things of the evil one." The call began officially with the sounding of a shofar by Robert Weinger, a master shofar blower in Israel's West Bank.[2] Garlow reminded listeners that the call was not open to the media or the public.

Mike Johnson was Garlow's first guest that day, and he spoke at some length, giving clear testimony of his faith, his view of American society, and his hopes for the future. The immediate reason for the call was the state of the Republican-led house, which was in turmoil because Kevin McCarthy had been voted out of his leadership position.

The views that Johnson expressed were as radical as Garlow's. He introduced himself and then made a profession of faith—explaining how he had come to deepen his own beliefs after his father, a firefighter, survived a terrible explosion. He then discussed the tenuous situation in the House, explaining his deep sense of uncertainty, and asserting that though the Lord had always given him a general "sense for where things are going to lead," at that point he really didn't know. He continued: "All I know is that the Lord has directly spoken to my heart and told me to be prepared for a shaking."

Soon Johnson began his prayer request: "What we need is a spiritual intervention from the God of the universe, the God in whom we Trust." Johnson digressed with a brief history lesson, referencing the phrase that has adorned the House of Representatives since 1962, asking: "Why did they put 'In God We Trust' above the marble above the speaker's head?" He explained that it had been installed during the Cold War as a reminder to Americans that they were different from the Soviets, whose Marxist worldview "begins with the idea that there is no God." But Johnson was adamant: "We *are* different. We *are* a nation subservient to Him. The reason that we became the great nation that we did, as everybody on this call knows, was because *that* was the foundation, that we hold truths to be self-evident, because God created us all equally and gave us our rights." Now, he warned, "our nation has abandoned that."[3]

When he got to the specifics of his request, Johnson said: "This is an inflection point. We are at a civilizational moment. The only question is: Is God going to allow our nation to enter a time of judgment for our collective sins, which his mercy and grace have held back for some time? Or is he going to give us one more chance to restore the foundations and return to Him?" He affirmed that what the nation really needed was a revival. But more immediately, Johnson said, "what we are going to need is a prayer for divine intervention in the hearts and among the members of this body [the House] . . . We will not be able to do it without the Lord's help . . . This is going to have to bring people to their knees."

Before Representative Johnson got off the call, Garlow prompted him to say something about whether this might be a time of judgment for America. Johnson gave a stark reminder about the "terrible state that we're in," citing a loss of faith in institutions, low church attendance, and a culture that is "so dark and depraved that it almost seems irredeemable."

He noted that "the number of people who do not believe in absolute truth is now above the majority for the first time. . . . We're losing the country."[4] Johnson did not mention himself as a possible replacement for McCarthy. But by the end of the month, on October 25, 2023, whether by divine intervention or sheer GOP desperation, he was confirmed as the new Speaker of the House.

Johnson's relative obscurity turned out to be an asset. Being mostly unknown allowed him to appear less radical than he was. As Jonathan Blitzer put it, writing in *The New Yorker*, "Johnson's power has followed from his discretion."[5] At the World Prayer Network, Johnson's ascension received little attention because the meetings in the aftermath of October 7, 2023, were dominated by the massacre and hostage-taking in Israel. While there would be a small schism on the Hard Right over the war in Gaza, the World Prayer Network group, like most right-wing Christian organizations in the United States, strongly supported Netanyahu and everything he stood for.[6]

This chapter is about right-wing Christian nationalism and Christian supremacy in the United States. Religion has been a pervasive theme throughout the book already—from Yoram Hazony's assertion that "this was a Christian nation, historically and according to its laws, and it's going to be a Christian nation again," to the Postliberal Catholics' "integration from within." Here, I explore how New Right intellectualism intersects with and overlaps with Christianity—and especially Protestant Christianity.

The New Right movement that materialized under the first Trump administration and then grew in power after January 6, 2021, was in many respects hard for American liberals to see and appreciate. This was partly because the movement was given cover by Trump's anti-intellectualism, and partly because liberals (and establishment types, too) have difficulty conceiving of perspectives and world views that differ so significantly from their own and seem so outlandish and extreme.

These blind spots also concern religion. The early twenty-first century was a time of spiritual turmoil, realignment, and dealignment in the United States, and it took some dramatic turns during the Trump era.[7] The Bronze Agers were part of this cultural foment; so were the

"Hour-is-laters," the integralists, the Dimes Square avant-garde, and the people pining for old-fashioned nationalism. As with the world of conservative intellectualism, the conservative Christian world saw dramatic rearrangements and reorientations after Trump's electoral victory in 2016. Across the Christian right, establishment figures were put on their heels, new leaders, previously obscure, were brought into the halls of power, and new ideas were granted authority from those on high. In this chapter I bring some light to the religious undercurrents—and Christian nationalist arguments—that shaped the right between 2016 and 2024 and consider how they relate to the New Right intellectual world we have explored heretofore.

Christianity in the United States is varied and dispersed: It extends across a vast proliferation of denominations and religious communities that span the full political spectrum. Though it takes harder and softer forms, Christian nationalism is pervasive in many of these communities, where it has, in some version or another, been cultivated for decades. It is distinct from other expressions of Christianity in that it is political and seeks political domination. The writer Katherine Stewart puts the matter clearly: "It does not seek to add another voice to America's pluralistic democracy, but to replace our foundational democratic principles and institutions with a state grounded on a particular version of Christianity."[8] Christian nationalists believe that America is a Christian nation (indeed, God's chosen nation), and must be defended as such. Kristin Kobes Du Mez, author of the book *Jesus and John Wayne: How White Evangelicals Corrupted a Faith and Fractured a Nation* (2020), adds another key layer to this story: "Evangelical support for Trump was no aberration, nor was it merely a pragmatic choice. It was, rather, the culmination of evangelicals' embrace of militant masculinity, an ideology that enshrines patriarchal authority and condones the callous display of power, at home and abroad. . . . Evangelicals did not cast their vote despite their beliefs, but because of them."[9]

In what follows, we will see more evidence for these claims, coming from various quarters. I discuss three distinctive Christian nationalist (or Christian supremacist) traditions and sensibilities, moving from the more mainstream and familiar to the unfamiliar and hard-line. My aim is to provide illustrative snapshots of the Christian nationalist world to take and knit into our cumulative understanding of the New Right.

Christian Founding Story Hour

Right-wing intellectuals have rich traditions of nationalist, far-right reactionary, and constitutional thought to draw on in their characterizations of American ideals; so too with Christian nationalists. American political history is full of claims about America being a "Christian nation" with a "Christian founding," and there is also—contrary to the liberal imagination—some good evidence for such assertions. In right-wing circles, Americans are culturally primed to believe that America was founded as a Christian country, that Christianity is fundamental to American civic identity, that America enjoys a world-historical situation analogous to the Israelites in the Hebrew Bible/Old Testament, and that God's favor is bestowed or denied according to Americans' adherence to Christian values.

These are some of the beliefs that characterize what we might call Christian Founding Era (or CFE) doctrine, and which are pervasive on the American right. CFE ideas have gained popularity since the 1960s. Around the time that Barry Goldwater won the Republican nomination at the Cow Palace Convention, the GOP began to consolidate its role as the political bastion of religious conservatism. Ronald Reagan's "moral majority" rose in response to the social turmoil of the 1960s and 1970s—turmoil that involved the Cold War and Vietnam War, the civil rights movement with its bold left-wing Christian influences, women's liberation, and the gay rights movement. Against this background of change and rebellion, a reactive, white, masculinist Christian nationalism asserted itself. This strain of conservative religiosity came to be known variously as "New Christian Right," the "New Religious Right," the "New Religious Political Right," or simply the "religious right." It was the age of televangelists like Pat Robertson and Jerry Falwell and the formation of many new antifeminist, anti-LGBTQ religious organizations.[10] The Federalist Society was also formed around this time. The New Christian Right comprised the strong social and moral leg of establishment, Buckley/Reagan style conservatism.

The New Christian Right of the 1980s also had its own prehistory. Arguments about the intimate relationship between the Christian faith and American civic life go back to before the founding, and contentious arguments about this were part of founding-era debates.[11] CFE doctrine consistently obscures the complexity of that history and those debates, and outright rejects the religious pluralism of the present. The parallels here with Claremont- and Hillsdale-style political thinking are evident, and the two narratives are mutually reinforcing, and mutually radicalizing.

———

I was witness to a broad spectrum of Christian nationalist sentiment and argumentation at the ISI/Claremont Institute conference I attended in Fort Lauderdale in February 2023—the one where Robby George (whom I do not consider a Christian nationalist) was the keynote, and where I saw so many other figures from the New Right, like Michael Anton, Yoram Hazony, and Charles Kesler.

On the final day of the conference, February 24, there was a panel called "Christian Nationalism and the American Regime," sponsored by Hazony's Edmund Burke Foundation and chaired by Clifford Humphrey, the Hillsdale PhD and then-director of religious coalitions for the foundation. The panel included Ben Crenshaw (at the time a PhD candidate at Hillsdale), as well as Stephen Wolfe, author of the controversial book *The Case for Christian Nationalism* (2022). "Christian nationalism" had been used frequently among academics and in the liberal commentariat during this period—mostly as a pejorative—and Wolfe's book was the first overt, book-length defense of the concept. The inevitable controversy surrounding the book mushroomed when Wolfe's podcasting partner's racist and misogynist online activity was discovered (this, recall, was the spur to the far right's NETTR debate). We will come back to Wolfe and his book.

Crenshaw's brief presentation, which was about Christian nationalism and the American founding, offered a useful sampling of CFE doctrine.[12] Crenshaw rehearsed some of the most common arguments for the idea of a distinctly Christian founding. He was working within a long and contentious tradition that includes scholars like John Fea and Mark David Hall on the more moderate end, and popular writers like David Barton—a defender of Christian nationalism who has been discredited by numerous historians—on the extreme.[13]

Crenshaw began by quoting from a famous letter from John Adams to the militia of Massachusetts in October 1798. The conclusion reads: "We have no Government armed with Power capable of contending with human Passions unbridled by morality and Religion. Avarice, Ambition, Revenge or Galantry, would break the strongest chords of our Constitution as a Whale goes through a Net. Our Constitution was made only for a moral and religious People. It is wholly inadequate to the government of any other."[14]

This letter is one of several texts often cited by conservatives in defense of Christian nationalism because it offers such a clear and unequivocal account of Adams's attitude toward religiosity and good government. Crenshaw argued that Adams, like the majority of Americans during the era, had the Christian religion in mind when he spoke of morality and religion.

Then Crenshaw went further, building toward the argument that America was founded as a Christian nation and in effect had a Christian nationalist founding. He covered three areas: the American people, the laws and institutions, and the culture and mores, all at the time of the founding. He took up the most controversial argument first, concerning the religiosity of ordinary people. He argued that church involvement was much higher than other scholars have claimed. Next, he turned to the role that Christianity played in early American laws and institutions, making some arguments resonant with what we saw in Vermeule's *Common Good Constitutionalism* concerning the Christian character of early American legal institutions and provisions. Then he homed in on early state constitutions.

Crenshaw described how the early colonies had established churches, and how this continued in several states even after 1776. Focusing on New Hampshire's state constitution of 1784, he argued that, for the earliest citizens of the state, religious practice was seen—in the vein of the

Adams letter—to be crucial to civic virtue and self-government, and also that religious liberty (the freedom to choose one's form of worship) was not considered to be in conflict with religious establishment (in short, people could have religious freedom even if there was an established state church). Crenshaw argued that the references to God in these documents should be understood as references to the Christian deity, and not to some rationalist deity or theistic rationalism, as liberals so often argue. And he discussed how the debate around religious establishment at the time of the founding typically concerned allowing religious liberty among competing Christian denominations, and not broader forms of religious pluralism.

In the final part of his talk, Crenshaw spoke about public norms and opinions of the founding era. He mentioned a number of civic institutions that have a spiritual dimension—like congressional prayers, national holidays, pledges, and other symbolism—then discussed the national days of prayer and thanksgiving that were established in the earliest days of the Republic. He explained how during their presidencies, Madison and Jefferson, both of whom were religious skeptics, declared national days of thanksgiving, even though they had said in private that it went against the separation of church and state—a clear demonstration of the Christian constraints of the founding era.

Crenshaw's talk in Fort Lauderdale included a smattering of standard fare CFE arguments. Other such claims include the idea that early Americans understood the revolution to have a religious valence (the early Puritans were fighting for their right to practice their chosen denomination of Christianity, not to throw off the yoke of religion), and that the Establishment Clause was not meant to deny Christianity a privileged position, but to ensure that no single domination took over. Most states, after all, already had established churches.

These claims are true, with some caveats and in a way, and so was Crenshaw's basic conclusion that at the time of the founding America was constituted by Christians, who presumably meant to establish a society based largely on Christian morality.

The problems arise when Crenshaw and others extrapolate to make more sweeping and totalizing claims—saying, for example, as

Crenshaw did, that Christianity was *the* public religion, and *the* source of American public morality, and that the early Americans sought to establish "a nation whose political institutions, laws, morals, and cultural mores are grounded on the truths of the Christian religion." Those statements may not sound so different from what came before, but they are just totalizing enough to conceal the relevant controversy.

And even if we, like Crenshaw and so many others, constrain ourselves to the founding era and so ignore the 250 or so years of subsequent liberalizing change, the controversy is genuine. It was there from the beginning.

———

Crenshaw's talk was entirely lopsided—as these arguments so often are—and so it occluded the liberal position, which has its own favorite bevy of founding-era quotes, arguments, and laws.

For example, take the Virginia Statute for Religious Freedom, which Jefferson helped to draft. During this process, efforts were made to insert "Jesus Christ" into the preamble of the law, right before the more generic words "the holy author of our religion." Jefferson, along with James Madison, rejected that effort, and the law was passed by a broad majority in 1786—without specific mention of Jesus. In his autobiography, he wrote about how this was proof that they "meant to comprehend, within the mantle of its protection, the Jew and the Gentile, the Christian and Mahometan, the Hindoo, and infidel of every denomination."[15] I love this passage because it offers such a forceful and expansive embrace of genuine pluralism. Jefferson was proud of his success, and the statute influenced the Bill of Rights. His role in passing Virginia's statute for religious freedom was inscribed on his tombstone.

Or consider texts like George Washington's Letter to the Hebrew congregation in Newport, from 1790, which asserted that "the Citizens of the United States of America have a right to applaud themselves for having given to mankind examples of an enlarged and liberal policy: a policy worthy of imitation. All possess alike liberty of conscience and immunities of citizenship." Washington further declared that the US government gives "to bigotry no sanction, to persecution no assistance" and "requires only that they who live under its protection should demean themselves as good citizens, in giving it on all occasions their effectual support."[16] The beautiful conclusion to the letter reads: "May the Children of the Stock of Abraham, who dwell in this land, continue to merit and enjoy the good will of the other Inhabitants; while every one shall sit in safety under his own vine and figtree, and there shall be none to make him afraid. May the father of all mercies scatter light and not darkness in our paths, and make us all in our several vocations useful here, and in his own due time and way everlastingly happy."

There's also the Treaty of Tripoli, between the United States and Tripoli (now Libya) in 1797, which in article 11 stated explicitly that "the United States of America is not, in any sense, founded on the Christian religion" and "has in itself no character of enmity against the laws, religion, or tranquility, of Mussulmen (Muslims)." This treaty was negotiated by a representative of President Washington, was read aloud on the Senate floor on May 29, passed through Congress unanimously (by all present), and signed into law by President John Adams on June 10, 1797.[17]

During the Q&A at the Christian Nationalism panel, I asked Crenshaw about the liberal flipside to CFE doctrine. Religious freedom and pluralism were both there from the start and, furthermore, were a source of patriotic love for many Americans. Why was he ignoring the other part of this history? Crenshaw had a reasonable enough response. He said that what I was talking about was "Virginia supremacy," and that this Jeffersonian outlook had almost completely eclipsed the other side of the story, the "Christian founding" side. He said that in his work he was trying to rectify this imbalance by highlighting alternative arguments. In other words, the Jeffersonian, liberal vision is all around us; it is the water we swim in, and that we take for granted, whereas these other views needed to be recovered.[18]

Those are fair points, even if they were absent from his original talk. Crenshaw was undoubtedly correct that in mainstream liberal contexts, the pluralistic (or secular) liberal account is dominant, sometimes to the point of excluding good historical arguments about American Christianity.

The deeper questions lurking here, though, concerned the present. Which vision of America—the Christian or the pluralist—should be embraced and celebrated today? Crenshaw and his fellow panelists seemed quite willing to deny or obscure the pluralistic arguments of the founding, and they seemed to be doing so in the service of a present-day political movement. In 2024 Crenshaw welcomed the idea of a "Christian Prince" for the *American Reformer* website. "Support for Trump could help pave the way for future Christian statesmanship," he wrote, "whether constitutional or post-constitutional." Crenshaw insisted that standing by Trump would translate into support for a future Christian Prince "when the time comes to restore order and good rule to America." He acknowledged that the process would "inevitably require difficult and painful policies that separate friends from enemies."[19]

This is how arguments that start with Christian Founding Era doctrine tip into hardened, unconstitutional Christian nationalism. It's one thing to explore history and reveal some long-forgotten truths. It's quite another to impose a reductive version of the past—or a newfangled Postliberal theocracy—onto the present. Especially after 250 plus years of pluralistic transformation.

Sociologists Andrew Whitehead and Samuel Perry consider Christian nationalism to be a cultural framework—"a collection of myths, traditions, symbols, narratives, and value systems—that idealizes and advocates a fusion of Christianity with American civic life." They continue: "Understood in this light, Christian nationalism contends that America has been and should always be distinctively 'Christian' from top to bottom—in its self-identity, interpretations of its own history, sacred symbols, cherished values and public policies—and it aims to keep it this way."[20] It's a very short intellectual leap from the CFE doctrine to the Christian nationalism that they describe.

Prophets, Apostles, Revival, and Warfare

Though the scene that unfolded at the Capitol on January 6, 2021, could not have been more different from the mood at the Fort Lauderdale conference two years later, on January 6 we did catch a glimpse of the kind of "difficult and painful policies" that might be required to install a Crenshaw-style "Christian Prince" in the United States of America.

I watched what was happening at the Capitol on TV. We were living in Frederick, Maryland, at the time, so nowhere nearby, but it felt like watching an act of desecration. I remember thinking, naively: Why isn't Trump putting a stop to this? At the time, I recognized some of the far right symbology but was also perplexed by what I saw—and not just the QAnon Shaman, but also all the other religious iconography—the shofars, for example, and the "Appeal to Heaven" flags. This was due to my own blind spots; experts on right-wing Christianity were soon able to show how this symbology provided visual evidence for the Christian nationalist dimensions of the day.[21] The role that Christian nationalism played on January 6—and in the broader story of Trump's rise—is one of the great neglected stories of the era.

When Representative Mike Johnson—a Southern Baptist—spoke to the World Prayer Network in October 2023, he spoke in a variety of registers. He discoursed about the phrase "In God We Trust" that has adorned the House of Representatives since 1962, and he did so using CFE concepts and language. And he also spoke about a "time of judgment for our collective sins," something you might well hear in Southern Baptist circles. But then he also spoke about the coming of a "shaking," and the need for a revival and divine intervention. This was more in the arena of charismatic, revivalist Christianity. Johnson is comfortable in all three worlds and demonstrates the extent to which traditional denominational lines matter less and less.

Both Garlow and Johnson are fellow travelers with part of a Christian revivalism that is quite distinct from New Right intellectualism, and from the Christian Founding Era arguments. It involves different people, different ideas and practices, and arguably a quite different set of motives. Scholars have various ways of describing this sector; I will refer to it as the independent Charismatic network. Another relevant term here is the New Apostolic Reformation (NAR), which is a subset of the broader network.

The independent Charismatic network played an outsized role in organizing and supporting the Capitol insurrection. While John Eastman was busy writing his memos and organizing fake slates of electors, the independent Charismatics and other Christian groups were organizing on behalf of the president too. In his book *The Violent Take It by Force* (2024), religion scholar Matthew Taylor wrote that "the distinctive prophecy-driven, charismatic spirituality of the New Apostolic Reformation (NAR) provided the Christian stage-setting to January 6, tying together what would otherwise seem like a bizarre array of Christian expressions." Taylor's book provides an exhaustive account of how independent Charismatic groups and leaders hosted major rallies and "Stop the Steal" marches, engaged in "spiritual warfare" for Trump, and formed a significant presence in DC that day. Three of the six permits issued for protests at the Capitol were made out to Charismatic groups. Taylor calls the Charismatic nondenominational subset of American Christianity the "amorphous, tumultuous Wild West of the modern church."[22]

Though this is just one slice of the Christian landscape in America— most Christians, be they Catholic or Protestant, belong to a formal denomination of Christianity—it is one of the few forms of Christianity that is growing, both in the United States and globally. Scholars have estimated that there were 312 million Independent Charismatics in the world in 2020 (contrasted with 44 million in 1970).[23]

So what exactly are we talking about here?

Pentecostalism is a subset of Protestantism that emphasizes direct personal experience of God. (Sarah Palin was the first Pentecostal to join a major party ticket.) The independent subset of Pentecostalism is distinct for its rejection of typical denominational governance. Rather than standard top-down church hierarchies, the independents form a loosely organized network of people, many of whom see themselves as present-day apostles and prophets—i.e., individuals whom God speaks through directly.[24] More than other forms of Pentecostalism, the independent churches are invested in recreating, in the words of Taylor, "the miraculous environment of the early church and creating a revival movement towards what they understand to be the end times."[25] Further, Taylor writes, "*Independent Charismatic communities are the epicenter of Christian Trumpism.*"[26]

One of the elements of the Independent Charismatic world that Taylor emphasizes as crucial to understanding popular Christian attachment to Trump is modern-day prophecy. Trump has benefited from Charismatic prophesies that go back almost two decades now (Taylor cites a 2007 prophecy by a South African prophet Kim Clement that said, "Trump shall become a trumpet"; there were also hundreds of prophets who proclaimed in 2020 that Trump would be reelected). Citing studies from 2022, Taylor writes:

> Belief in modern-day prophecy—and particularly, belief in prophecies about Donald Trump—was both strongly correlated with belief in Trump's claims of election fraud and a major accelerant for extreme political views, including an openness to supporting violence or lawbreaking in the pursuit of political goals. This should not surprise anyone too much: If you believe—truly believe—that God is intervening directly in American politics and anointing presidents, then democracy and the will of the people must logically be secondary and subordinate to the will of God.[27]

Taylor is always careful to note just how big and complicated Evangelicalism is in America, but his work also demonstrates the special import of the independent Charismatic network to Trumpism.

The story of how Trump and Trumpism came to have such deep ties to the Charismatic sector of American Christianity is fascinating. Trump was not a typical candidate for the Republican nomination, and if there is one thing besides his fame that smoothed his path for victory in 2016, it was that he had cultivated ties in the evangelical movement for years. His main contact was the televangelist Paula White. Taylor calls White "the fulcrum on which an epochal shift in American religious politics tilted." As the investigative journalist Sarah Posner has explained, Trump was always "more like a televangelist than a politician," and he seemed to respect White from the moment he met her.[28] When 2016 came around, Trump leaned on his connections to White to solidify his candidacy. As Posner explained to me, "It was not unheard of for Republican candidates to reach out to the Charismatic world (recall Sarah Palin). Trump just did it more and better and placed White at the center of his evangelical outreach."[29]

Paula White and the early involvement of Charismatic Christians in the Trump campaign created an early permission structure for Trumpism among evangelicals somewhat analogous to what was happening for intellectuals in the blog pages of the *Journal of American Greatness*. In those early days, mainstream evangelicals were generally uncomfortable with Trump as a candidate and tended to stay aloof, which had the effect of amplifying the role of independent Charismatics in Trump's orbit. And because they showed loyalty early, they enjoyed outsized influence in Trump's version of the GOP, and as such throughout the country. Taylor used the analogy of the fringe becoming the rug.[30] As we have seen throughout this book, a similarly dramatic reorientation took place among conservative intellectuals.

Those who study the Christian right had a name for what was happening and explained the movement's political doctrine—and Trump's ideology—in terms of Christian nationalism. Some on the right protested this characterization. Others—notably Congresswoman Marjorie Taylor Greene—started to embrace the label openly. In an interview on July 23, 2022, at the Turning Point USA Student Action Summit in Florida, she said: "We need to be the party of nationalism and I'm a Christian, and I say it proudly, we should be Christian nationalists."[31]

Experts like Posner, Taylor, and Kristin Kobes Du Mez agree that the connection between Trump and the Christian right is not entirely or even primarily transactional; it is much more sincere and emotionally charged, and Trump is often seen as a vessel of the divine. Posner observed that Trump is a culmination of decades of political organizing on the Christian right. "He became their savior," she wrote, "because he spoke the language that tied them and him—and the grievances of the alt-right—together against 'political correctness,' civil and human rights, and at its core, the entire arduous project of maintaining a pluralistic, secular, liberal democracy."[32] The New Right gave intellectuals a justificatory rationale for Trumpism; the evangelical right helped to provide that for conservative Christians. In both cases the fringe became the weave, and in both cases the fabrics stayed intact, and were even strengthened and reinforced, after January 6, 2021, at which time the new "Lost Cause" narrative gained momentum.

One important wrinkle here is that the independent Charismatics are more transnational than nationalist. This is a multiracial, multi-ethnic network seeking global Christian supremacy, and it is more open to women in leadership than other Christian groups. Taylor suggested to me that the nondenominational character of the movement naturally decenters adherents, detaches them from denominational identities, and so reduces the salience of ethnic and theological categories. All identity categories are "subsumed under a generic and quite intentionally de-cultured 'Christian' identity."[33] But because the independent Charis-matic network is multiracial and global does not mean that it is politically moderate. On the contrary, there are strong connections between Amer-ican Pentecostals, Charismatics, and Christian Zionism, and, with some important exceptions, this subset of American Christianity supports an aggressive and rhetorically violent form of Christian nationalism.[34]

Many independent Charismatic leaders, for example, embrace a doc-trine called the Seven Mountain Mandate, or 7M, an idea that origi-nated within Dominion Theology.[35] Dominion Theology supports the idea of pervasive Christian political and cultural domination, whereby Christians are justified in taking over whole societies, and even the world. Some of the most prominent Dominionist intellectuals in Amer-ica historically have been Calvinist Christian Reconstructionists (like Rousas John Rushdoony, whom we will meet again shortly). 7M is a Charismatic, Pentecostal variation on Dominion Theology that delin-eates the seven distinctive "mountains" that are ripe for Christian take-over and control: family, religion, education, media, entertainment, business, and government. This is the Charismatic version of Yarvin's destruction of the Cathedral and "Retire All Government Employees," of Catholic "integration from within," or of Rufo and Roberts's "march through the institutions." Several prominent members of the Domin-ionist movement, like the influencer Charlie Kirk and the prophet Lance Wallnau, identify openly as Christian nationalists.[36]

Another popular prophecy in independent circles, also promoted by Wallnau, likens Trump to the Persian king Cyrus (this is sometimes called the "Cyrus Anointing"). In the Hebrew Bible, God uses Cyrus, the great Persian king from the sixth century BCE (who was not Jewish), to help liberate the Israelites from Babylon. According to the Cyrus Anointing, Trump is the new Cyrus who will save the Christians from liberal secularism. "Sometimes," Lance said in 2018, "God can anoint a wrecking ball."[37] Kevin Roberts of the Heritage Foundation, who is Catholic, has appealed to the Cyrus theory.[38]

Finally, in addition to the Seven Mountain Mandate and the idea of Trump-as-Cyrus, apostles and prophets within the Charismatic networks often speak of politics in terms of "spiritual warfare," "discipling nations," and Christian colonialism.[39] As Taylor wrote in his book, the crux of the problem of the independent Charismatic sector today concerns its "theologies of violence, the ideation of violence, and the romanticization of spiritual violence that have grown up in Charismatic evangelicalism. It is about the culture of violent rhetoric that has spread from there into broader American Christianity and into American politics."[40] This is a movement that rejects, in the strongest possible terms, the idea of church-state separation, and seeks to dominate and control all areas of public life. More than other, older versions of the Christian Right, the independent Charismatic ecosystem empowers individuals to take matters into their own hands, as spiritual warriors for Jesus.[41]

Stephen Wolfe, operating in an entirely different mode and register, is also interested in empowering Christians—and especially Christian men—to dominate America.

Stephen Wolfe's Big Bad Book

Yes, atheism will be crushed.
And we'll do it citing scripture, Tradition, and Plato.

—STEPHEN WOLFE, OR @PERFINJUST

Ben Crenshaw's discussion of the Christian founding was part of a panel at the ISI/Claremont conference that included a presentation by Stephen Wolfe, whose *The Case for Christian Nationalism* was published in fall 2022. Wolfe represents a highly cerebral version of Christian nationalism grounded in Calvinist theology. This is far away from the Charismatic world, but just as extreme (if not more so), and there are a few points of contact.

Wolfe is certainly part of the New Right. He graduated from West Point in 2008 and was active duty for five years, attaining the rank of captain.[42] He earned a master's degree in political science at Louisiana State University in 2016, and another master's degree in philosophy in 2019. He earned his PhD in political science from LSU in 2020. His dissertation was called "Protestant Experience and Continuity of Political Thought in Early America, 1630–1789." It was an erudite defense of Protestantism as "not just another competing source or tradition among others in the founding era," but rather as the tradition that "supplied the underlying principles of early American political thought." At LSU, he worked with a well-regarded conservative professor named James Stoner. (Fun fact: In 2013, my husband and I were offered faculty positions in the political science department at LSU; on another timeline, I could have been Wolfe's teacher.) After graduating in 2020, Wolfe held a postdoctoral fellowship with Robby George's James Madison Program in American Ideals and Institutions.[43] *The Case for Christian Nationalism* was published by Canon Press on November 1, 2022.

Canon is not an academic or a mainstream press; rather, it is Douglas Wilson's press. Wilson is a theologian in the Reformed Presbyterian (Calvinist) tradition of Christianity, also known as Christian Reconstructionism. Christian Reconstructionism in the United States traces back to thinkers like Gary North, David Chilton, and, most especially, the aforementioned Rousas John Rushdoony—a major theologian of Dominion theology, who wrote from an austere Calvinist perspective.[44] This is a narrow but influential group of Christian thinkers who are committed to "restoring" full Christian dominance to America—which means a fundamental transformation of the regime. As Jerome Copulsky wrote in his book *American Heretics* (2024): "Christian Reconstructionists believed that restoration of law and order would require a return to the ultimate source of law and order—submission to the sovereignty of the triune God. 'Christ or chaos, God's law or tyranny' was their slogan." Copulsky goes on to explain that Rushdoony's ideas were extremely influential on the New Christian Right in the 1980s, even though no one admitted it at the time. He asks: "Why did they refuse to admit his influence on their thinking?" His answer: "Because Rushdoony was a fearless advocate of theocracy."[45]

Douglas Wilson is also a highly controversial figure in his own right, thanks to: his advocacy of theocracy in the town of Moscow, Idaho; concerns about his handling of sexual assault cases in his community and teachings that involve the subordination of women; and a Canon Press pamphlet called *Southern Slavery, As It Was* (1996), which contained claims like "slavery produced in the South a genuine affection between the races that we believe we can say has never existed in any nation before the War or since."[46] Wolfe does not identify as a Dominionist or a Reconstructionist, but he is certainly Calvinist, and Canon was the press that he chose for his book.

The Case for Christian Nationalism features a blurb from Yoram Hazony on its cover that says "A Pioneering Work . . . Relentlessly Innovative." That is one way of putting it. As noted previously, there was a good deal of controversy surrounding Wolfe's book upon publication, when his podcast partner at the time, Thomas Achord, was outed as a white nationalist.[47] This caused controversy for Wolfe not only because of the friendship, but also because his book can easily be read as a defense of "Kinism," or racial and ethnic chauvinism. Wolfe offers a strong defense of love of one's own in the book, and, while he offers the occasional repudiation of white supremacy, he does "use the terms *ethnicity* and *nation* almost synonymously," and claims that "no nation (properly speaking) is composed of two or more ethnicities."[48] Mark David Hall, who is not exactly hawkish against Christian nationalism, noted that the book is peppered with references to notions like "blood relations," "the *volk*," "community in blood," and "the principle of similarity."[49]

To be clear, though, Wolfe's book was not just some unthinking screed or manifesto. Wolfe is a highly learned person with deep knowledge of the tradition he works within. His book is situated largely within the Reformed, Calvinist conservative tradition of Protestant political thought. He claims from the outset to be a political theorist, not a theologian, which means that he is less interested in the political implications of given passages of scripture (which he rarely cites), and more in how Calvinist thinkers of the past—mainly sixteenth- and seventeenth-century authors—have sought to reconcile biblical teachings with the real world. As Hall explained in his review of the book, "Wolfe proceeds on the assumption that the Reformed theological tradition is true, and so makes 'little effort' to make biblical or more broadly theological arguments to support it." Hall continues: "Unless one assumes the truth of Reformed theology, there is little reason to read this work."

In some respects, the American Calvinists are the true opposites of the independent Charismatic types. You will not find Wolfe taking part in revelatory prophecies or talking of "shakings"; this is someone invested in high Calvinist theology and the religious life of the mind. But as with the revivalists, Wolfe's thinking stands in stark opposition to mainstream American liberalism. And as with Christian Founding Era doctrine, Wolfe's reading of the past dismisses all modern Enlightenment influences as deeply misguided. Indeed, Wolfe's version of Christianity is so austere that it is not altogether clear whom his audience is. Hall suggests that it "includes Douglas Wilson and some of his followers, but I'm not sure it extends much beyond this quirky collection of patriarchal Calvinists," and that Wolfe is not a Christian nationalist in the sense that the term is typically understood (especially by its critics)—i.e., as involving a nationalist takeover of the country. Rather, Hall argues, Wolfe is committed to local and regional forms of Christian nationalism; the book ought perhaps to have been titled "The Case for Patriarchal Christian Localism."[50] There is not a whiff of internationalism in Wolfe's work, to the point where he opposes Christian Zionism (and has been accused of antisemitism for it).[51]

Readers who are curious about Wolfe's political theology should consult the book for themselves, and the many reviews written by experts, including a two-part review titled "Treatise or Tweet?" by one of Wolfe's intellectual mentors, Glenn Moots.[52] What I can say with confidence is that in the more than four hundred pages of his tome—as well as all over social media—in addition to the genteel, localist man of learning, Wolfe plays the chauvinist edgelord and provocateur. Hall and others suggest that Wolfe's book will be of interest only to people in the Re-formed tradition, but that is credulous. The book is also BAPism for Protestants, a red-pill for the Christian crowd.

It would be tedious—especially so late in this journey—to enumer-ate the ways in which Wolfe's work has affinities with Hard Right think-ing. But two points are worth emphasizing: First, Wolfe's politics are deeply misogynist. His work is utterly Schmittian, and for him the enemy is the contemporary liberal regime, which he prefers to call, echoing BAP, "gynocracy." Wolfe writes: "We live under a gynocracy—a rule of women. This may not be apparent on the surface, since men still run many things. But the governing virtues of America are feminine vices, associated with certain feminine virtues, such as empathy, fair-ness, and equality."[53]

While it is true that there are strong whiffs of Kinism in the book, Wolfe, like BAP, goes full throttle with the reactionary misogyny.

Wolfe argues explicitly for a patriarchal, male-exclusive politics where women are kept out. In civil affairs, Wolfe says, echoing another far right misogynist subculture, that "men should go their own way" (MGTOW). He includes the occasional Scott Yenor–like footnote about how, for example, restrictive Covid policies have "exacerbated women's already fragile mental health."[54] On social media, he is on the record asserting that he does not affirm women's right to vote.[55]

Second, Wolfe is dedicated to a reactionary aestheticized politics of domination. His book includes encomiums to the possibilities of "Great men," the possibilities of "heroic masculinity," and new feats of the will, and, more specifically, to the possibility of a great "Christian Prince" who will lead the whole to greatness and do "everything in his power to make his people's culture, as a whole, Christian." The book includes pleas for revolution against the current regime and acknowledges that if a minority of Christians can constitute a secure government "for true justice and the complete good," then they do not have to care about the consent of non-Christians. He says that non-Christians deserve justice, peace, and safety, but not political equality; heretics and atheists will be treated harshly. He concludes his chapter on revolution with a call to arms reminiscent of the fascist Eliade: "We are gripped by a slavish devotion to our secularist captors. But we do not have to be like this. We have the power and the right to act. Let us train the will and cultivate our resolve."[56] He recommends starting locally, in the states.[57]

The concluding section of Wolfe's book—an epilogue entitled "Now What?"—is by far the most manifesto-like. It consists of a series of pseudo-Nietzschean aphoristic observations that include further meditations on gynocracy ("The rise of Christian nationalism necessitates the fall of gynocracy"), virulent attacks against secular liberal elites as "enemies of the human race," extended disquisitions on the evils of the "Globalist American Empire" (he uses the acronym "GAE," borrowed from Darren Beattie of Revolver News and Raw Egg Nationalist); and the need for self-overcoming in the face of our modern sentiments ("We have to retrain the mind by the strength of will. We might *feel*, for example, that it is wrong for public space to be exclusively Christian, but it still ought to be. . . . We must overcome ourselves").[58]

There are good, historically informed accounts of fascism out there, several of which include lists of archetypal features of fascist movements—things like "nostalgia for a purer, mythic, often rural past; cults of tradition and cultural regeneration . . . the universalizing of some groups as authentically national, while dehumanizing all other groups . . . anti-modernism; fetishized patriarchal masculinity."[59] Wolfe knows how to check those boxes.

———

In Fort Lauderdale, Wolfe and his fellow panelists did not focus on the fascist factor in *The Case for Christian Nationalism*. Wolfe used his time to clarify his concept of "complacent self-love," which is a nice, almost Rousseauian, idea that he uses in the book to defend the idea of the basic goodness of Christian life and of the self, and so too of the nation. And he spent some time clarifying what he means by the Christian Nation and Christian nationalism. He emphasized that he was not working in the Reconstructionist or Dominionist or Postmillennial traditions, but within the tradition of magisterial Protestantism and Classical protestant theology. He said that he did not believe America had a special covenant with God, he was not arguing against natural law, nor was he arguing for direct theocracy—in fact, he explained, he was against the idea of pastors and church magistrates participating in politics. Instead, Wolfe explained, what he seeks is a nation that is "self-consciously Christian."[60] Generally speaking, at the ISI/Claremont conference, Wolfe reined himself in.

That did not stop the audience from taking up some of the bait in his book. The first person to ask a question after the panel ended was Nathan Pinkoski. He wondered what the panelists' thoughts were about terms like "ethnic nationalism" and "ethno-nationalism." Pinkoski recognized that these categories had "negative connotations," and conceded that he probably wouldn't want to fight the battle to return to a world of *racial* nationalism. But he "might fight the battle on the other front and point to countries in the world that define themselves in terms of an *ethnos*." What were the panelists' thoughts on this, he wondered. Wolfe took the question and dutifully disavowed the idea of race and DNA as the basis for nationalism, preferring instead a phenomenological account emphasizing commonalities of place and historical experiences and struggle. It was prudently done.

———

The rest of my day at the ISI conference was quite strange. Immediately after the panel, a woman came up to me to try to explain how the Enlightenment was not a major influence on the founders. She was displeased when I strongly disagreed. Clifford Humphrey and I sat together at lunch and spoke at length about foundationalism, Christian nationalism, and the meaning of the Constitution. He was so nice and friendly. Humphrey basically said that he defended Christian nationalism because Christian moral standards were foundational to decent living and to the American Constitutional order. And he took strong issue with the current liberal norms dominating American life, which I took to mean "wokeness" and "cancel culture." I believe he called them the new blasphemy laws. I thought that was an exaggeration, and I said so. If you misspoke today, you might be faced with social consequences, or maybe even professional ones—but you would not be fined or held criminally accountable or whipped, and you might even be rewarded in other social settings and circles, like the ones we were sitting in.

He pushed back, asking where I thought the standards for rules and norms came from, suggesting that I must be a moral relativist. I said that while I believed in principles, I thought that they did change over time, and ultimately had to be negotiated by democratic peoples—and that such shifts were not arbitrary impositions. In our system, people had to show up, reason things through, persuade and campaign hard, protest and organize, and win free and fair elections. At one point he tried to put me in the majoritarian, winner-takes-all Stephen Douglas camp in a manner reminiscent of the 1776 Report. We were both frustrated. I was reminded how hard it is to defend liberal pluralism and epistemology against bull-headed self-certainty and fundamentalism.

The exchange with Humphrey also conjured up a time in graduate school when we were discussing the possibility that all human knowledge is mediated knowledge—mediated through our prophets, traditions, texts, history, languages, brains, and so forth—such that access to the full truth remains utterly elusive. In the thick of this very grad school moment, one of my more conservative and religious classmates became animated and exclaimed something along the lines of "but there *must* be *true knowledge*! Like, *out there*!" His point was that mediated knowledge was not good enough—for truth to be truth, it had to be independent, otherworldly, permanent and absolute truth, the kind that Richard Weaver, Harry Jaffa, and Congressman Johnson were all so taken by.

Humphrey would surely have agreed with them; for my part, I still don't understand how you get unmediated access to that kind of truth, and I like the mediated versions just fine. I think they are rich and wonderful. And more true.

In any case, after that I attended a Claremont Institute panel called "What the Right Can Learn from the Left," featuring Michael Anton, Glenn Ellmers, Kevin Slack, and Ryan Williams. This was a weird panel, where the speakers derived lessons from Marx, the New Left of the post-1960s, and Foucault. Mostly the panel was boring, but Slack, a professor at Hillsdale College (the one who taught the online course called "The American Left: From Liberalism to Despotism"), did say some astonishing things. At one point he plugged Darren Beattie for his relentless mockery of the Globalist American Empire (or GAE) and suggested that this sort of ridicule was a terrific model for the New Right. He said that every time you see somebody ridiculous, you should show up and protest. He gave the example of the "LBBTQI+ crowd," saying that making fun of it was crucial. It was vile and hateful.[61] He recounted how he went to counterprotest one of these groups at his local library with a bunch of young New Right types and was delighted because "you can see how intimidated the rainbow people were." In the end he wasn't encouraging ridicule so much as intimidation.

Slack argued that it is important to get involved in local government, "control the sheriff's office," so that they don't enforce things like Covid mandates. He noted that taking the Michigan state house was probably unrealistic, but that it would be good to join local associations, like rifle associations. "Most every young guy I know has an AR-15 and they go out and train. And I don't mean with the FBI which is to say the militia, but they lift weights together and they're trying to form the true bonds that would be the basis for a true Republicanism and political power." He said that in the red states, they should exercise the power that they have, asking "Why do you have any progressive professors at the University of Idaho period? Get 'em! Why is Scott Yenor having to fight for a job at Boise State? . . . In our red states, we've got to parry or purge!" It should surprise no one that Slack is a proponent of Red Caesarism.[62]

―――――

That's about when I ducked out. The conference was not over, but I had booked my flight home for early in the evening, knowing that I would miss the Robby George keynote; the conference organizers had told me that it would be posted online. Michael Anton and Ryan Williams begged off early, too. I know because right after the panel they came out to the front of the hotel, and stood a few feet away from where I sat waiting for my Uber. With their luggage, they soon got into a big, official-looking SUV. I thought to myself, "I wonder if they are off to visit the DeSantis campaign?"

Months later I learned that indeed they were. Anton and Williams planned to have dinner that night with Arthur Milikh and Scott Yenor in Palm Beach, just north of Fort Lauderdale, and then would spend the weekend at the "Governor's Blueprint Retreat," at the Four Seasons Resort. Anton and Williams had discussed their plans via email with Yenor, who was using his public university's email account. The exchanges—and many others—were subject to public information requests, which in 2024 led to some interesting news stories in *The New York Times* and *The Guardian*, including about their role in the anti-DEI campaign run by Christopher Rufo, as well as Yenor and Williams's membership in the Society for American Civic Renewal, alongside Charles Haywood and Nathan Fischer. These men were later dubbed the "TheoBros."[63] They were friendly with JD Vance.[64]

As regards their early departure from the ISI event, Williams expressed some concern about missing Robby George, but then he said, "I must be honest in saying I'd rather us just dine together in Palm Beach than sit through Robbie and a rubber chicken hotel dinner." Anton heartily agreed ("Absolutely"). On Saturday and Sunday, the four men were scheduled to attend DeSantis's retreat, for which they had pitched a panel called "How to Counter the Regime with Red States," which included tips on how to make the state into a counterrevolutionary force "against the woke regime."[65] The idea was that states could serve as a good testing ground for restoring America (in the end, of course, they wouldn't need to resort merely to state-level action).

When they drove by, I thought about waving from my little bench, but I couldn't see them through the dark tinted windows, and I don't think they would have waved back.

It was still astonishing to me that these men, and the other New Right leaders I discuss in this book, had attained such tremendous ideological authority within the GOP. People outside the Claremonter camp had their own paths into Trumpism. But ones nearest to my own intellectual universe, people like Kesler, Anton, BAP and Beattie, had done so based largely on their Straussian credentials—some by peddling extravagant rhetoric about wokeness and the end of Western civilization, others leading a descent into the gutters of race science, misogyny, and nouveau conspiracism. It was a clear trajectory of intellectual decline and unraveling, catalyzed by a long-cultivated style of intellectual hubris. Strauss himself was a complex figure, who inspired students of all political persuasions, but his focus on esotericism and the supremacy of ancient philosophy also, at least in hindsight, came at a cost.

Christopher Hitchens once wrote: "The cynicism of Strauss's theory and practice was summarized in his antithesis between Athens and Jerusalem. I am certain to vulgarise the recondite here, but Straussians believe in religion and not in God."[66] This formulation brings us a long way to understanding the friendliness that some New Right intellectuals came to have toward Christian nationalism, and to radicalism more generally. Strauss's dichotomies, both Athens vs. Jerusalem and Ancients vs. Moderns, fostered an either/or mode of thought that actively made room both for true believers—the more fanatical, the better—as well as for anyone who, educated in Straussian schools of esoteric dissembling and *thymos*, came to believe in their own superiority. But this model didn't always make room for others—for people who were more quietly pious, or more questioning than strident, or who thought in terms beyond Strauss's either/or. In some of these circles, anyone who believed in modern liberty and pluralism—anyone who came to believe that people might learn, even in the face of the deepest intellectual and spiritual differences, to live together in some kind of civil truce or peace—was seen at best as shallow and naïve, and at worst as a harbinger of the Last Man or the Longhouse.

None of this was based on careful thinking about anything. Rather, it was based on hyped-up formulas, macho abstract doctrines, "Straussian lullabies," and nostalgic myths that calcified over time, reifying dogmatism and alienating anyone who dared to disagree.

And so it was that by 2024 the Claremonters, as well as their more genuinely devout NatCon and Postliberal colleagues, were cooperating with the likes of Donald Trump, with sincere extremists like those who constitute the Charismatic world, and with creeps like Stephen Wolfe. It was, in the end, the Enlightenment philosophers who made them do it.

13

Conclusion: *Ecce Furor*

There's something grander and bigger than liberalism, and that's to
be seen in the philosophy of the ancients. Plato and Aristotle are the
leaders, but there are a number of them. . . . I would describe what you
learn from the ancients as learning how to live in the land of virtue,
and the beauties and the difficulties of that land. . . . And liberalism
knows essentially nothing of the land of virtue.

—HARVEY MANSFIELD, JULY 6, 2022

I. Mansfield at AEI

ON JULY 6, 2022, I had a front row seat for a quiet spectacle unfolding
at the American Enterprise Institute, the conservative think tank in
Washington, DC. I was there for an afternoon of panels organized in
honor of Harvey C. Mansfield Jr.—idol to Michael Anton, advisor to
Costin Alamariu, and one of the great American conservative professors
of his generation. It was also a reunion of sorts for a good number of
prominent Straussians after years of Covid-related isolation. The event
had been organized by Yuval Levin and Bill Kristol, both of whom had
been students of Mansfield at Harvard. Mansfield was sitting in the front
row, too.

AEI is one of those places that feels overflowing with money: The
building is gorgeous and the art is real. It had been over a decade since
I had gone to conservative summer camp in Charlottesville, but the
feeling here was basically the same. On the surface, the day's event was
pleasant and contained, but anyone familiar with the people in attendance
would have felt the simmering tensions, muted only by the esteem

enjoyed by the elderly honoree. Mansfield had recently turned ninety years old and had been teaching in Harvard's Department of Government for sixty years. That milestone inspired the celebration, where a dozen or so of his notable former students gathered to sing his praises. But the commemoration was also a rare moment that brought figures of the New Right, like Charles Kesler, in public contact with the other side—with the old establishment conservatism, including some, like Bill Kristol, from the neocon Never Trump camp.[1] In addition to Kesler, Peter Berkowitz was a panelist—another Straussian (and senior fellow at the Hoover Institute) who had served in the first Trump administration, as the director of policy planning in the State Department.[2] The air was thick with anticipation. What would be said, by whom? Would tempers flare? And that is only to mention the controversies that were likely of interest to those who had chosen to attend. Harvey Mansfield, after all, was a controversial figure in his own right.[3]

Critics would have been amused but unsurprised by the constitution of the audience: Nearly all white, overwhelmingly male, and with a strong showing from young Republicans in navy blazers and khakis. They would perhaps have been entertained by the sight of ninety-year-old Harvey periodically nodding off during the proceedings, supported by his "spectacular" (his word) third wife Anna.[4] Even so, the overall mood was one of scholarly gravitas, as well as of respect and gratitude for a wonderful teacher. During some of the talks, I felt a wash of recognition for my younger, more Straussian self—and for the part of me that still just loves this stuff and always will.

The second panel was the one to watch for anyone interested in contemporary American politics. The panel was ostensibly devoted to "Tocqueville and America," but it pitted the two Trump advocates, Kesler and Berkowitz, against two critics, Bryan Garsten of Yale University and Yuval Levin of AEI (with Levin acting as moderator). Kristol had introduced the first panel of the day. When it came time for this one, he left the room.

The panelists hewed mainly to the Tocquevillian theme, but in a quiet and tactful way Yale's Garsten confronted Kesler. He used his time not only to praise Mansfield, but also to raise big Lincolnian questions about the preservation of American institutions. Garsten reminded the audience that the problem of conservative populism in America was not new, noting how Mansfield was someone who used to offer loud warnings about its dangers.[5] Garsten summarized the warning: "It's a dangerous game to try to ride the tiger," he said. "You might end up inside it." He added: "Are we going to be overcome by the democratic impatience with forms and formalities so much so that constitutionalism as a source of conservatism gets put aside?"[6]

Garsten did not mention Trump or Trumpism, but the source of his concern was obvious, and during the Q&A he faced pushback from Kesler, who suggested that Trump "in a way" represented a "democratic upsurge" that had happened because "the old constitution . . . had fallen into a certain kind of disrepair, or even deliberate diminishment and abandonment." Kesler argued that the populism was partly "proconstitutional, even though it takes an angry form in many cases." This was a rehash of *The Crisis of the Two Constitutions*—a book that replicated the same Manicheanism, in more genteel form, of "charge the cockpit or you die" and "the hour is late" Red Caesarism.

Each group of the MAGA New Right that we have been concerned with in this book offered a full slate of positions—spanning from Kesleresque refinement to Kevin Slack's reckless vulgarity—but each camp worked toward its own hard restorationists's vision of the future. The Claremonters said they wanted a return to the vision of the founders—a small-government Republican vision that respects traditional religion, manly statesmanship, self-government, and federalism. If that didn't work, then Red Caesarism would have to do. The National Conservatives sought to protect the true American nation—a Christian, mostly white, socially conservative nation, and one where the hordes of woke neo-Marxists would be defeated for good. For the American Postliberals and Catholic integralists, the ultimate endgame was spiritual; the secularist enemies would be defeated for the sake of the common good, which included orderly hierarchical politics, economic melioration, and the soul's salvation. The Hard Right wanted to smash the liberal status quo, come what may.

There was significant variation between the New Right modes, but in each instance, what we saw was a group of theoretically-minded people who turned into, or always were, ideologues fighting an existential battle against liberal democratic pluralism and its freedoms.

Each of these Ideas First visions refused to contend honestly with the realities of historical change and contemporary pluralism. But change and pluralism were real, and many people supported the transformation. Which meant that the New Right would require an authoritarian turn. Many were willing to take that risk, and it certainly helped that they were so caught up in their own ideas, so "high on their own supply." They had, one after another, become like G. K. Chesterton's madman.

"If you argue with a madman," the English critic wrote, "it is extremely probable that you will get the worst of it; for in many ways his mind moves all the quicker for not being delayed by the things that go with good judgment." The madman is not held back by a sense of humor, or by charity, or even by reality and the "dumb certainties of experience." Chesterton concludes: "He is the more logical for losing certain sane affections. Indeed, the common phrase for insanity is in this respect a misleading one. The madman is not the man who has lost his reason. The madman is the man who has lost everything except his reason."[7] The MAGA New Right was full of madmen like this, who were also angry, who then got a taste of power and influence, too.

At the Mansfield event at AEI, Kesler's argument was staked on the doubtful proposition that the aims of "progressive constitutionalism" are altogether different from those of the founders' constitution—and, furthermore, that brazen, Trump-style political means could serve genuinely restorative, constitutional ends. In his final response to Kesler, Garsten probed further: "Under what conditions [could] populism be expected to generate a new appreciation for constitutionalism? Or does it create habits and practices that will, in the end, do just the reverse? In other words, to what extent can we separate means and ends? Can we have that [populist] style of politics and hope that it leads us to a very different style of politics at some point in the future?" I do not take these to be merely rhetorical questions, and I don't think he did either. But Garsten's questioning pointed to just how tenuous Kesler's claims were in the case of Trump, given his dubious character, his demagoguery and vengefulness, and his plain disinterest in democracy, constitutionalism, and bridging divides.

To speak in a more classical idiom: you would need a more magnanimous, great-souled person to achieve what Kesler had hoped for from Trump.

But the Mansfield fête was never going to be the place for *thymotic* fireworks, and that was the extent of the confrontation between Kesler and Garsten. When Mansfield himself took to the podium at the end of that July afternoon, he made his little speech about conservative isles of virtue, took a few more formulaic swipes against liberals and liberalism, and concluded with a petty jab against Obama (for his ambition and "senseless assertiveness"). I have seldom been so glad to no longer be part of something as when I walked out of the AEI building and into the DC sunshine that day.

II. NatCon 4

If AEI was the Superego of right-wing intellectualism in the early 2020s, NatCon was the Ego and angry Id. Two years later, on July 8, 2024, I went back to that part of DC, just a few blocks north of the White House and about a half mile away from AEI to the Capital Hilton hotel, hoping to get into NatCon 4. We had recently moved back to DC by this point, so it was just a trip across town. I went with my friend Jerome.

This iteration of the conference boasted six US senators on the roster of speakers, with Josh Hawley and JD Vance set to give keynotes.[8] Steve Bannon had originally been listed but then had to report to prison. The NatCon group seemed to have consolidated institutional support in DC, as well as with partners like Hungary's Danube Institute. And though Peter Thiel was off the donor's list, the Heritage Foundation, Jim DeMint's Conservative Partnership Institute, and Thomas Klingenstein were all still listed as big donors, with the Claremont Institute, Hillsdale College, and other smaller groups on the program now, too.[9] A major new theme of the conference (in addition to surefire hits like "Big Tech and Big Porn," "Separation of Church and State Has Failed," and "Corporations Against Conservatism") was "Lawfare: The Criminalization of Politics." That panel included John Yoo, author of the so-called Bush Torture Memos, and John Eastman, who gave a talk on "Living in the

Shadow of Lawfare."[10] Chris DeMuth opened the conference with a pointed declaration: "Welcome to the mainstream!" Hawley concluded the day by declaring himself a Christian Nationalist: "Some will say now I am calling America a Christian nation—and so I am. Some will say I'm advocating Christian nationalism—and so I do. . . . My question is, is there any other kind worth having?"[11] Douglas Wilson—the theologian from Moscow, Idaho—was a new addition to the NatCon roster. A young writer named Mana Afsari wrote about NatCon 4 and said that "everyone, young and old, was dressed to the nines." She noted that Curtis Yarvin was in attendance, too.[12]

National Conservatism, which began as a group of Trump-supporting misfits, was now the heart of the party. And beyond the bevy of American senators, there were also representatives from across the foreign far right: several constituents from the recently defeated Tory Party in Britain; a substantial delegation from Modi's India; the expatriate crown prince of Iran, Reza Pahlavi; Gladden Pappin and Balázs Orbán from Hungary; and Ryszard Legutko of Poland, who was there to receive an award.

Among the speakers, the fringiest contingent this time around included Paul Gottfried, Jonathan Keeperman (aka L0m3z), and Jack Posobiec, whose speech was titled "This Year We Can Save Western Civilization."[13] Posobiec had taken to calling the left "Unhumans," and he published a book by that title with War Room Books the day before he spoke at the conference. Vance provided a blurb for the book.[14]

David Azerrad of Hillsdale College was allotted time to speak and took advantage of it in a speech called "Enemies of the State: The Left's Schmittian Politics." Azerrad, who was originally from Montreal and whom I knew from my time in Texas (he did his PhD at the University of Dallas with some of my Alberta friends), had become a far-right provocateur, happy to denounce all the left as the enemy; in 2023 he denounced Martin Luther King in Paul Gottfried's *Chronicles* magazine.[15] At NatCon, he channeled a younger Mansfield (or perhaps Senator Hawley, who had recently released a book on *Manhood*): "America has always been manly. We took on the Red Coats, tamed the West, won two World Wars and put a man on the moon. Manliness is as American as apple pie. And I would say to all of you: What does it say about the failure of the right to engage on this issue that young men need to turn for manly advice to a scumbag like Andrew Tate, who's currently awaiting trial for human trafficking and rape charges?"

This pearl-clutching about Tate struck me as droll. The rest of Azerrad's performance involved, in the words of journalists Annika Brockschmidt and Ben Lorber, "an unabashedly White nationalist and male supremacist speech, for which he received one of the only standing ovations at the conference."[16]

I was not in attendance for Azerrad's or anyone else's NatCon speeches. I tried to get a press pass but was turned away. I offered to pay and they said no. When I showed up in person that Monday morning, they gallantly shepherded me over to the ladies' line (that was a conference first; the line was short)—but then the director of the conference confirmed that I was not getting in. Jerome and some other friends were admitted. I spent a bit of time in the hotel lobby, headed home, and watched some of the talks online later. There are worse things than not attending NatCon.

III. Masculinist Furies

Only the real political junkies were paying attention to NatCon 4, which was also held during the same week as the NATO summit and right before the GOP convention. It was a strange time in the United States—or that's how it seemed to me in the thick of the hot DC summer. President Biden had had a catastrophic debate performance in June that left Democrats and many others feeling desperate and anxious, and there was no end in sight to the campaign's relentless, exhausting, drip drip drip stagnation. If Aristotle was right that pity and fear together are two of the key ingredients to tragedy, then it is fair to say that I, at least, was in a tragic mood, feeling both pity and fear acutely, and for the country at large. And in the narrative that was brewing in my mind, the men of the New Right had crystallized into something like the ancient Greek Furies—only with the gender dynamics inverted, or perhaps dressed in drag. It was an image that, once it came, I could not shake. So much of what happened on the New Right was so excruciatingly performative and online, and yet also visceral and raw. So much of it had to do with masculinity, and the masculinist furies clearly had the upper hand against a campaign like Biden's.

The Furies, or Erinyes (sometimes euphemized as the *Eumenides*, or "kindly ones"), were ancient goddesses of vengeance, who upheld ancient curses and old forms of justice—hounding anyone who acted with ingratitude or insolence, especially toward their parents or blood relatives. In Greek mythology and Athenian theater, they represented the earthly chthonic gods—the world of the old laws, to them—and were often embattled with the newer and younger gods of Olympus. Aeschylus ties them emotionally to Clytemnestra and the anguished women of Mycenae whose husbands had been away at war for so long. And while the Furies were spiritually reactionary, they weren't without their charms, because they spoke for abiding human things: the desire for hard justice, the need for common sense and respect, and the need for not all things to change. The Olympian gods, for their part, were a mixed bag: some fickle, some cruel, some wise, some mischievous. More progressive, a bit flighty and out of touch. More like liberals.

In the third play of Aeschylus's *Oresteia*—the only extant tragic trilogy from ancient Greece, beloved by Bobby Kennedy—the Furies form the play's wretched chorus and together haunt the protagonist, Orestes. Orestes is the son of the king and hero Agamemnon and queen Clytemnestra, and he has just avenged his father's murder by slaying the queen, thereby feeding into a generational cycle of violence. At one point he wavers, Hamlet-like, but he goes ahead with the matricide, spurred on by the god Apollo. The Furies swoop in fast and are unforgiving. They take the side of women, domesticity, and daughters in the binary world that the plays explore, haunting and tormenting Orestes because mother-killing is just so deeply wrong. They do not care that he had his reasons. They just chase him down, full of rage and hate, out for blood on behalf of the dead queen and the mother-child bond.

The masculinist Furies of the twenty-first century, with their anger, their reactionary values, and their all-or-nothing takes, found a comfortable home on the American New Right. Many ancient themes were being made explicit, as in Reno's *Return of the Gods* and the newly open embrace of Christian nationalism; at NatCon 4 there was much excitement about laws dictating the display of the Ten Commandments in public schools. The GOP as defined by Trump and Trumpism wanted badly to represent men and MAGA masculinity—from PUA-obsessed Michael Anton and Manosphere anons like Raw Egg Nationalist, to Josh Hawley and Brett Kavanaugh—and even to hound and chase out women from public life. The right's *thymotic* chest-thumping lined up with popular culture—from Jordan Peterson's lobsters to Johnny Depp's online hordes—and together they formed a living mirror to the old Furies' raging laments. By 2024 masculinist fervor come to saturate the movement.

In the strange corners of the culture war that I was watching, this newly rekindled gender struggle had a bizarre peak just prior to the publication of a new translation of Homer's *Iliad*, in 2023.[17] This was not just any new translation; rather, it was Emily Wilson's translation, and Wilson's *Odyssey*, from 2018, was the first major translation of that book into English by a woman.[18] The *Odyssey* translation was a bestseller and a major event in the publishing world, and Wilson gained a kind of mythic stature in the (normie, liberal) reading public. One might have expected the Bronze Agers to have been pleased to see Homer getting so much attention. I loved Wilson's *Odyssey* for its quick pace and simple elegance, but the Wilson translations made the men of the Hard Right mad. In 2022 a group of them decided that Wilson represented the Longhouse and everything "gynocracy," and they presumed that Homer shared in their prejudices, too. *IM-1776* published a piece titled "Homer's Brazen Vandalizers: How Female Academics are ruining the Classics" by a man named Abdullah Yousef; it argued that Homer portrayed the famously wily Odysseus as an unquestionable and simply inspiring hero.[19] In April 2023, ahead of the publication of Wilson's *Iliad*, Yousef led the charge once more. "Seeing a lot of morons talk about Homer again, so just to repeat: there's an active agenda, predominantly through neutered and effeminate translation and re-writing, to reinterpret all classical works as never disturbing the false holiness of the gynocratic world of today." A few months later, a man named Max Meyer attempted to dissect Wilson's translations based on his single year of ancient Greek in college.[20] His thread went viral and gained nearly three million views.

It is hard to overstate the idiocy of these attacks, which, in addition to their ugly treatment of Wilson, reduced Homer to a machismo-propagating hack. Yousef and Meyer wrote as though Homer never questioned heroic valor, even though almost the whole power and beauty of the Homeric poetry consists in its throttling ambiguity about themes like war, honor, manly virtue, and mortality.

Emily Wilson published her *Iliad* in September 2023, but the misogyny of the New Right never abated. At NatCon 4 it was expressed in what the writer Sarah Jones called "an explicit obsession with white Christian fertility, which consumes the speakers and animates the crowd perhaps more than any other subject."[21] None of it should have been surprising. From the very start, Trumpism involved open boasting or worse about pussy-grabbing; it turned into a violent effort to overturn a democratic election; in some quarters—like its academic conferences—it encouraged training with AR-15s to intimidate fellow citizens at public libraries.

IV. Summer Reversals

The fury of the New Right was on full display when a young man tried to assassinate Donald Trump at a campaign rally in Pennsylvania on July 13, 2024, just a week or so after NatCon. A local man, Corey Comperatore, was killed. I obviously do not mean to blame the New Right for the gunman (who was a registered Republican and clearly deranged, but whose motives were unclear). But I do mean to recall Trump's defiant response, and that of his followers: After being forced to the ground by his Secret Service members, Trump rose to his feet with his fist raised, enraged, and yelled "FIGHT!" The scene, skillfully captured by photographers, offered the perfect distillation of the movement's macho energy. In the immediate aftermath, this *thymos* coursed through the (online) body politic, and Trump's status soared. On X, Elon Musk endorsed Trump within the hour and declared, "Last time America had a candidate this tough was Theodore Roosevelt." Sohrab Ahmari went further:

"I'll be honest: If a bullet grazed my ear, I would not have it in me to get up, pump my first, and urge my supporters to 'fight'! That's evidence of a truly extraordinary man. World-historical in the way Napoleon was for the 19th century."[22] Stephen Wolfe said that the photo captured "courage and victory" such that "a new possibility of being has opened before young men." He concluded: "The future is rightwing."[23] Within days the online right was blaming diversity, equity, and inclusion initiatives for the attack, since some of the agents on site that day were women, and so was the head of the Secret Service at the time.[24] Ahmari asserted: "That footage of the overweight Secret Service agent struggling to re-holster her pistol is yet another everything-is-broken moment."[25] Even Trump did not sink that low.

The attempt on Trump's life set off a dynamic few weeks in American history, full of reversals and upsets. That same week, on July 15, Trump announced that Senator JD Vance would be his running mate. It was a bold choice that seemed designed to please the New Right, since Vance had been a darling of the movement from its earliest days, and a fixture in New Right spaces of all kinds. Vance, who published his memoir *Hillbilly Elegy* in June 2016, converted to Catholicism in 2019 (the same year he converted to Trumpism) and was ideologically closest to Post-liberal thinkers like Deneen and Vermeule. He was a speaker at Deneen's book launch for *Regime Change* and has cited him as an intellectual influence. Peter Thiel was his mentor and financial backer, and he was on the record as a supporter of Viktor Orbán. But unlike Deneen and Vermeule, and more like Thiel, Vance never kept his distance from the New Right's more activist and imprudent expressions. He went to the Nat-Con conferences. He gave speeches at Claremont Institute events. He appeared on niche podcasts like *Jack Murphy Live* and the *American Moment*, where he made claims that harmonized with Hard Right positions on everything from getting red-pilled for Trump and Claremont-style "hour-is-lateism," to the misery of modern professional women. The phrase that caught the country's imagination, about how the country was run by "a bunch of childless cat ladies who are miserable at their own lives . . . and so they want to make the rest of the country miserable, too," revealed Vance's saturation in New Right thinking. The line, and others that Vance used, might as well have come from *Bronze Age Mindset* or *The Case for Christian Nationalism*.[26]

On July 21, 2024, Joe Biden withdrew as presidential candidate, and Vice President Harris gained the nomination soon after. Suddenly, the gender dynamics of the campaign were transformed, and Vance's culture-warrior style seemed, briefly, like a liability. Harris asked Minnesota governor Tim Walz to be her running mate. With his working-class background, modest career as coach and teacher, and easy demeanor, Walz drew a dramatic contrast with Vance.

Vance seemed to get more frustrated by the day. Soon after the Walz announcement, he and his mostly male staff—clearly in a performative mood—approached Harris's official plane, Air Force Two, on a tarmac in Wisconsin. He did not end up confronting or even speaking to the vice president but did post a photo on X about the stunt, joking, "This Entourage reboot is going to be awesome."[27] At a press conference in Michigan later that day, Charlie Langton of Fox News questioned him: "You've been criticized for being a little too serious, even angry sometimes," he began. "What makes you smile? What makes you happy?" Vance replied that, while he was enjoying himself on the campaign trail, he was also "angry about what Kamala Harris has done to this country and done to the American southern border." He said that "what's going on in this country is a disgrace" and that "both things can be true. I think most Americans can joke around and [be] pissed off about the direction of this country."[28] By the end of the summer, Vance and Trump were spreading gross conspiracies about Haitian migrants in Springfield, Ohio—Vance's own district—leading to bomb threats and closures in the community.[29] "If I have to create stories so that the American media actually pays attention to the suffering of the American people, then that's what I'm going to do," the senator said.[30]

I guess it's what they call a noble lie.

But Trump and Vance were offering something politically effective, and even the writers at *The New York Times* agreed that Vance outshone Governor Walz during their debate.[31] Soon Vance got to step onto the Air Force Two plane as vice president of the United States.

V. Absentee Goddess

In hindsight, the summer of 2024 looks like the flubbed deus ex machina moment in our collective history: the moment where the pod bros and George Clooney and Nancy Pelosi, like the Goddess Athena in Aeschylus, took noble action on behalf of democracy, forced Biden out, and tried to save the day.[32] But it didn't work. The switch to Harris offered a brief reprieve from the tragic gloom, but the forces at play were beyond what the liberals were equipped for. By the end of the campaign— if not long before—liberals like me were angry, too. Angry about Biden's decision to run again, and about the Democratic Party's failure to run a proper primary, which felt like a huge slap in the face for anyone who believes in democracy. Angry about the party's approach to inflation and the cost of groceries—which amounted to little more than denial. Angry about Biden's unfettered support for Israel and the war in Gaza. Angry about Elon Musk. Angry about cloying campaign ads featuring, for example, Julia Roberts reminding women that their ballots were secret (GOP women were clearly in the thrall of their wife-beater husbands, the ad implied).[33]

The outcome of the election did not help temper any of that rage.

Aeschylus's *Oresteia* trilogy includes a true deus ex machina, and culminates in something like a paean to democratic Athens. The political hero of the play is the goddess Athena, who resolves Orestes's tragic contest with the Furies by setting up the first major trial by jury in Athens. The tone here is very contemporary: Democratic processes to the rescue! After some good civics lessons—and terrible legal arguments— the vote is split. Athena gets the deciding vote, and she, the goddess of wisdom, tips the scales in favor of Orestes, which is also a vote for Apollo and his sophistry, and for Athens's masculinist, rationalistic politics.[34] And so, while there is relief for Orestes, the Furies lose, and it seems that mother-murder will go unavenged. The goddesses are poised to slink away back to the netherworlds to tend their festering wounds. But that is not how it ends up. Instead, Athena's final, drawn-out gesture is to try to assuage the angry Furies—an acknowledgment of the ignominies they have endured. The only thing that saves the final play from devolving into total rah-rah jingoism, besides the gravitas of all that came before, is Athena's gentleness: "You do still have your rights. . . . Soothe down the seething storm-waves of your rage."[35]

Athena offers the Furies a new perch in the city: "You shall have / a cavern-dwelling in this land, where you shall take / your seats on glistening stones beside your altars, / and receive due worship from these citizens." They are given recognition, and a modicum of dignity—honored properly as deities of marriage and family, receiving the "first fruits of the fertile Athenian land" as sacrifices. Athena beseeches the citizens "You should always treat these kind ones / kindly and respect them: that way / you shall keep your land and city / glorious in the ways of justice."[36]

From 2016 to 2024 the psychodramatic landscape in America was an almost perfect reversal of the *Oresteia* with respect to gender and who represents the old and the new—and, of course, with regards to who won out in the end. In our story, after the 2024 election, the masculinist furies prevailed, ready for vengeance, and no bright-eyed Athena appeared to vote them down, offer peace, or bind up the nation's wounds. Our lessons are more brutal, and we will have to forge our own way.

VI. Whose Renaissance?

The election of Trump in 2016 began to reveal just how much we liberals had taken for granted, and just how fragile our understandings of the world had been. In 2017 the philosopher Charles Mills wrote of an "aggressively resurgent anti-Enlightenment, which bears some affinities to traditional conservatism and the nineteenth-century counter-Enlightenment but is now more explicitly racialized than before." He continued: "So this is no longer a time when self-styled post-Enlightenment critics—taking for granted liberal-democratic guarantees—can afford to be sneering at Enlightenment norms. The protections of those rights and freedoms can no longer be assumed." Since then (and sadly since Mills's death in 2021), the illiberal right's renaissance has only grown in scope, power, and counterrevolutionary extremism. By 2024, the New Right obviously could no longer be ignored.

Yet still liberals were caught off-guard. In January 2024, Constanze Stelzenmüller described how liberal rationalism and modernism had become a genuine liability to America's leaders in the Democratic Party. She wrote of the Biden team's hyperrationalism, and of their "precise and nuanced analysis of the dynamics of global strategic linkages and interdependencies." The downside to all the expertise was that these wonkish, hypercompetent elites "had no answers—no feeling, even— for the seemingly archaic aspects of politics. Anger, hatred, enmity: these are its blind spots," she wrote.[37] The early months of the second Trump administration further illuminated this mass failure of liberal psychology and moral imagination: We wouldn't know the furies if they were knocking down our own front doors. And then suddenly they were.

In February 2025, as Elon Musk and his Department of Government Efficiency set out to purge and replace the federal government, Patrick Deneen delivered the *First Things* Inaugural Neuhaus Lecture at New College, Florida. It was emblematic of the New Right's antimodern radicalism. "I think the most urgent question for us to explore today," he concluded, "is the possibility that we must think through and assist in developing a fourth wave of modernity." This new "truly postliberal age" would be "made not of the salty waters of liberal modernity but refreshed, and perhaps even replaced, with the purer waters of premodernity, our classical and Christian heritage."[38]

Even as Musk did his worst, much of America did not even seem awake to the possibility that Deneen was describing. If I'm right that the New Right puts Ideas First, liberals and the Democrats seem to put them last—having incubated them in an AI lab, tested them against a dozen polls, and assigned them to a celebrity to rehearse. This means that Trump's second big win was also a failure of leadership and principle among liberals; in the end, of course, ideas and principles do matter a great deal, and we need good ones to prevail. One of the most frustrating experiences for any liberal observer of the New Right was to witness, again and again, the incredible contrast between the coarse brazenness of its ideologues and the tepid intellectual reserve (and cluelessness, and cowardice) of so many centrist and liberal leaders, both within academia and beyond. Of course there are exceptions, but not nearly enough.

So what is to be done? What might an Athena for our own age have to say?

In the short term, it is clear that Americans who oppose Trump and the New Right will have to keep engaging and pushing back however they can, and as their circumstances allow—in protests, civil actions, and lawsuits, running for election at every level, and putting pressure on Congress to restore their own authority in our constitutional order.

In the longer term, and on the theoretical plane, let me venture that, contra Deneen's "purer waters of premodernity," our era calls for liberal renaissance and reinvention. Some of the academic work here is well underway.[39] But most of it isn't academic work; it's political and practical work that involves, as Arendt said, "thinking what we are doing," talking to one another, and acting together in the world. Not everyone is going to do this the same way, but it should be done with courage and ethical resolve.

When a ninety-year-old Harvey Mansfield told the audience at AEI that "liberalism knows essentially nothing of the land of virtue," he was wrong, but it is not hard to understand why he said it. Liberalism was invented in part to sidestep and quell the flames of ideological fanaticism. Partly as a result of that history, liberals have for far too long accepted a minimalist self-understanding that avoids all talk of virtue and ethical vision; they have similarly refused to acknowledge and cultivate the moral worlds and traditions that sustain our lives. This is understandable, but it is time to do better: to step up, have a bit of ambition, and admit that liberalism could be something wonderful, and in truth it already is. If you look around the modern liberal world—even at Harvard—you will encounter talented, courageous, and truth-telling liberal people everywhere. It is also true that liberals do not always speak fluidly about the Aristotelian mean, the tripartite soul, Machiavellian *virtù*, or secret esoteric gardens. Oh well. People are allowed to have other loves and love languages, other ideas about the good, the true, the beautiful, about being human, and being alive. Part of the work of the liberal renaissance is to make these facts plain.

The reimagining will also require that liberals become more upfront about the core ideas and ideals of liberalism: about what liberalism values and why, in language that can be broadly understood. To borrow from someone we have come to know in these pages:

> The best way to counter the degradations of American institutional life is to remind the public of the fundamental purpose of those institutions, and to communicate that purpose. What is the purpose of the university? What is the purpose of a school? What system of government will guide us toward human happiness? These questions provoke doubt and anxiety in the current regime. And no wonder. The idea of happiness, properly understood, can be revolutionary.[40]

It was Christopher Rufo who said that, and it's true. The difference between a liberal outlook and that of Rufo, though, is that liberal purposes (and liberal happiness) will always be plural and messy: more Mardi Gras or renaissance fair than country club gala or debutante ball. But if liberals cannot both articulate and fight in solidarity for our aspirations—what we value and live and work for, our visions for individual and collective happiness, and our beliefs and programs for what is right and fair—then why should anyone else do it for us? They will not. And there will always be plenty of people eager to impose their order on us, or willing to send us careening back into premodernity— and not just its "purer waters," but also its storms of ideological conflict and bloody strife.

To the antiliberals and others on the Postliberal right who say that we are already there, that liberal tyranny and oppression is already mainstream, I say: You have lost your way and should walk with more care. You take the liberal world for granted, too. This has allowed you to don the language of grievance and oppression far too lightly, without having given enough thought to what oppression actually means—the kind of oppression that doesn't let you love who you want to, or vote in free elections, or not be disappeared. It is unseemly, and it is unmanly, and some of you will miss your liberalism when it's gone.

To liberals and progressives, the message has to be different, because the problems are different. They have to do less with gross state violence and disregard for human decency and more to do with what Jonathan Rauch has called "coercive conformity" or what Tocqueville called "soft despotism." It is not a general problem but a rather narrow one having mainly to do with insular academics and elites. Whatever we call it, when it comes to this subset, conservatives who complain about liberal intolerance have a point. If deep moral pluralism is to be a modern liberal aspiration—and I think it must be—then all liberals must cultivate a hardened but steadfast toleration for worldviews that we find incomprehensible, deeply offensive, or dangerous. We do not have to like it, and we do not have to be sweet—as Sarah Schulman has written, "conflict is not abuse"—but we must do it, as a matter of intellectual integrity, a guard against the tyrannical drives that lurk within, and a pledge of humility and hope for a truly diverse future.[41] Maximal accommodation for different outlooks should be our watchword; curiosity is a good one, too.

In that vein, there are many things to be learned from the New Right. If I were to play Athena in the unfolding drama of our age, and was in a magnanimous mood, I would ask Americans to think about the ways in which the New Right intellectuals have succeeded in shaking up the status quo—on economics, trade, localism, technocracy and managerialism, campus silos and campus bureaucracies, and the crisis of masculinity to which the entire New Right movement is such a loud testament. These are all areas where Americans could learn from one another across political divides, and in some cases they already have. The mistake here would not be listening too much; it would be to fall for the New Right's Schmittian filth about friends and enemies and America being irreparably divided.

As Athena, I might also recommend some aspects of Patrick Deneen's "mixed constitutionalism." Deneen's ideas about liberalism are bogus, but some of his ideas about mixing up the American social order are good: moving some federal agencies from DC to other parts of the country, for example, or finding other ways to reinvigorate places that are struggling.[42] I also agree with Deneen that it is "high time to revisit the question of national service." This would not just involve military service but could also mean giving people opportunities to work on infrastructure projects, environmental repair, and social services. Think the Civilian Conservation Corps—the goal being, in Deneen's words, "the mingling of people from a variety of walks of life."[43] Deneen also supports increased funding for public schools, with much more support for education in the trades. Amen to that. Let's add a big child tax credit—for all children, in all kinds of families—to the list. We could tax the billionaires and millionaires to make it happen. Sohrab Ahmari's ideas about unions and workers sound good, too. Athena knows there is no shortage of other interesting policy ideas in the center and on the left. When it comes to inequality, poverty, and the shrinking middle class, what are lacking are ambition and will.

As magnanimous Athena, I would also take a "patriotic education" page out of the New Right handbook. I would propose a hybrid version of it—traditional and woke—in K–12 education, something like the Hillsdale Curriculum meets the authors of 1619. States, educators, and parent groups would be charged with sorting out the details for their own regions, schools, and kids. It would inspire real patriotism to see these matters hashed out in town halls everywhere. Imagine if America could do something collective to elevate the profession of the teacher.

As for higher education, I would tear up the patriotic education page and instead promote history, great books, and liberal humanism, broadly conceived—not as a replacement but as a well-funded alternative option to what dominates already (i.e., STEM and preprofessional specialization). I would commit to building new liberal education programs in big state schools all over the country, with a genuinely pluralistic, aka "mixed," character. The purposes here would be mainly old-fashioned and Socratic. The initiatives would ensure exposure to fine works of art, literature, and history and would treat questions—What is justice? What is love? What does it mean to live well?—as foundational. But this new liberal education would also recognize that politics and activism are legitimate concerns for young people, as is religion. Such an education would necessarily vary widely from region to region. As Athena, I wouldn't dictate the curriculum or allow state legislatures to touch it. I would insist that faculty do that work, and I would pay them well to do it. Would such programs duplicate what universities already do in some instances? Oh yes. But I still suspect that, if it were done well, there would be no shortage of faculty to hire, nor of students to enroll.

You don't have to be a goddess to see that everything about this style of education could serve as a rampart against some of our most urgent problems, from spiritual malaise and masculinist charlatans to cutthroat careerism and the onslaught of AI.

The programs I have described are hardly unprecedented. Bryan Garsten has initiated a nonpartisan civics programs at Yale that is worth imitating, and between 2016 and 2024, major new public civics initiatives were started in red states all over the country.[44] These latter were all, so far as I could tell, directed by white men, and some of the programs had an insular partisan or reactionary bent, but they were a boon to humanities hiring. As part of my own Olympian strategy, I would aim for something better, though—a modern humanistic renaissance, where young people could get out of their silos and cocoons and have the chance to be broadly and richly educated. As an olive branch to the right, I would ask conservatives, including those discussed in this book (well, except a few) to direct the programs. I would make these new perches contingent, however, on their sharing leadership with a woman academic (or woke neo-Marxist) for the duration of their tenure. All this would doubtless initiate a cycle of hiring and curricular battles the likes of which, even in America, we have never seen. At one school they would read *The Federalist* and Annette Gordon-Reed; at another, James Baldwin and Hannah Arendt. As Athena, I'd push for Homer and the Bible everywhere. Wouldn't it be grand?

VII. Interregnum

The *Oresteia* won first prize at the City Dionysia in 458 BCE. It was the Golden Age of Athens; the Greek allies had been victorious in the Greco-Persian wars, Pericles ruled, and Socrates was around twelve years old. But Aeschylus wrote as though the city were at a fragile dawn—and as though it needed the protection of the gods and poets.

And that was probably true: By the end of the century, Athens had been defeated by Sparta, and it never fully recovered.

The United States is almost a quarter of a millennium old, but in many ways, it is still a young democracy, where basic civil rights have been legally protected for only sixty years, and other core liberal rights for far less. It is hard to tell today whether we are living through the tragic end of the American experiment in liberty and pluralism or on the cusp of a new way through. As the chorus of worn-down, elderly men in Aeschylus's *Agamemnon* say at the start of the *Oresteia*, "The scales of Justice weigh out gain / to those who've learned from pain: / but as for what the future bears, / you'll hear as it occurs. / Let be: it will emerge as bright / as when the dawn brings light."[45]

They are right: The truth will come. For them—graybeards past their prime, feckless and unable to act—that meant palace intrigue and murder, the dissolution of the city, a cruel tyranny, and then the implausible, last-minute intervention of the goddess.

I hope our fate is otherwise. Let's work to make it so.

NOTES

Chapter 1

1. See Michael Anton, *The Stakes: America at the Point of No Return* (Regnery, 2020), 341–51.

2. Patrick J. Deneen, *Regime Change: Toward a Postliberal Future* (Sentinel, 2023).

3. Jill Covlin and Bill Barrow, "Trump's Vow to Only Be a Dictator on His First Day Back in Office," *AP News*, December 7, 2023, https://apnews.com/article/trump-hannity-dictator -authoritarian-presidential-election-f27e7e9d7c13fabbe3ae7dd7f1235c72#.

4. Michael Anton/Publius Decius Mus, "The Flight 93 Election," *Claremont Review of Books*, September 5, 2016, https://claremontreviewofbooks.com/digital/the-flight-93-election/.

5. R. R. Reno, *Return of the Strong Gods: Nationalism, Populism, and the Future of the West* (Regnery Gateway, 2021), xv–xvii.

6. On Declarationism, see Ken I. Kersch, "Beyond Originalism: Conservative Declarationism and Constitutional Redemption," *Maryland Law Review* 71, no. 1 (2011), https:// digitalcommons.law.umaryland.edu/mlr/vol71/iss1/12.

7. Joshua Tait, "Conservatives or Counterrevolutionaries?," *To Live Is to Maneuver*, August 25, 2024, https://joshuatait.substack.com/p/conservatives-or-counterrevolutionaries.

8. Ian Ward, "Patrick Deneen: The New Right's Man in the Ivory Tower," *Politico*, June 8, 2023, https://www.politico.com/news/magazine/2023/06/08/the-new-right-patrick-deneen -00100279.

9. On the complex history of this concept, see Jerome E. Copulsky, *American Heretics: Religious Adversaries of Liberal Order* (Yale University Press, 2024), chap. 4.

10. The Trump era set off a wide-ranging and fruitful discussion of American fascism among scholars and in the wider public. That discussion informs my work, but it is not my focus. Two classics on the subject that I have found useful are Umberto Eco, "Ur-Fascism," *New York Review of Books*, June 22, 1995, https://www.nybooks.com/articles/1995/06/22/ur-fascism/; and Robert O. Paxton, *The Anatomy of Fascism* (Vintage, 2005). Also see Sarah Churchwell, "American Fascism: It Has Happened Here," *New York Review of Books*, June 22, 2020, https://www.nybooks .com/online/2020/06/22/american-fascism-it-has-happened-here/. For insight into the contemporary debate, see John Ganz's *Unpopular Front* Substack and Daniel Steinmetz-Jenkins, ed., *Did It Happen Here? Perspectives on Fascism and America* (Norton, 2024).

11. See Elisabeth Zerofsky, "How the Claremont Institute Became a Nerve Center of the American Right," *New York Times*, August 3, 2022, https://www.nytimes.com/2022/08/03 /magazine/claremont-institute-conservative.html; and Graeme Wood, "How Bronze Age Pervert Charmed the Far Right," *Atlantic*, August 3, 2023, https://www.theatlantic.com/magazine /archive/2023/09/bronze-age-pervert-costin-alamariu/674762/.

12. See George Hawley, "The Myth of Republican Radicalism," *Fusion*, November 1, 2023, https://www.fusionaier.org/post/the-myth-of-republican-radicalism. Hawley argues that

partisan polarization is increasing, but on the whole, identity-based radicalization is not. These arguments are also part of his book, *The Moderate Majority: Real GOP Voters and the Myth of Mass Republican Radicalization* (De Gruyter, 2024).

13. Lee Atwater, a Republican strategist and consultant, explained the whitewashing, "coded" character of the strategy vividly and at some length in an infamous interview from 1981. See Rick Perlstein, "Exclusive: Lee Atwater's Infamous 1981 Interview on the Southern Strategy," *Nation*, November 13, 2012, https://www.thenation.com/article/archive/exclusive-lee-atwaters-infamous-1981-interview-southern-strategy/.

14. See George H. Nash, *The Conservative Intellectual Movement in America Since 1945* (ISI Books, 2006), 111–14. Presidents Warren G. Harding, Calvin Coolidge, and Herbert Hoover exemplified this original conservative style.

15. John Ganz, "The Forgotten Man," *Baffler*, December 15, 2017, https://thebaffler.com/latest/the-forgotten-man-ganz. For more on Rothbard, see John Ganz, *When the Clock Broke: Con Men, Conspiracists, and How America Cracked Up in the Early 1990s* (Farrar, Straus and Giroux, 2024), chap. 3. There was also a strong antidemocratic element to the Old Right, especially on the part of intellectuals like H. L. Mencken, Frank Chodorov, and Alfred Jay Nock. See Matthew Continetti, *The Right: The Hundred-Year War for American Conservatism* (Basic Books, 2022), 25–30.

16. See Rick Perlstein, "I Thought I Understood the American Right. Trump Proved Me Wrong," *New York Times*, April 11, 2017, https://www.nytimes.com/2017/04/11/magazine/i-thought-i-understood-the-american-right-trump-proved-me-wrong.html.

17. In the early contest between "interventionist" and "containment" conservatism, Buckley decided that, in the words of historian George Nash, "he would rather take his chances later with a powerful domestic State than adopt a foreign policy that would allow Communism to conquer the world." Nash, *The Conservative Intellectual Movement*, 113.

18. See Geoffrey Kabaservice, *Rule and Ruin: The Downfall of Moderation and the Destruction of the Republican Party* (Oxford University Press, 2012), xvii–xix, for an explanation of "movement conservatism."

19. Matthew Continetti notes (in *The Right*, 231–232), that at bottom this movement was populist, socially conservative, and activist. It "did not care about elite validation. It wanted results." Its enemies, he writes, were "compromise, gradualism, and acquiescence in a corrupt system."

20. See Lee Edwards, "The Conservative Consensus: Frank Meyer, Barry Goldwater, and the Politics of Fusionism," Heritage Foundation, January 22, 2007, https://www.heritage.org/political-process/report/the-conservative-consensus-frank-meyer-barry-goldwater-and-the-politics.

21. Gary Dorrien, *Imperial Designs* (Routledge, 2004), 23.

22. Continetti, *The Right*, 259–65. For a compelling account of the growth of the Christian Right over the twentieth century, see Kristin Kobes Du Mez, *Jesus and John Wayne: How White Evangelicals Corrupted a Faith and Fractured a Nation* (Liveright, 2020).

23. For more on the Birchers, see David Austin Walsh, *Taking America Back: The Conservative Movement and the Far Right* (Yale University Press, 2024), chap. 6.

24. For various brief treatments of this history, see Erick Trickey, "Long Before QAnon, Ronald Reagan and the GOP Purged John Birch Extremists from the Party," *Washington Post*, January 15, 2021, https://www.washingtonpost.com/history/2021/01/15/john-birch-society-qanon-reagan-republicans-goldwater/; Matthew Dallek, "Debunking a Longstanding Myth About William F. Buckley," *Politico*, March 31, 2023, https://www.politico.com/news/magazine/2023/03/31/buckley-john-birch-society-00087893; Alvin Felzenberg, "Buckley vs. Birchers: No Myth," *National Review*, April 23, 2023, https://www.nationalreview.com/2023/04/buckleys-battle-with-the-birchers-was-no-myth/.

25. Paleoconservatives like Paul Gottfried felt the sting of Buckley's rebukes. See Gottfried's collaborative work with Richard B. Spencer, *The Great Purge: The Deformation of the Conservative Movement* (Washington Summit Publishers, 2015).

26. See Ganz, *When the Clock Broke*, 101. Ganz calls attention to a great Rothbard quote: "With the inspiration of the death of the Soviet Union before us, we now know that it can be done. With Pat Buchanan as our leader, we shall break the clock of social democracy. We shall break the clock of the Great Society. We shall break the clock of the welfare state. We shall break the clock of the New Deal. . . . We shall repeal the twentieth century."

27. Du Mez, *Jesus and John Wayne*, 3.

28. Cas Mudde, "The Populist Zeitgeist," *Government and Opposition* 39, no. 4 (2004): 543.

29. See Jan-Werner Müller, *What Is Populism?* (University of Pennsylvania Press, 2016).

30. See J. Eric Oliver and Wendy M. Rahm, "Rise of the Trumpenvolk: Populism in the 2016 Election," *ANNALS of the American Academy of Political and Social Science* 661, no. 1 (2016): 201.

31. See Thomas Zimmer, "Democracy Faces a Reactionary Counter-Mobilization," *Democracy Americana*, Substack, November 29, 2022, https://thomaszimmer.substack.com/p/democracy-faces-a-reactionary-counter.

32. January 6 is the most obvious example here. Conservatives will often justify their failure to win majorities by appealing to the pat notion that "we're a republic, not a democracy." That claim has rhetorical power, but the constitution's counter-majoritarian measures were meant to temper the majority's will, not overrule it. See George Thomas, "'America Is a Republic, Not a Democracy' Is a Dangerous—and Wrong—Argument," *Atlantic*, November 2, 2020, https://www.theatlantic.com/ideas/archive/2020/11/yes-constitution-democracy/616949/.

33. From Matthew McManus, "Another Kingdom Is Possible: A Review of Kevin Vallier's *All the Kingdoms of the World*," Institute for Christian Socialism, May 14, 2024, https://www.christiansocialism.com/2024/05/14/another-kingdom-is-possible-a-review-of-kevin-valliers-all-the-kingdoms-of-the-world/.

34. See Julian Coman, "The Pastor Versus the Populist: Hungary's New Faith Faultline," *Guardian*, December 29, 2019, https://www.theguardian.com/world/2019/dec/29/pastor-v-populist-viktor-orban-hungary-faith-faultline.

35. See David A. Graham, "The New Lost Cause," *Atlantic*, October 18, 2021, https://www.theatlantic.com/ideas/archive/2021/10/donald-trumps-new-lost-cause-centers-january-6/620407/.

36. Masha Gessen, *Surviving Autocracy* (Riverhead Books, 2020), 108.

37. Adam Kirsch, ed., *The Republic of Plato*, trans. Allan Bloom (Basic Books, 2016).

38. Ralph Waldo Emerson, "Plato; or, the Philosopher," *Ralph Waldo Emerson*, accessed October 1, 2024, https://emersoncentral.com/texts/representative-men/plato-or-the-philosopher/.

39. See Roosevelt Montás, *Rescuing Socrates: How the Great Books Changed My Life and Why They Matter for a New Generation* (Princeton University Press, 2021), for a fuller, and non-Straussian, version of this kind of experience with Plato. See also Pierre Hadot, *Philosophy as a Way of Life: Spiritual Exercises from Socrates to Foucault* (Blackwell, 1995).

40. For more on the practice of esotericism, see Arthur Melzer, *Philosophy Between the Lines: The Lost History of Esoteric Writing* (University of Chicago Press, 2014). Also note that Strauss was not devoted to the Western tradition in a dogmatic way. He once wrote, for example, that "the greatest minds to whom we ought to listen are by no means exclusively the greatest minds of the West. It is merely an unfortunate necessity which prevents us from listening to the greatest minds of India and China: we do not understand their languages, and we cannot learn all languages." Leo Strauss, *Liberalism Ancient and Modern* (University of Chicago Press, 1995), 7.

41. Richard Weaver, *Ideas Have Consequences* (University of Chicago Press, 1948), 2, 2, 4, 1–7.

42. Francis Fukuyama and Bill Kristol are the obvious examples here. Other prominent liberal or anti-Trump thinkers whom Strauss has influenced are Bill Galston, Bryan Garsten, Arthur Melzer, Jeffrey Tulis, Catherine Zuckert, and Michael Zuckert.

43. Nadezhda Mandelstam and Maria Stepanova, *Hope Against Hope*, trans. Max Hayward (Everyman's Library, 2023). See also Clive James, "Last Will and Testament" (a review of Primo Levi's *The Damned and the Saved*), *New Yorker*, May 23, 1988, 88–92; the epigraph to this book comes from this essay by James.

44. Matthew Rose, *A World after Liberalism* (Yale University Press, 2022), 137.

Chapter 2

1. Richard Norton Smith quotes a typical line from Goldwater: "Forget the urban East . . . I'd like to win this goddamned election without New York. Then we could tell New York to kiss our ass and we could really start a conservative party." "How the 1964 Republican Convention Sparked a Revolution From the Right," *Politico*, October 21, 2014.

2. See Nicholas Buccola, *One Man's Freedom: Goldwater, King, and the Battle over an American Ideal* (Princeton University Press, 2025), 10, 382n18. The quote is from a 1955 speech to the New York State Young Republicans.

3. Barry M. Goldwater et al., *The Conscience of a Conservative*, ed. C. C. Goldwater, rev. ed. (Princeton University Press, 2007). L. Brent Bozell was the ghostwriter for Goldwater's book. Bozell would later break with mainstream conservatism to become a radical Francoist and precursor to the integralist faction of the MAGA New Right. He was also one of the founders of the arch-conservative Catholic *Triumph* magazine. See José Pedro Zúquete and George Hawley, "Iberian Vistas: Franco, Salazar, and American Conservatives," *Political Studies Review*, October 1, 2024, https://doi.org/10.1177/14789299241280469.

4. See Louis Menand, "He Knew He Was Right," *New Yorker*, March 18, 2001, https://www.newyorker.com/magazine/2001/03/26/he-knew-he-was-right.

5. Menand, "He Knew He Was Right." See also Rick Perlstein, *Before the Storm: Barry Goldwater and the Unmaking of the American Consensus* (Bold House Books, 2009), 402, 444; and Theodore Harold White, *The Making of the President 1964* (Atheneum, 1965).

6. Rick Perlstein, "How the 1964 Republican Convention Sparked a Revolution from the Right," *Smithsonian Magazine*, August 2008, https://www.smithsonianmag.com/history/1964-republican-convention-revolution-from-the-right-915921/.

7. Bill Van Niekerken, "When SF Mourned Martin Luther King Jr., 50 Years Ago," *San Francisco Chronicle*, April 3, 2018, https://www.sfchronicle.com/chronicle_vault/article/When-SF-mourned-Martin-Luther-King-Jr-50-years-12798143.php.

8. C-SPAN, "Governor Nelson Rockefeller Addresses the '64 Convention," https://www.c-span.org/video/?c3807346/user-clip-governor-nelson-rockefeller-addresses-64-convention.

9. White, *Making of the President*, 200, 201. See also Charles J. Holden, "The Republican National Convention That Shocked the Country," *Time*, July 17, 2024, https://time.com/6991064/rnc-history-1964-republican-convention/.

10. Tim O'Rourke, "Chronicle Covers: The Goldwater Conservatives' Huge Cow Palace Win," *San Francisco Chronicle*, July 15, 2016, https://www.sfchronicle.com/chronicle_vault/article/Chronicle-Covers-The-Goldwater-conservatives-8353277.php.

11. Matthew Delmont, "How Jackie Robinson Helped Defeat a Trump-Like Candidate," *Atlantic*, March 19, 2016, https://www.theatlantic.com/politics/archive/2016/03/goldwater-jackie-robinson/474498/.

12. See Perlstein, "1964 Republican Convention." Perlstein recounts how at the time, Pat Brown, the Democratic governor of California, told the press that the "stench of fascism is in the air."

13. See Buccola, *One Man's Freedom*, chap. 7, for a thorough treatment of King and Goldwater during this time. The chapter begins with a discussion of King's decision to denounce Goldwater (312–13).

14. Perlstein, "1964 Republican Convention."

15. Anton, "The Flight 93 Election"; Rush Limbaugh, "The Shaming of the Never Trumpers," *Rush Limbaugh Show*, September 7, 2016, https://www.rushlimbaugh.com/daily/2016/09/07/the_shaming_of_the_never_trumpers/.

16. Anton, "The Flight 93 Election."

17. Rush Limbaugh, "We Have Not Lost Our Country," *Rush Limbaugh Show*, November 9, 2016, https://www.rushlimbaugh.com/daily/2016/11/09/we_have_not_lost_our_country/.

18. Harry V. Jaffa, *Crisis of the Strauss Divided: Essays on Leo Strauss and Straussianism, East and West* (Rowman & Littlefield, 2012), 7–8.

19. See Strauss and The Leo Strauss Center, "Courses: Audio & Transcripts," accessed October 2, 2024, https://leostrausscenter.uchicago.edu/audio-transcripts/courses-audio-transcripts/.

20. The standard account of these differences is Catherine H. Zuckert and Michael Zuckert, *The Truth about Leo Strauss: Political Philosophy and American Democracy* (University of Chicago Press, 2006), 20–23, 228–59.

21. Robert Kraynak, "Moral Order in the Western Tradition," *Review of Politics* 71 (March 1, 2009): 181.

22. Eric P. Newcomer, "The Harvey Mansfield Story," *Harvard Crimson*, March 1, 2012, https://www.thecrimson.com/article/2012/3/1/harvey-mansfield-scrutiny-FM/.

23. Elaine Woo, "Harry V. Jaffa dies at 96; shaped modern American conservative movement," *Los Angeles Times*, January 15, 2015, https://www.latimes.com/local/obituaries/la-me-harry-jaffa-20150116-story.html.

24. Harry V. Jaffa, *Crisis of the House Divided: An Interpretation of the Issues in the Lincoln-Douglas Debates, 50th Anniversary Edition*, enl. ed. (University of Chicago Press, 2009).

25. The fact that Lincoln was a political actor—one who was open to compromise with the South until quite late and led his country into war—is in some tension with Jaffa's abstract, theory-oriented portrait.

26. Harry V. Jaffa, *A New Birth of Freedom: Abraham Lincoln and the Coming of the Civil War* (Rowman & Littlefield, 2004).

27. Thomas Merrill, "The Claremont Institute, Harry Jaffa, and the Temptation of Theory," *Bulwark*, July 30, 2024, https://www.thebulwark.com/p/the-claremont-institute-harry-jaffa-and-the-temptation-of-theory.

28. See Harry Jaffa, "The American Founding as the Best Regime," July 4, 2007, https://www.csub.edu/~mault/jaffa.htm; Merrill, "The Claremont Institute."

29. Jaffa, "The American Founding as the Best Regime."

30. Michael Zuckert, in his review of Jaffa's second Lincoln book, points out that whereas Strauss was a thinker of dualities, Jaffa thought in terms of unities. Jaffa "collapses Athens and Jerusalem, poetry and philosophy, and goes a long way toward assimilating Strauss's ancients and moderns." He continues: "What Strauss has put asunder Jaffa attempts to join together." See Michael P. Zuckert, "Jaffa's New Birth: Harry Jaffa at Ninety," *Review of Politics* 71, no. 2 (April 2009): 210, https://doi.org/10.1017/S003467050900031X.

31. Brian Gaffney, "Jaffa on That Goldwater Speech," Philadelphia Society, 2014, https://phillysoc.org/collections/tributes/tributes-to-harry-jaffa/jaffa-on-that-goldwater-speech/. Hess credits Jaffa with the line about extremism but also writes, "I had the opportunity to make it famous in the acceptance speech, which I wrote for the senator." Karl Hess, Charles Murray,

and Marcus Raskin, *Mostly on the Edge: An Autobiography*, ed. Karl Hess Jr. (Prometheus, 1999), 170. For more on Goldwater's speech, see White, *Making of the President 1964*, 214–20.

32. Gaffney, "Jaffa on Goldwater"; Philip Jaffa, "My Father and the Birth of Modern Conservatism," *Bulwark*, July 30, 2024, https://www.thebulwark.com/p/my-father-and-the-birth-of-modern-conservatism.

33. Martin Luther King, Jr., *The Autobiography of Martin Luther King, Jr.*, ed. Clayborne Clarson (Grand Central Publishing, 2001), 247.

34. For more on this theme, see Menand, "He Knew He Was Right."

35. On ruthlessness and its connection to the illiberal temperament, see Joshua L. Cherniss, *Liberalism in Dark Times: The Liberal Ethos in the Twentieth Century* (Princeton University Press, 2021).

36. Menand, "He Knew He Was Right." See also Ed Kilgore, "The Spirit of Goldwaterism," *Washington Monthly*, April 18, 2014, http://washingtonmonthly.com/2014/04/18/the-spirit-of-goldwaterism/.

37. George F. Will, "Goldwater: A Man Who Won the Future," *Washington Post*, March 27, 1994, https://www.washingtonpost.com/archive/opinions/1994/03/27/goldwater-a-man-who-won-the-future/667e6b62-23dd-4b38-a86f-3a029e3cf465/.

38. Paul Gottfried, "The Right Lesson," *American Conservative*, November 17, 2008, https://www.theamericanconservative.com/the-right-lesson/.

39. Gottfried, "The Right Lesson."

40. Harry Jaffa, "Harry Jaffa on Barry Goldwater," *New York Magazine*, October 12, 2012, https://nymag.com/news/politics/elections-2012/barry-goldwater-campaign-2012-10/.

41. See Joseph R. Fornieri, "Harry V. Jaffa's Contribution to Lincoln Studies and American Statesmanship," *Journal of the Abraham Lincoln Association* 37, no. 2 (Summer 2016), http://hdl.handle.net/2027/spo.2629860.0037.205; Mike Sabo, "The Soul of Politics: Harry V. Jaffa, Prudence, and Statesmanship," *Public Discourse*, December 8, 2021, https://www.thepublicdiscourse.com/2021/12/79386/.

42. Harry V. Jaffa, "Lincoln and the Cause of Freedom," *National Review*, September 21, 1965, 828. See also Frank S. Meyer, "Lincoln Without Rhetoric," *National Review*, August 24, 1965; and Frank S. Meyer, "Again on Lincoln," *National Review*, January 25, 1966.

43. See Matthew Sitman and Sam Adler-Bell, "Jaffa vs. Kendall," *Know Your Enemy*, May 29, 2021, https://www.patreon.com/posts/jaffa-vs-kendall-51840426; Willmoore Kendall and George W. Carey, *Basic Symbols of the American Political Tradition* (Louisiana State University Press, 1970); and Harry V. Jaffa, "Equality as a Conservative Principle," *Loyola of Los Angeles Law Review* 8 (June 1, 1975): 471–505.

44. See Merrill, "The Claremont Institute."

45. Allan Bloom, *The Closing of the American Mind: How Higher Education Has Failed Democracy and Impoverished the Souls of Today's Students* (Simon and Schuster, 1987); William F. Buckley, *God and Man at Yale: The Superstitions of "Academic Freedom"* (Regnery, 2002).

46. In his discussion of the 1960s, Bloom draws an astonishing equivalence between the New Left in America and the right-wing pro-Hitler groups in 1930s Germany, concluding that "the unthinking hatred of 'bourgeois society' was exactly the same in both places." Bloom, *Closing of the American Mind*, 314.

47. Lawrence W. Levine's critical assessment of Bloom's book, entitled *The Opening of the American Mind* (Beacon, 1997), begins with a humorous list of copycat books.

48. See Damon Linker, "The Intellectual Face of Anti-Gay Bigotry," *The Week*, January 23, 2015, https://theweek.com/articles/535248/intellectual-face-antigay-bigotry; Nathan Robinson, "Conservative Hero's Dark Side: How an 'Intellectual' Icon's Real Legacy Got Sanitized," *Salon*, January 20, 2015, https://www.salon.com/2015/01/20/conservative_heros_dark_side_how_an_intellectual_icons_legacy_got_sanitized/.

49. Ken Masugi, "Harry V. Jaffa's Call for Liberation," *First Things*, March 2, 2015, https://www.firstthings.com/web-exclusives/2015/03/harry-v-jaffas-call-for-liberation.

50. Harry V. Jaffa, "Humanizing Certitudes and Impoverishing Doubts: A Critique of *The Closing of the American Mind* by Allan Bloom," *Interpretation: A Journal of Political Philosophy* 16, no. 1 (Fall 1988), https://interpretationjournal.com/shop/humanizing-certitudes-impoverishing-doubts-critique-closing-american-mind-allan-bloom-harry-v-jaffa/.

51. See "The Egg-Head's Egger-On" and "Bloom's Way," both in Christopher Hitchens, *Unacknowledged Legislation: Writers in the Public Sphere* (Verso, 2000).

52. Bloom, *Closing of the American Mind*, 248.

53. As Maudemarie Clark, a Nietzsche scholar, observed in her review of Arthur Melzer's book on esotericism, too often the Socratic skepticism that Straussians profess to admire becomes a "mask for Straussian certainties concerning which truths have to be hidden from which people"—or worse, a *disinvitation* to actual philosophizing. Maudemarie Clark, "Philosophy and Esotericism," *Perspectives on Political Science* 44, no. 4 (2015): 212–20, https://doi.org/10.1080/10457097.2015.1080085.

54. Regardless of its accuracy concerning their work, Martha Nussbaum's critique of Judith Butler resonates with my experiences in the Straussian world: "In this way obscurity creates an aura of importance. It also serves another related purpose. It bullies the reader into granting that, since one cannot figure out what is going on, there must be something significant going on, some complexity of thought." Martha Nussbaum, "The Professor of Parody," *New Republic*, February 22, 1999, https://newrepublic.com/article/150687/professor-parody. In her book *Wild Faith* (Hachette, 2022), Talia Lavin describes in vivid detail how conspiracism works in Christian nationalist communities (see chap. 1, "Devils in the Dining Room").

Chapter 3

1. Friedrich Nietzsche, "On the Uses and Abuses of History for Life," in *Untimely Meditations*, trans. R. J. Hollingdale (Cambridge University Press, 1997), 69.

2. The institute's influence on US populism began earlier. See Steve Teles, "How the Progressives Became the Tea Party's Mortal Enemy: Networks, Movements, and the Political Currency of Ideas," in *The Progressives' Century*, ed. Stephen Skowronek, Stephen M. Engel, and Bruce A. Ackerman (Yale University Press, 2016). The administrative state has been a focus of Claremont Institute affiliates like Ken Masugi, Ronald Pestritto, and John Marini for decades. Throughout the twentieth century, other conservatives made their peace with the administrative state or even positively embraced it. See Ken I. Kersch, *Conservatives and the Constitution* (Cambridge University Press, 2019); Johnathan O'Neill, *Conservative Thought and American Constitutionalism Since the New Deal* (Johns Hopkins University Press, 2022).

3. See David Folkenflik, "Voice of America CEO Accused of Fraud, Misuse of Office All in One Week," NPR, January 8, 2021, https://www.npr.org/2021/01/08/953999556/voice-of-america-ceo-accused-of-fraud-misuse-of-office-all-in-one-week.

4. See Asawin Suebsaeng, "Steve Bannon's Long Love Affair with War," *Daily Beast*, January 31, 2017, https://www.thedailybeast.com/articles/2017/01/31/steve-bannon-s-long-love-affair-with-war.

5. See Michael Anton, "Draining the Swamp," *Claremont Review of Books* (Winter 2019), https://claremontreviewofbooks.com/draining-the-swamp1/.

6. Rosie Gray, "The Populist Nationalist on Trump's National Security Council," *Atlantic*, March 24, 2017, https://www.theatlantic.com/politics/archive/2017/03/does-trumps-resident-intellectual-speak-for-his-boss/520683/.

7. Claremont Institute, *Annual Report*, 2024, 11.

8. Timothy Shenk, "The Dark History of Donald Trump's Rightwing Revolt," *Guardian*, August 16, 2016, https://www.theguardian.com/news/2016/aug/16/secret-history-trumpism -donald-trump.

9. Livy, *The History of Rome*, trans. B. O. Foster (Loeb Classical Library, 1919), vol. 4, 8.9 and 10.28.

10. Tina Nguyen, "Is This the Most Powerful Man in Trump's Administration?," *Vanity Fair*, February 23, 2017, https://www.vanityfair.com/news/2017/02/michael-anton-white-house -machiavelli; Peter Maass, "Trump Official Obsessed Over Nuclear Apocalypse, Men's Style, Fine Wines in 40,000 Posts on Fashion Site," *Intercept*, February 16, 2017, https://theintercept .com/2017/02/16/trump-official-obsessed-over-nuclear-apocalypse-mens-style-fine-wines-in -40000-posts-on-fashion-site/.

11. Mark Landler, "A National Security Aide's Departing Wish: Cooking for the State Dinner," *New York Times*, April 25, 2018, https://www.nytimes.com/2018/04/24/us/politics /michael-anton-white-house-state-dinner.html; Maass, "Trump Official Obsessed." As Anton put it to Maass, "At least I'm a self-aware hypocrite."

12. Gray, "Populist Nationalist."

13. Maass, "Trump Official Obsessed"; Nguyen, "Is This the Most Powerful Man in Trump's Administration?"

14. "Tom Wolfe and Me," *City Journal*, June 8, 2018, https://www.city-journal.org/article /tom-wolfe-and-me/.

15. Jordyn Pair, "Anton Speaks on Recent Elections, Political Hostility," *Hillsdale Collegian*, November 29, 2018, https://hillsdalecollegian.com/2018/11/anton-speaks-recent-elections -political-hostility/.

16. Bruce Cole, "The Dandy," *Humanities* 29, no. 2 (March/April 2008), https://www.neh .gov/humanities/2008/marchapril/feature/the-dandy.

17. "In Memoriam: Harry V. Jaffa, 1918–2015," Claremont McKenna College, January 12, 2015, https://www.cmc.edu/news/in-memoriam-harry-v-jaffa-cmc-professor-emeritus-of -government.

18. Michael Anton, "Harry V. Jaffa: An Appreciation," *Claremont Review of Books* 15, no. 1 (Winter 2014/15), https://claremontreviewofbooks.com/harry-v-jaffa-an-appreciation/.

19. Anton, "Harry V. Jaffa."

20. See Montás, *Rescuing Socrates*, 23–29, for a discussion of some of this history. The Association for Core Texts and Courses (ACTC) keeps a long list of these programs. See "College Great Books Programs," accessed October 4, 2024, https://www.coretexts.org/programs /college-great-books. Of course many, if not most, humanities courses in the country incorporate "Great Books" into their curricula.

21. Bloom, *Closing of the American Mind*, 344.

22. See Mark Lilla, "The Lure of Syracuse," *New York Review of Books*, September 20, 2001, https://www.nybooks.com/articles/2001/09/20/the-lure-of-syracuse/; Nick Romeo and Ian Tewksbury, "When Philosopher Met King: On Plato's Italian Voyages," *Aeon*, December 21, 2020, https://aeon.co/essays/when-philosopher-met-king-on-platos-italian-voyages.

23. See Hans-Georg Gadamer, "Back from Syracuse?," trans. John McCumber, *Critical Inquiry* 15, no. 2 (January 1989): 429, https://doi.org/10.1086/448491.

24. Thoughtful Straussians argue that the ancients recognized the injustice of gender inequality but, as pragmatic realists, made their peace with it. For some good considerations of gender in ancient thought, see Arlene W. Saxonhouse, "The Philosopher and the Female in the Political Thought of Plato," *Political Theory* 4, no. 2 (1976): 195–212, https://www.jstor.org/stable /190629; Anne-Marie Schultz, "Feminism in Ancient Philosophy," in *The Oxford Handbook of Feminist Philosophy*, ed. Kim Q. Hall and Ásta (Oxford University Press, 2021), 25–37, https://doi

.org/10.1093/oxfordhb/9780190628925.013.2; and Dana Jalbert Stauffer, "Aristotle's Account of the Subjection of Women," *Journal of Politics* 70, no. 4 (2008): 929–41, https://doi.org/10.1017/s0022381608080973.

25. Harvey Mansfield, "November 18, 1986 speech on a proposal to establish Women's Studies as a field of concentration," in "Harvard Faculty Speeches, 1975–2006," *Contemporary Thinkers*, November 18, 1986, https://contemporarythinkers.org/harvey-mansfield/teaching/harvard-faculty-speeches-1975-2006/. The counter to this argument was obvious: that the universities had for centuries been patriarchal, male-dominated institutions; carving out space for thinking about women and gender was about counterbalance and intellectual pluralism, not bias. Mansfield would tell you that this sort of context-seeking is typical of the womanly mind. See Harvey C. Mansfield, *Manliness* (Yale University Press, 2006), 29–30, 117, 199, 239, 240.

26. Mansfield, *Manliness*, ix.

27. Mansfield, *Manliness*, 29, 70.

28. Laura Bates, *Men Who Hate Women* (Simon and Schuster, 2020), 62.

29. Michael Anton, "A Woman in Full," *Claremont Review of Books* 15, no. 2 (Spring 2015), https://claremontreviewofbooks.com/a-woman-in-full/.

30. Michael Anton, "Socrates as Pickup Artist: An Interpretation of Xenophon's Memorabilia III 11," *Perspectives on Political Science* 44, no. 1 (2015): 40–54, https://doi.org/10.1080/10457097.2014.973736.

31. Maass, "Trump Official Obsessed."

32. JAG authors, "JAG Recovered: Who Are We?" February 19, 2017, https://perma.cc/VHH7-52QG.

33. Peggy Noonan, "A Party Divided, and None Too Soon," *Wall Street Journal*, June 2, 2016, https://www.wsj.com/articles/a-party-divided-and-none-too-soon-1464907737. The 100,000 figure comes from my interview with Krein on March 14, 2023. See also Shenk, "The Dark History."

34. See JAG authors, "Notice to Our Readers," 2016, https://perma.cc/KN6E-BV4P. The fullest publicly available archive that I know of was at the *Jackson Gazette* site, which saved 70 or so of the 125 original posts. For a list of the posts, see JAG, "JAG Recovered," 2016, https://perma.cc/Q67Z-KKDJ; "JAG Recovered: Who Are We?," 2016, https://perma.cc/37EZ-TNTZ. A full permanent archive of these posts is available at JAG, "Jackson Gazette | Page 1," 2016, https://perma.cc/B55J-S82T; "Page 2," https://perma.cc/H4YS-BUXV; "Page 3," https://perma.cc/6HBJ-UPVT; "Page 4," https://perma.cc/L6LB-J6FC; "Page 5," https://perma.cc/FV7F-D7AA; "Page 6," https://perma.cc/4TWP-9VRN; "Page 7," https://perma.cc/3YZX-6CXL; "Page 8," https://perma.cc/L24X-BUSX.

35. JAG, "Notice."

36. Anton would later try to have "Toward a Sensible, Coherent Trumpism" published at the *Claremont Review of Books* (Charles Kesler rejected it). See Zerofsky, "How the Claremont Institute Became a Nerve Center." John Marini, known on the site as "Cato the Elder," also republished some of his writings from the site. See Anton, "Draining the Swamp."

37. Kelefa Sanneh, "A New Trumpist Magazine Débuts at the Harvard Club," *New Yorker*, February 25, 2017, https://www.newyorker.com/news/news-desk/a-new-trumpist-magazine-debuts-at-the-harvard-club; Eliana Johnson, "Meet the Harvard Whiz Kid Who Wants to Explain Trumpism," *Politico*, January 3, 2017, https://www.politico.com/story/2017/01/trump-intellectual-harvard-233150.

38. JAG, "Jackson Gazette | Page 8"; Julius Krein, "Notes on the Origins and Future of Trumpism," 2016, https://perma.cc/V5JY-NC75.

39. See Julius Krein, "James Burnham's Managerial Elite," *American Affairs Journal* 1, no. 1 (February 2017), https://americanaffairsjournal.org/2017/02/james-burnhams-managerial-elite/.

40. Jared Taylor, "Personal Recollections of Sam Francis," *Occidental Quarterly* (Summer 2005): 55.

41. Krein interview with author, March 14, 2023.

42. Nicole Hemmer, *Partisans: The Conservative Revolutionaries Who Remade American Politics in the 1990s* (Basic Books, 2022), 64.

43. Ed Kilgore, "Pat Buchanan, a Vindicated Extremist, Packs It In," *Intelligencer*, January 25, 2023, https://nymag.com/intelligencer/2023/01/pat-buchanan-a-vindicated-extremist-packs-it-in.html. For more on Buchanan, see Ganz, *When the Clock Broke*; and Hemmer, *Partisans*, 64.

44. Continetti, *The Right*, 288–89; Hemmer, *Partisans*, 75; Nicole Hemmer, "The Man Who Won the Republican Party Before Trump Did," *New York Times*, September 8, 2022, https://www.nytimes.com/2022/09/08/opinion/pat-buchanan-donald-trump.html.

45. He was not the first to do so; he credited Michael Brendan Dougherty and Rush Limbaugh with the discovery. See Krein, "Notes on Origins"; Samuel Francis, "From Household to Nation," *Chronicles Magazine*, 1996, https://chroniclesmagazine.org/web/from-household-to-nation/, https://chroniclesmagazine.org/web/from-household-to-nation/; Damon Linker, "Sam Francis: The Dangerous Apostle of Right-Wing Populism," *Unpopulist*, March 15, 2024, https://www.theunpopulist.net/p/sam-francis-the-dangerous-apostle. For more on Francis's white supremacy, see Shenk, "The Dark History."

46. Charles Krauthammer, "Buchanan Explained," *Washington Post*, March 1, 1992, https://www.washingtonpost.com/archive/opinions/1992/03/01/buchanan-explained/c1cf4bdb-071b-4508-bae2-2422ee3846e4/.

47. Francis, "From Household to Nation." See Ganz's *The Year the Clock Broke* for a fuller depiction of these characters and this era.

48. Krein, "Notes on Origins."

49. See Samuel Francis, "The Phrase 'America First,'" *Chronicles Magazine*, December 1, 1991, https://chroniclesmagazine.org/columns/principalities-powers/the-phrase-america-first/.

50. Krein, "Notes on Origins."

51. Krauthammer, "Buchanan Explained."

52. Dinesh D'Souza, "Racism: It's a White (and Black) Thing," *Washington Post*, September 24, 1995, https://www.washingtonpost.com/archive/opinions/1995/09/24/racism-its-a-white-and-black-thing/46284ab5-417c-4c0c-83e1-029d51655d91/. On D'Souza's possible motives, see Laurence Auster, "Race and Reality," *Washington Post*, October 7, 1995, https://www.washingtonpost.com/archive/opinions/1995/10/07/race-and-reality/b3e42928-753d-4dac-8588-7cf5b04143cd/.

53. Publius Decius Mus, "Slouching Towards Caesarism," *Jackson Gazette*, 2016, https://perma.cc/UXQ3-WGJW.

54. Krein, "Notes on Origins."

55. Publius Decius Mus, "Trump, Sullivan and Caesarism," *Jackson Gazette*, 2016, https://perma.cc/3AM5-UJPN.

56. Decius calls Muslim immigration "the biggest disaster" within the broader disaster of "Mass Third World immigration," and a "Towering Inferno Within the Poseidon Adventure," in "A Litmus Test for 'New People,'" *Jackson Gazette*, 2016, https://perma.cc/VK2J-8DK5.

57. Anton's immigration conspiracism is evident in Publius Decius Mus, "When There Are No Good Guys," *Jackson Gazette*, 2016, https://perma.cc/Z8JD-5RA6.

58. Publius Decius Mus, "Solidaristic Conservatism: A Reply to Ahmari," *Jackson Gazette*, 2016, https://perma.cc/WQ59-VLQT.

59. Publius Decius Mus, "Toward a Sensible, Coherent Trumpism," 2016, https://perma.cc/B8M5-RCWE.

60. Harry Jaffa cites the passage from Lincoln's speech in *Crisis of the House Divided*, 315–16.

61. Publius Decius Mus, "Toward a Sensible, Coherent Trumpism"; National Archives, "Dred Scott v. Sandford (1857)," July 27, 2021, https://www.archives.gov/milestone-documents /dred-scott-v-sandford.

62. Abraham Lincoln, "Speech on the Dred Scott Decision," Teaching American History, accessed May 21, 2025, https://teachingamericanhistory.org/document/speech-on -the-dred-scott-decision-3/.

63. Lincoln, "Speech on the Dred Scott Decision."

64. See Publius Decius Mus, "The Unilateral Disarmament of High-Minded Losers," *Jackson Gazette*, 2016, https://perma.cc/3WA4-TUSA; "Restatement on Sulla," *Jackson Gazette*, 2016, https://perma.cc/ZV93-GXSG; "Trump's Bathroom Break," *Jackson Gazette*, 2016, https:// perma.cc/NPN4–5NCM.

65. See Livy, *History of Rome*, vol. 3, 6.14–20.

66. Gladden Pappin, "Gladden J. Pappin Harvard Profile," 2022, https://scholar.harvard.edu /pappin/home; Elizabeth W. Green, "Gladden J. Pappin '04," *Harvard Crimson*, June 5, 2003, https://www.thecrimson.com/article/2003/6/5/people-in-the-news-gladden-j/; Daniel Oppenheimer, "Gladden Pappin Wants to Make Conservatism Great Again," *Texas Monthly*, December 16, 2020, https://www.texasmonthly.com/news-politics/gladden-pappin-wants-to -make-conservatism-great-again/.

67. Kinga Kincső Antal, "'I See Hungary's Clear Vision in Foreign Policy,'" *Hungarian Conservative*, August 17, 2023, https://perma.cc/TS8M-485V; Mátyás Kohán, "Gladden Pappin: Within the West, Hungary Has Set the Standard for a Reasonable Approach," *Mandiner*, April 14, 2023, https://mandiner.hu/kulfold/2023/04/gladden-pappin-hungary-foreign-policy -interview.

68. See, for example, Manlius Capitolinus, "The GOP's Grand Bargain Fizzles," 2016, https:// perma.cc/884L-YLLV; "Trumpian Accomplishments, Part I: The End of Big Data," 2016, https://perma.cc/JQ5K-YXJC; "Trump and the Eclipse of Weberian Politics," 2016, https:// perma.cc/D2G9–8V9T.

69. Manlius Capitolinus, "Trumpian Accomplishments."

70. Pappin wrote his article before the Trump campaign partnered with Cambridge Analytica, the data firm run by Robert and Rebekah Mercer, as well as Steve Bannon, in May 2016, but Trump had begun to assemble a sophisticated data modeling team months earlier. See Kenneth P. Vogel and Darren Samuelsohn, "Trump Quietly Builds a Data Juggernaut," *Politico*, May 1, 2016, https://www.politico.com/story/2016/01/trump-builds-data-juggernaut-217391; Joshua Green, *Devil's Bargain: Steve Bannon, Donald Trump, and the Storming of the Presidency* (Penguin, 2017); Issie Lapowsky, "What Did Cambridge Analytica Really Do for Trump's Campaign?," *Wired*, October 26, 2017, https://www.wired.com/story/what-did-cambridge-analytica -really-do-for-trumps-campaign/.

71. American Greatness, "Our Declaration of Independence from the Conservative Movement," July 21, 2016, https://amgreatness.com/2016/07/21/declaration-independence -conservative-movement/.

72. Sanneh, "A New Trumpist Magazine."

73. Anne-Marie Slaughter, "Toward an All-*American Affairs*," *American Affairs* 1, no. 3 (Fall 2017), https://americanaffairsjournal.org/2017/08/toward-american-affairs/.

74. Julius Krein, "I Voted for Trump. And I Sorely Regret It," *New York Times*, August 17, 2017, https://www.nytimes.com/2017/08/17/opinion/sunday/i-voted-for-trump-and-i-sorely -regret-it.html. See also Isaac Chotiner, "An Interview with Julius Krein," *Slate*, August 18, 2017, https://slate.com/news-and-politics/2017/08/an-interview-with-julius-krein.html.

75. Bill Scheuerman puts it clearly in his review of Bernd Rüthers's book, *Carl Schmitt im Dritten Reich*: "Schmitt engaged in an endless series of despicable racist diatribes from the very first days of the Nazi regime until the Allies violently destroyed it in 1945." Further, "Schmitt's book on Hobbes is held to be his anti-Nazi book, but it contains rampant antisemitism." Bill Scheuerman, "Review: Carl Schmitt and the Nazis," *German Politics & Society*, no. 23 (1991): 71–79, https://www.jstor.org/stable/23735189.

76. Carl Schmitt, *Political Theology: Four Chapters on the Concept of Sovereignty*, trans. G. Schwab (University of Chicago Press, 2005, originally published in 2022).

77. Donald J. Trump, "Trump on Truth Social on X," March 21, 2025, https://perma.cc/8JAE-XRFZ.

78. See Gladden Pappin, "Pappin Tweet on X," April 13, 2023, https://perma.cc/4WB2-4HMU.

Chapter 4

1. Patrick J. Deneen, "Leaving Washington," *Front Porch Republic*, October 9, 2012, https://www.frontporchrepublic.com/2012/10/leaving-washington/; Rod Dreher, "Deneen Leaving Georgetown for a Catholic University," *American Conservative*, January 23, 2012, https://www.theamericanconservative.com/deneen-leaving-georgetown-for-a-catholic-university/; Patrick J. Deneen, "Why I Am Leaving Georgetown," *Front Porch Republic*, January 23, 2012, https://web.archive.org/web/20120127063113/https:/www.frontporchrepublic.com/2012/01/why-i-am-leaving-georgetown/.

2. Deneen, "Leaving Washington."

3. Deneen, "Leaving Washington."

4. Deneen, *Regime Change*, 25; Patrick Deneen, "Replace the Elite," *First Things*, March 1, 2020, https://www.firstthings.com/article/2020/03/replace-the-elite.

5. J. D. Vance, "How I Joined the Resistance," *Lamp*, April 1, 2020, https://thelampmagazine.com/blog/how-i-joined-the-resistance; Simon van Zuylen-Wood, "The Radicalization of J. D. Vance," *Washington Post*, January 4, 2022, https://www.washingtonpost.com/magazine/2022/01/04/jd-vance-hillbilly-elegy-radicalization/; Ian Ward, "The Seven Thinkers and Groups That Have Shaped JD Vance's Unusual Worldview," *Politico*, July 18, 2024, https://www.politico.com/news/magazine/2024/07/18/jd-vance-world-view-sources-00168984.

6. Van Zuylen-Wood, "The Radicalization of J. D. Vance"; Ian Ward, "Patrick Deneen: The New Right's Man in the Ivory Tower," *Politico*, June 8, 2023, https://www.politico.com/news/magazine/2023/06/08/the-new-right-patrick-deneen-00100279.

7. Damon Linker, "America Doesn't Need Regime Change," *Notes from the Middleground*, June 6, 2023, https://damonlinker.substack.com/p/america-doesnt-need-regime-change.

8. Mark Bittman, "Wendell Berry, American Hero," *Opinionator*, New York Times, April 24, 2012, https://archive.nytimes.com/opinionator.blogs.nytimes.com/2012/04/24/wendell-berry-american-hero/.

9. Joshua Rothman, "Rod Dreher's Monastic Vision," *New Yorker*, April 24, 2017, https://www.newyorker.com/magazine/2017/05/01/rod-drehers-monastic-vision.

10. Wendell Berry, "Preserving Wildness," *Home Economics* (Counterpoint Press, 1987), 141.

11. Berry calls his version of economics the "loving economy." See Wendell Berry, *What Are People For? Essays* (Counterpoint, 2010); Wendell Berry and Paul Kingsnorth, *The World-Ending Fire: The Essential Wendell Berry* (Counterpoint, 2019).

12. Alexis de Tocqueville, *Democracy in America*, trans. Harvey C. Mansfield and Delba Winthrop (University of Chicago Press, 2002). See especially vol. 2, chaps. 3 and 4.

13. Barack Obama, "Instagram Reading List 2018," Instagram, December 28, 2018, https://www.instagram.com/barackobama/p/Br7ziuvgzCf/.

14. Patrick J. Deneen, "The Alternative Tradition in America," *Front Porch Republic*, July 6, 2009, https://www.frontporchrepublic.com/2009/07/the-alternative-tradition-in-america/.

15. Patrick J. Deneen, "Who Closed the American Mind?," *The Imaginative Conservative*, May 29, 2013, https://theimaginativeconservative.org/2013/05/who-closed-american-mind-allan-bloom-patrick-deneen.html; Ward, "Patrick Deneen."

16. Deneen has long been against marriage equality. Patrick J. Deneen, "Against (Gay) Marriage," *Front Porch Republic*, June 1, 2009, https://www.frontporchrepublic.com/2009/06/against-gay-marriage/.

17. Bloom, *Closing of the American Mind*, introduction.

18. A good place to start on these questions is Richard Rorty. See his *Philosophy and Social Hope* (Penguin, 2000); and *Achieving Our Country* (Harvard University Press, 1999).

19. Bloom, *Closing of the American Mind*, 326.

20. Bloom, *Closing of the American Mind*, 327.

21. Hitchens, "The Egg-Head's Egger-On."

22. See Leo Strauss, *Natural Right and History* (University of Chicago Press, 1965), 4, https://press.uchicago.edu/ucp/books/book/chicago/N/bo49994271.html.

23. See Bloom, *Closing of the American Mind*, 100, for a critique of feminism's "longing for the unlimited" that reads as a preview to Deneen's argument. Bloom also describes rock music as a "longing for a world without restraint."

24. Patrick J. Deneen, *Why Liberalism Failed* (Yale University Press, 2018), 3.

25. For a wonderful expression of Bloom's liberalism, see Allan Bloom, "Raymond Aron: Last of the Liberals," *New Criterion*, September 1, 1985, https://newcriterion.com/article/raymond-aron-last-of-the-liberals/.

26. Ezra Klein, "Transcript: Ezra Klein Interviews Patrick Deneen," *New York Times*, May 13, 2022, https://www.nytimes.com/2022/05/13/podcasts/transcript-ezra-klein-interviews-patrick-deneen.html.

27. Deneen, *Why Liberalism Failed*, 128.

28. See Patrick Deneen, "Against Great Books," *First Things*, January 1, 2013, https://www.firstthings.com/article/2013/01/against-great-books.

29. See Laura K. Field, "Revisiting 'Why Liberalism Failed,'" Niskanen Center, December 21, 2020, https://www.niskanencenter.org/revisiting-why-liberalism-failed-a-five-part-series/.

30. Klein, "Transcript."

31. See Samuel Goldman, "The Inevitability of Liberal Failure?," *Russell Kirk Center*, January 15, 2018, https://kirkcenter.org/reviews/the-inevitability-of-liberal-failure/. For a description of the radical right's critique of liberalism, see Matthew Rose, *A World After Liberalism: Philosophers of the Radical Right* (Yale University Press, 2021), 9–10, 50–51; James M. Patterson, "Into the Reactionary Abyss—James M. Patterson," *Law & Liberty*, August 15, 2024, https://lawliberty.org/into-the-reactionary-abyss/.

32. Deneen, *Why Liberalism Failed*, 1.

33. Deneen, *Why Liberalism Failed*, 19.

34. See Bloom, *Closing of the American Mind*, 113; also Field, "Revisiting," part 3.

35. The political theorist Jason Blakely offers an opposite approach: "The history of liberalism is richer and more complex than its critics typically allow, and it can always take on new, unexpected meanings—as it certainly has in the United States. Liberalism should be thought of more like a literary genre, with new forms and innovations continually emerging." Jason

Blakely, "The Integralism of Adrian Vermeule," *Commonweal*, October 5, 2020, https://www
.commonwealmagazine.org/not-catholic-enough.

36. Deneen, *Why Liberalism Failed*, 187.

37. Jennifer Szalai, "If Liberalism Is Dead, What Comes Next?," *New York Times*, January 17,
2018, https://www.nytimes.com/2018/01/17/books/review-why-liberalism-failed-patrick
-deneen.html.

38. Deneen came close to admitting as much in the interview with Klein in 2022. Klein,
"Transcript."

39. Patrick J. Deneen, *Conserving America: Essays on Current Discontents* (St. Augustine's
Press, 2016), 11.

40. Adrian Vermeule, "Integration from Within," *American Affairs Journal*, February 20, 2018,
https://americanaffairsjournal.org/2018/02/integration-from-within/.

41. See Leon Wieseltier, "Christianism," *Liberties*, April 1, 2022, https://libertiesjournal.com
/articles/christianism/.

42. See Patrick Deneen, "Patrick Deneen Integralism Both/And Tweet," September 17, 2020,
https://perma.cc/YL3B-BCUX.

43. Patrick J. Deneen, *Why Liberalism Failed* (Yale University Press, 2019, paperback edition),
xxiii–xxiv.

44. See Kevin Vallier, *All the Kingdoms of the World: On Radical Religious Alternatives to
Liberalism* (Oxford University Press, 2023), 12.

45. "Mission Statement," *First Things*, June 21, 2007, Internet Archive, https://web.archive
.org/web/20070621111929/http:/www.firstthings.com/article.php3?id_article=9.

46. See Vallier, *All the Kingdoms of the World*, 12–14.

47. Vallier, *All the Kingdoms of the World*; and Romanus Cessario, "Non Possumus," *First
Things*, February 1, 2018, https://www.firstthings.com/article/2018/02/non-possumus. Cessario asked, "Should putative civil liberties trump the requirements of faith?" His answer was
"no."

48. See R. R. Reno, "Judaism, Christianity, and First Things," *First Things*, January 12, 2018,
https://www.firstthings.com/web-exclusives/2018/01/judaism-christianity-and-first-things.

49. Various, "Against the Dead Consensus," *First Things*, March 21, 2019, https://www
.firstthings.com/web-exclusives/2019/03/against-the-dead-consensus.

50. Sohrab Ahmari, "Against David French-Ism," *First Things*, May 29, 2019, https://www
.firstthings.com/web-exclusives/2019/05/against-david-french-ism.

51. Benjamin Wallace-Wells, "David French, Sohrab Ahmari, and the Battle for the Future
of Conservatism," *New Yorker*, September 12, 2019, https://www.newyorker.com/news/the
-political-scene/david-french-sohrab-ahmari-and-the-battle-for-the-future-of-conservatism.

52. Ahmari, "Against David French-Ism."

53. Ahmari, "Against David French-Ism."

54. See Copulsky, *American Heretics*.

55. William Galston, "What Is National Conservatism?," *Persuasion*, February 8, 2021,
https://www.persuasion.community/p/what-is-national-conservatism.

Chapter 5

1. For more on Thiel's intellectual context and connections to the Straussian world, see Peter
Augustine Lawler, "Is Peter Thiel a Prophet We Can Believe In?," *Law & Liberty*, September 30,
2014, https://lawliberty.org/is-peter-thiel-a-prophet-we-can-believe-in/.

2. See Andrew Granato, "How Peter Thiel and the Stanford Review Built a Silicon Valley
Empire," *Stanford Politics*, November 27, 2017, https://stanfordpolitics.org/2017/11/27/peter

-thiel-cover-story/; Max Chafkin, *Contrarian* (Bloomsbury, 2022). For more on Johnson, see Tina Nguyen, *The MAGA Diaries: My Surreal Adventures Inside the Right-Wing* (Atria/One Signal, 2024); Isaac Stanley-Becker and Beth Reinhard, "JD Vance in Texts with Far-Right Figure: Profane and Off-the-Cuff," *Washington Post*, August 7, 2024, https://www.washingtonpost.com /politics/2024/08/07/jd-vance-charles-johnson-texts/.

3. See Peter Thiel, "The Star Trek Computer Is Not Enough," YouTube, 2019, https://youtu .be/7JRyy2MM-rI?si=nKhyXyFK7vqWGN6j.

4. One relevant encapsulation of Thiel's outlook is his popular essay "The Straussian Moment" (2007). This grandiose essay presents several perverse claims with stunning confidence. An example: Thiel says that it is only since 9/11 that we have been forced to "awaken from that very long and profitable period of intellectual slumber and amnesia that is so misleadingly called the Enlightenment"—apparently having forgotten the entire twentieth century, including the Holocaust.

5. See Granato, "How Peter Thiel." As Granato notes, Thiel made a major donation to the 2016 Trump campaign one week after the leak of the *Access Hollywood* tape.

6. Thiel, "The Star Trek Computer Is Not Enough."

7. See Peter Thiel and Blake Masters, *Zero to One: Notes on Startups, or How to Build the Future* (Crown Currency, 2014).

8. See "Peter Thiel: Google Is Working with Chinese Communist Government but Not US Military," *Fox News*, July 16, 2019, https://www.foxnews.com/video/6059526990001.

9. Chafkin, *Contrarian*, 287–90.

10. See the donor list on the program for the Orlando conference at NatCon, "National Conservatism Conference 2 Program 2021," November 31, 2021, https://nationalconservatism .org/natcon-2-2021/.

11. Michael Anton, "The Trump Doctrine," *Foreign Policy*, April 20, 2019, https://foreignpolicy .com/2019/04/20/the-trump-doctrine-big-think-america-first-nationalism/.

12. ISI, "Conservative Book of the Year Award," *Intercollegiate Studies Institute*, 2019, https:// isi.org/alumni/conservative-book-of-the-year-award/.

13. Roni Dori, "The Case for Nationalism, by the Israeli Credited with Shaping Trump's Foreign Policy," *Haaretz*, October 30, 2020, https://www.haaretz.com/israel-news/2020-10-30 /ty-article-magazine/.highlight/a-case-for-nationalism-by-the-israeli-credited-with-shaping -trumps-foreign-policy/0000017f-e128-d568-ad7f-f36bd0700000.

14. Marilyn H. Marks, "In a Nation's Service," *Princeton Alumni Weekly*, January 21, 2016, https://paw.princeton.edu/article/nations-service-0.

15. Hazony describes this period of life in depth and offers his own life as something like a proof of concept for a devoted conservative existence. Yoram Hazony, *Conservatism: A Rediscovery* (Regnery Gateway, 2022), concluding chapter.

16. Hazony, *Conservatism*, 381, 364–67.

17. Yoram Hazony, "Farewell from a 'Non-Kahanist,'" *Jerusalem Post*, November 8, 1990. JDL has been classified as a right-wing terrorist group by the FBI since 2001 (FBI, "Terrorism 2000/2001," accessed October 9, 2024, https://www.fbi.gov/stats-services/publications/ terror).

18. See Dori, "Case for Nationalism."

19. Julian Borger and Oliver Holmes, "US Says Israeli Settlements No Longer Considered Illegal in Dramatic Shift," *Guardian*, November 18, 2019, https://www.theguardian.com/world /2019/nov/18/us-israeli-settlements-no-longer-considered-illegal-palestinian-land-mike -pompeo.

20. Dori, "Case for Nationalism."

21. Dori, "Case for Nationalism"; Marks, "In a Nation's Service."

22. Hazony moved on to found and preside over the Herzl Institute in Jerusalem ("Institute Mission," *Herzl Institute—Machon Herzl*, accessed October 8, 2024, https://herzlinstitute.org /en/institute-mission/). For more on the funding sources for these organizations, see Na'ama Lanski and Daphna Berman, "Storm in a Neo-Con Teapot," *Haaretz*, November 29, 2007, https://www.haaretz.com/2007-11-29/ty-article/storm-in-a-neo-con-teapot/0000017f-e60c -d62c-a1ff-fe7f3c9c0000; Zack Beauchamp, "How an Israeli Thinker Became One of Trumpism's Foremost Theorists," *Vox*, October 26, 2020, https://www.vox.com/21355993/trump -israel-yoram-hazony-nationalism-tikvah.

23. Dori, "Case for Nationalism."

24. See Constanze Stelzenmüller, "America's Policy on Europe Takes a Nationalist Turn," *Financial Times*, January 30, 2019, https://www.ft.com/content/133ef614-23b3-11e9-b20d -5376ca5216eb; Anton, "The Trump Doctrine."

25. Yoram Hazony, *The Virtue of Nationalism* (Basic Books, 2018), 6.

26. Hazony, *The Virtue of Nationalism*, 6.

27. Hazony, *The Virtue of Nationalism*, 101, 226.

28. Hazony, *The Virtue of Nationalism*, 3, 42–50.

29. Hazony, *The Virtue of Nationalism*, 154.

30. Dori, "Case for Nationalism."

31. Stelzenmüller, "America's Policy."

32. Hazony, *The Virtue of Nationalism*, 22.

33. Hazony, *The Virtue of Nationalism*, 26.

34. Furthermore, the Protestant Reformation is often associated with the development of liberal democratic freedoms—a connection Hazony ignores.

35. Suzanne Schneider, "Light Among the Nations," *Jewish Currents*, September 28, 2023, https://jewishcurrents.org/light-among-the-nations. Schneider suggests that Hazony's nationalism amounts to something more like idol worship.

36. Dori, "Case for Nationalism."

37. Park MacDougald, "Are You a Nationalist or an Imperialist?," *Intelligencer*, September 21, 2018, https://nymag.com/intelligencer/2018/09/yoram-hazony-virtue-of-nationalism-review.html.

38. See, for example, Hazony's arguments about state formation in early modern philosophy (*The Virtue of Nationalism*, 76–77). For a straightforward counterargument, see section 119 of John Locke, *Second Treatise of Government*, ed. C. B. Macpherson (Hackett, 1980). For an account of the many problems with Hazony's treatment of Locke, see Michael Harding, "An Unjust Treatment of Locke," *Political Science Reviewer* 43, no. 1 (January 2019): 249–55.

39. For a glimpse of the intraright tension here, compare Hazony's speech in Brussels in 2023, "Ukraine and the Brotherhood of Nations," Brussels National Conservatism Conference, March 23, 2022, YouTube, https://www.youtube.com/watch?v=qFpnM4V5Sjk, to the letter by various contributors in Sohrab Ahmari's *Compact* magazine, "Away from the Abyss," March 31, 2022, https://www.compactmag.com/article/away-from-the-abyss/.

40. See Kathryn Joyce, "Right-Wing Switchback: 'National Conservatives' Dump Want to Claim Ukraine," *Salon*, April 13, 2022, https://www.salon.com/2022/04/13/right-wing -switchback-national-conservatives-want-to-claim-ukraine/.

41. See especially part 3 of the book, "Anti-Nationalism and Hate," 190–223, where Hazony offers a lopsided account of the history of the region.

42. Hazony, *The Virtue of Nationalism*, 103.

43. Schneider, "Light Among the Nations."

44. See Isabel Debre and Almudena Calatrava, "President Milei's Surprising Devotion to Judaism and Israel Provokes Tension in Argentina and Beyond," *AP News*, June 3, 2024, https:// apnews.com/article/milei-judaism-hezbollah-israel-hamas-war-netanyahu-d8831369a6 bc8a96205d4080d2b2045b.

45. See Geert Wilders, "The Resurgence of National Pride and the Future of Europe," *Parlementaire Monitor*, June 3, 2013, https://www.parlementairemonitor.nl/9353000/1/j9vvij 5epmj1ey0/vjacryghemyc.

46. "*Trump: You Know What I Am? I'm a Nationalist*," YouTube, 2018, https://www.youtube .com/watch?v=sazitj4x6YI; Quint Forgey, "Trump: 'I'm a Nationalist,'" *Politico*, October 22, 2018, https://www.politico.com/story/2018/10/22/trump-nationalist-926745.

47. Aaron Blake, "Trump's Embrace of a Fraught Term—'Nationalist'—Could Cement a Dangerous Racial Divide," *Washington Post*, October 23, 2018, https://www.washingtonpost.com /politics/2018/10/23/trumps-embrace-fraught-term-nationalist-could-cement-dangerous -racial-divide/.

48. Emma Green, "The Nationalists Take Washington," *Atlantic*, July 17, 2019, https://www .theatlantic.com/politics/archive/2019/07/national-conservatism-conference/594202/.

49. For more on Brog, see Judy Maltz, "Inside the Evangelical Money Flowing into the West Bank," *Haaretz*, December 9, 2018, https://www.haaretz.com/israel-news/2018-12-09/ty -article-magazine/.premium/inside-the-evangelical-money-flowing-into-the-west-bank /0000017f-f4b0-d460-afff-fff6add90000; Jacob Kornbluh, "He Was the Head of Christians United for Israel. Now He's Running as a Jewish Candidate for Congress," *Forward*, May 9, 2022, https://forward.com/news/501610/david-brog-nevada-election-christians-united-for-israel -congress/.

50. Christopher DeMuth, "Trumpism, Nationalism, and Conservatism," *Claremont Review of Books* (Winter 2019), https://claremontreviewofbooks.com/trumpism-nationalism-and-conservatism/.

51. DeMuth's essay was framed as a review of a popular book by David Goodhart, *The Road to Somewhere: The Populist Revolt and the Future of Politics* (Hurst, 2017).

52. In 2022 DeMuth told Michael Continetti: "We do not believe that America is a creedal nation, that America is defined by an idea; we actually believe that America is defined by hundreds of years of tradition and incremental changes and adaptation to new conflicts, and we believe it goes back hundreds of years before that to the emergence of Anglo-American common law which was incorporated pretty thoroughly into the American constitutional order." "Nationalize or Not? Matthew Continetti and Chris DeMuth Debate the Future of Conservatism," YouTube, 2022, https://www.youtube.com/watch?v=D13ULbBXr48.

53. William Galston, "What Is National Conservatism?," *Persuasion*, February 8, 2021, https://www.persuasion.community/p/what-is-national-conservatism.

54. Michael Anton, "Downsides of Hard and Soft Imperialism—National Conservatism Conference," YouTube, 2019, https://www.youtube.com/watch?v=Ry5aFZZuft0.

55. Charles Kesler, "Nationalism, Creed, & Culture," YouTube, 2020, https://www.youtube .com/watch?v=yb-i3oAmPt0.

56. Patrick Deneen, "Sustainable Conservatism—National Conservatism Conference," YouTube, 2019, https://www.youtube.com/watch?v=_nKKO2FW0OM.

57. See Yoram Hazony and Patrick Deneen, "Judaism and Free Speech on Campus Post-October 7, 2023," YouTube, 2024, https://www.youtube.com/watch?v=3iLVjP2ZdpM.

58. Julius Krein, "A Strategy for National Development," YouTube, 2019, https://www .youtube.com/watch?v=q0208KXDQT8.

59. Thomas Meaney, "Trumpism After Trump: Will the Movement Outlive the Man?," *Harper's*, February 2020, https://harpers.org/archive/2020/02/trumpism-after-trump/.

60. Oren Cass and Richard Reinsch, "Should America Adopt An Industrial Policy?," YouTube, 2019, https://www.youtube.com/watch?v=CsGxRmjiiPQ.

61. Tucker Carlson, "Big Business Hates Your Family—National Conservatism Conference," YouTube, 2019, https://www.youtube.com/watch?v=AXGoWtK1NnY. His speech was called "Big Business Hates Your Family."

62. JD Vance, "Beyond Libertarianism—National Conservatism Conference," YouTube, 2019, https://www.youtube.com/watch?v=dmVjKIEC8rw.

63. Senator Josh Hawley, "The Promise of the Republic—National Conservatism Conference," YouTube, 2019, https://www.youtube.com/watch?v=DkIapXCfPGE.

64. See Meaney, "Trumpism After Trump."

65. Yoram Hazony, "On Nationalism and Scripture," YouTube, 2019, https://www.youtube.com/watch?v=zzsNnqXDkRc.

66. Stephen Collinson, "Trump vs. 'the Squad' Makes Watershed Moment in Racial Politics," CNN, July 16, 2019, https://www.cnn.com/2019/07/16/politics/donald-trump-squad-ilhan-omar-racist/index.html.

67. See "Lydia Brimelow," Southern Poverty Law Center, accessed October 8, 2024, https://www.splcenter.org/fighting-hate/extremist-files/individual/lydia-brimelow. The VDARE website became inoperative in 2024: "White Nationalist Website VDARE Suspends Operations Amid Legal Scrutiny," Southern Poverty Law Center, September 18, 2024, https://www.splcenter.org/hatewatch/2024/09/18/white-nationalist-website-vdare-suspends-operations-amid-legal-scrutiny.

68. Peter Brimelow, "'East Is East and West Is West,'" Unz Review, June 21, 2019, https://www.unz.com/article/east-is-east-and-west-is-west/.

69. David Brog, "Roots of American Nationalism," YouTube, 2024, https://www.youtube.com/watch?v=2xNfChzwH3w.

70. Zack Beauchamp, "Amy Wax, 'National Conservatism,' and the Dark Dream of a Whiter America," Vox, July 23, 2019, https://www.vox.com/policy-and-politics/2019/7/23/20679172/amy-wax-white-national-conservatism-yoram-hazony-racism.

71. Yoram Hazony, "Hazony Tweet Beauchamp/Wax," Twitter, July 19, 2019, https://perma.cc/A9TP-2RDE; Zack Beauchamp, "Beauchamp Amy Wax Tweet," Twitter, July 19, 2019, https://perma.cc/LH8T-SWCX.

72. On Wax's attendance in 2018, see Paul Gottfried, "The Eleventh Annual H. L. Mencken Club Conference," Internet Archive, accessed March 22, 2025, https://web.archive.org/web/20190625114325/http://hlmenckenclub.org/2018-conference. Mencken conference schedules for 2008–2019 are preserved on the Internet Archive. Peter Brimelow was a speaker every year between 2008 and 2017, with the exception of 2013. Other regular attendees included Lee Congdon, John Derbyshire, Carl Horowitz, James Kalb, Robert Paquette, Steve Sailer, and Richard Spencer. See HLM Club, "The Mencken Club," "Conferences" tab, accessed March 22, 2025.

73. Paul Gottfried, "Presidential Address," delivered November 8, 2019, Internet Archive, https://web.archive.org/web/20191226180327/http://hlmenckenclub.org/2019-texts.

74. Yoram Hazony, "Guilt by Association at Rome's National Conservatism Conference," Spectator, February 8, 2020, https://www.spectator.co.uk/article/guilt-by-association-at-rome-s-national-conservatism-conference/.

75. Chris DeMuth, "Full Interview: Viktor Orbán at the National Conservativism Conference in Rome," Remix News, February 6, 2020, https://rmx.news/article/full-interview-viktor-orban-at-the-national-conservativism-conference-in-rome/.

76. Some of these manipulations include changing thresholds for parties to participate and gain seats; redistricting of the whole country to benefit Fidesz; state and oligarchic control of media; limiting oppositions' air time; rewriting of the constitution after 2010; threatening to fire individuals who do not vote for the party; and changing election rules to minimize minority participation. Tímea Drinóczi and Agnieszka Bień-Kacała, "Illiberal Constitutionalism: The Case of Hungary and Poland," German Law Journal 20, no. 8 (December 2019): 1140–66, https://doi.org/10.1017/glj.2019.83; Robert Sata and Ireneusz Pawel Karolewski, "Caesarean Politics

in Hungary and Poland," *East European Politics* 36, no. 2 (April 2, 2020): 206–25, https://doi.org
/10.1080/21599165.2019.1703694; Zack Beauchamp, "It Happened There: How Democracy
Died in Hungary," *Vox*, September 13, 2018, https://www.vox.com/policy-and-politics/2018/9
/13/17823488/hungary-democracy-authoritarianism-trump; and Anne Applebaum, *The Twilight of Democracy* (Penguin, 2021), 96–101.

77. Emily Schultheis, "Viktor Orbán: Hungary Doesn't Want 'Muslim Invaders,'" *Politico*,
January 8, 2018, https://www.politico.eu/article/viktor-orban-hungary-doesnt-want-muslim
-invaders/; DeMuth, "Full Interview."

78. Yoram Hazony, "After the Revolution—What Happens Next?," YouTube, 2022, https://
www.youtube.com/watch?v=EEtlCMFSWpw.

79. Larry Buchanan, Quoctrung Bui, and Jugal K. Patel, "Black Lives Matter May Be the
Largest Movement in U.S. History," *New York Times*, July 3, 2020, https://www.nytimes.com
/interactive/2020/07/03/us/george-floyd-protests-crowd-size.html.

80. "UConn Study: At Least 96% of Black Lives Matter Protests Were Peaceful," *WSHU*,
October 19, 2020, https://www.wshu.org/news/2020-10-19/uconn-study-at-least-96-of-black
-lives-matter-protests-were-peaceful.

81. See Melissa Pamer, "Los Angeles 1992 Riots: By the Numbers," *NBC Los Angeles*, April 21,
2012, https://www.nbclosangeles.com/news/local/los-angeles-1992-riots-by-the-numbers
/1950945/.

82. T. Greg Doucette documented video footage of hundreds of examples of police brutality
against protestors during this time. See "T. Greg Doucette 2020 Police Brutality Thread," Twitter, July 18, 2020, https://x.com/greg_doucette/status/1284526898991828992.

83. Tom Cotton, "Send in the Troops," *New York Times*, June 3, 2020, https://www.nytimes
.com/2020/06/03/opinion/tom-cotton-protests-military.html.

84. Brennan Center for Justice, "Trump's Insurrection Act Threat," April 21, 2022, https://
www.brennancenter.org/our-work/analysis-opinion/trumps-insurrection-act-threat.

85. Rishika Dugyala, "NYT opinion editor resigns after outrage over Tom Cotton op-ed,"
Politico, June 7, 2020, https://www.politico.com/news/2020/06/07/nyt-opinion-bennet
-resigns-cotton-op-ed-306317.

86. Clayborne Carson, ed., *The Autobiography of Martin Luther King, Jr.* (Warner Books,
2001), 247.

87. Will Higgins, "April 4, 1968: How RFK Saved Indianapolis," *Indy Star*, April 2, 2015,
https://www.indystar.com/story/life/2015/04/02/april-rfk-saved-indianapolis/70817218/.

88. Daniel Mendelsohn, "J.F.K., Tragedy, Myth," *New Yorker*, November 22, 2013, https://
www.newyorker.com/books/page-turner/j-f-k-tragedy-myth; David Brooks, "The Education
of Robert Kennedy," *New York Times*, November 26, 2006, https://www.nytimes.com/2006/11
/26/opinion/26brooks.html.

89. Higgins, "April 4, 1968: How RFK Saved Indianapolis."

90. Shortly after President Kennedy's assassination, Jackie Kennedy reportedly gave RFK a
book by Edith Hamilton called *The Greek Way* that became a solace to him. See Brooks, "The
Education of Robert Kennedy"; Mendelsohn, "J.F.K., Tragedy, Myth."

91. Alan Taylor, "The Riots That Followed the Assassination of Martin Luther King Jr.," *Atlantic*, April 3, 2018, https://www.theatlantic.com/photo/2018/04/the-riots-that-followed-the
-assassination-of-martin-luther-king-jr/557159/.

92. Higgins, "How RFK Saved Indianapolis"; Joe Scarborough, "RFK: Bending History,"
Internet Archive, https://web.archive.org/web/20071025062559/http:/www.joescarborough
.com/view.asp?ID=31.

93. Mendelsohn, "J.F.K., Tragedy, Myth."

94. To get a sense of the complexity here, see the interview that James Baldwin had with Kenneth Clark after a visit with Bobby Kennedy in 1963: "A Conversation with James Baldwin," YouTube, 2020, https://www.youtube.com/watch?v=zhop-eFB0sI.

Chapter 6

1. Connie Bruck, "How Hollywood Remembers Steve Bannon," *New Yorker*, April 24, 2017, https://www.newyorker.com/magazine/2017/05/01/how-hollywood-remembers-steve-bannon; Stephen K. Bannon, "Fox Faces Its Uncertain Future: The Minor Murdochs Take Command," *Breitbart*, August 6, 2016, https://www.breitbart.com/the-media/2016/08/06/fox-faces-uncertain-future-minor-murdochs-take-command/; Asawin Suebsaeng, "Steve Bannon's Long Love Affair with War," *Daily Beast*, January 31, 2017, https://www.thedailybeast.com/articles/2017/01/31/steve-bannon-s-long-love-affair-with-war; Michael Crowley, "Why the White House Is Reading Greek History," *Politico*, June 21, 2017, https://politi.co/2sjcsQi; J. Lester Feder, "This Is How Steve Bannon Sees the Entire World," *Buzzfeed*, November 16, 2016, https://www.buzzfeednews.com/article/lesterfeder/this-is-how-steve-bannon-sees-the-entire-world. See also Green, *Devil's Bargain*.

2. Osita Nwanevu, "Steve Bannon Boasts About His Love of Thucydides for All the Wrong Reasons," *Slate*, June 21, 2017, https://slate.com/news-and-politics/2017/06/steve-bannon-likes-thucydides-for-all-the-wrong-reasons.html.

3. Kori Schake, "The Summer of Misreading Thucydides," *Atlantic*, July 18, 2017, https://www.theatlantic.com/international/archive/2017/07/the-summer-of-misreading-thucydides/533859/.

4. Myke Cole, "How the Far Right Perverts Ancient History—and Why It Matters," *Daily Beast*, March 3, 2019, https://www.thedailybeast.com/how-the-far-right-perverts-ancient-historyand-why-it-matters; Ishaan Tharoor, "Why the West's Far-Right—and Trump Supporters—Are Still Obsessed with an Ancient Battle," *Washington Post*, November 7, 2016, https://www.washingtonpost.com/news/worldviews/wp/2016/11/07/why-the-wests-far-right-and-trump-supporters-are-still-obsessed-with-an-ancient-battle/; Ainara Tiefenthäler and Natalie Reneau, "Video: Swastikas, Shields and Flags: Branding Hate in Charlottesville," *New York Times*, August 15, 2017, https://www.nytimes.com/video/us/100000005360556/white-supremacist-symbols-charlottesville.html.

5. Sarah Posner, "How Steve Bannon Created an Online Haven for White Nationalists," *Mother Jones*, August 22, 2016, https://www.motherjones.com/politics/2016/08/stephen-bannon-donald-trump-alt-right-breitbart-news/.

6. Matt Flegenheimer, "Hillary Clinton Says 'Radical Fringe' Is Taking Over G.O.P. Under Donald Trump," *New York Times*, August 25, 2016, https://www.nytimes.com/2016/08/26/us/politics/hillary-clinton-speech.html.

7. "Donald Trump's New York Times Interview," *New York Times*, November 23, 2016, https://www.nytimes.com/2016/11/23/us/politics/trump-new-york-times-interview-transcript.html.

8. Patrice Taddonio, "How Steve Bannon Engineered President Trump's Travel Ban," *Frontline*, May 22, 2017, https://www.pbs.org/wgbh/frontline/article/watch-how-steve-bannon-engineered-president-trumps-travel-ban/; Terry Gross, "'Hatemonger' Paints Trump Advisor Stephen Miller as a 'Case Study in Radicalization,'" *NPR*, August 24, 2020, https://www.npr.org/2020/08/24/905403716/hatemonger-paints-trump-advisor-stephen-miller-as-a-case-study-in-radicalization.

9. Thucydides and Victor Davis Hanson, *The Landmark Thucydides*, ed. Robert B. Strassler, trans. Richard Crawley (Free Press, 1998), 4.80.

10. Shane Goldmacher, "Trump Taps Aide Stephen Miller to Write Inaugural Address," *Politico*, December 26, 2016, https://www.politico.com/story/2016/12/trump-miller-inauguration -speech-232967.

11. Politico Staff, "2017 Donald Trump Inauguration Speech Transcript," *Politico*, January 20, 2017, https://www.politico.com/story/2017/01/full-text-donald-trump-inauguration-speech -transcript-233907.

12. McKay Coppins, "The Outrage Over Family Separation Is Exactly What Stephen Miller Wants," *Atlantic*, June 19, 2018, https://www.theatlantic.com/politics/archive/2018/06/stephen -miller-family-separation/563132/; Piper French, "Will the Families Separated by Trump Ever Be Reunited?," *Intelligencer*, February 27, 2024, https://nymag.com/intelligencer/article /separated-families-border-trump-zero-tolerance-immigration.html; Julie Hirschfeld Davis and Michael D. Shear, "How Trump Came to Enforce a Practice of Separating Migrant Families," *New York Times*, June 16, 2018, https://www.nytimes.com/2018/06/16/us/politics/family -separation-trump.html.

13. Tom McCarthy, "'Trump Is 100% Right': David Horowitz, the Thinker Who Sponsored Stephen Miller," *Guardian*, June 20, 2018, https://www.theguardian.com/us-news/2018/jun/20 /donald-trump-david-horowitz-stephen-miller-family-separation-border-policy.

14. Reeves Wiedeman, "The Duke Lacrosse Scandal and the Birth of the Alt-Right," *Intelligencer*, April 14, 2017, https://nymag.com/intelligencer/2017/04/the-duke-lacrosse-scandal -and-the-birth-of-the-alt-right.html.

15. Graeme Wood, "Richard Spencer Was My High-School Classmate," *Atlantic*, May 14, 2017, https://www.theatlantic.com/magazine/archive/2017/06/his-kampf524505/.

16. Wiedeman, "Duke Lacrosse Scandal."

17. George Hawley, *Making Sense of the Alt-Right* (Columbia University Press, 2017). See also Tamir Bar-On, "Richard B. Spencer and the Alt Right," in *Key Thinkers of the Radical Right: Behind the New Threat to Liberal Democracy*, ed. Mark Sedgwick (Oxford University Press, 2019), chap. 14.

18. Wood, "Richard Spencer Was My High-School Classmate."

19. Josh Harkinson, "Meet the White Nationalist Trying to Ride the Trump Train to Lasting Power," *Mother Jones*, October 2016, https://www.motherjones.com/politics/2016/10/richard -spencer-trump-alt-right-white-nationalist/.

20. Wood, "Richard Spencer Was My High-School Classmate"; Harkinson, "Meet the White Nationalist."

21. Wood, "Richard Spencer Was My High-School Classmate."

22. Hawley, *Making Sense of the Alt-Right*, 67.

23. C. J. Ciaramell, "Some Well-Dressed White Nationalists Gathered in DC Last Weekend," *Vice*, October 29, 2013, https://www.vice.com/en/article/some-well-dressed-white-nationalists -gathered-in-dc-last-weekend/.

24. Bar-On, "Richard B. Spencer and the Alt Right."

25. Hawley, *Making Sense of the Alt-Right*, 51–53.

26. Hawley, *Making Sense of the Alt-Right*.

27. Jacob Siegel, "Paul Gottfried, the Jewish Godfather of the 'Alt-Right,'" *Tablet*, November 30, 2016, https://www.tabletmag.com/sections/news/articles/spencer-gottfried-alt-right.

28. Derbyshire was fired from the *National Review* in 2012 for publishing an anti-Black, racist column in *Taki* magazine. See Dylan Byers, "National Review Fires John Derbyshire," *Politico*, April 7, 2012, https://www.politico.com/blogs/media/2012/04/national-review-fires-john -derbyshire-119887.

29. The audio files for some speeches have been preserved on the Internet Archive. See HLM Club, "Conference Audio Recordings," Internet Archive, accessed March 22, 2025, https://web .archive.org/web/20160118180618/http:/hlmenckenclub.org/hlmc-audio/.

30. Clay Risen, "William H. Regnery II, 80, Dies; Bankrolled the Rise of the Alt-Right," Obituary, *New York Times*, July 16, 2021, https://www.nytimes.com/2021/07/16/obituaries/william-h-regnery-ii-dead.html; Aram Roston and Joel Anderson, "This Man Used His Inherited Fortune to Fund the Racist Right," *Buzzfeed*, July 23, 2017, https://www.buzzfeednews.com/article/aramroston/hes-spent-almost-20-years-funding-the-racist-right-it.

31. See Hawley, *Making Sense of the Alt-Right*, 59.

32. Joshua Tait, "The Rise of the Alt-Right," *Tablet*, August 11, 2023, https://www.tabletmag.com/sections/news/articles/what-was-alt-right.

33. Daniel Lombroso and Yoni Applebaum, "White Nationalists Salute the President-Elect: 'Hail Trump!,'" *Atlantic*, November 21, 2016, https://www.theatlantic.com/politics/archive/2016/11/richard-spencer-speech-npi/508379/.

34. See HLM Club, "The 9th Annual H. L. Mencken Club Conference," Internet Archive, accessed March 22, 2025, https://web.archive.org/web/20191226180254/http://hlmenckenclub.org/2016-conference. Beattie's name was not listed on the program but the title of his talk was.

35. Madeline Conway, "'Scholars and Writers for America' Group Endorses Trump," *Politico*, September 30, 2016, https://www.politico.com/story/2016/09/donald-trump-scholars-writers-endorsement-228987; Likhitha Butchireddygari, "Professor Who Predicted Trump's Win Explains How He Knew," *Chronicle*, November 11, 2016, https://www.dukechronicle.com/article/2016/11/professor-who-predicted-trumps-win-explains-how-he-knew-what-comes-next; Keith Lawrence, "What Can We Expect on Nov. 8, and After?," *Duke Today*, November 2, 2016, https://today.duke.edu/2016/11/what-can-we-expect-nov-8-and-after.

36. Claremont Institute, "Publius Fellowship Alumni," accessed October 9, 2024, https://www.claremont.org/publius-fellowship-alumni/; Marc Fisher and Isaac Stanley-Becker, "The Claremont Institute Triumphed in the Trump Years. Then Came Jan. 6," *Washington Post*, July 24, 2022, https://www.washingtonpost.com/nation/2022/07/24/claremont-john-eastman-trump/.

37. See HLM Club, "9th Annual Conference." For Beattie's speech, see "Intelligensia and the Right," https://www.documentcloud.org/documents/4780191-Intelligentsia-and-the-Right/.

38. Darren Beattie, "Duke Foolish to Condemn Perfectly-Reasonable 'Travel Ban,'" *Chronicle*, March 6, 2017, https://www.dukechronicle.com/article/2017/03/duke-foolish-to-condemn-perfectly-reasonable-travel-ban; Samantha Neal, "Experts Debate Merits, Flaws of Trump's Immigration Ban," *Chronicle*, April 14, 2017, https://www.dukechronicle.com/article/2017/04/experts-debate-merits-flaws-of-trumps-immigration-ban.

39. Benjamin R. Teitelbaum, *War for Eternity: Inside Bannon's Far-Right Circle of Global Power Brokers* (Dey Street Books, 2020), 187–99, 163–99.

40. Joseph Brean, "Naive Philosopher or Far-Right Propagandist?," *National Post*, October 4, 2018, https://nationalpost.com/news/toronto/university-of-toronto-controversially-awards-doctorate-translator-of-sanctioned-russian-neo-fascist; Thomas Chatterton Williams, "The French Origins of 'You Will Not Replace Us,'" *New Yorker*, November 27, 2017, https://www.newyorker.com/magazine/2017/12/04/the-french-origins-of-you-will-not-replace-us.

41. See Josh Vandiver, "The Radical Roots of the Alt-Right," *Political Extremism and Radicalism in the Twentieth Century* (Gale Cengage, 2018).

42. Teitelbaum, *War for Eternity*, 199.

43. Jessica Mazzola, "I'm a Leftist, Not a Nazi," *NJ.com*, September 27, 2017, https://www.nj.com/essex/2017/09/who_is_new_jerseys_alt-right_professor.html.

44. Carol Schaeffer, "Jason Jorjani Fancied Himself an Intellectual Leader of a White Supremacist Movement—Then It Came Crashing Down," *Intercept*, March 18, 2018, https://theintercept.com/2018/03/18/alt-right-jason-jorjani/.

45. Rosie Gray, "An Alt-Right Leader Sets Up Shop in Northern Virginia," *Atlantic*, January 12, 2017, https://www.theatlantic.com/politics/archive/2017/01/a-one-stop-shop-for-the

-alt-right/512921/; Mark Townsend, "Infiltrator Exposes Generation Identity UK's March Towards Extreme Far Right," *Observer*, August 24, 2019, https://www.theguardian.com/world/2019/aug/24/generation-identity-uk-far-right-extremists.

46. "Mayor: Richard Spencer-Attended-Torch-Lit Protest in Charlottesville, Va. 'Hearkens Back to the Days of the KKK,'" *CBS News*, May 15, 2017, https://www.cbsnews.com/news/charlottesville-protest-richard-spender-kkk-robert-e-lee-statue/.

47. Jonah Engel Bromwich and Alan Blinder, "What We Know About James Alex Fields," *New York Times*, August 13, 2017, https://www.nytimes.com/2017/08/13/us/james-alex-fields-charlottesville-driver-.html.

48. Sasha Ingber, "Neo-Nazi James Fields Gets 2nd Life Sentence for Charlottesville Attack," NPR, July 15, 2019, https://www.npr.org/2019/07/15/741756615/virginia-court-sentences-neo-nazi-james-fields-jr-to-life-in-prison.

49. Jeremy W. Peters and Maggie Haberman, "Bannon Was Set for a Graceful Exit. Then Came Charlottesville," *New York Times*, August 21, 2017, https://www.nytimes.com/2017/08/20/us/politics/steve-bannon-fired-trump-departure.html; Andrew Prokop, "Steve Bannon's Exit from the Trump White House, Explained," *Vox*, August 18, 2017, https://www.vox.com/policy-and-politics/2017/8/18/16145188/steve-bannon-fired-resigns.

50. Schaeffer, "Jason Jorjani."

51. Jessica Mazzola, "NJIT Prof Suspended Over Video of Him Discussing Hitler's Legacy," *NJ.com*, September 26, 2017, https://www.nj.com/essex/2017/09/college_suspends_professor_plagued_by_alt-right_co.html.

52. Teitelbaum, *War for Eternity*, 266.

53. Eliana Johnson, "Trump Speechwriter's Ouster Sparks Racially Charged Debate," *Politico*, August 23, 2018, https://www.politico.com/story/2018/08/23/trump-think-tank-racism-claremont-794070; Andrew Kaczynski, "Speechwriter Who Attended Conference with White Nationalists in 2016 Leaves White House," CNN, August 19, 2018, https://www.cnn.com/2018/08/19/politics/darren-beattie-mencken-club/index.html.

54. Jake Sherman and John Bresnahan, "Matt Gaetz Appears to Run Afoul of House Ethics Rules," *Politico*, July 22, 2020, https://www.politico.com/news/2020/07/22/gaetz-florida-house-ethics-rules-377098.

55. Michael Anton, "Are the Kids Al(t)Right?," *Claremont Review of Books* (Summer 2019), https://claremontreviewofbooks.com/are-the-kids-altright/.

56. Anton, "Are the Kids Al(t) Right?"

57. Curtis Yarvin (as Mencius Moldbug), "Did Barack Obama Go to Columbia?," *Unqualified Reservations*, October 31, 2008, https://www.unqualified-reservations.org/2008/10/did-barack-obama-go-to-columbia/.

58. Joseph Bernstein, "Alt-White: Here's How Breitbart and Milo Smuggled White Nationalism into the Mainstream," *Buzzfeed*, October 5, 2017, https://www.buzzfeednews.com/article/josephbernstein/heres-how-breitbart-and-milo-smuggled-white-nationalism#.eh5ZrNkN7; James Pogue, "Inside the New Right, Where Peter Thiel Is Placing His Biggest Bets," *Vanity Fair*, April 20, 2022, https://www.vanityfair.com/news/2022/04/inside-the-new-right-where-peter-thiel-is-placing-his-biggest-bets.

59. Jacob Siegel, "The Red Pill Prince," *Tablet*, March 31, 2022, https://www.tabletmag.com/sections/news/articles/red-pill-prince-curtis-yarvin.

60. Curtis Yarvin, "Salvador as a Startup State," *Gray Mirror*, September 2, 2023, https://graymirror.substack.com/p/salvador-as-a-startup-state.

61. Joshua Tait, "Mencius Moldbug and Neoreaction," in *Key Thinkers of the Radical Right: Behind the New Threat to Liberal Democracy*, ed. Mark Sedgwick (Oxford University Press, 2019), 187–88.

62. Matt McManus, "Yarvin's Case Against Democracy," *Commonweal*, January 27, 2023, https://www.commonwealmagazine.org/curtis-yarvin-thiel-carlyle-monarchism-reactionary. As McManus rightly notes, "Yarvin's writing is of a very low intellectual quality, even compared with other neo-reactionaries."

63. Damon Linker, "The Intellectual Right Contemplates an American Caesar," *The Week*, July 28, 2021.

64. Suzanne Schneider, "Beyond Athens and Jerusalem," *Strange Matters*, no. 3 (Spring 2024), https://strangematters.coop/fascist-economic-debates-peter-thiel-curtis-yarvin/.

65. See Curtis Yarvin, "A Brief Explanation of the Cathedral," *Gray Mirror*, January 21, 2021, https://graymirror.substack.com/p/a-brief-explanation-of-the-cathedral.

66. Rosie Gray, "How Bronze Age Pervert Built an Online Following and Injected Anti-Democracy, Pro-Men Ideas Into the GOP," *Politico*, July 16, 2023, https://www.politico.com/news/magazine/2023/07/16/bronze-age-pervert-masculinity-00105427. The idea that liberalism—especially "woke" liberalism—is a new religion is pervasive on the New Right. It is based on a fundamental misunderstanding of liberalism. See Laura K. Field, "What the Reactionary Right Gets Dead Wrong About Modern Liberal Democracy," *Bulwark*, July 30, 2024, https://www.thebulwark.com/p/what-the-reactionary-right-gets-dead-wrong-about-modern-liberal-democracy.

67. Mencius Moldbug, "An Open Letter to Progressives, Chapter 9: How to Uninstall a Cathedral," *Unqualified Reservations*, June 12, 2008, https://www.unqualified-reservations.org/2008/06/ol9-how-to-uninstall cathedral/; Curtis Yarvin, "Coriolanus and the Conservatives," *Gray Mirror*, March 2, 2021, https://graymirror.substack.com/p/coriolanus-and-the-conservatives.

68. Yarvin, "A Brief Explanation of the Cathedral."

69. See Anton, "Are the Kids Al(t)Right?"; Gray, "How Bronze Age Pervert Built an Online Following"; Damon Linker, "Down the Straussian Rabbit Hole," *Notes from the Middleground*, February 22, 2023, https://damonlinker.substack.com/p/down-the-straussian-rabbit-hole.

70. Wood, "How Bronze Age Pervert Charmed the Far Right."

71. Gray, "Alt-Right Leader Sets Up Shop."

72. Anton, "Are the Kids Al(t)Right?"

73. Anton, "Are the Kids Al(t) Right?"

74. Wood, "How Bronze Age Pervert Charmed the Far Right."

75. Bronze Age Pervert, *Bronze Age Mindset*, part 2, sec. 33 (independently published, 2018).

76. On BAP and masculinity, see Josh Vandiver, "Metapolitics, Masculinity, and Technology in the Rise of 'Bronze Age Pervert,'" in *Contemporary Far-Right Thinkers and the Future of Liberal Democracy* (Routledge, 2021).

77. Bronze Age Pervert, *Bronze Age Mindset*, sec. 77. "The increase of chaos, confusion and pressure on the Leviathan will lay it low: imagine even a world where the people, under relentless assault of contradictory and wild claims, would lose all faith in the media and government and doctors and believe nothing they hear through official channels anymore."

78. @proteinpilled, "BAP on the Gynocratic Longhouse 1," https://x.com/proteinpilled/status/1494085031001837570; "BAP on the Gynocratic Longhouse 2," https://x.com/proteinpilled/status/1494085713561800705; and "BAP on the Gynocratic Longhouse 3," https://x.com/proteinpilled/status/1494086451411173376, all on Twitter, February 16. 2022; "Bronze Age Aesthetics on Twitter: 'BAP on the Gynocratic Longhouse . . . ,'" February 16, 2022, https://web.archive.org/web/20220607013524/https:/twitter.com/proteinpilled/status/1494085031001837570.

79. Friedrich Nietzsche, *Thus Spoke Zarathustra: A Book for Everyone and Nobody*, trans. Graham Parkes (Oxford University Press, 2008), part 2, "The Stillest Hour"; Friedrich Nietzsche and Duncan Large, *Ecce Homo: How One Becomes What One Is* (Oxford University Press, 2007), Foreword.

80. Beattie, "Intelligensia and the Right."

81. Nietzsche, *Thus Spoke Zarathustra*, part 4, "The Cry of Need."

82. Nietzsche, *Thus Spake Zarathustra*, part 4, "The Sorcerer."

83. See Friedrich Nietzsche, *The Will to Power*, trans. Walter Kaufmann and R. J. Hollingdale (Vintage, 1968), sec. 983; or Giorgio Colli and Mazzino Montinari, *Friedrich Nietzsche—Samtliche Werke: Kritische Studienausgabe in 15 Banden* (De Gruyter, 1999), vol. 11, 289. On Jesus, see Friedrich Nietzsche, *The Twilight of the Idols and the Anti-Christ: Or How to Philosophize with a Hammer*, ed. Michael Tanner, trans. R. J. Hollingdale (Penguin Classics, 1990), bk. *The Antichrist*, especially sec. 42.

84. SPLC, "Racist Book, Camp of the Saints, Gains in Popularity," Southern Poverty Law Center, March 21, 2001, https://www.splcenter.org/fighting-hate/intelligence-report/2001/racist-book-camp-saints-gains-popularity.

85. Cathy Young, "Do American 'National Conservatives' Condone Orbán's White Nationalism?," *Bulwark*, July 28, 2024, https://www.thebulwark.com/p/do-american-national-conservatives-condone-orbans-white-nationalism.

86. Michael Edison Hayden, "Stephen Miller's Affinity for White Nationalism Revealed in Leaked Emails," Southern Poverty Law Center, November 12, 2019, https://www.splcenter.org/hatewatch/2019/11/12/stephen-millers-affinity-white-nationalism-revealed-leaked-emails; Jason Richwine, "IQ and Immigration Policy" (PhD diss., Harvard University, 2009).

87. Jason Richwine and Amy Wax, "Low-Skill Immigration: A Case for Restriction," *American Affairs Journal*, November 20, 2017, https://americanaffairsjournal.org/2017/11/low-skill-immigration-case-restriction/; Dylan Matthews, "Heritage Study Co-Author Opposed Letting in Immigrants with Low IQs," *Washington Post*, May 8, 2013, https://www.washingtonpost.com/news/wonk/wp/2013/05/08/heritage-study-co-author-opposed-letting-in-immigrants-with-low-iqs/; Aaron Blake, "Jason Richwine Resigns from Heritage Foundation," *Washington Post*, May 10, 2013, https://www.washingtonpost.com/news/post-politics/wp/2013/05/10/jason-richwine-resigns-from-heritage-foundation/.

88. Christopher Mathias, "Trump Has Appointed 2 White Nationalists to Government Roles Since Losing the Election," *Huffington Post*, November 19, 2020, https://www.huffpost.com/entry/trump-appoints-white-nationalists-darren-beattie-jason-richwine_n_5fb6eedbc5b67f34cb398973.

89. For more on Murphy, see Laura K. Field, "The Decay at the Claremont Institute Continues," *Bulwark*, April 20, 2022, https://www.thebulwark.com/p/the-decay-at-the-claremont-institute-continues; Michael Edison Hayden, "Jack Posobiec's Rise Tied to White Supremacist Movement," Southern Poverty Law Center, July 8, 2020, https://www.splcenter.org/hatewatch/2020/07/08/jack-posobiecs-rise-tied-white-supremacist-movement.

Chapter 7

1. Tocqueville, *Democracy in America*, vol. 2, 252.

2. Claremont Institute, "John C. Eastman," accessed October 11, 2024, https://beta.claremont.org/bio/john-c-eastman/.

3. NOM, "National Organization for Marriage Names John Eastman Chairman of the Board," *NCR*, September 28, 2011, https://www.ncregister.com/news/national-organization-for-marriage-names-john-eastman-chairman-of-the-board; NOM, "About Us—National Organization for Marriage," accessed October 11, 2024, https://nationformarriage.org/about-us/.

4. John Eastman, "John Eastman for Attorney General—the Campaign for Our Agenda Continues," Internet Archive, June 9, 2010, https://web.archive.org/web/20100715163044/http:/www.eastmanforag.com/news/the-campaign-for-our-agenda-continues; John Eastman, "Eastman AG Website Permalink," June 9, 2010, https://perma.cc/EK7B-UR8Z.

5. C-SPAN, "John Eastman at January 6 Rally," January 6, 2021, https://www.c-span.org/video/?c4953961/user-clip-john-eastman-january-6-rally.

6. Eastman's involvement was uncovered by Bob Woodward and Robert Costa, in *Peril* (Simon & Schuster, 2021).

7. See Ryan Goodman et al., "Comprehensive Timeline on False Electors Scheme in 2020 Presidential Election," *Just Security*, May 15, 2024, https://www.justsecurity.org/81939/timeline-false-electors/.

8. United States Government, "Select January 6th Committee Final Report and Supporting Materials Collection," GovInfo, December 22, 2022, https://www.govinfo.gov/app/details/GPO-J6-REPORT/.

9. Eastman's involvement was reported at the time and was further clarified during the January 6 hearings. Peter Baker, Maggie Haberman, and Annie Karni, "Pence Reached His Limit with Trump. It Wasn't Pretty," *New York Times*, January 13, 2021, https://www.nytimes.com/2021/01/12/us/politics/mike-pence-trump.html; Scott Wong, "Takeaways from Day 3 of Jan. 6 Hearings: Lawyer Eastman Told Trump Election Plot Wasn't Legal," *NBC News*, June 16, 2022, https://www.nbcnews.com/politics/congress/takeaways-day-3-jan-6-hearings-lawyer-eastman-told-trump-election-plot-rcna34034.

10. John Eastman and Tom Klingenstein, "The John Eastman Interview," *TomKlingenstein.com*, June 21, 2023, https://tomklingenstein.com/the-john-eastman-interview/; Charles Murray, "Steve Sailer Loves America," *TomKlingenstein.com*, June 19, 2024, https://tomklingenstein.com/steve-sailer-loves-america/.

11. Colby Itkowitz, Beth Reinhard, and Clara Ence Morse, "In Vance, Trump Finds a Kindred Spirit on Election Denial and Jan. 6," *Washington Post*, July 17, 2024, https://www.washingtonpost.com/politics/2024/07/17/vance-trump-january-6-election-denial/.

12. Graham, "The New Lost Cause."

13. Luke O'Brien, "The Far-Right Helped Create the World's Most Powerful Facial Recognition Technology," *HuffPost*, April 7, 2020, https://www.huffpost.com/entry/clearview-ai-facial-recognition-alt-right_n_5e7d028bc5b6cb08a92a5c48; Ben Schreckinger, "The Alt-Right Comes to Washington," *Politico*, May 8, 2020, https://politi.co/2OaVQ5u.

14. Chuck DeVore, "79 Days to Inauguration Taskforce Report," Texas Public Policy Foundation, October 20, 2020, 3, https://www.texaspolicy.com/79-days-to-inauguration-taskforce-report/.

15. Christian Vanderbrouk, "Notes on an Authoritarian Conspiracy: Inside the Claremont Institute's '79 Days to Inauguration' Report," *Bulwark*, November 8, 2021, https://www.thebulwark.com/p/notes-on-an-authoritarian-conspiracy-inside-the-claremont-institutes-79-days-to-inauguration-report.

16. Andrew Busch, "Sleepwalking Into Secession," *American Mind*, August 18, 2020, https://americanmind.org/memo/sleepwalking-into-secession/.

17. Michael Anton, "The Coming Coup?," *American Mind*, September 4, 2020, https://americanmind.org/salvo/the-coming-coup/.

18. American Mind Editors, "Stop the Coup," *American Mind*, September 12, 2020, https://americanmind.org/memo/stop-the-coup/.

19. Michael Anton, "Game-On for the Coup?," *American Mind*, November 4, 2020, https://americanmind.org/salvo/game-on-for-the-coup/.

20. "The Steal Is on. What Republicans Must Do Next to Guarantee Victory," *Revolver News*, November 4, 2020, https://revolver.news/2020/11/president-trump-must-stop-the-steal/; Seth Cohen, "Revolver News, a Right-Wing Website Endorsed by Trump, Calls for Shooting Protestors," *Forbes*, September 9, 2024, https://www.forbes.com/sites/sethcohen/2020/09/24/revolvernews-a-right-wing-website-endorsed-by-trump-calls-for-shooting-protestors/.

21. Ryan Williams et al., "The Fight Is Now," *American Mind*, November 5, 2020, https://americanmind.org/salvo/the-fight-is-now/, emphasis added.

22. Williams et al., "The Fight Is Now."

23. On "counterfeit facts" as a preferable descriptor to "alternative facts," see Patrick Thaddeus Jackson, *Facts and Explanations in International Studies . . . and Beyond* (Routledge, 2024).

24. Patrick Deneen, "Patrick Deneen Election Denial Tweet," December 9, 2020, https://perma.cc/N2Z8–3P7A.

25. See Emmy M. Cho and Isabella B. Cho, "Harvard Law School Organizations Petition to Denounce Professor Adrian Vermeule's 'Highly Offensive' Online Rhetoric," *Harvard Crimson*, January 13, 2021, https://www.thecrimson.com/article/2021/1/13/harvard-law-school-petition-vermeule/.

26. For screenshots of these tweets, see the appendix to Harvard Letter Writers, "Harvard Student Letter Vermeule," 2021, https://perma.cc/J33V-AXWG.

27. Kyle Cheney, "John Eastman, Architect of Trump's 2020 Election Plot, Should Be Disbarred, Judge Rules," *Politico*, March 27, 2024, https://www.politico.com/news/2024/03/27/john-eastman-disbarred-00149468; Alexandra Berzon et al., "Inside the Movement Behind Trump's Election Lies," *New York Times*, October 28, 2024, https://www.nytimes.com/interactive/2024/10/28/us/politics/inside-the-movement-behind-trumps-election-lies.html.

28. "John Eastman Testimony During Georgia Senate Election Hearing," YouTube, 2020, https://www.youtube.com/watch?v=IHt6UEc_tQ8. See also Luke Broadwater and Alan Feuer, "John Eastman Pressed Pennsylvania Legislator to Throw Out Biden Votes," *New York Times*, May 12, 2022, https://www.nytimes.com/2022/05/11/us/politics/john-eastman-trump-2020-election.html.

29. See Jonathan Adler, "Additional Filings in and Additional Thoughts on the Texas Election Suit," *Reason*, December 9, 2020, https://reason.com/volokh/2020/12/09/additional-filings-in-and-additional-thoughts-on-the-texas-election-suit/.

30. Michael S. Schmidt and Maggie Haberman, "The Lawyer Behind the Memo on How Trump Could Stay in Office," *New York Times*, October 2, 2021, https://www.nytimes.com/2021/10/02/us/politics/john-eastman-trump-memo.html; John Eastman, "Trump Lawyer's Full Memo on Plan for Pence to Overturn the Election," CNN, September 21, 2021, https://www.cnn.com/2021/09/21/politics/read-eastman-full-memo-pence-overturn-election/index.html.

31. See "Results of Lawsuits Regarding the 2020 Elections," Campaign Legal Center, accessed October 11, 2024, https://campaignlegal.org/results-lawsuits-regarding-2020-elections.

32. "Read Pence's Full Letter Saying He Can't Claim 'Unilateral Authority' to Reject Electoral Votes," *PBS News*, January 6, 2021, https://www.pbs.org/newshour/politics/read-pences-full-letter-saying-he-cant-claim-unilateral-authority-to-reject-electoral-votes.

33. See John Eastman, "Setting the Record Straight on the POTUS 'Ask,'" *American Mind*, accessed October 11, 2024, https://americanmind.org/memo/setting-the-record-straight-on-the-potus-ask/; Eric Cortellessa, "John Eastman Told Trump That Pence Jan. 6 Plan Was Illegal," *Time*, June 16, 2022, https://time.com/6188491/john-eastman-jan-6-testimony-trump/; John Eastman, "Trying to Prevent Illegal Conduct from Deciding an Election Is Not Endorsing a 'Coup,'" *American Greatness*, October 1, 2021, https://amgreatness.com/2021/09/30/trying-to-prevent-illegal-conduct-from-deciding-an-election-is-not-endorsing-a-coup/; Schmidt and Haberman, "The Lawyer Behind the Memo."

34. Chris Cillizza, "Analysis: The Single Most Damning Email Exchange in the New January 6 Committee Filing," CNN, March 3, 2022, https://www.cnn.com/2022/03/03/politics/trump-january-6-committee-eastman-email/index.html.

35. Kyle Cheney, "Select Committee Points to Evidence Trump Lawyer's Election-Related Efforts Resumed After Jan. 6," *Politico*, June 14, 2022, https://www.politico.com/news/2022/06

/14/select-committee-points-to-evidence-trump-lawyers-election-related-efforts-resumed
-after-jan-6-00039649.

36. See Hugo Lowell, "Trump Lawyer John Eastman Sought Presidential Pardon After January 6," *Guardian*, June 16, 2022, https://www.theguardian.com/us-news/2022/jun/16/trump
-lawyer-john-eastman-presidential-pardon.

37. "I've decided that I should be on the pardon list, if that's still in the works," wrote Eastman. Aaron Blake, "What John Eastman and 'the Pardon List' Means," *Washington Post*, June 17, 2022, https://www.washingtonpost.com/politics/2022/06/17/john-eastman-pardon-list/.

38. Maggie Haberman, "In Videotaped Testimony, Barr Dismissed Trump's Claims of Fraud," *New York Times*, June 10, 2022, https://www.nytimes.com/2022/06/09/us/bill-bar
-testimony-trump-january-6.html.

39. J. Michael Luttig, "Opening Statement January 6 Hearing," *Politico*, June 16, 2022, https://
www.politico.com/news/2022/06/16/j-michael-luttig-opening-statement-jan-6-hearing
-00040255.

40. Marshall Cohen, "Who Are the Trump Co-Conspirators in the 2020 Election Interference Indictment?," CNN, August 1, 2023, https://www.cnn.com/2023/08/01/politics/co
-conspirators-trump-indictment/index.html.

41. "State Bar Court Hearing Judge Recommends John Eastman's Disbarment," State Bar of California press release, March 27, 2024, https://www.calbar.ca.gov/About-Us/News/News
-Releases/state-bar-court-hearing-judge-recommends-john-eastmans-disbarment.

42. Laura K. Field, "The Author of the 'Coup Memos' Sticks to His Story," *Bulwark*, July 31, 2023, https://www.thebulwark.com/p/john-eastman-sticks-to-his-story; Laura K. Field, "John Eastman: The Dems Made Me Do It," *Bulwark*, August 10, 2023, https://www.thebulwark.com
/p/john-eastman-the-dems-made-me-do.

43. Charles R. Kesler, as quoted in Fisher and Stanley-Becker, "The Claremont Institute Triumphed in the Trump Years."

44. Sophie Ellman-Golan, "Beattie Screenshots January 6, 2021," Twitter, accessed October 30, 2024, https://perma.cc/R9NW-GTZU.

45. Michael Anton, "The Continuing Crisis," *Claremont Review of Books* (Winter 2021), https://claremontreviewofbooks.com/the-continuing-crisis/.

46. Jonathan Chait, "The Future of Conservatism Is Flight 93 Elections Forever," *Intelligencer*, February 23, 2021, https://nymag.com/intelligencer/article/trump-conservatism
-republican-michael-anton-flight-93-election-january-6-insurrection.html.

47. Glenn Ellmers, "'Conservatism' Is No Longer Enough," *American Mind*, March 24, 2021, https://americanmind.org/salvo/why-the-claremont-institute-is-not-conservative-and-you
-shouldnt-be-either/; John Ganz, "The Week in Fascism," *Unpopular Front*, July 23, 2022, https://
www.unpopularfront.news/p/the-week-in-fascism; Merrill, "The Claremont Institute."

48. Christopher Flannery, "John Eastman Is an American Hero," *American Greatness*, August 5, 2022, https://amgreatness.com/2022/08/04/john-eastman-is-an-american-hero/. For more on Flannery, see Laura K. Field, "What the Hell Happened to the Claremont Institute?," *Bulwark*, July 13, 2024, https://www.thebulwark.com/p/what-the-hell-happened-to-the
-claremont-institute.

49. Roger Kimball, "The January 6 Insurrection Hoax," *Imprimis*, October 1, 2021, https://
imprimis.hillsdale.edu/january-6-insurrection-hoax/.

50. CMC, "Charles R. Kesler | Claremont McKenna College," accessed October 11, 2024, https://www.cmc.edu/academic/faculty/profile/charles-r-kesler.

51. R. Shep Melnick, "Claremont's Constitutional Crisis," *Law & Liberty*, March 29, 2021, https://lawliberty.org/book-review/claremonts-constitutional-crisis/.

52. Eastman, "Setting the Record Straight"; Charles R. Kesler, "After January 6th," *Claremont Review of Books* (Winter 2020/2021), https://claremontreviewofbooks.com/after-january-6th/.

53. See Campaign Legal Center, "Results of Lawsuits Regarding the 2020 Elections," accessed October 11, 2024, https://campaignlegal.org/results-lawsuits-regarding-2020-elections.

54. Brian Stelter, "This Infamous Steve Bannon Quote Is Key to Understanding America's Crazy Politics," CNN, November 16, 2021, https://www.cnn.com/2021/11/16/media/steve-bannon-reliable-sources/index.html.

55. Joseph M. Bessette, "A Critique of the Eastman Memos," *Claremont Review of Books* (Fall 2021), https://claremontreviewofbooks.com/critique-eastman-memos/.

56. John Yoo, "The 'Claremont Question,' with Charles Kesler and John Yoo," *Ricochet*, March 17, 2022, https://ricochet.com/podcast/powerline/the-claremont-question-with-charles-kesler-and-john-yoo/.

57. Fisher and Stanley-Becker, "The Claremont Institute Triumphed"; Zerofsky, "How the Claremont Institute Became a Nerve Center."

58. Field, "The Decay at the Claremont Institute Continues." Raw Egg Nationalist continued to publish regularly with *American Mind*, including after his identity was discovered. See Gregory Davis, "Egg-Sposed: We Reveal the Identity of Far Right Bodybuilder 'The Raw Egg Nationalist,'" *HOPE Not Hate*, June 20, 2024, https://hopenothate.org.uk/2024/06/20/egg-sposed-we-reveal-the-identity-of-far-right-bodybuilder-the-raw-egg-nationalist/.

59. This equates circumstances today with a time when millions of people were enslaved. It was a talking point for associates of Claremont Institute. See Emma Green, "The Conservatives Dreading—and Preparing for—Civil War," *Atlantic*, October 1, 2021, https://www.theatlantic.com/politics/archive/2021/10/claremont-ryan-williams-trump/620252/; Angelo Codevilla, "The Cold Civil War," *Claremont Review of Books*, Spring 2017, https://claremontreviewofbooks.com/the-cold-civil-war/; Charles R. Kesler, "America's Cold Civil War," *Imprimis*, October 22, 2018, https://imprimis.hillsdale.edu/americas-cold-civil-war/; Tom Klingenstein, "A Cold Civil War," *TomKlingenstein.com*, October 26, 2022, https://tomklingenstein.com/a-cold-civil-war/; Cameron Joseph, "This Super PAC Wants to Win the 'Cold Civil War' Against 'Woke Communists,'" *Vice*, November 30, 2021, https://www.vice.com/en/article/claremont-institute-thomas-klingenstein-super-pac/.

60. Charles R. Kesler, *Crisis of the Two Constitutions: The Rise, Decline, and Recovery of American Greatness* (Encounter Books, 2021), 382, 398, 383, 384.

61. Melnick, "Claremont's Constitutional Crisis."

62. Rich Lowry, "The Flight 93 Post-Election," *National Review*, January 15, 2021, https://www.nationalreview.com/2021/01/the-flight-93-post-election/; Rich Lowry, "The Crash of the Flight 93 Presidency," *Politico*, January 13, 2021, https://www.politico.com/news/magazine/2021/01/13/the-crash-of-the-flight-93-presidency-459140.

63. Charles R. Kesler, "America's Constitutional Crisis," *Law & Liberty*, May 3, 2021, https://lawliberty.org/americas-constitutional-crisis/.

64. Yoo, "The 'Claremont Question,'"; Andy Kroll, "Revealed: The Billionaires Funding the Coup's Brain Trust," *Rolling Stone*, January 12, 2022, https://www.rollingstone.com/politics/politics-news/devos-bradley-claremont-trump-election-fraud-insurrection-1274253/; O'Brien, "The Far-Right Helped Create."

65. See Laura K. Field, "A Reply to the Claremont Institute's Claim That 'America Is Not Racist,'" Niskanen Center, June 26, 2020, https://www.niskanencenter.org/a-reply-to-the-claremont-institutes-claim-that-america-is-not-racist/.

66. Charles Kesler, "Call Them the 1619 Riots," *New York Post*, June 19, 2020, https://nypost.com/2020/06/19/call-them-the-1619-riots/.

67. See also the signatories of "Liberty and Justice for All: An Open Letter to Fellow Citizens in Defense of American Institutions," *National Review*, September 10, 2020, https://www.nationalreview.com/2020/09/liberty-and-justice-for-all-an-open-letter-to-fellow-citizens-in-defense-of-american-institutions/.

68. Radley Balko painstakingly debunked this conspiracy theory, which was laundered into the mainstream by Coleman Hughes in Bari Weiss's *Free Press* publication in 2023. See Radley Balko, "The Retconning of George Floyd," *The Watch*, January 31, 2024, https://radleybalko.substack.com/p/the-retconning-of-george-floyd.

69. Roger Kimball, "Commentary: The George Floyd Narrative, Unraveled," *Ohio Star*, October 22, 2023, https://theohiostar.com/commentary/commentary-the-george-floyd-narrative-unraveled/ohstarstaff/2023/10/22/.

70. Sohrab Ahmari, "Worse than War: My Night Besieged by Looters and Thugs in NYC," *New York Post*, June 2, 2020, https://nypost.com/2020/06/02/worse-than-war-my-night-besieged-by-looters-and-thugs-in-nyc/.

71. Sohrab Ahmari, "Jan. 6 Looks Different Through the Lens of 'American Carnage,'" *New York Times*, January 6, 2022, https://www.nytimes.com/2022/01/06/opinion/jan-6-trump-us.html.

72. Gladden Pappin, "'The Trouble with Trumpism' Tweet," Twitter, January 6, 2022, https://x.com/gjpappin/status/1479097736481972230; Gladden Pappin, "Pappin on X," January 6, 2022, https://perma.cc/3HLJ-BAG4.

Chapter 8

1. Christopher Rufo, "Critical Race Theory Has Infiltrated the Federal Government," Fox News, YouTube, 2020, https://www.youtube.com/watch?v=rBXRdWflV7M.

2. Christopher F. Rufo, "Obscene Federal 'Diversity Training' Scam Prospers—Even under Trump," *New York Post*, July 16, 2020, https://nypost.com/2020/07/16/obscene-federal-diversity-training-scam-prospers-even-under-trump/; Christopher Rufo, "Rufo Tweet August 2020," August 28, 2020, https://perma.cc/44MX-7BQ4; and Christopher F. Rufo, "Nuclear Consequences," *Christopher F. Rufo*, September 14, 2024, https://christopherrufo.com/p/nuclear-consequences.

3. Benjamin Wallace-Wells, "How a Conservative Activist Invented the Conflict over Critical Race Theory," *New Yorker*, June 18, 2021, https://www.newyorker.com/news/annals-of-inquiry/how-a-conservative-activist-invented-the-conflict-over-critical-race-theory.

4. Betsy DeVos, *Hostages No More: The Fight for Education Freedom and the Future of the American Child* (Center Street, 2022), 258–59; Laura Meckler, "With His 1776 Commission on Patriotism, Trump Helped Spark a Culture War," *Washington Post*, September 2, 2024, https://www.washingtonpost.com/politics/2024/09/02/trump-1776-commission-education/.

5. Claremont Institute, "2017 Lincoln Fellows," accessed October 11, 2024, https://www.claremont.org/2017-lincoln-fellows/; Brian Stelter, "Fox News Segment Prompts Trump to Target Diversity Training," CNN, September 6, 2020, https://www.cnn.com/2020/09/06/media/donald-trump-fox-news-critical-race-theory/index.html.

6. Wallace-Wells, "How a Conservative Activist Invented the Conflict."

7. Trump White House, "Executive Order on Combating Race and Sex Stereotyping—The White House," accessed October 12, 2024, https://trumpwhitehouse.archives.gov/presidential-actions/executive-order-combating-race-sex-stereotyping/.

8. Hailey Fuchs, "Trump Attack on Diversity Training Has a Quick and Chilling Effect," *New York Times*, October 13, 2020, https://www.nytimes.com/2020/10/13/us/politics/trump

-diversity-training-race.html; John Murawski, "No Critical Race Theory in Schools? Here's the Abundant Evidence Saying Otherwise," *Real Clear Investigations*, December 22, 2021, https://www.realclearinvestigations.com/articles/2021/12/22/no_critical_race_theory_in_schools_heres_the_abundant_evidence_saying_otherwise_808528.html. CRT was growing in popularity as a framework for understanding but it does not make the essentialist claims Rufo was constantly attributing to it.

9. See Samuel Hoadley-Brill, "Chris Rufo's Critical Race Theory Reporting Is Filled with Errors, and He Doesn't Seem to Care," *Flux*, July 26, 2021, https://flux.community/samuel-hoadley-brill/2021/07/chris-rufo-obsessed-critical-race-theory-he-also-doesnt-understand-it/. As Zack Beauchamp wrote in a review of Rufo's 2023 book, "His worldview is built on a foundation of exaggerations and misrepresentations—distortions that make it difficult to trust even his basic factual assertions, let alone his big-picture analysis of American society." Zack Beauchamp, "Chris Rufo's Dangerous Fictions," *Vox*, September 10, 2023, https://www.vox.com/23811277/christopher-rufo-culture-wars-ron-desantis-florida-critical-race-theory-anti-wokeness.

10. Fuchs, "Trump Attack on Diversity Training."

11. For an illustrative deep dive into some of the complications and unintended consequences of DEI, see Nicholas Confessore, "The University of Michigan Doubled Down on D.E.I. What Went Wrong?," *New York Times*, October 16, 2024, https://www.nytimes.com/2024/10/16/magazine/dei-university-michigan.html. See also Musa al-Gharbi, *We Have Never Been Woke: The Cultural Contradictions of a New Elite* (Princeton University Press, 2024).

12. Various, "The 1619 Project," *New York Times*, August 14, 2019, https://www.nytimes.com/interachttps://www.nytimes.com/interactive/2019/08/14/magazine/1619-america-slavery.html.

13. The more careful conservative analysts admitted this. See Lucas Morel, "A Review of the 1619 Project Curriculum," Heritage Foundation, December 15, 2020, https://www.heritage.org/progressivism/report/review-the-1619-project-curriculum. In 2020 the *Times* reported that more than four thousand teachers had used the teaching material in their classrooms. In 2022 the National Center for Education Statistics estimated that there were around 3.7 million teachers in America. See Jake Silverstein, "On Recent Criticism of the 1619 Project," *New York Times*, October 16, 2020, https://www.nytimes.com/2020/10/16/magazine/criticism-1619-project.html; National Center for Education Statistics, "The NCES Fast Facts Tool Provides Quick Answers to Many Education Questions," accessed November 4, 2024, https://nces.ed.gov/fastfacts/display.asp?id=372.

14. See, for example, Robby Soave, "Yes, the 1619 Project Actually Suggests That Year Was America's True Founding, and Nikole Hannah-Jones Admits It," *Reason*, September 23, 2020, https://reason.com/2020/09/23/1619-project-nikole-hannah-jones-1776-founding-race-new-york-times/; Jake Silverstein, "Why We Published the 1619 Project," *New York Times*, December 20, 2019, https://www.nytimes.com/interactive/2019/12/20/magazine/1619-intro.html; Phil Magness, "Down the 1619 Project's Memory Hole," *Quillette*, September 19, 2020, https://quillette.com/2020/09/19/down-the-1619-projects-memory-hole/; Nikita Stewart, "Why Can't We Teach Slavery Right in American Schools?," *New York Times*, August 19, 2019, https://www.nytimes.com/interactive/2019/08/19/magazine/slavery-american-schools.html; Morel, "A Review of the 1619 Project Curriculum."

15. "The 1619 Project Exposed: A Special Edition of the American Mind Podcast," *American Mind*, April 27, 2020, https://americanmind.org/audio/the-1619-project-exposed-a-special-edition-of-the-american-mind-podcast/.

16. New Criterion Editors, "1619 & All That," *New Criterion*, December 18, 2019, https://newcriterion.com/article/1619-all-that/.

17. Allen Guelzo, "Preaching a Conspiracy Theory," *City Journal*, December 8, 2019, https://www.city-journal.org/article/preaching-a-conspiracy-theory/.

18. See Frederick Douglass, "Oration of Frederick Douglass Delivered on the Occasion of the Unveiling of the Freedmen's Monument in Memory of Abraham Lincoln," April 14, 1876, in

The Essential Douglass, Nick Buccola (Hackett: 2016); Laura K. Field, "Frederick Douglass' 1876 Report," Niskanen Center, January 27, 2022, https://www.niskanencenter.org/frederick-douglass-1876-report/.

19. Cory Turner, "Week 1: Why America's Schools Have a Money Problem," NPR, April 18, 2016, https://www.npr.org/2016/04/18/474256366/why-americas-schools-have-a-money-problem; Daphne Kenyon, Bethany Paquin, and Semida Munteanu, "Public Schools and the Property Tax: A Comparison of Education Funding Models in Three U.S. States," Lincoln Institute of Land Policy, April 12, 2022.

20. See Neil Gross, *Why Are Professors Liberal and Why Do Conservatives Care?* (Harvard University Press, 2013).

21. Mary Ellen Flannery, "State Funding for Higher Education Still Lagging," National Education Association, October 25, 2022, https://www.nea.org/nea-today/all-news-articles/state-funding-higher-education-still-lagging.

22. Benjamin Schmidt, "The Humanities Are in Crisis," *Atlantic*, August 23, 2018, https://www.theatlantic.com/ideas/archive/2018/08/the-humanities-face-a-crisisof-confidence/567565/; Tyler Austin Harper, "The Humanities Have Sown the Seeds of Their Own Destruction," *Atlantic*, December 19, 2023, https://www.theatlantic.com/ideas/archive/2023/12/humanities-university-conservative-critics/676890/.

23. See Yascha Mounk, *The Identity Trap: A Story of Ideas and Power in Our Time* (Penguin Press, 2023).

24. Rita Felski, *The Limits of Critique* (University of Chicago Press, 2015), 9, 10, 9, 4, 10. Felski writes: "What afflicts literary studies is not interpretation as such but the kudzu-like proliferation of a hypercritical style of analysis that has crowded out alternative forms of intellectual life." Earlier, quoting Oxford's Helen Small, she named some of these alternative forms: "the work of the humanities is frequently descriptive, or appreciative, or provocative, or speculative, more than it is critical."

25. Montás, *Rescuing Socrates*, 3, 107, 87, 87, 34.

26. See Nietzsche, "On the Uses and Abuses of History for Life."

27. See, for example, Hillsdale College, "The Good, the True, and the Beautiful," *Hillsdale College*, March 10, 2016, https://www.hillsdale.edu/hillsdale-blog/academics/classical-liberal-arts/good-true-beautiful/.

28. "White House Conference on American History," YouTube, 2020, https://www.youtube.com/watch?v=0RLdpptscHs.

29. Hillsdale College, "Larry P. Arnn," accessed October 11, 2024, https://gradschool.hillsdale.edu/Profiles/Larry-P-Arnn/; and "Course Catalog | Hillsdale College Online Courses," accessed October 12, 2024, https://online.hillsdale.edu/.

30. C-SPAN, "White House Conference on American History," September 17, 2020, https://www.c-span.org/video/?476072-1/white-house-conference-american-history.

31. Trump White House, "Executive Order 13958—Establishing the President's Advisory 1776 Commission," November 2, 2020, https://www.presidency.ucsb.edu/documents/executive-order-13958-establishing-the-presidents-advisory-1776-commission.

32. See Matthew Spalding, "The Farewell Address: Washington's Forgotten Legacy" (ProQuest Dissertations & Theses, 1995), https://www.proquest.com/openview/ea8eabe2d79a6b dfbefb10e1a8f598b2/1.

33. Meckler, "With His 1776 Commission."

34. See Trump White House, "President Donald J. Trump Is Protecting America's Founding Ideals by Promoting Patriotic Education," November 2, 2020, https://trumpwhitehouse.archives.gov/briefings-statements/president-donald-j-trump-protecting-americas-founding-ideals-promoting-patriotic-education/.

35. Nicole Hoplin and Ron Robinson, *Funding Fathers: The Unsung Heroes of the Conservative Movement* (Regnery, 2008), 177.

36. Hillsdale College, "Hillsdale College: History," accessed October 12, 2024, https://www.hillsdale.edu/about/history/; Erik Eckholm, "In Hillsdale College, a 'Shining City on a Hill' for Conservatives," *New York Times*, February 1, 2017, https://www.nytimes.com/2017/02/01/education/edlife/hillsdale-college-great-books-constitution-conservatives.html.

37. Mary Catherine Meyer, "Kirk Should Be on the Liberty Walk," *Hillsdale Collegian*, February 25, 2016, https://hillsdalecollegian.com/2016/02/25637/.

38. Hillsdale College, "Collections," accessed October 11, 2024, https://lib.hillsdale.edu/about/collections/.

39. Robyn Meredith, "Scandal Rocks a Conservative Campus," *New York Times*, November 15, 1999, https://www.nytimes.com/1999/11/15/us/scandal-rocks-a-conservative-campus.html.

40. Hillsdale College, "Larry P. Arnn."

41. See Hillsdale College, "Barney Charter School Initiative," accessed November 5, 2024, https://k12.hillsdale.edu/Schools/BCSI/.

42. Hillsdale College, "Hillsdale College Homepage," accessed October 12, 2024, https://www.hillsdale.edu/.

43. See "About Online Courses | Hillsdale College Online Courses," accessed March 25, 2025, https://online.hillsdale.edu/about.

44. Hillsdale College, "The Young Jane Austen: Northanger Abbey," accessed October 11, 2024, https://online.hillsdale.edu/courses/promo/jane-austen.

45. See Landmark Legal, "About Landmark Legal Foundation," accessed October 11, 2024, https://landmarklegal.org/about-landmark-legal-foundation/.

46. Arnn was no longer on this board as of 2014. Center for Individual Rights, "CIR Board of Directors," August 10, 2013, https://web.archive.org/web/20130810074731/http://cir-usa.org/board.html; "Board," Center for Individual Rights, March 15, 2016, https://web.archive.org/web/20160315174641/https://www.cir-usa.org/board/.

47. Tim Mak, "Heritage Foundation Gets Tough: Think Tank Puts Punch Behind Its Conservative Ideas," *Washington Examiner*, September 13, 2013, https://www.washingtonexaminer.com/politics/183856/heritage-foundation-gets-tough-think-tank-puts-punch-behind-its-conservative-ideas/; "About," Intercollegiate Studies Institute, accessed October 8, 2024, https://isi.org/about/.

48. SPLC, "The Council for National Policy: Behind the Curtain," Southern Poverty Law Center, May 17, 2016, https://www.splcenter.org/hatewatch/2016/05/17/council-national-policy-behind-curtain.

49. See Andrea Suozzo Roberts et al., "Hillsdale College, Full Filing—Nonprofit Explorer," ProPublica, May 9, 2013, https://projects.propublica.org/nonprofits/organizations/381374230/202341329349308244/full; Matthew Miller, "Donations Soar 85 Percent at Trump-Supporting Michigan College Since 2017," *mlive*, September 13, 2023, https://www.mlive.com/news/2023/09/as-hillsdale-colleges-national-profile-rose-in-the-waning-days-of-the-trump-era-donations-spiked.html.

50. See Thomas Novelly, "Trump Chooses DeVos over Arnn for Education Secretary," *Hillsdale Collegian*, December 1, 2016, https://hillsdalecollegian.com/2016/12/trump-chooses-devos-arnn-education-secretary/.

51. Hillsdale College, "Hillsdale College Launches Van Andel Graduate School of Government in Washington, DC," *Spaces4Learning*, September 25, 2019, https://spaces4learning.com/Articles/2019/09/25/Hillsdale-College-DC.aspx.

52. Rob Crilly, "Trump's 1776 Commission Hears Plea to Make Judeo-Christian Principles Central to American Story," *Washington Examiner*, January 5, 2021, https://www.washingtonexaminer.com/news/1844625/trumps-1776-commission-hears-plea-to-make-judeo-christian-principles-central-to-american-story/; Federal Register, "President's Advisory

1776 Commission," January 12, 2021, https://www.federalregister.gov/documents/2021/01/12/2021-00525/presidents-advisory-1776-commission; Joshua Tait, "The Origins of Trump's Slapdash, Last-Second '1776 Report,'" *Bulwark*, January 22, 2021, https://www.thebulwark.com/p/the-origins-of-trumps-slapdash-last-second-1776-report.

53. See "1776 Commission Meeting 2 Recording," US Department of Education January 15, 2021, https://www.ed.gov/sites/ed/files/about/bdscomm/list/1776/011521-meeting.mp3.

54. Pierre-Antoine Louis and Nikole Hannah-Jones, "'No People Has a Greater Claim to That Flag than Us': Interview with Nikole Hannah-Jones," *New York Times*, September 6, 2019, https://www.nytimes.com/2019/09/06/us/nikole-hannah-jones-interview.html.

55. Meckler, "With His 1776 Commission."

56. Meckler, "With His 1776 Commission," 10.

57. Trump White House, "1776 Commission Report," 15, https://trumpwhitehouse.archives.gov/briefings-statements/1776-commission-takes-historic-scholarly-step-restore-understanding-greatness-american-founding/.

58. See, for example, U.S. Department of the Treasury, "Racial Inequality in the United States," September 20, 2024, https://home.treasury.gov/news/featured-stories/racial-inequality-in-the-united-states.

59. Trump White House, "1776 Commission Report," 37, emphasis mine.

60. Kesler's fullest discussion of slavery takes place in chap. 10, "From Citizenship to Multiculturalism." See Kesler, *Crisis of the Two Constitutions*, 225.

61. Kesler, *Crisis of the Two Constitutions*, 84.

62. See Jaffa, "Equality as a Conservative Principle," 492.

63. Kesler, *Crisis of the Two Constitutions*, 100.

64. Melnick, "Claremont's Constitutional Crisis."

65. Christopher Caldwell, *The Age of Entitlement: America Since the Sixties* (Simon & Schuster, 2020).

66. Jonathan Rauch, "Did the Civil Rights Movement Go Wrong?," *New York Times*, January 17, 2020, https://www.nytimes.com/2020/01/17/books/review/christopher-caldwell-age-of-entitlement.html.

67. Christopher Caldwell, "There Goes Robert E. Lee," *Claremont Review of Books* (Spring 2021), https://claremontreviewofbooks.com/there-goes-robert-e-lee/.

68. Reno, *Return of the Strong Gods*.

69. Deneen, *Regime Change*, 201–3, quote on 202 (emphasis in original).

70. See al-Gharbi, *We Have Never Been Woke*; and Jason Blakely, "The Thin Line Between 'Postliberalism' and Theocracy," *Chronicle of Higher Education*, August 2, 2023, https://www.chronicle.com/article/the-thin-line-between-postliberalism-and-theocracy.

71. See Hillsdale College, "Hillsdale College Releases 1776 Curriculum," *Hillsdale College*, accessed October 11, 2024, https://www.hillsdale.edu/news-and-media/press-releases/hillsdale-college-releases-1776-curriculum/.

72. See Hillsdale K–12, "FAQ," accessed October 11, 2024, https://k12.hillsdale.edu/About/FAQ/.

73. Elissa Salamy, "Hillsdale College's 1776 Curriculum Focuses on 'Evidence,' Says Assistant Provost," WUTV, July 23, 2021, https://wutv29.com/news/nation-world/hillsdale-colleges-1776-curriculum-focuses-on-evidence-says-assistant-provost.

74. Adam Hochschild, "History Bright and Dark," *New York Review of Books*, May 25, 2023, https://www.nybooks.com/articles/2023/05/25/history-bright-and-dark-hillsdale-1776-curriculum-1619-project/.

75. Richard Delgado and Jean Stefancic, *Critical Race Theory: An Introduction*, 2nd ed. (NYU Press, 1984).

Chapter 9

1. Sessions shared the original notes with me. David Sessions, "David Sessions Tweet Clubhouse Meeting," May 11, 2022, https://perma.cc/FG8W-YUPF. See Helen Roy, "Helen Roy David Sessions Tweet," May 11, 2022, https://perma.cc/HL5Y-PVHZ; Matthew Peterson, "Matthew Peterson David Sessions Clubhouse Notes," Twitter, May 11, 2022, https://perma.cc/3HH6-MSZJ; "Rufo Peterson Shideler Poulos Williams Sessions Clubhouse Notes," March 19, 2021, https://perma.cc/9FP6-2FTH.

2. Williams was the president of the institute. Peterson and James Poulos founded and edited the *American Mind* (and Peterson had been the institute's vice president of education). Fischer was a friend and business partner to Peterson. Reaboi had been a Lincoln Fellow in 2012 and was a fellow at the institute. Shideler attended the Lincoln Fellows program in 2017, alongside Rufo.

3. Samuel Hoadley-Brill, "Christopher Rufo: Professional Bullshit Artist," *Conceptual Disinformation*, May 25, 2021, https://conceptualdisinformation.substack.com/p/chris-rufo-professional-bullshit.

4. Books in this genre include Helen Pluckrose and James Lindsay, *Cynical Theories: How Activist Scholarship Made Everything about Race, Gender, and Identity—and Why This Harms Everybody* (Pitchstone Publishing, 2022); Richard Hanania, *The Origins of Woke: Civil Rights Law, Corporate America, and the Triumph of Identity Politics* (Broadside Books, 2023); Yascha Mounk, *The Identity Trap: A Story of Ideas and Power in Our Time* (Penguin Press, 2023).

5. Michelle Alexander, *The New Jim Crow: Mass Incarceration in the Age of Colorblindness*, 10th anniversary ed. (New Press, 2020).

6. Ta-Nehisi Coates, "The Case for Reparations," *Atlantic*, May 22, 2014, https://www.theatlantic.com/magazine/archive/2014/06/the-case-for-reparations/361631/.

7. "What Happened in Ferguson?," *New York Times*, August 13, 2014, https://www.nytimes.com/interactive/2014/08/13/us/ferguson-missouri-town-under-siege-after-police-shooting.html.

8. The "long march" idea was first developed by Rudi Dutschke, a German sociologist and activist, in the 1960s. It is sometimes associated with the cultural theories of the Italian Marxist Antonio Gramsci. See Herbert Marcuse, *Counterrevolution and Revolt* (Beacon Press, 1972), 55–56.

9. Christopher F. Rufo, *America's Cultural Revolution: How the Radical Left Conquered Everything* (Broadside Books, 2023).

10. For more on Rufo's dishonesty, see Wallace-Wells, "How a Conservative Activist Invented the Conflict Over Critical Race Theory"; Beauchamp, "Chris Rufo's Dangerous Fictions."

11. Beauchamp, "Chris Rufo's Dangerous Fictions." See also Jonathan Chait, "Conservatives Have a New Master Theory of American Politics," *Intelligencer*, July 26, 2023, https://nymag.com/intelligencer/2023/07/long-march-through-institutions-conservatives-rufo-milikh-claremont-desantis-trump.html.

12. Christopher Rufo, "Laying Siege to Elite Institutions," *City Journal*, May 24, 2022, https://www.city-journal.org/article/laying-siege-to-the-institutions.

13. Rufo, *America's Cultural Revolution*, 280.

14. Rufo, *America's Cultural Revolution*, 282.

15. Samantha Lock, "Donald Trump's CPAC Speech Transcript in Full," *Newsweek*, March 1, 2021, https://www.newsweek.com/donald-trump-cpac-speech-transcript-full-gop-biden-facebook-1572719.

16. Tyler Kingkade, Brandy Zadrozny, and Ben Collins, "'Held Hostage': How Critical Race Theory Moved from Fox News to School Boards," *NBC News*, June 15, 2021, https://www.nbcnews.com/news/us-news/critical-race-theory-invades-school-boards-help-conservative

-groups-n1270794; John Nichols, "The School Board Culture War," *Nation*, May 20, 2022, https://www.thenation.com/article/society/the-school-board-culture-war/.

17. Sanford, "Trump's February 28th Speech."

18. Manhattan Institute, "Woke Schooling: A Toolkit for Concerned Parents," *Manhattan Institute*, June 17, 2021, https://manhattan.institute/article/woke-schooling-a-toolkit-for-concerned-parents/.

19. Carly Mayberry, "Hillsdale College's '1776' Curriculum Contrasts 1619 Project," *Newsweek*, August 18, 2021, https://www.newsweek.com/college-launches-1776-curriculum-counter-critical-race-theory-1620714.

20. Sarah Schwartz, "Map: Where Critical Race Theory Is Under Attack," *Education Week*, June 11, 2021, https://www.edweek.org/policy-politics/map-where-critical-race-theory-is-under-attack/2021/06.

21. Hannah Natanson and Moriah Balingit, "Caught in the Culture Wars, Teachers Are Being Forced from Their Jobs," *Washington Post*, June 16, 2022, https://www.washingtonpost.com/education/2022/06/16/teacher-resignations-firings-culture-wars/.

22. Sarah Mervosh and Giulia Heyward, "The School Culture Wars: 'You Have Brought Division to Us,'" *New York Times*, August 18, 2021, https://www.nytimes.com/2021/08/18/us/schools-covid-critical-race-theory-masks-gender.html.

23. See Valerie Hopkins, "Campus in Hungary Is Flagship of Orban's Bid to Create a Conservative Elite," *New York Times*, June 28, 2021, https://www.nytimes.com/2021/06/28/world/europe/hungary-orban-university.html.

24. Lauren Kent and Samantha Tapfumaneyi, "Hungary's PM Bans Gender Study at Colleges Saying 'People Are Born Either Male or Female,'" CNN, October 19, 2018, https://www.cnn.com/2018/10/19/europe/hungary-bans-gender-study-at-colleges-trnd/index.html; Benjamin Novak, "Pushed from Hungary, University Created by Soros Shifts to Vienna," *New York Times*, November 15, 2019, https://www.nytimes.com/2019/11/15/world/europe/university-soros-vienna-orban.html; Benjamin Novak, "Hungary Transfers 11 Universities to Foundations Led by Orban Allies," *New York Times*, April 28, 2021, https://www.nytimes.com/2021/04/27/world/europe/hungary-universities-orban.html.

25. "Facebook Live Dreher Deneen in Hungary," Facebook, June 28, 2021, https://www.facebook.com/watch/live/?v=158843492853549&ref=watch_permalink.

26. National Conservatism, "Conference Schedule Natcon 2021," *National Conservatism Conference*, 2021, https://nationalconservatism.org/natcon-2-2021/conference-schedule/.

27. Lisa Lerer, "The Unlikely Issue Shaping the Virginia Governor's Race: Schools," *New York Times*, October 12, 2021, https://www.nytimes.com/2021/10/12/us/politics/virginia-governor-republicans-schools.html.

28. Karen Tumulty, "McAuliffe Ended up Dancing to Youngkin's Choreography," *Washington Post*, November 3, 2021, https://www.washingtonpost.com/opinions/2021/11/03/mcauliffe-ended-up-dancing-youngkins-choreography/.

29. Christopher Rufo, "Rufo Tweet Youngkin," September 2, 2021, https://perma.cc/8F2E-8D5H.

30. Lisa Lerer and Reid J. Epstein, "G.O.P. Attack Involving Toni Morrison Novel Inflames Virginia Contest," *New York Times*, October 27, 2021, https://www.nytimes.com/2021/10/27/us/politics/beloved-toni-morrison-virginia.html.

31. Brendan Farrington and Anthony Izaguirre, "Florida Expands 'Don't Say Gay'; House OKs Anti-LGBTQ Bills," *AP News*, April 19, 2023, https://apnews.com/article/desantis-florida-dont-say-gay-ban-684ed25a303f83208a89c556543183cb.

32. Leah Watson, "Lessons Learned from Our Classroom Censorship Win Against Florida's Stop W.O.K.E. Act," ACLU, November 29, 2022, https://www.aclu.org/news/free-speech/lessons-learned-from-our-classroom-censorship-win-against-floridas-stop-w-o-k-e-act.

33. Farrington and Izaguirre, "Florida Expands 'Don't Say Gay.'"

34. Staff, "Gov. DeSantis Proposes Reestablishing Florida State Guard Civilian Volunteer Force," *News4Jax*, December 2, 2021, https://www.news4jax.com/news/florida/2021/12/02/gov-desantis-proposes-reestablishing-florida-state-guard-civilian-volunteer-force/.

35. Kathryn Joyce, "The Far Right's National Plan for Schools: Plant Charters, Defund Public Education," *Salon*, March 17, 2022, https://www.salon.com/2022/03/17/the-far-rights-national-plan-for-schools-plant-charters-defund-public-education/; Katie LaGrone, "Classical Education Charter Schools on the Rise in Florida with Help from Small, Conservative Michigan College," *ABC Action News Tampa Bay*, August 11, 2022, https://www.abcactionnews.com/news/state/classical-education-charter-schools-on-the-rise-in-florida-with-help-from-small-conservative-michigan-college.

36. Doug Lederman, "Hillsdale Leader's Slurs of Teacher Preparation Stoke Tennessee Controversy," *Inside Higher Ed*, July 5, 2022, https://www.insidehighered.com/news/2022/07/05/hillsdale-leaders-comments-teachers-spur-tenn-controversy.

37. See Joyce, "The Far Right's National Plan." For further perspective on charter schools and classical schools, see Emma Green, "Have the Liberal Arts Gone Conservative?," *New Yorker*, March 11, 2024, https://www.newyorker.com/magazine/2024/03/18/have-the-liberal-arts-gone-conservative.

38. Valerie Strauss, "DeSantis Moves to Turn a Progressive Fla. College Into a Conservative One," *Washington Post*, January 7, 2023, https://www.washingtonpost.com/education/2023/01/07/new-college-florida-desantis-rufo/.

39. Christopher Rufo, "University DEI Programs Work Against Liberal Education," *New York Times*, July 27, 2023, https://www.nytimes.com/2023/07/27/opinion/christopher-rufo-diversity-desantis-florida-university.html.

40. Michelle Goldberg, "This Is What the Right-Wing Takeover of a Progressive College Looks Like," *New York Times*, April 29, 2023, https://www.nytimes.com/2023/04/29/opinion/new-college-florida-republican-desantis.html.

41. Carlos Suarez and Nicquel Terry Ellis, "Students, Professors Report Chaos as Semester Begins at New College of Florida," CNN, August 26, 2023, https://www.cnn.com/2023/08/26/us/new-college-of-florida-chaos-reaj/index.html.

42. Zack Beauchamp, "Ron DeSantis Is Following a Trail Blazed by a Hungarian Authoritarian," *Vox*, April 28, 2022, https://www.vox.com/policy-and-politics/2022/4/28/23037788/ron-desantis-florida-viktor-orban-hungary-right-authoritarian; Ishaan Tharoor, "The Orbanization of America," *Washington Post*, May 18, 2022, https://www.washingtonpost.com/world/2022/05/18/cpac-hungary-lgbtq-orban-florida-desantis/.

43. See Christopher Rufo, "What Conservatives See in Hungary," *Compact*, July 28, 2023, https://www.compactmag.com/article/what-conservatives-see-in-hungary/; Creede Newton, "Contracts Between Hungarian Nonprofit and Christopher Rufo, Others, Raise Foreign Agent Concerns: Expert," SPLC, December 13, 2023, https://www.splcenter.org/resources/hatewatch/contracts-between-hungarian-nonprofit-and-christopher-rufo-others-raise-foreign-agent/.

44. NatCon, "National Conservatism Conference 3 Program 2022 Miami," accessed April 25, 2025, https://nationalconservatism.org/natcon-3-2022/.

45. Kevin Richert, "Boise State Professor Scott Yenor Takes a Florida-Based Job with a Conservative Think Tank," *Idaho Capital Sun*, February 9, 2023, https://idahocapitalsun.com/2023/02/09/boise-state-professor-scott-yenor-takes-a-florida-based-job-with-a-conservative-think-tank/.

46. Disney challenged this in court, and it was settled in March 2024. Mike Schneider, "Settlement Reached Lawsuit Between Disney and Florida Gov. Ron DeSantis' Allies," *AP News*, March 27, 2024, https://apnews.com/article/disney-florida-ron-desantis-settlement-91040178ad4708939e621dd57bc5e494.

47. Maggie Taylor, "The Enduring Power and Impact of Dove's 'Real Beauty' Campaign," *Strixus*, February 22, 2023, https://strixus.com/entry/the-enduring-power-and-impact-of-doves-real-beauty-campaign-18095.

48. Thank you to Danny Fine for help with this section. See also Rebecca Leber, "The weird Republican turn against corporate social responsibility," *Vox*, December 10, 2022, https://www.vox.com/energy-and-environment/2022/12/10/23496712/esg-gop-climate-corporate-responsibility.

49. Deborah Nason, "'Sustainable Investing' Is Surging, Accounting for 33% of Total U.S. Assets under Management," CNBC, December 21, 2020, https://www.cnbc.com/2020/12/21/sustainable-investing-accounts-for-33percent-of-total-us-assets-under-management.html; Lauren Cohen, Umit G. Gurun, and Quoc Nguyen, "It's Time to Change How ESG Is Measured," *Harvard Business Review*, July 10, 2024, https://hbr.org/2024/07/its-time-to-change-how-esg-is-measured.

50. "Texas Comptroller Glenn Hegar Announces List of Financial Companies That Boycott Energy Companies," Texas Comptroller of Public Accounts, August 24, 2022, https://comptroller.texas.gov/about/media-center/news/20220824-texas-comptroller-glenn-hegar-announces-list-of-financial-companies-that-boycott-energy-companies-1661267815099.

51. Karen Rives, "Half of Anti-ESG Bills in Red States Have Failed in 2023 as Campaign Pushes On," *S&P Global*, June 28, 2023, https://www.spglobal.com/marketintelligence/en/news-insights/latest-news-headlines/half-of-anti-esg-bills-in-red-states-have-failed-in-2023-as-campaign-pushes-on-76276575.

52. *American Reformer*, "About Page," accessed October 12, 2024, https://perma.cc/6J2U-8AL9.

53. John Hyatt, "How Vivek Ramaswamy Became a Billionaire," *Forbes*, August 21, 2023, https://www.forbes.com/sites/johnhyatt/2023/08/21/how-vivek-ramaswamy-became-a-billionaire/.

54. Strive, "Strive—Invest in Excellence," accessed October 12, 2024, https://strive.com/the-strive-story.

55. "2ndVote Value Investments Appoints Andy Puzder as Executive Chairman of the Board of Directors," *Business Wire*, December 6, 2021, https://www.businesswire.com/news/home/20211206005238/en/2ndVote-Value-Investments-Appoints-Andy-Puzder-as-Executive-Chairman-of-the-Board-of-Directors.

56. 2nd Vote Funds, "2ND VOTE FUNDS to Close Its 2ndVote Life Neutral ETF (LYFE) and 2ndVote Society Defended ETF (EGIS)," August 2, 2023, https://finance.yahoo.com/news/2nd-vote-funds-close-2ndvote-214900811.html/.

57. Andy Puzder, "ESG Investing Is an Attack on the Free Market—NatCon 3," YouTube, September 11, 2022, https://www.youtube.com/watch?v=7vUoBceqLG0&t=797s.

58. Mike Pence, "Republicans Can Stop ESG Political Bias," *Wall Street Journal*, May 26, 2022, https://www.wsj.com/articles/only-republicans-can-stop-the-esg-madness-woke-musk-consumer-demand-free-speech-corporate-america-11653574189.

59. "Biden Uses First Veto to Defend Rule on ESG Investing," *Reuters*, March 20, 2023, https://www.reuters.com/business/sustainable-business/biden-vetoes-resolution-block-labor-dept-rule-esg-investing-2023-03-20/.

60. Gladden Pappin, "Gladden Pappin Tweet on Heritage and Hungary," April 12, 2024, https://perma.cc/UNG5-BVM2.

61. Kevin Roberts, "The Second American Revolution," YouTube, 2022, https://www.youtube.com/watch?v=kbh-4q2nr4k.

62. This followed on the heels of the creation of Heritage Action—an activist sister organization to the think tank—in 2010. Jennifer Steinhauer and Jonathan Weisman, "In the DeMint Era at Heritage, a Shift from Policy to Politics," *New York Times*, February 24, 2014, https://www.nytimes.com/2014/02/24/us/politics/in-the-demint-era-at-heritage-a-shift-from-policy-to-politics.html; Eliana Johnson and Nancy Cook, "The Real Reason Jim DeMint Got the Boot," *Politico*, May 2, 2017, https://www.politico.com/story/2017/05/02/why-jim-demint-was-ousted-from-heritage-237876.

63. Heritage Foundation, "Trump Administration Embraces Heritage Foundation Policy Recommendations," January 23, 2018, https://www.heritage.org/impact/trump-administration -embraces-heritage-foundation-policy-recommendations; Katie Glueck, "Trump's Shadow Transition Team," *Politico*, November 22, 2016, https://www.politico.com/story/2016/11 /trump-transition-heritage-foundation-231722.

64. Kim R. Holmes, "Donald Trump: At Home in Postmodern America," *Public Discourse*, December 14, 2015, https://www.thepublicdiscourse.com/2015/12/16133/; "Heritage Foundation Taps Kim Holmes as Executive Vice President," Heritage Foundation, February 6, 2018, https://www.heritage.org/press/heritage-foundation-taps-kim-holmes-executive-vice-president; Kim Holmes, "The Problem of Nationalism," Heritage Foundation, December 13, 2019, https://www.heritage.org/conservatism/commentary/the-problem-nationalism.

65. Holmes, "The Problem of Nationalism"; Kim Holmes, "Why American Exceptionalism Is Different from Other Countries' 'Nationalisms,'" Heritage Foundation, September 29, 2020, https://www.heritage.org/american-founders/commentary/why-american -exceptionalism-different-other-countries-nationalisms. See also Kim R. Holmes, "The Fallacies of the Common Good," *New Criterion*, December 22, 2021, https://newcriterion.com/article /the-fallacies-of-the-common-good/.

66. Kay Coles James, "How America Can Stand for Peace While Demanding Justice," Heritage Foundation, May 31, 2020, https://www.heritage.org/civil-society/commentary/how -america-can-stand-peace-while-demanding-justice.

67. Andrew R. Kloster, "Whither Heritage?," *American Conservative*, March 23, 2021, https:// www.theamericanconservative.com/whither-heritage/; Josh Hammer, "Yesterday's Man, Yesterday's Conservatism," *New Criterion*, December 22, 2021, https://newcriterion.com/article /yesterdays-man-yesterdays-conservatism/.

68. Graham, "The New Lost Cause."

69. Shikha Dalmia, "Faced with Trump, Libertarianism Shrugged," *Bulwark*, November 8, 2024, https://www.thebulwark.com/p/how-trump-killed-libertarianism. See Andrew Kirell, "Anti-'Cancel Culture' Reason Magazine Accused of Canceling Columnist for Being Too Anti-Trump," *Daily Beast*, December 2, 2020, https://www.thedailybeast.com/anti-cancel-culture -reason-magazine-accused-of-canceling-shikha-dalmia-for-being-too-anti-trump; Shikha Sood Dalmia, "After 15 Years, the Curtains Came Down for Me at Reason . . . ," Facebook, December 1, 2020, https://www.facebook.com/shikha.sood.dalmia/posts/10157660285662918. The Liberty Fund experienced its own controversies, with tragic consequences. See Damon Linker, "A Libertarian Tragedy in Indianapolis," *The Week*, January 26, 2022, https://theweek.com /libertarian/1009440/a-libertarian-tragedy-in-indianapolis; Adam Wren, "The Pursuits of Liberty," *Indianapolis Monthly*, January 23, 2022, https://www.indianapolismonthly.com /longform/the-pursuits-of-liberty/.

70. NR Symposium, "Conservatives against Trump," *National Review*, January 21, 2016, https://www.nationalreview.com/2016/01/donald-trump-conservatives-oppose-nomination /; Editors, "The Promise of Ron DeSantis," *National Review*, May 25, 2023, https://www .nationalreview.com/2023/05/the-promise-of-ron-desantis-2/.

71. "My First Vote for Trump," *National Review*, November 5, 2024, https://www.national review.com/2024/11/my-first-vote-for-trump/.

72. Thank you to Stephanie Slade for helpful insights into these institutional dynamics.

73. Jason Wilson, "Revealed: The Extremist Maga Lobbying Group Driving Far-Right Republican Policies," *Guardian*, May 23, 2024, https://www.theguardian.com/us-news/article /2024/may/23/conservative-partnership-institute-republican-laws.

74. "The Meticulous, Ruthless Preparations for a Second Trump Term," *Economist*, July 13, 2023, https://www.economist.com/briefing/2023/07/13/the-meticulous-ruthless -preparations-for-a-second-trump-term.

75. Heritage Foundation, "Mandate for Leadership: The Conservative Promise, Project 2025," 2023, https://perma.cc/XQ23-PYCZ.

76. See Thomas Zimmer, "What 'Project 2025' Would Do to America," *Democracy Americana*, February 29, 2024, https://thomaszimmer.substack.com/p/what-project-2025-would-do-to-america.

77. These programs are based at the Foundation for Excellence in Higher Education (FEHE Network), https://excellenceinhighered.org/network/. See Gareth Gore, *Opus* (Simon and Schuster, 2024), 222–27, 291ff.

78. For example, Pinkoski referred throughout to Pope Pius XII's "Summi Pontificatus," an encyclical "On the Unity of Human Society." At one point he quotes this sentence from para. 72: "A disposition in fact of the divinely sanctioned order, divides the human race into social groups, nations or states, which are mutually independent in organization and in the direction of their internal life." But then he omits the qualification that immediately follows: "But for all that, the human race is bound together by reciprocal ties, moral and juridical, into a great commonwealth directed to the good of all nations and ruled by special laws which protect its unity and promote its prosperity." Similarly, compare Pinkoski's quote of para. 49 with the beautiful part that he ignores (including para. 50). Pope Pius XII, *Summi Pontificatus*, encyclical, October 20, 1939, Vatican.va, https://www.vatican.va/content/pius-xii/en/encyclicals/documents/hf_p-xii_enc_20101939_summi-pontificatus.html.

79. Nathan Pinkoski, "Catholicism and the Necessity of Nationalism," YouTube, 2022, https://www.youtube.com/watch?v=LtmGrXbKoQY.

80. Nathan Pinkoski, "Spiritual Death of the West," *First Things*, May 1, 2023, https://www.firstthings.com/article/2023/05/spiritual-death-of-the-west; L0m3z, "What Is the Longhouse?," *First Things*, February 16, 2023, https://www.firstthings.com/web-exclusives/2023/02/what-is-the-longhouse.

81. Deneen, "Patrick Deneen Tweet on L0m3z," September 19, 2023, https://perma.cc/Q9HZ-3SW5.

82. See L0m3z, "What Is the Longhouse?"; Jason Wilson, "Revealed: US University Lecturer Behind Far-Right Twitter Account and Publishing House," *Guardian*, May 14, 2024, https://www.theguardian.com/world/article/2024/may/14/far-right-twitter-identity-revealed; Ali Breland, "The Far Right's New 'Badge of Honor,'" *Atlantic*, June 10, 2024, https://www.theatlantic.com/technology/archive/2024/06/doxxing-far-right-influencers-anonymity/678645/; "Jonathan Keeperman: Dissident Artists and Publishing Are Creating a New Culture," YouTube, 2024, https://www.youtube.com/watch?v=2dHtMM-8myU; Paul Gottfried, "Waving Goodbye to an Expendable Ally," YouTube, 2024, https://www.youtube.com/watch?v=4JxCNsw69ck.

83. Hamilton Center, "Center Based Faculty," Internet Archive, May 2023, https://web.archive.org/web/20230530021304/https://hamilton.center.ufl.edu/people/center-based-faculty/; Garrett Shanley, "A GOP-Backed Center Stoked Faculty Paranoia at the U. of Florida. Then Ben Sasse Got Mad," *Chronicle of Higher Education*, November 4, 2024, https://www-chronicle-com.eu1.proxy.openathens.net/article/oath-of-fealty.

84. See Christopher Caldwell, "How to Think About Vladimir Putin," *Imprimis*, March 9, 2017, https://imprimis.hillsdale.edu/how-to-think-about-vladimir-putin/.

85. David Reaboi, "Reaboi Tweet Re: Putin," February 26, 2022, https://perma.cc/RKK3-8NKR.

86. For more on Hazony's choices here, see chap. 5, 108–110.

87. Michael Walzer, "Notes on a Dangerous Mistake," *Liberties*, January 2, 2024, https://libertiesjournal.com/articles/notes-on-a-dangerous-mistake/.

88. Its mission was to promote "a strong social-democratic state that defends community—local and national, familial and religious—against a libertine left and a libertarian right." Aponte

was out within a few months. See "Losing the Plot: The 'Leftists' Who Turn Right," *In These Times*, December 12, 2023, https://inthesetimes.com/article/former-left-right-fascism -capitalism-horseshoe-theory.

89. Sohrab Ahmari, "The Return of Liberal Nationalism," *Compact*, May 12, 2022, https:// www.compactmag.com/article/the-return-of-liberal-nationalism/.

90. Various, "Away From the Abyss," *Compact*, March 31, 2022, https://www.compactmag .com/article/away-from-the-abyss/.

91. "National Conservatism: A Statement of Principles," *National Conservatism*, accessed October 12, 2024, https://nationalconservatism.org/national-conservatism-a-statement-of -principles/. Signatories included Michael Anton, Larry Arnn, David Azerrad, Rod Dreher, Paul Gottfried, Victor Davis Hanson, Tom Klingenstein, Arthur Milikh, Joshua Mitchell, Matthew Peterson, Nathan Pinkoski, David Reaboi, Christopher Rufo, Peter Thiel, Scott Yenor, and Ryan Williams. And it included a growing set of New Right influencers: Rachel Bovard, Josh Hammer, Julie Kelly, Charlie Kirk, Michael Knowles, Amanda Milius, and Saurabh Sharma.

92. Ahmari was consistent on this point. See Sohrab Ahmari, "Trump Will Have to Choose: Populism or Elon Musk," *New Statesman*, August 15, 2024, https://www.newstatesman.com /comment/2024/08/trump-will-have-to-choose-populism-or-elon-musk.

93. Heritage began cultivating ties to Hungary. Flora Garamvolgyi and David Smith, "Republicans to Meet Allies of Hungary's Viktor Orbán on Ending Ukraine Aid," *Guardian*, December 10, 2023, https://www.theguardian.com/us-news/2023/dec/10/hungary-viktor-orban -republicans-ukraine-aid; Pappin, "Gladden Pappin Tweet on Heritage and Hungary."

Chapter 10

1. Intercollegiate Studies Institute, "Johnny Burtka Appointed as New President of the Intercollegiate Studies Institute," September 1, 2020, https://www.prnewswire.com/news-releases /johnny-burtka-appointed-as-new-president-of-the-intercollegiate-studies-institute -301122433.html.

2. Jeffery Tyler Syck, "From 'Educating for Liberty' to Fawning Over Nationalism," *Dispatch*, July 22, 2024, https://thedispatch.com/article/from-educating-for-liberty-to-fawning-over -nationalism/; Susan Hanssen, "ISI Still Stands for Timeless Truths," *American Conservative*, September 13, 2024, https://www.theamericanconservative.com/isi-still-stands-for-timeless -truths/.

3. Burtka published an op-ed in *Newsweek* in 2021 suggesting that the APG Summit was designed as a response to the supposed sidelining of the Claremont Institute by the American Political Science Association (John Burtka, "Building America's Counter-University," *Newsweek*, October 6, 2021, https://www.newsweek.com/building-americas-counter-university -opinion-1635721). For more on this controversy, see Laura K. Field, "The Claremont Institute's Bogus Censorship Charge," *Bulwark*, October 18, 2021, https://www.thebulwark.com/p/the -claremont-institutes-bogus-censorship-charge; Ryan Williams, "APSA Caves to the Mob," *Newsweek*, October 1, 2021, https://www.newsweek.com/apsa-caves-mob-opinion-1634485; Ryan Quinn, "Claremont Institute, Home of 'Stop the Steal' Lawyer, Returns to Political Science Conference," *Inside Higher Ed*, September 10, 2024, https://www.insidehighered.com /news/faculty-issues/academic-freedom/2024/09/10/claremont-home-stop-steal-lawyer -back-apsa.

4. ISI, "All the information you need about APG," author record of email, February 23, 2023, https://perma.cc/5NMR-69GT.

5. See Francie Diep, "Fears of Politicization Dog Another Florida Public University's Presidential Search," *Chronicle of Higher Education*, May 3, 2023, https://www.chronicle.com/article /fears-of-politicization-dog-another-florida-public-universitys-presidential-search.

6. See Daniel Kennelly, "Florida's Higher Education Reforms," *City Journal*, February 17, 2023, https://www.city-journal.org/article/floridas-higher-education-reforms/.

7. For more on George's connections to Luis Tellez and the broader conservative Catholic world, see Kevin Spinale, "'Sustained by Faith': An Interview with Robert P. George," *America Magazine*, November 7, 2011, https://www.americamagazine.org/issue/793/article/sustained -faith; "Spotted History Aside, Opus Dei Forges Close Campus Links," *Daily Princetonian*, February 13, 2005, https://www.dailyprincetonian.com/article/2005/03/spotted-history-aside -opus-dei-forges-close-campus-links; Gore, *Opus*, 223–27; Stanley Kurtz, "The Princeton Way," *National Review*, April 11, 2005, https://www.nationalreview.com/2005/04/princeton-way -stanley-kurtz/; Max Blumenthal, "Princeton Tilts Right," *Nation*, February 23, 2006, https:// www.thenation.com/article/archive/princeton-tilts-right/.

8. Robert P. George, "Leaders Should Be Servants," YouTube, 2023, https://www.youtube .com/watch?v=a-t2ptfJvaA.

9. Robert P. George, "Election 2024 Facebook Post," Facebook, October 25, 2024, https:// perma.cc/262T-ZLS4.

10. Vallier, *All the Kingdoms of the World*, 25.

11. Brooke Masters, "Adrian Vermeule's legal theories illuminate a growing rift among US conservatives," *Financial Times*, October 14, 2022, https://www.ft.com/content/5c615d7d-3b1a -47a2-86ab-34c7db363fe4.

12. Robert P. George, "Facebook Celebration of Adrian Vermeule Conversion," Facebook, August 20, 2016, https://www.facebook.com/photo.php?fbid=10209417000154599&set=a .1088932776192.2015840.1012638420&type=3&theater.

13. See "Emily Dickinson Townsend Vermeule," *Harvard Gazette*, June 3, 2004, https://news .harvard.edu/gazette/story/2004/06/emily-dickinson-townsend-vermeule/.

14. Masters, "Adrian Vermeule's Legal Theories."

15. He subsequently resigned in protest of the academy's political biases.

16. Cass R. Sunstein and Adrian Vermeule, *Law and Leviathan: Redeeming the Administrative State* (Harvard University Press, 2020), https://www.hup.harvard.edu/books/9780674247536.

17. See, for example Adrian Vermeule, "Publius as an Exportable Good," *New Rambler Review*, December 3, 2015, https://newramblerreview.com/book-reviews/law/publius-as-an -exportable-good.

18. Adrian Vermeule, "The Publius Paradox," *Modern Law Review*, July 23, 2018, Harvard Public Law Working Paper No. 18-50, http://dx.doi.org/10.2139/ssrn.3218332.

19. Eric Posner and Adrian Vermeule, "A 'Torture' Memo and Its Tortuous Critics," *Wall Street Journal*, July 6, 2004, https://www.wsj.com/articles/SB108906730725255526; Eric Posner and Adrian Vermeule, "Tyrannophobia," University of Chicago Public Law & Legal Theory Working Paper no. 276, 2009; Adrian Vermeule, "Optimal Abuse of Power," *Northwestern Law Review* 109, no. 3 (2015): https://scholarlycommons.law.northwestern.edu/nulr /vol109/iss3/4.

20. Adrian Vermeule, "Finding Stable Ground," *First Things*, November 4, 2016, https://web .archive.org/web/20200819022516/https://firstthings.com/blogs/firstthoughts/2016/11 /finding-stable-ground.

21. For more on Gregory, see Mark Lilla, *The Shipwrecked Mind: On Political Reaction* (New York Review Books, 2016).

22. Adrian Vermeule, "A Christian Strategy," *First Things*, November 1, 2017, https://firstthings .com/a-christian-strategy/.

23. See William Galston, "What Is Integralism?," November 4, 2022, *Persuasion*, https://www .persuasion.community/p/what-is-integralism, for a helpful short primer on Catholic integralism.

24. See Gerardus Maiella, "Molina on Civil and Ecclesiastical Power," *Josias*, July 8, 2020, https://thejosias.com/2020/07/08/molina-on-civil-and-ecclesiastical-power/.

25. Joshua Tait, "The Myth of Antonio Salazar," *Reason*, April 26, 2021, https://reason.com/2021/04/26/the-myth-of-antonio-salazar/; James Patterson, "An Awkward Alliance: Neo-Integralism and National Conservatism," Acton Institute, October 12, 2024, https://www.acton.org/religion-liberty/volume-35-number-1-2/awkward-alliance-neo-integralism-and-national-conservatism.

26. Copulsky, *American Heretics*, 178–92; Jeet Heer, "Tilting at Franco," *The Time of Monsters*, August 16, 2021, https://jeetheer.substack.com/p/tilting-at-franco.

27. Vallier, *All the Kingdoms of the World*, 10, 16. Vallier called this an "ingenious move." It allowed him to dissociate from politics and controversy, even while there was nothing philosophically or theologically stopping traditionalists from embracing Catholic integralism while at the same time, for example, attacking Pope Francis.

28. Vallier, *All the Kingdoms of the World*, 12.

29. Adrian Vermeule, "Liberalism's Fear," *Josias*, May 9, 2018, https://thejosias.com/2018/05/09/liberalisms-fear/; Vermeule, "Integration from Within"; Adrian Vermeule, "Ralliement: Two Distinctions," *Josias*, March 16, 2018, https://thejosias.com/2018/03/16/ralliement-two-distinctions/.

30. Vallier, *All the Kingdoms of the World*, 5.

31. As Waldstein put it on *The Josias* blog, "since man's temporal end is subordinated to his eternal end, the temporal power must be subordinated to the spiritual power." Edmund Waldstein, "Integralism in Three Sentences," *Josias*, October 17, 2016, https://thejosias.com/2016/10/17/integralism-in-three-sentences/.

32. Heer, "Tilting at Franco."

33. Vermeule, *Common Good Constitutionalism*, 116.

34. George Schwab, *The Challenge of the Exception: An Introduction to the Political Ideas of Carl Schmitt Between 1921 and 1936* (Praeger, 1989), 15, 18–25.

35. See Carl Schmitt and Tracy B. Strong, *Political Theology: Four Chapters on the Concept of Sovereignty*, trans. George Schwab (University of Chicago Press, 2006), 62. Schmitt approvingly cites Donoso Cortés. "Liberalism, with its contradictions and compromises, existed for Donoso Cortés only in that short interim period in which it was possible to answer the question 'Christ or Barabbas?' with a proposal to adjourn and appoint a commission of investigation."

36. Carl Schmitt, Tracy B. Strong, and Leo Strauss, *The Concept of the Political*, trans. George Schwab (University of Chicago Press, 2007).

37. Adrian Vermeule, "Our Schmittian Administrative Law," *Harvard Law Review* 122, no. 4 (February 2009).

38. Eric A. Posner and Adrian Vermeule, *Executive Unbound* (Oxford University Press, 2011), 4, 17.

39. Eric A. Posner and Adrian Vermeule, "Demystifying Schmitt," *The Oxford Handbook of Carl Schmitt*, ed. J. Meierhenrich and O. Simons (Oxford University Press, 2013), abstract and 624.

40. Adrian Vermeule, "All Human Conflict Is Ultimately Theological," *Church Life Journal*, July 26, 2019, https://churchlifejournal.nd.edu/articles/all-human-conflict-is-ultimately-theological/.

41. Mark A. Graber, "The Executive Unbound: After the Madisonian Republic; The System of the Constitution," *Perspectives on Politics* 11, no. 4 (December 2013): 1159, https://doi.org/10.1017/S1537592713002351; Richard Pious, "The Executive Unbound: After the Madisonian Republic," *Presidential Studies Quarterly* 41, no. 4 (December 2011): 865; Chris Edelson, "The Executive Unbound: After the Madisonian Republic," *Political Research Quarterly* 127, no. 2 (Summer 2012): 311.

42. Vermeule, "All Human Conflict."

43. Vermeule's first example was the Obama administration's "relentless" actions against the Little Sisters of the Poor ("the main point was to stage a public, sacramental celebration of the justice of liberal power and the overcoming of reactionary opposition"). Of *Obergefell*, Vermeule wrote that "a conspicuous conflict with the settled *mores* of millennia was, of course, the point."

44. Vermeule cites Carl Schmitt, *Roman Catholicism and Political Form* (Greenwood, 1996), 17.

45. On some of these points, see Heinrich Meier, *Carl Schmitt and Leo Strauss: The Hidden Dialogue*, trans. J. Harvey Lomax (University of Chicago Press, 2006), 72–87.

46. Adrian Vermeule, "Against Originalism," *Atlantic*, March 31, 2020, https://www .theatlantic.com/ideas/archive/2020/03/common-good-constitutionalism/609037/.

47. Vermeule, *Common Good Constitutionalism*, 5, 12, 116.

48. Vermeule, *Common Good Constitutionalism*, 7.

49. Vermeule, *Common Good Constitutionalism*, 7, 59; see also 134, 138.

50. I have written elsewhere about how Vermeule's treatment of freedom is parallel to that of Edmund Waldstein. See Laura K. Field, "Forced to be Free? America's Postliberals on Freedom and Liberty," in *Far-Right Newspeak and the Future of Liberal Democracy*, ed. A. James McAdams and Samuel Piccolo (Routledge, 2024), 145–65.

51. See Vermeule, *Common Good Constitutionalism*, 53–56.

52. Micah Schwartzman and Richard Schragger, "What Common Good?," *American Prospect*, April 7, 2022, https://prospect.org/culture/books/what-common-good-vermeule-review/.

53. Vermeule, *Common Good Constitutionalism*, 55.

54. See Vermeule, *Common Good Constitutionalism*, 54, 180.

55. Vermeule, *Common Good Constitutionalism*, 39.

56. Vermeule's sleight of hand vis-à-vis American history is most evident in a subsection of chapter 1 titled "Moral Readings of the Constitution," 38–43.

57. Vermeule, *Common Good Constitutionalism*, 39.

58. Deneen, *Why Liberalism Failed*, 101, 27.

59. Patrick J. Deneen, "A Good That Is Common," *Postliberal Order*, November 17, 2021, https://www.postliberalorder.com/p/a-good-that-is-common.

60. Josh Hammer, "Common Good Originalism," *American Mind*, May 6, 2020, https:// americanmind.org/features/waiting-for-charlemagne/common-good-originalism/; Josh Hammer, "Undoing the Court's Supreme Transgression," *American Mind*, June 19, 2020, https:// americanmind.org/memo/undoing-the-courts-supreme-transgression/; Josh Hammer, "Who's Afraid of the Common Good?," *American Mind*, November 23, 2020, https:// americanmind.org/salvo/whos-afraid-of-the-common-good/; Hadley Arkes et al., "A Better Originalism," *American Mind*, March 18, 2021, https://americanmind.org/features/a-new -conservatism-must-emerge/a-better-originalism/; Josh Hammer, "The Telos of the American Regime," *American Mind*, April 7, 2021, https://americanmind.org/features/a-new-conservatism -must-emerge/the-telos-of-the-american-regime/.

61. Hammer, "Undoing the Court's Supreme Transgression."

62. Josh Hammer, "Conservatives Must Make Their Arguments in Moral Language," *Daily Wire*, June 3, 2019, https://www.dailywire.com/news/hammer-conservatives-must-make-their -arguments-josh-hammer.

63. Arkes et al., "A Better Originalism."

64. Hammer, "The Telos of the American Regime"; Josh Hammer, "Manly Originalism," *American Mind*, May 19, 2022, https://americanmind.org/features/a-human-event/manly -originalism/.

65. Josh Hammer, "Common Good Originalism: Our Tradition and Our Path Forward," *SSRN Scholarly Paper* (Social Science Research Network, June 3, 2021), 917, 953, https://papers.ssrn.com/abstract=3860301. See Hammer's discussion of the Preamble on 929.

66. Kim R. Holmes, "The Fallacies of the Common Good," *New Criterion*, January 2022, https://newcriterion.com/article/the-fallacies-of-the-common-good/.

67. Josh Hammer, "Yesterday's Man, Yesterday's Conservatism," *New Criterion*, December 22, 2022, https://newcriterion.com/article/yesterdays-man-yesterdays-conservatism/. See also Hammer, "Why Is Everyone Talking About the Claremont Institute?," *Newsweek*, August 4, 2022, https://www.newsweek.com/why-everyone-talking-about-claremont-institute-opinion-1731040.

68. William Baude and Stephen E. Sachs wrote in *Harvard Law Review* 136, no. 3 (January 2023), 861–906, that "the book might be best understood as what Vermeule once called a 'constitutional manifesto': a work of 'movement jurisprudence' whose political aims come into conflict with theoretical rigor." Jeffrey A. Pojanowski and Kevin C. Walsh wrote, in the *Notre Dame Law Review* 98, no. 1 (November 2022), 403, that "in reading and rereading the book, we found ourselves frustrated with it, notwithstanding the apparent agreement we shared with the author at some abstract level of principle. And that abstraction, it turns out, is just the problem with the book's application of the classical legal tradition to constitutional law. All the right concepts are there for a sound approach to constitutionalism. . . . Too often, though, the only thing missing from this theory of constitutional law was a law, namely the Constitution of the United States." See also Peter J. Wallison, "Review: Common Good Constitutionalism," *American Enterprise Institute—AEI*, December 1, 2022, https://www.aei.org/articles/review-common-good-constitutionalism/; James M. Patterson, "Uncommonly Bad Constitutionalism—James M. Patterson," *Law & Liberty*, April 28, 2022, https://lawliberty.org/book-review/uncommonly-bad-constitutionalism/.

69. Sohrab Ahmari and Veritas Center Conference, "Restoring a Nation," *Institutes and Centers*, April 8, 2022, https://institutes.franciscan.edu/restoring-a-nation/.

70. Michael Lind, "Michael Lind What Would Hamilton Do," National Conservatism Conference, Miami 2022, accessed October 12, 2024, https://nationalconservatism.org/natcon-3-2022/presenters/michael-lind/; "America's Forgotten Common-Good Traditions," YouTube, 2022, https://www.youtube.com/watch?v=3DIiCzyeqVw.

71. Rachel Bovard, "What's New in the New Right?," YouTube, 2022, https://www.youtube.com/watch?v=1WR7xE7Bka8.

72. Harvard JLPP, "CGC Symposium," *Harvard Journal of Law & Public Policy*, August 30, 2022, https://journals.law.harvard.edu/jlpp/symposia/cgc-symposium/.

73. Linda C. McClain and James E. Fleming, "Toward a Liberal Common Good Constitutionalism for Polarized Times," *SSRN Scholarly Paper*, Social Science Research Network, November 28, 2023, 1125, https://papers.ssrn.com/abstract=4647284. See also Sotirios Barber, James E. Fleming, and Stephen Macedo, "The Constitution, the Common Good, and the Ambition of Adrian Vermeule," *Constitutionalist*, January 26, 2021, https://theconstitutionalist.org/2021/01/26/the-constitution-the-common-good-and-the-ambition-of-adrian-vermeule-by-sotirios-barber-stephen-macedo-and-james-fleming/.

74. "Religion's Refusal to Die," *AEI*, April 2023, https://www.aei.org/events/religions-refusal-to-die/; "Religion's Refusal to Die Video," YouTube, 2023, https://www.youtube.com/watch?v=xtBQAmMGzMg.

75. Deneen, *Regime Change*, xiii–xiv. Emphasis my own.

76. See Becca Rothfeld, "The New Conservative Arguments for an Un-Modern America," *Washington Post*, July 28, 2023, https://www.washingtonpost.com/books/2023/07/28/patrick-deneen-regime-change-sohrab-ahmari-tyranny-inc-review/; Pew Research Center, "Public Opinion on Abortion," May 13, 2024, https://www.pewresearch.org/religion/fact-sheet/public

-opinion-on-abortion/; Gabriel Borelli, "About Six-in-Ten Americans Say Legalization of Same-Sex Marriage Is Good for Society," Pew Research Center, November 15, 2022, https://www.pewresearch.org/short-reads/2022/11/15/about-six-in-ten-americans-say-legalization-of-same-sex-marriage-is-good-for-society/.

77. Rothfeld, "The New Conservative Arguments." See also Jason Blakely, "The Thin Line Between 'Postliberalism' and Theocracy," *Chronicle of Higher Education*, August 2, 2023, https://www.chronicle.com/article/the-thin-line-between-postliberalism-and-theocracy.

78. See Deneen, *Regime Change*, 153–57, 185. As Jeff Isaac wrote, "It is dangerous because Deneen speaks out of both sides of his mouth, gesturing at some very radical and even violence-provoking ideas while issuing muted caveats that might afford him plausible deniability." Jeffrey C. Isaac, "When 'Postliberalism' Means Reaction: On Patrick J. Deneen's 'Regime Change,'" *Los Angeles Review of Books*, October 7, 2023, https://lareviewofbooks.org/article/when-postliberalism-means-reaction-on-patrick-j-deneens-regime-change.

79. Jennifer Szalai, "When 'Regime Change' Means Returning America to an Idealized Past," *New York Times*, June 7, 2023, https://www.nytimes.com/2023/06/07/books/review/regime-change-patrick-deneen.html.

80. On Machiavellian means, see Deneen, *Regime Change*, 165, 168, 174, 185, 187, 189. For Deneen's passage on mobs, see 165; he is quoting Machiavelli's Discourses on Livy, book 1, chap. 4.

81. Deneen, *Regime Change*, xiv.

82. Julius Krein, "A Populism Deferred," *American Conservative*, December 8, 2020, https://www.theamericanconservative.com/a-populism-deferred/.

83. See James M. Patterson, "The Realignment That Wasn't," *Law & Liberty*, November 9, 2023, https://lawliberty.org/the-realignment-that-wasnt/; Gladden Pappin, "Requiem for the Realignment," *American Affairs Journal*, February 20, 2023, https://americanaffairsjournal.org/2023/02/requiem-for-the-realignment/.

84. See chapter 9, 218.

85. Sohrab Ahmari and Matthew Schmitz, "He's Still the One," *Compact*, September 27, 2022, https://www.compactmag.com/article/he-s-still-the-one/.

86. Sohrab Ahmari, "I Was Wrong: The GOP Will Never Be the Party of the Working Class," *Newsweek*, August 14, 2023, https://www.newsweek.com/i-was-wrong-gop-will-never-party-working-class-opinion-1819644. See also Ahmari, "The Undead Consensus," *Compact*, May 5, 2022, https://www.compactmag.com/article/the-undead-consensus/. Ahmari singles out Senators Hawley, Rubio, and Vance.

87. Michelle Goldberg, "The Right-Winger Calling for Social Democracy," *New York Times*, August 21, 2023, https://www.nytimes.com/2023/08/21/opinion/columnists/sohrab-ahmari-social-democracy.html.

88. Sohrab Ahmari, *Tyranny, Inc.: How Private Power Crushed American Liberty—and What to Do About It* (Forum Books, 2023). See also Isaac, "When 'Postliberalism' Means Reaction."

89. See Jacob Heilbrunn, *America Last: The Right's Century-Long Romance with Foreign Dictators* (Liveright, 2024); "About," *Hungarian Conservative*, accessed October 12, 2024, https://www.hungarianconservative.com/about/.

90. See Vermeule, "Liberalism's Fear."

91. Vermeule gave a speech in honor of Legutko in Poland in 2018 at the invitation of the Polish consul general. He went to Poland again for an event in honor of Legutko in 2022, this time accompanied by Deneen. See Adrian Vermeule, "In Honor of Ryszard Legutko," *Postliberal Order*, November 17, 2021, https://www.postliberalorder.com/p/in-honor-of-ryszard-legutko. Legutko spoke at NatCon 1 in 2019, the NatCon conference in Brussels in 2022, and NatCon 3 in 2024, where he was awarded a prize.

92. See Vermeule, "Liberalism's Fear."

93. See Vermeule, "In Honor of Ryszard Legutko."

94. See "Facebook Live Dreher Deneen in Hungary," Facebook, June 28, 2021, https://www
.facebook.com/watch/live/?v=158843492853549&ref=watch_permalink. This quote comes
from toward the end of the interview, around 1:09. I have lightly edited Deneen's words for
clarity.

95. See Patrick J. Deneen and Gladden Pappin, "Dispatch from Budapest," *Postliberal Order*,
August 5, 2022, https://www.postliberalorder.com/p/dispatch-from-budapest.

96. Orbán has been explicit in other contexts about his own redefinition of liberty. See
"Interview with Chris DeMuth," YouTube, 2020, https://www.youtube.com/watch?v
=9WP8xzxH7YY.

97. Deneen whitewashes Orbánism in *Regime Change*, 94, 182. See also Isaac, "When 'Postliberalism' Means Reaction."

98. See Tímea Drinóczi and Agnieszka Bień-Kacała, "Illiberal Constitutionalism: The Case
of Hungary and Poland," *German Law Journal* 20, no. 8 (December 2019): 1140–66, https://doi
.org/10.1017/glj.2019.83; Miklós Bánkuti, Gábor Halmai, and Kim Lane Scheppele, "Hungary's
Illiberal Turn: Disabling the Constitution," *Journal of Democracy* 23, no. 3 (2012): 138–46,
https://muse.jhu.edu/pub/1/article/480981; Liana Fix and Constanze Stelzenmüller, "Germany's New Normal?," *Foreign Affairs*, October 10, 2023, https://www.foreignaffairs.com
/germany/germanys-new-normal.

99. See Gladden Pappin, "Within the West, Hungary Has Set the Standard for a Reasonable
Approach," *Postliberal Order*, November 17, 2021, https://www.postliberalorder.com/p/within
-the-west-hungary-has-set-the; Magyar Külügyi Intézet, "The Hungarian Institute of International Affairs Is Reorganized Approach," *Postliberal Order*, April 14, 2023, https://hiia.hu/en/the
-hungarian-institute-of-international-affairs-is-reorganized/.

100. Ahmari, *Tyranny, Inc.*, 1, 211n1; William A. Galston, "Democracy Promotion in a World
Growing More Dangerous," *Wall Street Journal*, April 13, 2021, https://www.wsj.com/articles
/democracy-promotion-in-a-world-growing-more-dangerous-11618355267; "Reversing the
Tide Task Force on US Strategy to Support Democracy and Counter Authoritarianism," Freedom House, accessed October 12, 2024, https://freedomhouse.org/democracy-task-force
/special-report/2021/reversing-the-tide/introduction.

101. Sohrab Ahmari, "The New Racist Right Are Uniquely Dangerous," *New Statesman*,
April 10, 2024, https://www.newstatesman.com/comment/2024/04/the-new-racist-right-are
-uniquely-dangerous.

102. Sohrab Ahmari, "The Poverty of Catholic Intellectual Life," *Liberties*, Spring 2024.

103. See "Religion's Refusal to Die"; and Patrick Deneen, "We Are All Postliberals Now,"
YouTube, February 15, 2025, https://www.youtube.com/live/xOOnn04XE1o.

104. Sohrab Ahmari, "The Rise of the Unabomber Right," *New Statesman*, June 14, 2023, https://
www.newstatesman.com/comment/2023/06/unabomber-american-right-ted-kaczynski.

105. Sohrab Ahmari, "Trump Will Have to Choose: Populism or Elon Musk," *New Statesman*,
August 15, 2024, https://www.newstatesman.com/comment/2024/08/trump-will-have-to
-choose-populism-or-elon-musk; Sohrab Ahmari, "Elon Musk Has Created a Cesspool. Https://T
.Co/B3d5riv7LX," X, July 9, 2024, https://x.com/SohrabAhmari/status/1810612672733327709;
Sohrab Ahmari, "Elon Musk Owns Donald Trump Now," *New Statesman*, August 28, 2023, https://
www.newstatesman.com/politics/2023/08/elon-musk-owns-donald-trump-now.

106. Sohrab Ahmari, "Too Online, Too Rigid, Too Weird: Why Ron DeSantis Failed," *New
Statesman*, January 21, 2024, https://www.newstatesman.com/uncategorized/2024/01/too
-online-too-rigid-too-weird-why-ron-desantis-failed.

107. Sohrab Ahmari, "The Rise of the Barbarian Right," *Liberties*, Autumn 2024.

Chapter 11

1. John F. Kennedy, "Remarks on the 50th Anniversary of the Children's Bureau, 9 April 1962," JFK Library, accessed October 12, 2024, https://www.jfklibrary.org/asset-viewer/archives /jfkwha-085-001.

2. Allison Pecorin, "Senate Democrats Hold Moment of Silence in Memory of George Floyd," *ABC News*, accessed October 12, 2024, https://abcnews.go.com/Politics/senate -democrats-hold-moment-silence-memory-george-floyd/story?id=71069405.

3. Nikki McCann Ramirez, "Man Boobs and Raw Eggs: The Most Absurd Moments from Tucker Carlson's Ball-Tanning Special," *Rolling Stone*, October 5, 2022, https://www.rollingstone .com/politics/politics-news/tucker-carlson-end-of-men-most-absurd-moments-1234606090/.

4. Media Matters Staff, "Alex Jones: Tucker Carlson Filmed Part of His 'End of Men' Documentary on My Land," *Media Matters for America*, April 18, 2022, https://www.mediamatters.org /alex-jones/alex-jones-tucker-carlson-filmed-part-his-end-men-documentary-my-land.

5. Chris Hamby and Jim Morris, "Industry vs. Government Science," *Salon*, July 30, 2013, https://www.salon.com/2013/07/30/industry_vs_government_science/.

6. See Norah Mackendrick, *Better Safe than Sorry* (University of California Press, 2018).

7. For example, see Peter Attia, "Aging Better," Johns Hopkins Medicine February 2024, https://www.hopkinsmedicine.org/news/articles/2024/02/aging-better; or Ashwin Rodrigues, "Wellness Should Be Just a Hobby," *New York Times*, November 10, 2024, https://www .nytimes.com/2024/11/10/opinion/wellness-bro-science.html.

8. Raw Egg Nationalist, "Ecce Homos," *American Mind*, June 6, 2022, https://americanmind .org/salvo/ecce-homos/.

9. See Nietzsche, *On the Genealogy of Morals and Ecce Homo*, trans. Walter Kaufmann (Vintage, 1989).

10. Raw Egg Nationalist, *The Eggs Benedict Option* (Antelope Hill, 2022).

11. Raw Egg Nationalist, "Digging for Victory," *American Mind*, October 20, 2022, https:// americanmind.org/salvo/digging-for-victory/.

12. Leonid Sharashkin, "The Socioeconomic and Cultural Significance of Food Gardening in the Vladimir Region of Russia" (ProQuest Dissertations & Theses, 2008), https://www .proquest.com/docview/304531394/abstract/?accountid=8285.

13. See Simon Clarke, *Making Ends Meet in Contemporary Russia: Secondary Employment, Subsidiary Agriculture and Social Networks* (Edward Elgar, 2002).

14. Raw Egg Nationalist, *The Eggs Benedict Option*, 25, 75–76. The "Planetary Health Diet" was an initiative put out by the EAT, a nonprofit organization, and *The Lancet* medical journal that is pitched as a "global reference diet" to "benefit both people and planet." Iain Shepherd, "The Planetary Health Diet," EAT, February 11, 2019, https://eatforum.org/learn-and-discover/the-planetary-health-diet/.

15. Josh Harkinson, "Meet the White Nationalist Trying to Ride the Trump Train to Lasting Power," *Mother Jones*, October 27, 2016, https://www.motherjones.com/politics/2016/10 /richard-spencer-trump-alt-right-white-nationalist/.

16. Hannah Gais et al., "White Nationalist Book Publishers Revealed," Southern Poverty Law Center, June 13, 2022, https://www.splcenter.org/hatewatch/2022/06/13/white -nationalist-book-publishers-revealed.

17. Richard Darré, *A New Nobility of Blood and Soil*, Antelope Hill Publishing, accessed October 12, 2024, https://antelopehillpublishing.com/product/a-new-nobility-of-blood-and -soil-by-richard-w-darre/.

18. See Field, "The Decay at the Claremont Institute Continues."

19. Raw Egg Nationalist, "Ecce Homos"; "Raw Egg Nationalist—JML #077," YouTube, 2021, https://www.youtube.com/watch?v=6wKScRWkHJ8.

20. BAP and REN, "Caribbean Rhythms with BAP—Episode 108—Raw Egg Nationalist," podcast, 2022, https://html5-player.libsyn.com/embed/episode/id/23011655/height/90 /theme/custom/thumbnail/yes/direction/forward/tdest_id/1582403/render-playlist/no /custom-color/000000/.

21. BAP and REN. See also Field, "The Decay at the Claremont Institute Continues."

22. Wood, "How Bronze Age Pervert Charmed the Far Right."

23. Zerofsky, "How the Claremont Institute Became a Nerve Center."

24. Ali Breland, "Is the Bronze Age Pervert Going Mainstream?," *Mother Jones*, October 2, 2023, https://www.motherjones.com/politics/2023/10/bronze-age-pervert-costin -alamariu/.

25. For an overview of Alamariu's convoluted attempt to connect all this historically, see Dustin Sebell, "An Achilles Without a Zeus: Liberalism and the Predicaments of 'Nietzschean Vitalism,'" *Political Science Reviewer* 48, no. 1 (May 30, 2024): 336–40, https://politicalscience reviewer.wisc.edu/index.php/psr/article/view/832.

26. See Costin Vlad Alamariu, *Selective Breeding and the Birth of Philosophy* (Self-published, 2023), chap. 1, 58ff.

27. Sebell, "An Achilles Without a Zeus."

28. Costin Vlad Alamariu, "The Problem of Tyranny and Philosophy in the Thought of Plato and Nietzsche" (ProQuest Dissertations & Theses, 2015), 247, https://www.proquest.com /docview/1760093792/abstract/?accountid=8285. (On the rejection of irony as a literary tool, see 249n15.)

29. In an email exchange, Kathryn Paige Harden, a professor of psychology at the University of Texas and expert in developmental genetics (and a friend of mine), explained it to me as follows: "It does not make sense to talk about 'Black Africans' as if they are a single group. BAP seems to be recycling an already outrageous claim from an old blog post by Razib Khan, a population geneticist who also wrote for the paleoconservative *Taki's Magazine*. Africa is incredibly diverse genetically: Two African populations can be more genetically different than Europeans are from East Asians. Regarding his characterization of Richard Lewontin, Lewontin had little data, by modern standards, but the remarkable amount of human genomic data collected and analyzed since then has basically validated his core argument: Most genetic variation is within human populations, not between them. It's also ironic that he's saying that Cavalli-Sforza disproved Lewontin, because Cavalli-Sforza was absolutely insistent that his work proved that 'races' don't exist."

30. See "Alamariu Dissertation Report Tweet," accessed October 13, 2024, https://perma.cc /YF55-Y7Y6.

31. See Ronald Beiner, "Do the Straussians Now Own Costin Alamariu?" in *Radical Right Ideologues in the Age of Trump: Heralds of Nihilism* (forthcoming with Routledge).

32. See Breland, "Is the Bronze Age Pervert Going Mainstream?"; P. Andrew Sandlin, "The Old Bronze Age Mindset Meets the New 'Christian Vitalism,'" *CultureChange*, October 13, 2023, https://pandrewsandlin.substack.com/p/the-old-bronze-age-mindset-meets?utm_medium =reader2; Blake Smith, "Bronze Age Pervert's Dissertation on Leo Strauss," *Tablet*, February 14, 2023, https://www.tabletmag.com/sections/arts-letters/articles/bronze-age-pervert-dissertation -leo-strauss; Oliver Traldi, "Bronze Age Pervert's Guide to Philosophy," *Quillette*, November 25, 2023, https://quillette.com/2023/11/25/bronze-age-perverts-guide-to-philosophy/; Michael Millerman, "The Mask of Philosophy," *IM-1776*, October 27, 2023, https://im1776.com/2023 /10/27/selective-breeding-review/.

33. "Rufo Congratulating Alamariu," September 18, 2023, https://perma.cc/YM34-3LEL; and "Hanania Congratulating Alamariu," September 16, 2023, https://perma.cc/J6AT -8CJ6.

34. Nekrasova Dasha, "Dasha Costin Dissertation Tweet," September 15, 2023, https://perma.cc/8JNG-49UG; Costin Alamariu, "Alamariu Nekrasova Dissertation Tweet," September 17, 2023, https://perma.cc/YF5S-Y7Y6.

35. Dasha Nekrasova and Anna Khachiyan, "Red Scare Podcast: Welcome to the Longhouse," July 28, 2022, https://redscarepodcast.libsyn.com/welcome-to-the-longhouse-teaser.

36. Dasha Nekrasova and Anna Khachiyan, "Red Scare Podcast: Bronze Age Podcast w/ Bronze Age Pervert," comments section, accessed October 13, 2024, https://redscarepodcast.libsyn.com/bronze-age-podcast-w-bronze-age-pervert-teaser.

37. Nekrasova and Khachiyan, "Red Scare Podcast: Bronze Age Podcast."

38. Joseph Bernstein, "'Look at What We're Doing with Your Money, You Dick': How Peter Thiel Backed an 'Anti-Woke' Film Festival," *BuzzFeed*, March 3, 2022, https://www.buzzfeednews.com/article/josephbernstein/peter-thiel-anti-woke-film-festival-trevor-bazile.

39. Julia Yost, "New York's Hottest Club Is the Catholic Church," *New York Times*, August 9, 2022, https://www.nytimes.com/2022/08/09/opinion/nyc-catholicism-dimes-square-religion.html.

40. See "Cath-Pilled Shoplifting Theory with Dasha Nekrasova of Red Scare," YouTube, 2019, https://www.youtube.com/watch?v=E2L3g5YPaGk; Carina Imbornone, "Dasha Nekrasova Believes in God, Wellbutrin, and Sigmund Freud," *Interview Magazine*, February 18, 2020, https://www.interviewmagazine.com/film/dasha-nekrasova-softness-of-bodies-amazon.

41. Email for the event forwarded to author. See also J. Arthur, "The Right-Wing Avant-Garde in American Fiction," *Verso*, accessed October 12, 2024, https://www.versobooks.com/blogs/news/the-right-wing-avant-garde-in-american-fiction.

42. See Mike Crumplar, "All in Good Fun," *Crumpstack*, June 11, 2023, https://mcrumps.substack.com/p/all-in-good-fun; Mike Crumplar, "My Own Dimes Square Fascist Humiliation Ritual," *Crumpstack*, August 3, 2022, https://mcrumps.substack.com/p/my-own-dimes-square-fascist-humiliation.

43. Sailer has been on Bronze Age Pervert's podcast and on *Red Scare*.

44. Richard Wolin, *Heidegger in Ruins: Between Philosophy and Ideology* (Yale University Press, 2023), 11–12, 314–18.

45. See Bruce Lincoln, *Secrets, Lies, and Consequences: A Great Scholar's Hidden Past and His Protégé's Unsolved Murder* (Oxford University Press, 2023), chaps. 2 and 4. For more on the fascist discourse regarding the "new man," Lincoln directs us to Jorge Dagnino, Paul Stocker, and Matthew Feldman, eds., *The "New Man" in Radical Right Ideology and Practice, 1919–45* (Bloomsbury, 2018), https://www.bloomsbury.com/uk/new-man-in-radical-right-ideology-and-practice-191945-9781474281096/.

46. Lincoln, *Secrets, Lies, and Consequences*, 24–25.

47. Lincoln, *Secret, Lies, and Consequences*, 34.

48. Sophia Nguyen, "The Plagiarism Allegations Against Ex-Harvard President Claudine Gay, Explained," *Washington Post*, January 5, 2024, https://www.washingtonpost.com/books/2024/01/04/claudine-gay-plagiarism-examples-harvard/.

49. See Tyler Austin Harper, "America's Colleges Are Reaping What They Sowed," *Atlantic*, May 2, 2024, https://www.theatlantic.com/ideas/archive/2024/05/college-activism-hypocrisy/678262/; Tyler Austin Harper, "The Real Harvard Scandal," *Atlantic*, January 3, 2024, https://www.theatlantic.com/ideas/archive/2024/01/claudine-gay-harvard-plagiarism/677007/.

50. Nguyen, "The Plagiarism Allegations"; Ian Ward, "We Sat Down with the Conservative Mastermind Behind Claudine Gay's Ouster," *Politico*, January 3, 2024, https://www.politico.com/news/magazine/2024/01/03/christopher-rufo-claudine-gay-harvard-resignation-00133618.

51. Christopher Rufo, "Rufo DEI Victory Lap Tweet," accessed October 13, 2024, https://perma.cc/VKH7-MJNQ.

52. Christopher Rufo, "The New Right Activism," *IM-1776*, January 4, 2024, https://im1776 .com/manifesto-counterrevolution/.

53. Rod Dreher and Mark Granza, "'Since the Hungarian Project Seems to Have Become Very Relevant for the Right in the West, I Thought It Made Sense for Me to Be Here,'" *Hungarian Conservative*, February 14, 2023, https://www.hungarianconservative.com/articles/interview /hungary_orban_conservatism_dreher_granza_interview_left_cancel_culture/.

54. "Mission Statement," *IM-1776*, accessed October 12, 2024, https://im1776.com/mission -statement/.

55. "IM—Phase II: The Art & Literature Foundation," *IM-1776*, accessed October 12, 2024, https://im1776.com/art-and-literature-foundation/.

56. The Claremont Institute has also supported the IM 1776 group. Jason Wilson, "Ron DeSantis Ally Chris Rufo Has Close Ties with 'Dissident Right' Magazine," *Guardian*, February 21, 2024, https://www.theguardian.com/world/2024/feb/21/chris-rufo-im-1776-far-right -desantis.

57. Jason Wilson, "US Businessman Is Wannabe 'Warlord' of Secretive Far-Right Men's Network," *Guardian*, August 22, 2023, https://www.theguardian.com/world/2023/aug/22/charles -haywood-claremont-institute-sacr-far-right.

58. Ruth Marcus, "Why a New Conservative Brain Trust Is Resettling Across America," *New York Times*, July 4, 2024, https://www.nytimes.com/2024/07/04/us/claremont-institute -trump-conservatives.html.

59. Rod Dreher, "Thomas Achord Confesses," *American Conservative*, November 28, 2022, https://www.theamericanconservative.com/thomas-achord-confesses/; Alastair Roberts, "On Thomas Achord," *Alastair's Adversaria*, November 27, 2022, https://alastairadversaria.com/2022 /11/27/the-case-against-thomas-achord/.

60. Daniel Miller and Charles Haywood, "No Enemies to the Right? DC Miller vs Charles Haywood," *IM-1776*, December 13, 2022, https://im1776.com/2022/12/13/no-enemies-to-the -right/, emphasis added.

61. Rod Dreher, "Sometimes You Do Have to Punch Right," *Rod Dreher's Diary*, September 28, 2023, https://roddreher.substack.com/p/sometimes-you-do-have-to-punch-right; "On 'No Enemies to the Right' Twitter Space," YouTube, 2023, https://www.youtube.com/watch?v =cHbVRuJTapo; Neil Shenvi, "No Enemies to the Right? Thoughts on Christian Political Engagement," *Neil Shenvi—Apologetics*, July 21, 2023, https://shenviapologetics.com/no-enemies -to-the-right-thoughts-on-christian-political-engagement/.

62. Ryan Bort, "DeSantis Influencers Rally Behind Unmasked Antisemite," *Rolling Stone*, June 28, 2023, https://www.rollingstone.com/politics/politics-news/desantis-influencers -defend-unmasked-antisemite-pedro-gonzalez-1234780062/.

63. Cameron Joseph, "Trump's Favorite Extreme Think Tank Is Jumping Ship for DeSantis," *Vice*, March 27, 2023, https://www.vice.com/en/article/claremont-institute-desantis/.

64. Alec Dent, "The New Right Finds a Home at the Intersection of Populism and Elitism," *Dispatch*, August 5, 2022, https://thedispatch.com/article/the-new-right-finds-a-home-at-the/.

65. David French, "The Lost Boys of the American Right," *New York Times*, August 13, 2023, https://www.nytimes.com/2023/08/13/opinion/masculinity-right-young-men.html.

66. Christopher Mathias, "Trump Has Appointed 2 White Nationalists to Government Roles Since Losing the Election," *HuffPost*, November 20, 2020, https://www.huffpost.com /entry/trump-appoints-white-nationalists-darren-beattie-jason-richwine_n_5fb6eedbc5 b67f34cb398973.

67. Clifford Humphrey, "Humphrey to Rufo on NETTR," September 23, 2023, https://perma .cc/Q3JM-8TLB.

Chapter 12

1. World Prayer Network, "WPN Call 279 | Mike Johnson, Jody Hice—Congress Update: Concurrent Resolution and Motion to Vacate," *Well Versed*, October 4, 2023, https://wellversedworld.org/media/ps8jt9w/wpn-call-279-mike-johnson-jody-hice-congress-update-concurrent-resolution-and-motion-to-vacate.

2. Naomi Zeveloff, "Robert Weinger Left an Affluent Life in California to Devote Himself to the Humble Shofar," *Forward*, September 26, 2016, https://forward.com/israel/350548/how-an-american-executive-dropped-everything-to-become-israels-shofar-king/.

3. World Prayer Network, "WPN Call 279," minutes 18:00–19:30. For a fuller account of the inscription story, see Du Mez, *Jesus and John Wayne*, 11–13, 35–37.

4. World Prayer Network, "WPN Call 279," minutes 19:30–26:00.

5. Jonathan Blitzer, "How Mike Johnson Went from Relative Obscurity to Speaker of the House," *New Yorker*, October 25, 2023, https://www.newyorker.com/news/daily-comment/how-mike-johnson-went-from-relative-obscurity-to-speaker-of-the-house.

6. Jaclyn Diaz, "Conservative Christians Are Lending Support—and Cash—to Israel at War," NPR, May 26, 2024, https://www.npr.org/2024/05/26/1244131702/conservative-christians-are-lending-support-and-cash-to-israel-at-war. Will Sommer, "Candace Owens Departs Ben Shapiro's Website after Antisemitic Commentary," *Washington Post*, March 22, 2024, https://www.washingtonpost.com/style/media/2024/03/22/candace-owens-antisemitism-daily-wire-shapiro/.

7. See, for example, Tara Isabella Burton, *Strange Rites: New Religions for a Godless World* (Public Affairs, 2020); Daniel N. Gullotta, "Witches Are Back. Why?," *Bulwark*, November 8, 2024, https://www.thebulwark.com/p/spiritual-divide-witches-men-women-church.

8. Katherine Stewart, *The Power Worshippers: Inside the Dangerous Rise of Religious Nationalism* (New York: Bloomsbury Publishing, 2022), 3.

9. Du Mez, *Jesus and John Wayne*, 4, 3.

10. For example, the American Coalition for Traditional Values (ACTV), Concerned Women for America (CWA), American Freedom Council (AFC), and the secretive Council on National Policy (CNP). Michael Lienesch, *Redeeming America: Piety and Politics in the New Christian Right* (University of North Carolina Press, 1993), 1–3.

11. See Steven K. Green, *Inventing a Christian America: The Myth of the Religious Founding* (Oxford University Press, 2017). Green shows that Christian nationalist arguments have been pervasive in America since the early 1800s, and argues that the Christian nationalist identity was first forged after 1800 as early American sought to solidify their self-understanding—then as now against a background of turmoil and uncertainty.

12. This account of Crenshaw's talk and other panels at the conference is based on my personal records.

13. Some key texts that take up these questions include: Mark David Hall, "Did America Have a Christian Founding?," Heritage Foundation, accessed October 13, 2024, https://www.heritage.org/political-process/report/did-america-have-christian-founding; Mark David Hall, *Did America Have a Christian Founding? Separating Modern Myth from Historical Truth* (Thomas Nelson, 2020); John Fea, *Was America Founded as a Christian Nation? Revised Edition: A Historical Introduction*, rev. ed. (Westminster John Knox Press, 2016); David Barton and Glenn Beck, *The Jefferson Lies: Exposing the Myths You've Always Believed About Thomas Jefferson* (Thomas Nelson, 2012).

14. "From John Adams to Massachusetts Militia, 11 October 1798," *Founders Online*, National Archives, accessed May 26, 2025, http://founders.archives.gov/documents/Adams/99-02-02-3102.

15. "Thomas Jefferson and Religious Freedom," Monticello, accessed May 26, 2025, https://www.monticello.org/research-education/thomas-jefferson-encyclopedia/thomas-jefferson-and-religious-freedom/.

16. George Washington, "From George Washington to the Hebrew Congregation in Newport, 18 August, 1790," *Founders Online*, National Archives, accessed May 26, 2025, http://founders.archives.gov/documents/Washington/05-06-02-0135.

17. The public records are available at US GOV, "U.S. Legislative Information—5th Congress (1797–1799)," congress.gov, May 1, 1797, https://www.congress.gov/browse/5th-congress. See also Jacob Crane, "Reading American Secularism in the 1797 Treaty of Tripoli," *American Quarterly* 72, no. 2 (2020): 403–22, https://www.proquest.com/docview/2419140583/abstract/8B710E368D6D46B2PQ/1.

18. Crenshaw's argument runs parallel to Aaron Renn's idea of the "Negative World." See Kiera Butler, "To Understand JD Vance, You Need to Meet the 'TheoBros,'" *Mother Jones*, November–December 2024, https://www.motherjones.com/politics/2024/09/theobros-jd-vance-christian-nationalism/.

19. Ben R. Crenshaw, "Trump as Tragic Hero," *American Reformer*, June 19, 2024, https://americanreformer.org/2024/06/trump-as-tragic-hero/.

20. Andrew L. Whitehead and Samuel Perry, *Taking America Back for God: Christian Nationalism in the United States* (Oxford University Press, 2020).

21. See Thomas B. Edsall, "'The Capitol Insurrection Was as Christian Nationalist as It Gets,'" *New York Times*, January 28, 2021, https://www.nytimes.com/2021/01/28/opinion/christian-nationalists-capitol-attack.html; Emma Green, "A Christian Insurrection," *Atlantic*, January 8, 2021, https://www.theatlantic.com/politics/archive/2021/01/evangelicals-catholics-jericho-march-capitol/617591/.

22. Matthew D. Taylor, *The Violent Take It by Force: The Christian Movement That Is Threatening Our Democracy* (Broadleaf Books, 2024), 243, 105–6, 242, 20. See also Dale M. Coulter, "Neocharismatic Christianity and the Rise of the New Apostolic Reformation," *Firebrand*, January 18, 2021, https://firebrandmag.com/articles/neocharismatic-christianity-and-the-rise-of-the-new-apostolic-reformation.

23. Matthew D. Taylor, "Christian Nationalism Gone Global," *Revealer*, October 1, 2024, https://therevealer.org/christian-nationalism-gone-global/.

24. See Frederick Clarkson and André Gagné, "When It Comes to Societal Dominion, the Details Matter: A Reporter's Guide to the New Apostolic Reformation, Part II," Religion Dispatches, October 11, 2022, https://religiondispatches.org/when-it-comes-to-societal-dominion-the-details-matter-a-reporters-guide-to-the-new-apostolic-reformation-part-ii/. Clarkson and Gagné note that Ché Ahn, in his book *Modern Day Apostles* (2019), defines an apostle as "a Christlike ambassador with extraordinary authority called and sent out by Jesus Christ with a specific assignment to align the Church to bring Heaven's culture to earth and fulfill the mandate to disciple nations."

25. See Taylor's conversation on Brad Onishi's podcast, "Mike Johnson and the New Apostolic Reformation," *Straight White American Jesus*, October 30, 2023, https://www.straightwhiteamericanjesus.com/episodes/mike-johnson-and-the-new-apostolic-reformation/.

26. See Matthew D. Taylor, "It Matters That Roger Stone Just Called Donald Trump the Lord's 'Apostle,'" *Matthew D. Taylor Substack*, October 16, 2023, https://matthewdtaylor.substack.com/p/it-matters-that-roger-stone-just?utm_medium=reader2. Emphasis is Taylor's

27. Matthew D. Taylor, "Roger Stone and the Key to Trump's Evangelical Support," *Bulwark*, May 31, 2023, https://www.thebulwark.com/p/roger-stone-key-trump-evangelical-support.

28. Taylor, *The Violent Take It*, 16; Sarah Posner, *Unholy: Why White Evangelicals Worship at the Altar of Donald Trump* (Random House, 2020), 13ff.

29. Sarah Posner, email to author, September 18, 2024.

30. Taylor, *The Violent Take It*, 8, 45.

31. Amanda Tyler, "Marjorie Taylor Greene's Words on Christian Nationalism Are a Wake-up Call," CNN, July 27, 2022, https://www.cnn.com/2022/07/27/opinions/christian-nationalism-marjorie-taylor-greene-tyler/index.html.

32. Posner, *Unholy*, xvii–xviii. "The Trump-evangelical relationship represents an intense meeting of the minds, decades in the making, on the notion that America lies in ruins after the sweep of historic changes since the mid-twentieth century" (9–10).

33. Email exchange with author.

34. See Joseph Williams, "The Pentecostalization of Christian Zionism," *Church History* 84, no. 1 (March 2015): 159–94. Taylor, in an email to me, noted that the predominantly African American segments of the Independent Charismatic sphere tend to be less aggressive politically and far less likely to support Trump.

35. See Frederick Clarkson and André Gagné, "Christian Right Denialism Is More Dangerous than Ever: A Reporter's Guide to the New Apostolic Reformation," Religion Dispatches, September 7, 2022, https://religiondispatches.org/christian-right-denialism-is-more-dangerous-than-ever-a-reporters-guide-to-the-new-apostolic-reformation/. On the Seven Mountain Mandate, see also Bradley Onishi and Matthew Taylor, "Charismatic Revival Fury," podcast series, episode 3, Institute for Islamic, Christian, Jewish Studies, December 9, 2022, https://icjs.org/charismatic-revival-fury/.

36. See Tim Dickinson, "He Has a 7-Point Plan for a Christian Takeover—and Wants Doug Mastriano to Lead the Charge," *Rolling Stone*, September 29, 2022, https://www.rollingstone.com/politics/politics-features/lance-wallnau-doug-mastriano-christian-dominion-1234602214/.

37. Taylor, *The Violent Take It*, 160–61.

38. Rone Tempest, "Wyoming's 'Cowboy Catholic' Could Remake Government If Trump Wins," *WyoFile*, February 8, 2024, http://wyofile.com/wyomings-catholic-cowboy-could-remake-government-if-trump-wins/.

39. Onishi and Taylor, "Charismatic Revival Fury," episodes 3 and 4.

40. Taylor, *The Violent Take It*, 244.

41. Sarah Posner, email exchange with author.

42. Stephen Wolfe, "Protestant Experience and Continuity of Political Thought in Early America, 1630–1789," *LSU Doctoral Dissertations*, July 15, 2020, https://doi.org/10.31390/gradschool_dissertations.5344. See vita, 296.

43. Wolfe was a 2021–22 Garwood Postdoctoral Research Associate. See James Madison Program, "Spring Report 2022," Princeton University, https://jmp.princeton.edu/about/program-reports.

44. Copulsky, *American Heretics*, 216–32.

45. Copulsky, *American Heretics*, 217.

46. Jason Wilson, "'Make It a Christian Town': The Ultra-Conservative Church on the Rise in Idaho," *Guardian*, November 2, 2021, https://www.theguardian.com/world/2021/nov/02/christ-church-idaho-theocracy-us-america; Sarah Stankorb, "Inside the Church That Preaches 'Wives Need to Be Led with a Firm Hand,'" *Vice*, September 28, 2021, https://www.vice.com/en/article/inside-the-church-that-preaches-wives-need-to-be-led-with-a-firm-hand/.

47. Rod Dreher, "Thomas Achord Confesses."

48. Stephen Wolfe, *The Case for Christian Nationalism* (Canon Press, 2022), 135; James Clark, "'The Case for Christian Nationalism,'" *North American Anglican*, November 30, 2022, https://northamanglican.com/book-review-the-case-for-christian-nationalism/.

49. Hall published a book in 2024 called *Who's Afraid of Christian Nationalism: Why Christian Nationalism Is Not an Existential Threat to America or the Church* (Fidelis). For the Wolfe review, see Mark David Hall, "Stephen Wolfe's Gift," *American Reformer*, December 7, 2022, https://americanreformer.org/2022/12/stephen-wolfes-gift/. Hall quotes from *The Case for Christian Nationalism*, 138, 139, 140, 141.

50. In his review, Hall notes that Wolfe believes "the *United States*, as a whole, is lost" (quoting Wolfe, *The Case for Christian Nationalism*, 474). Hall, "Stephen Wolfe's Gift."

51. See Stephen Wolfe, "Love your people the way that Lindsay Graham loves Israel," October 4, 2024, https://perma.cc/U68K-MGUD; "Wolfe love your people like Babylon Bee loves Israel," October 22, 2024, https://perma.cc/88P4-M2NR; "Wolfe on Gaza destruction,"

February 5, 2025, https://perma.cc/5RKV-V7ZL; Stephen Wolfe, "Being invested in Israel/Gaza is distraction," February 21, 2025, https://perma.cc/855A-TQUW; Stephen Wolfe and Joel Berry, "Wolfe and Joel Berry exchange on Israel/Gaza," January 22, 2025, https://perma.cc/5V3V-NT2L.

52. Glenn Moots, "Treatise or Tweet? A Review of Stephen Wolfe's *The Case for Christian Nationalism* (Part 1)," *Public Discourse*, December 18, 2022, https://www.thepublicdiscourse.com/2022/12/86478/; Glenn Moots, "Treatise or Tweet? A Review of Stephen Wolfe's *The Case for Christian Nationalism* (Part 2)," *Public Discourse*, December 19, 2022, https://www.thepublicdiscourse.com/2022/12/86487/.

53. Wolfe, *The Case for Christian Nationalism*, 448.

54. Wolfe, *The Case for Christian Nationalism*, 291.

55. Stephen Wolfe, "Stephen Wolfe women's suffrage," February 7, 2022, https://perma.cc/N3FR-PL6J. See also "Wolfe miscegenation tweet 1," September 30, 2022, https://perma.cc/XT57-EB4Q; "Wolfe miscegenation tweet 2," September 30, 2022, https://perma.cc/Y6E6-ZVBW.

56. Wolfe, *The Case for Christian Nationalism*, 455, 346, 390–92.

57. Wolfe, *The Case for Christian Nationalism*, 176, 181, 473–74. As Hall notes, "One need not be Jefferson Davis to discern how such an approach might go astray." Hall, "Stephen Wolfe's Gift."

58. Wolfe, *The Case for Christian Nationalism*, 454, 456, 440–45 (on GAE), 455.

59. See Churchwell, "American Fascism"; Paxton, *Anatomy of Fascism*; John Ganz, "The Cross and the Flag," *Unpopular Front*, July 23, 2022, https://www.unpopularfront.news/p/the-cross-and-the-flag.

60. Author's conference notes.

61. He explained: "They're ugly, they're fat, and they're always hurt and vulnerable." He continued: "There's not a manly man among them. It's a bunch of overweight single moms with broken children." (Authors conference notes.)

62. In a 2023 essay for *The American Mind*, Slack outlined his schema for the New Right in colorful terms that included militant training for young men and the construction of a militant new language. Slack proclaimed that "the New Right has a monopoly on beauty." The essay included his visions of a new Caesar taking vengeance on the ruling powers through "mass dislocations" and the smashing of corporations. At one point Slack envisioned that "The lengthier stalks of kleptocratic wheat may be the harvest of righteous Fury." See Kevin Slack, "The Constitution, Citizenship, and the New Right," *American Mind*, June 15, 2023, https://americanmind.org/features/the-constitution-citizenship-and-the-new-right/. The essay was reprinted in Slack's book, *War on the American Republic* (Encounter, 2023).

63. This group included another "Wolfe"—William, who had worked in the first Trump administration—as well as Texas pastor Joel Webbon, and others like Josh Abbotoy and Brian Sauve. See Butler, "To Understand JD Vance, You Need to Meet the 'TheoBros.'" For more on this network, see Nicholas Confessore, "'America Is Under Attack': Inside the Anti-D.E.I. Crusade," *New York Times*, January 20, 2024, https://www.nytimes.com/interactive/2024/01/20/us/dei-woke-claremont-institute.html; Ruth Graham, "Why a New Conservative Brain Trust Is Resettling Across America" Jason Wilson, "Revealed: US Conservative Thinktank's Links to Extremist Fraternal Order," *Guardian*, March 11, 2024, https://www.theguardian.com/us-news/2024/mar/11/claremont-institute-society-for-american-civic-renewal-links.

64. See Josh Clemans, "Fischer Vance," July 15, 2024, https://perma.cc/UV6K-NK7R; Jason Wilson, "Revealed: Top Vance Aide Worked for Far-Right Consultancy with Extremist Links," *Guardian*, August 28, 2024, https://www.theguardian.com/us-news/article/2024/aug/28/jd-vance-far-right-aide.

65. "Yenor Williams Anton Milikh email record," November 12, 2024, https://perma.cc/YQ5C-BE5P.

66. Hitchens, "The Egg-Head's Egger-On."

Chapter 13

1. Michael Anton was not welcome at the AEI event (though Mansfield published a book the next year in which he thanked a list of "Machiavellian" friends that included Michael Anton and Gladden Pappin).

2. Hoover Institution, "Peter Berkowitz," accessed November 13, 2024, https://www.hoover .org/profiles/peter-berkowitz.

3. Mansfield's friends were reminded of his long role as a public intellectual and gadfly when, in anticipation of the AEI event, a graduate student in the government department at Harvard, Sophie Hill, gathered some of Mansfield's most noxious public statements for a satirical website, mansfieldat90.com. On the landing page for the website, Hill wrote: "let us celebrate the intellectual legacy of the renowned political theorist and Harvard professor, in his own words." She had a good deal to work with. The site allows you to click through quotes from Mansfield's long career and demonstrates plainly enough how his record is also one of plainspoken chauvinism and bigotry. "Mansfield at 90," accessed November 13, 2024, https:// mansfieldat90.com/.

4. American Enterprise Institute, "Harvey Mansfield at 90: A Conference on Major Themes of His Work," accessed May 28, 2025, https://www.aei.org/events/harvey-mansfield-at-90-a -conference-on-major-themes-of-his-work/; "Harvey Mansfield at 90: A Conference on Major Themes of His Work," YouTube, July 6, 2022, https://www.youtube.com/watch?v =PcVsVlIBTfs.

5. Immediately after Reagan's landslide victory in 1980, Mansfield wrote that the new president would "be well advised to find his conservatism in the constitution rather than to adopt a conservative populism. If he does the latter, he is likely to discover that the radical means of populism will overcome and outlast the conservative ends." See Steven Hayward, "Reagan's Unfinished Agenda," American Enterprise Institute, June 1, 2009, https://www.aei.org/articles /reagans-unfinished-agenda/.

6. "Harvey Mansfield at 90."

7. Thank you to Jack Pitney for bringing this passage to my attention. See Gilbert K. Chesterton, *Orthodoxy*, section II ("The Maniac"), Project Gutenberg, updated January 1, 2021, https://www.gutenberg.org/cache/epub/130/pg130.html.

8. National Conservatism, "Confirmed Speakers," accessed November 13, 2024, https:// nationalconservatism.org/natcon-4-2024/confirmed-speakers/.

9. National Conservatism, "About NatCon 4," accessed November 13, 2024, https:// nationalconservatism.org/natcon-4-2024/about/.

10. Nationalism Conservatism, "Schedule," *National Conservatism Conference, Washington 2024*, accessed November 13, 2024, https://nationalconservatism.org/natcon-4-2024/schedule/.

11. Annika Brockschmidt and Ben Lorber, "Persecution, Betrayal, and the Zero Sum Fight for Global Domination—Day 1 of NatCon 2024," *Religion Dispatches*, July 9, 2024, https:// religiondispatches.org/persecution-betrayal-and-the-zero-sum-fight-for-global-domination -day-1-of-natcon-2024/.

12. Mana Afsari, "The Last Boys at the Beginning of History," *The Point*, January 22, 2025, https://thepointmag.com/politics/last-boys-at-the-beginning-of-history/.

13. Nationalism Conservatism, "Schedule."

14. Jack Posobiec, Joshua Lisec, and Stephen K. Bannon, *Unhumans: The Secret History of Communist Revolutions* (War Room Books, 2024).

15. See David Azerrad, "American Conservatism Is Fiddling While Rome Burns, *American Conservative*, July 30, 2020, https://www.theamericanconservative.com/american-conservatism -is-fiddling-while-rome-burns/; Paul Peirce and Rich Cholodofsky, "Saint Vincent College Responds to Racism Claims Following Weekend Lecture," *TribLIVE.com*, April 14, 2022, https:// triblive.com/local/westmoreland/saint-vincent-college-responds-to-racism-claims-following

-weekend-lecture/; "David Azerrad at St. Vincent College," YouTube, 2022, https://youtu.be/PJAOstN6aC0?si=kBDI5jvPRsI_-Lz7; "From MLK to CRT," *Chronicles*, January 13, 2023, https://chroniclesmagazine.org/web/from-mlk-to-crt/.

16. Annika Brockschmidt and Ben Lorber, "'Pro-Life' Theater, Open White Nationalism, and Virility Fear—Day 3 of NatCon," *Religion Dispatches*, July 11, 2024, https://religiondispatches.org/pro-life-theater-open-white-nationalism-and-virility-fear-day-3-of-natcon/. See also Ben Lorber, "Ben Lorber on Azerrad 1," July 10, 2024, https://perma.cc/76FZ-N4L3; and Ben Lorber, "Ben Lorber on Azerrad 2," July 10, 2024, https://perma.cc/BU58-K3XC.

17. Homer, *The Iliad*, trans. Emily Wilson (Norton, 2023).

18. Homer, *The Odyssey*, trans. Emily Wilson (Norton, 2018).

19. Abdullah Yousef, "Classic Vandalism," *IM-1776*, August 5, 2022, https://im1776.com/2022/08/05/classic-vandalism/. Yousef also argues that Homer clearly had unambiguously positive feelings about war, which "was not seen by Homer as pointless, but glorious." As he explains, "falling in battle and beauty are one" in the Homeric poetry. You don't have to be Simone Weil to find this asinine.

20. Max Meyer, "Max Meyer Wilson Thread 1," August 23, 2023, https://perma.cc/D927-ASLB; Max Meyer, "Max Meyer Wilson Disclaimer," August 10, 2023, https://perma.cc/9YT6–42CS; Abdullah Yousef, "Yousef Wilson," April 23, 2023, https://perma.cc/X22D-GEVR.

21. Sarah Jones, "Women's Limited Role at the National Conservatism Conference," *Intelligencer*, July 11, 2024, https://nymag.com/intelligencer/article/women-national-conservatism-conference.html.

22. Elon Musk, "Musk Trump Teddy Roosevelt," July 13, 2024, https://perma.cc/R4MK-D5QL; Sohrab Ahmari, "Ahmari Trump Napoleon," July 13, 2024, https://perma.cc/ST96-GVA8; Dana Kennedy, "Elon Musk Goes All in for Trump After Pa. Rally Shooting: 'I Fully Endorse President Trump,'" *New York Post*, July 14, 2024, https://nypost.com/2024/07/13/us-news/elon-musk-goes-all-in-for-trump-after-pa-rally-shooting-i-fully-endorse-president-trump/; Josh Gerstein and Betsy Woodruff Swan, "The Right Is Attacking the Secret Service's Women Agents. Trump Hasn't Joined in," *Politico*, July 18, 2024, https://www.politico.com/news/2024/07/18/secret-service-women-trump-00169420.

23. Stephen Wolfe, "Wolfe Trump New Being," July 14, 2024, https://perma.cc/HER2-A7V4.

24. Hadas Gold, "Right-Wing Media Figures Blame Women in Secret Service and DEI for Security Failure in Trump Shooting," *CNN Business*, July 17, 2024, https://www.cnn.com/2024/07/17/media/secret-service-agents-women-trump-shooting/index.html; Gerstein and Swan, "The Right Is Attacking."

25. Sohrab Ahmari, "Ahmari Women in Secret Service," July 14, 2024, https://perma.cc/XJX5-K6HX.

26. Claremont Institute, "JD Vance: What to Do About Woke Capital," *American Way of Life*, May 19, 2021, https://dc.claremont.org/watch-jd-vance-on-woke-capital/; Jason Wilson, "Revealed: JD Vance Promoted Far-Right Views in Speech About Extremists' Book," *Guardian*, August 22, 2024, https://www.theguardian.com/us-news/article/2024/aug/22/jd-vance-speech-extremist-far-right-book; Laura K. Field, "JD Vance Has a Bunch of Weird Views on Gender," *Politico*, July 24, 2024, https://www.politico.com/news/magazine/2024/07/24/jd-vance-gender-views-00170673; "J.D. Vance—JML #070," YouTube, September 17, 2021, https://www.youtube.com/watch?v=PMq1ZEcyztY.

27. JD Vance, "Vance Entourage," August 7, 2024, https://perma.cc/2UQA-2TU9.

28. Tim Hains, "J.D. Vance to Reporter: 'I Smile at a Lot of Things . . . Right Now I Am Angry,'" *RealClearPolitics*, August 7, 2024, https://www.realclearpolitics.com/video/2024/08/07/jd_vance_to_reporter_i_smile_at_a_lot_of_thing_right_now_i_am_angry.html.

29. Mike DeWine, "I'm the Republican Governor of Ohio. Here Is the Truth About Springfield," *New York Times*, September 20, 2024, https://www.nytimes.com/2024/09/20/opinion/springfield-haitian-migrants-ohio.html.

30. Phil Helsel, "More than 30 Bomb Threats Made in Springfield, Ohio, After False Pets Claims," *NBC News*, September 16, 2024, https://www.nbcnews.com/news/us-news/30-bomb-threats-made-springfield-ohio-false-pets-claims-rcna171392.

31. "'Vance's Excellent Reviews Will Enrage Trump': 13 Writers on Who Won the Vice-Presidential Debate," *New York Times*, October 2, 2024, https://www.nytimes.com/2024/10/02/opinion/vance-walz-debate-scorecard.html.

32. Lois Beckett, "How the Ex-Obama Aides of Pod Save America Lost Faith in Candidate Biden," *Guardian*, July 12, 2024, https://www.theguardian.com/us-news/article/2024/jul/12/pod-save-america-biden-criticism; "Pelosi, Clooney, Democratic Senators Raise New Doubts About Biden," *Reuters*, July 10, 2024, https://www.reuters.com/world/us/biden-meets-union-leaders-democrats-calls-exit-race-continue-2024-07-10/.

33. Chris Gardner, "How Julia Roberts and George Clooney Came to Narrate Buzzy Political Ads," *Hollywood Reporter*, November 5, 2024, https://www.hollywoodreporter.com/news/politics-news/julia-roberts-political-ad-kamala-harris-vote-common-good-1236054509/.

34. By the strange logic (and biology) explored in the trial, wife-killing is worse than matricide. For more on this theme in the plays, see Emily Wilson, "Ah, how miserable!" *London Review of Books*, October 8, 2020, https://www.lrb.co.uk/the-paper/v42/n19/emily-wilson/ah-how-miserable.

35. Aeschylus, *The Oresteia: Agamemnon, Women at the Graveside, Orestes in Athens*, trans. Oliver Taplin (Liveright, 2018), *Orestes in Athens*, 823, 832.

36. *Orestes in Athens*, 804–7, 835, 991–94.

37. Constanze Stelzenmüller, "Flirting with Dictatorship," *Internationale Politik Quarterly*, January 10, 2024, https://ip-quarterly.com/en/flirting-dictatorship.

38. Deneen, "We Are All Postliberals Now."

39. See, for example, Helena Rosenblatt, *The Lost History of Liberalism: From Ancient Rome to the Twenty-First Century* (Princeton University Press, 2018); Joshua L. Cherniss, *Liberalism in Dark Times: The Liberal Ethos in the Twentieth Century* (Princeton University Press, 2021); Adrian Pabst, *Postliberal Politics: The Coming Era of Renewal* (Polity, 2021); Helene Landemore, *Open Democracy: Reinventing Popular Rule for the Twenty-First Century* (Princeton University Press, 2022); Danielle Allen, *Justice By Means of Democracy* (University of Chicago Press, 2023); Elizabeth Anderson, *Hijacked: How Neoliberalism Turned the Work Ethic against Workers and How Workers Can Take It Back* (Cambridge University Press, 2023); Samuel Moyn, *Liberalism against Itself: Cold War Intellectuals and the Making of Our Times* (Yale University Press, 2023); Bryan Garsten, "The Liberalism of Refuge," *Journal of Democracy*, 35, no. 2 (April 2024), https://www.journalofdemocracy.org/articles/the-liberalism-of-refuge/; Melvin L. Rogers, *The Darkened Light of Faith: Race, Democracy, and Freedom in African American Political Thought* (Princeton University Press, 2023); Daniel Chandler, *Free and Equal: What Would a Fair Society Look Like* (Knopf, 2024); Alexandre Lefebvre, *Liberalism as a Way of Life* (Princeton University Press, 2024); Matthew McManus, *The Political Theory of Liberal Socialism* (Routledge, 2024); Keidrick Roy, *American Dark Age: Racial Feudalism and the Rise of Black Liberalism* (Princeton University Press, 2024); Emma Planinc, *Regenerative Politics* (Columbia University Press, 2024); and Osita Nwanevu, *The Right of the People: Democracy and the Case for a New American Founding* (Random House, 2025).

40. Christopher Rufo, "The New Right Activism," *IM-1776*, January 4, 2024, https://im1776.com/manifesto-counterrevolution/.

41. See Sarah Schulman, *Conflict is Not Abuse: Overstating Harm, Community Responsibility, and the Duty of Repair* (Arsenal Pulp Books, 2016).

42. Deneen, *Regime Change*, 172.

43. Deneen, *Regime Change*, 174. Deneen recommends a service requirement; I prefer a well-incentivized voluntary approach.

44. On Garsten's initiatives, see Linda Prevost, "Yale launches Center for Civic Thought to promote thoughtful discourse," *YaleNews*, May 27, 2025, https://news.yale.edu/2025/05/27/yale-launches-center-civic-thought-promote-thoughtful-discourse. The new red state civic centers include: the School of Civic and Economic Thought at Arizona State; the Hamilton Center at the University of Florida; the UT Austin School of Civic Leadership; the School of Civic Life and Leadership at the University of North Carolina at Chapel Hill; and the Institute of American Civics at the University of Tennessee, Knoxville.

45. Aeschylus, *Agamemnon*, in *The Oresteia*, 12, 250–55.

INDEX

A NOTE ON THE TYPE

This book has been composed in Arno, an Old-style serif typeface in the classic Venetian tradition, designed by Robert Slimbach at Adobe.